Talking Philosophy

The result of twenty-five years of teaching philosophy to students of varied cultural and linguistic backgrounds, *Talking Philosophy* presents an informative and critical look at the basic terminology of twentieth-century Anglophone philosophy. It also examines the more important aspects of the terminology which philosophy shares with common discourse, and the language of argument generally.

Arranged thematically, the book begins with short definitions and discussions of expressions like 'discourse', 'sentence', 'proposition', and leads on through topics such as Identity, Meaning, Nonsense, and a variety of -isms and -ologies, to Logical Relations. Discussion is discursive and rarely neutral, and every paragraph is studded with aphorism and humour.

The many cross-references and a copious index enable the reader to find his way about with facility.

A. W. Sparkes is a Senior Lecturer in Philosophy at the University of Newcastle, New South Wales.

Talking Philosophy

A wordbook

A. W. Sparkes

London and New York

First published 1991
by Routledge
11 New Fetter Lane, London EC4P 4EE

Simultaneously published in the USA and Canada
by Routledge
a division of Routledge, Chapman and Hall, Inc.
29 West 35th Street, New York, NY 10001

Typeset in 10/12 Times
Printed in Great Britain by
Butler & Tanner Ltd, Frome and London

British Library Cataloguing in Publication Data
Sparkes, A. W.
   Talking philosophy: a wordbook.
   1. Philosophy. Language
   I. Title
   101'.4

Library of Congress Cataloging in Publication Data
Sparkes, A. W.
   Talking philosophy: a word book / A.W. Sparkes.
      p. cm.
   ISBN 0–415–04222–4. – ISBN 0–415–04223–2 (pbk.)
   1. Philosophy – Terminology. I. Title.
B49.S63   1991
101'.4–dc20   89–48900

ISBN 0–415–04222–4
      0–415–04223–2 pbk

To my sister

JILL ELIZABETH MEARA

'... how often you and I
Had tired the sun with talking, and sent him down the sky.'

Lux perpetua luceat ei.

Contents

Preface

Philosophy, like any other skilled activity, has a technical vocabulary. In this book, I attempt to give an account of the more important components of that vocabulary.

Such an attempt has inevitable shortcomings if it is done as briefly as I have done it here. The main problem is that how to define many of the terms is itself a matter of philosophical controversy. There is, for instance, considerable disagreement about the terms 'analytic' and 'synthetic' (p. 64) and it is quite impossible to formulate neutral controversy-free definitions of them.

For that reason, there is something disagreeably dogmatic about much of what I have to say here, but it should still be of some assistance. Although philosophers disagree strongly about the definitions of 'analytic' and 'synthetic', they *tend* to agree about which propositions are analytic and which are synthetic. Many philosophers would not be entirely happy about my remarks on 'sentence', 'proposition' and 'statement' (pp. 1–3), but most would agree that distinctions roughly similar should be drawn. There were two alternatives to writing the present book: writing no book at all and writing a book for each word.

At all events, the reasonably diligent student should soon be able to discover the points at which I have over-simplified. The purpose of this book is to provide some initial assistance. The references given in the text and the student's own reading will enable him/her to compensate for any inadequacies here.

Not all the words dealt with here are technical. Philosophy is, amongst other things, a systematic critique of argument and reasoning, so I have included many words which are familiar elements of non-philosophical argument, paying particular attention to words which are frequently used in a waffly, obfuscating, unclear fashion.

It would be a mistake to treat the technical terms of philosophy as the magical, secret language of an in-group. These terms are useful as most technical terms are useful: they provide reasonably brief, reasonably precise ways of saying things of importance in practising the trade.

A. W. S.

Acknowledgements

In the mid 1960s, Mr R. S. Walters of the University of New South Wales gave his students a one-page note on philosophical terminology. Later, while teaching at the University of Papua New Guinea, I obtained his permission to adapt that note for my own purposes. Over the years, the adaptation was re-adapted and re-adapted and grew into this book. I am sure that it is all the better for any grains of solid Waltersian sense which it may contain, but Mr Walters is in no way responsible for my errors, omissions and infelicities.

Neither an unreliable memory nor space available permits a complete list of the many other people who have helped me with criticisms and suggestions. Professor J. J. C. Smart, Professor John Kleinig and Dr J. D. McKenzie were particularly generous with their time and energy. (Professor Smart strongly objects to the remark about him in section 7.17, but he will just have to put up with that.) Amongst the others I must thank are my colleagues Dr D. W. Dockrill, Dr W. V. Doniela, Professor C. A. Hooker and Dr J. M. Lee. I am very grateful also to Dr Damian Grace, Mrs Cheryl Haynes, Dr A. R. Lacey, Dr M. B. Schedvin and Mrs Jacqueline Thorpe.

Mrs D. E. Nesmith typed the manuscript (and typed it and typed it and . . .). I am very grateful indeed for her patience and for her editorial assistance which saved me from many pitfalls. I am also very grateful to Mr Richard Stoneman, Ms Sarah Pearsall, and Ms Margaret Christie of Routledge.

I acknowledge quotations from the following works which are copyright (page-numbering, etc. refer to this book): W. V. Doniela 'Rationalism' (p. 196); Antony Flew *Thinking about Thinking* (p. 53); Herbert McCabe *Law, Love and Language* (p. 205); Val and Richard Routley 'Social Theories, Self Management and Environmental Problems' (pp. 44, 199–200); R. N. Spann 'Clichés and Other Bad Habits in Political Science' (p. 104); Paul Tillich *Systematic Theology* (p. 135); Mary Anne Warren 'On the Moral and Legal Status of Abortion' (p. 42); E. G. Whitlam 'Law Reform and Law and Order' (p. 51); Raymond Williams *Keywords* (p. 17); Judith Wright *Child with Dead Animal* (pp. 25, 43). Fuller details of these works will be found in the bibliography.

If I have inadvertently omitted any acknowledgement, I apologize for it. All quotations fall within the limits of fair dealing as defined by the appropriate legislation.

A. W. S.

1 Saying Things

1.1 DISCOURSE; EXPRESSION

(i) **'Discourse'** is a word with a variety of meanings. One of the more useful is as an omnibus word covering both **thought** and **talk. Political discourse** is **talk and thought about politics.** Statements, questions, imperatives, etc. are **elements of discourse** (sections 1.2, 1.5). Narratives, arguments, recipes, etc. are different kinds of **discourse-system. To discourse** of something is to talk about it, think about it, reason about it, etc.

(ii) The word **'expression'** can be used as a catch-all label covering any symbol or collection of symbols: e.g., a word, a sentence, a logical formula. For **place-holding expression**, see section 6.2.

1.2 SENTENCES AND PROPOSITIONS; QUESTIONS

A. Sentence, proposition, statement

(i) It is not very easy to say what a **sentence** is, even though it is quite easy to recognize one when it comes along. Whatever else a sentence may be, it is a grammatically structured collection of words.

A: 'Caesar invaded Britain in 55 BC.'
B: 'Did Caesar invade Britain in 55 BC?'
C: 'Abacinate, abaciscus, aback, abacus.'
D: 'Of out snakes lightly bottle unto over.'

A and B are sentences; C and D are not. C is a list; D is a jumble. (See Crystal, 1980, pp. 319–320; Fowler, 1968, pp. 546–547.) A sentence, as such, is a **grammatical** thing. Sentences may be well-formed or badly formed (section 6.5 (iii)), meaningful (significant) or meaningless (nonsensical) (section 3.3). But sentences, as sentences, do not have truth-value, i.e., a sentence, as a sentence, is neither true nor false (1.3). As sentences, as grammatical things, 'The sun rises in the east' and 'The sun rises in the west' are equal. It is **when they are used to assert**

propositions that the difference emerges. To use a sentence to assert a proposition is **to use that sentence assertively** (see section 1.4). A sentence which can be so used is an **indicative** sentence (section 1.5).

(ii) A **proposition** is whatever can be true or false (i.e., that which has **truth-value**). Propositions may be asserted or denied, considered, doubted, believed, argued for or against, confirmed, falsified, verified, etc. Different sentences may be used to **convey the same proposition** (i.e., may be used to say the same thing). The same sentence may be used to convey different propositions.

If Roaring Tom says: 'I can beat anyone in the house', and Bruising Jack says in reply: 'I can beat anyone in the house', they have uttered the same sentence, but they have not asserted the same proposition. On the other hand, suppose there are three people, Frank, Franz, and François. At roughly the same time and place, each looks out of a window and utters as follows:

> Frank: 'It's raining.'
> Franz: 'Es regnet.'
> François: 'Il pleut.'

They have uttered different sentences but they have asserted the same proposition. See section 10.3 (**equivalence of propositions**). In ordinary talk, 'proposition' tends to be used as a synonym of 'proposal'. Do not confuse that with the technical use.

(iii) A **statement** is the verbal assertion of a proposition. For that reason, statements have truth-value (section 1.3). See Flew, 1975, Ch. I. A statement may contain propositions which are not asserted:

> E: 'If the present Vice-Chancellor of Newcastle University committed the Jack-the-Ripper murders, he is more than a century old.'
> F: 'The present Vice-Chancellor of Newcastle University committed the Jack-the-Ripper murders.'
> G: 'The present Vice-Chancellor of Newcastle University is more than a century old.'

F and G are **components** of E, but one can assert E without asserting either F or G. As it happens, E is true, even though both F and G are false. (For **assert** see section 1.4.)

The question of the nature of sentences, propositions, and statements is *much* more complicated and more controversial than the above may suggest. See Lacey, 1976, pp. 197–199; Kneale and Kneale, 1962, pp. 49–54; Gale, 1967; Quine, 1970, Ch. I. Roughly speaking, **indicative sentence** (section 1.5) stands to **proposition** as **numeral** stands to **number**. Saying that does not clarify the relationship, but it does indicate the nature of its obscurity.

(iv) A **sentence-frame** is a set of words which, as it stands, is not a sentence, but will become a sentence if a gap in it is filled. 'Socrates is ....' is a sentence-frame. 'Socrates is wise.' and 'Socrates is the son of Sophroniskos.' are sentences. 'Who killed ...?' is a sentence-frame. 'Who killed Cock Robin?' and 'Who killed Roger Ackroyd?' are sentences. Some completions of sentence-frames result in logically untroublesome sentences. Some do not. Inserting 'Tom' in '... has a head-cold.' gives us a sentence which can be used to make an intelligible statement, but some have thought that inserting 'The number 7' produces not mere falsehood but nonsense. See sections 3.4B, 1.9D (**categories; category mistake; predicate**).

(v)

'The sky is blue.'

That is a **subject-predicate sentence**. It can be used simply to predicate (section. 1.9D) something (blueness) of something else (the sky). Not all sentences are like that, not even all **indicative** sentences (section 1.5). There are **existential sentences** which merely assert the existence of something ('There are crocodiles in that river.'), **conditional sentences** ('If the headlights were left on all night, the battery will be flat.' – see section 4.12), and lots of others (section 1.5).

B. Questions

(i) **'Erotetic'** means (whether you believe it or not) **of, like, or pertaining to questions. Erotetic logic** is the branch of logic concerned with the analysis of questions. See Hamblin, 1967; Prior and Prior, 1955.

(ii) A **rhetorical question** is a statement in question's clothing, i.e., a speaker makes an assertion, but, for emphasis, expresses it with an interrogative sentence rather than an indicative one. At a 'literary conference' held in Prague in 1949, Dylan Thomas was so exasperated by Stalinist propaganda that he shouted: 'I am a Communist, but am I also a bloody fool?' (Fitzgibbon, 1968, p. 247). He was not asking for information, he was giving it.

(iii) **Hypothetical questions** are questions which require the respondent to express an opinion on what would be true, right, or appropriate if some possibility (which is not or may not be actualized) were to be actualized (cf. section 4.15 on **counterfactuals**). They range from questions which anyone should be able to answer (e.g., 'What would you do if the house caught fire?') to questions which are totally unanswerable (e.g., 'If human beings were propagated like thistles, what would be the correct moral attitude when strange babies started growing amongst your gladioli?' (cf. J. J. Thomson, 1974, p. 15)). In the middle there are questions which no sensible person would answer categorically but which might provoke informative speculation (e.g., 'If William III and Mary II had had a child who survived them, would Britain and the

Netherlands now be a united kingdom?'). There are also questions which can be categorically answered but only in ways wide open to misunderstanding or distortion, e.g.:

> Tertius: 'Suppose the Vice-Chancellor had a fit of homicidal madness and came charging at you with an axe. Suppose you had a loaded gun. What would you do?'
>
> Quartus: 'I'd shoot him in the leg.'

Tertius then goes and tells the world that Quartus has admitted to being prepared to shoot the Vice-Chancellor. Sometimes, people say 'But that's a hypothetical question' in a way which suggests that all such questions are unanswerable. That is not true. It is, however, perfectly legitimate for someone to refuse to answer a question which cannot be answered in a non-misleading fashion. See also (v) below.

(iv) 'A **leading question**' does *not* mean *a difficult question*, or *a trick question*, or *a question which can be answered only in a way which embarrasses the person questioned*. A leading question is one which suggests the answer which is required. I have heard a radio interviewer say to someone who was objecting to some statement by a cabinet minister: 'And would you say that a person so prejudiced should not hold high office?' In media-parlance, this is called 'feeding questions' to the interviewee. The term 'leading question' is borrowed from the language of English law. A barrister is forbidden to put a leading question to a witness whom he has called, unless the witness shows himself hostile to the barrister and/or his client. See Fowler, 1968, p. 327; Mozley and Whiteley, 1977, pp. 189, 161; Osborn, 1976, pp. 198, 167.

(v) A question cannot be false (or true), but it can rest on false (or true) assumptions (section 5.5C). 'Why does a dead fish weigh more than a live fish?' rests on a false assumption, as does 'Why are all militant unions led by Pommy migrants?' This is sometimes called 'the **fallacy of many questions**' (or of **a complex question**), though, strictly, it is not a fallacy (see section 4.20). See Hamblin, 1970, pp. 38–40; Flew, 1975, pp. 98–101. Cf. **begging the question** (section 4.23).

1.3   TRUTH

A.   Truth-conditions; truth-claims

(i) 'What is the **truth-value** of that proposition?' means 'Is that proposition true or is it false?' If someone says, 'p has truth-value', he is not saying that p is true. He is saying that p is either true or false.

(ii) The **truth-conditions** of a proposition p are those conditions which must be satisfied if p is true. See also sections 5.1 and 5.4 (**verification principle** and **falsifiability**).

(iii) When someone makes a statement, he is alleging that **something is the** case or **is not the case**. That is his **truth-claim**. Sometimes, however, it may not be quite clear what truth-claim is being made. E.g., if someone says: 'There is something wrong with the steering-lock', it may not be clear what his truth-claim is, because of the **ambiguity** of 'steering-lock'. For **ambiguity**, see section 2.7.

B. Truth and falsehood

(i) If the province of philosophy is the fundamental, then truth is the arch-philosophical topic. The distinction between truth and falsehood is taken for granted in almost all discourse. It is ordinary and commonplace and extremely difficult to deal with. My remarks will be merely notes.

(ii)

'If someone believes that something is true, then it is true for him.'

This frequently made assertion is preposterous. Either 'It is true for him' means simply 'He believes that it is true' (which makes the assertion true but trivial) or the whole thing is absurd. Suppose Harry believes that it will rain tomorrow. If having the belief makes it true for him, then tomorrow the grass will be wet for him (but not for Tom who believes that the weather will be dry tomorrow). That is absurd, so the proposition that *if someone believes that something is true, then it is true for him* is also absurd.

(iii) Most philosophers agree that there is a *primary* sense of 'true' according to which the predicate '... is true' contrasts with the predicate '... is false'. In that sense, those predicates can be applied intelligibly only to *propositional* things, i.e., to propositions, statements, judgments, theories, beliefs, etc. A proposition, etc., which is *not a true* proposition (etc.) is nevertheless a *genuine* proposition (etc.). That primary sense of 'true' is distinguished from other senses according to which:

(1) Something is said to be **a true X** on the ground that, unlike something else which might *seem* to be an X but is not, it *does* satisfy the requirements for being an X. ('The grizzly is a true bear. The koala is not.' Notice that no one would say that the koala is *a false bear*, but only that it is *not a true bear*. See section 1.16B **(pseudo-)**.)

(2) Something is said to be **a true X** on the ground that it satisfies the requirements for being an X *to a pre-eminent degree*. Tom has many friends but only of Harry does he say, 'He is a true friend.' That does not imply that the others are 'false friends' or non-friends but merely that Harry's friendship is something very special.

'True' in these non-primary senses means much the same as 'real' (see section 1.16).

(iv) A lie may be a statement which is true, i.e., the truth can be told dishonestly. ('No dutiable goods to declare,' I say to the Customs officer, believing *mistakenly* that there are some dutiable goods in my luggage.) See also section 4.5B.

(v) There is a quite spurious use of the phrases '[a] true X', 'truly xious', frequently employed by totalitarians and by other muddle-heads and deceivers. According to this use a *true* X is something which the rest of us would, in our unenlightened way, regard as non-X or even anti-X. *True* democracy is accepting without question everything the Politburo or the Fuehrer says or does. The dissenter silenced in Siberia is more *truly* free than he would be if he were allowed to pursue his wicked dissenting ways, and *true* temperance is, as one of Aldous Huxley's characters says, 'much more refined' than 'just gross refusal to drink': 'True temperance is a bottle of claret with each meal and three double whiskies after dinner.' (Huxley, 1949, pp. 122–124.) See Flew, 1975, pp. 47–51, 81–82.

(vi) **Verisimilitude**. Literally: 'truthlikeness'. A narrative, theory, etc., **has verisimilitude** to the extent that it approaches the truth, reveals how things are, etc. See Popper, 1983, pp. 181–198. See also section 6.27 (**excluded middle**).

(vii) **Veridical**. Literally: 'truthtelling', applied not to persons but to narratives, perceptions (section 5.22B), arguments (with true conclusions), etc. 'Veridical' contrasts with '**falsidical**' (Quine, 1976, pp. 1–10). 'Virid' means *green*, so watch the spelling.

(viii) For further reading on **truth**, see Lacey, 1976, pp. 220–223; Pitcher, 1964. Each has a good bibliography.

1.4   ASSERT; UTTER; SAY

(i) Someone **asserts** the proposition p when he declares that the proposition p is true. (Strictly speaking, that is not quite accurate, but it comes close to accuracy and is certainly much clearer than the following which is, I think, accurate: 'Someone asserts the proposition p when he utters a verbal formula equivalent to p in such a manner that he commits himself to the truth of p.') The word 'assert' has a very strange history. See *SOED*.

The word 'assertion' can mean either **that which is asserted** or **the act of asserting it**. That little ambiguity is not likely to give much trouble. In this sense of 'assert', one can assert something tremulously or hesitantly; i.e., the typical philosophic use of the word differs from its use in certain branches of psychology. Do not confuse 'assert' with 'ascertain' which means 'to find out'. 'Assertation' is not a word in English (or, I strongly suspect, any other language).

(ii) Something is **uttered** if it is spoken, written, transmitted by semaphore or Morse, etc. If someone makes an assertion, he makes an **utterance**, but some utterances are not assertions (e.g., questions, exclamations, groans, etc.).

(iii) '**Say**' can be ambiguous between 'utter' and 'assert', but, if you assert that Tom says that tobacco is good for you, what *you* say does not mean that *he merely utters the words* 'Tobacco is good for you.' What it means is that *he has committed himself to the proposition* that tobacco is good for you. If Tom had said: 'Only a fool would think that tobacco is good for you', he has uttered those words, but if you were to say: 'Tom says that tobacco is good for you', you would be grossly misrepresenting him. Philosophers, like other argumentative writers, sometimes spend a paragraph or more expounding views which they intend to demolish in the next paragraph. Be careful that you do not attribute to a philosopher views which he has **merely** expounded. See also sections 1.6C (**context**); 1.6D(ii) (**in propria persona**).

1.5 INDICATIVE, INTERROGATIVE, IMPERATIVE

Traditional grammarians divide sentences (section 1.2A(i)) into three types:

(i) **Indicative** sentences are those which are typically used to *make statements* (see section 1.2A(iii)), e.g.: 'There is milk in the refrigerator.'

(ii) **Interrogative** sentences are those which are typically used *to ask questions*, e.g.: 'Does this train stop at Fassifern?'

(iii) **Imperative** sentences, according to many grammar books, are those used to **give orders or commands**. But that cannot be true. Someone who says: 'Oh Lord, hear my prayer, and let my cry come unto Thee' is speaking in the imperative, but he is not giving orders or commands. Actually, 'the imperative' is a rag-bag class including (amongst other things): **orders or commands** ('Right turn!' 'Go away!'), **requests** ('Would you please pass the butter'), **pieces of advice** ('Be careful'), and **instructions** (such as recipes). See Hare, 1971, pp. 1–43.

(iv) The indicative/interrogative/imperative classification is useful, but it has its rough and ready aspects. It is also incomplete. Ludwig Wittgenstein said, 'How many kinds of sentence are there? Say assertion, question and command? There are *countless* kinds' (*PI* I 23.1958, p. 11). That may be putting it a little high, but there are certainly sentences which slip through the traditional grammarians' net. If someone says 'I promise to pay you $5' or 'I name this ship the Queen Elizabeth', what is he doing? Quite obviously, he is not asking a question or issuing an imperative, but neither is he making a statement (i.e., saying something which can be true or false). What he is doing is *promising* or *naming* as the case may be. He is not reporting or describing an act of promising or naming, he is *actually performing* the act.

J. L. Austin (1911–1960) called such sentences **performatives** and divided the class of **indicatives** into **performatives** and **constatives** (those whose typical use is to make statements). See his papers 'Performative Utterances' (Austin, 1979, pp. 233–252) and 'Performative-Constative' (Searle, 1971, pp. 13–22). Certain difficulties about this distinction led Austin to develop his theory of *speech acts* (see Lacey, 1976, pp. 206–207; D. E. Cooper, 1973, Ch. VIII; Searle, 1969).

1.6   USE AND MENTION; QUOTATION AND CONTEXT

A.   Use and mention

(i)

The Nile is longer than the Murrumbidgee. (A)
The Nile is shorter than the Murrumbidgee. (B)

The same person might utter both those sentences with the intention of asserting two quite different and compatible (see section 10.2) propositions. That would be so if, when he utters (A), he is comparing two rivers, and if, when he utters (B), he is comparing *the names of* two rivers. But that is messy and confusing, and, although there is no self-contradiction involved, it has a worrying *look of* self-contradiction. To clear up the mess, we bring in some technical terminology:

In the first case, when the speaker is talking about two rivers, we say he is **using** the names of those rivers.

In the second case, when the speaker is talking about the names of two rivers, we say that he is *not* using those names, but **mentioning** them.

And, to make things clearer still, we have a *visual* device. When we **use** an expression, we leave it alone. When we **mention** it, we enclose it in inverted commas (sometimes called '**quotes**').
Thus:

The Nile is longer than the Murrumbidgee. (A$_1$)
'The Nile' is shorter than 'the Murrumbidgee'. (B$_1$)

Any sort of linguistic expression can be mentioned: words, phrases, sentences, statements, etc. (I owe the example to J. D. MacKenzie.)

(ii)   One alternative to the use of inverted commas is to **display** mentioned expressions by giving them a special position on the page. I have done that in this section with sentences (A), (B), (A$_1$) and (B$_1$). When logical formulae are being mentioned, external curved brackets function as mention-marks; e.g., '(p & q) is a compound'.

For clear introductory treatments of the use/mention distinction, see Quine, 1987, pp. 231–235, and T. J. Richards, 1978, pp. 16–17, 48–49. For something much more advanced, see Goddard and Routley, 1966.

There are some odd cases where it is difficult to say whether an expression is being used or mentioned. In such cases, **italics**, **boldface**, or **underlining** can be useful. Alston suggests regularly italicizing or underlining 'what follows "means" in "E means . . ." (or what follows "is" in "The meaning of E is . . ."). This is intended to reflect the fact that when expressions are put into this slot, they have a unique kind of occurrence, for which we shall use the term "exhibit" ' (Alston, 1964, p. 11, n. 2), e.g. (from *ibid*, p. 21):

The meaning of 'procrastinate' is *put things off*.

Notice that the technical use of the words 'use' and 'mention' is at variance with two common English idioms. In ordinary speech, Mr X might say to Mr Y: 'I was talking with Mr Z about who should be on the Committee. Your name was mentioned.' That is perfectly good English usage. Nevertheless, in terms of the technical use/mention distinction, Mr Z's name was *not* mentioned but *used*. In ordinary speech, 'Mr X used Mr Y's name' would normally be taken to mean that *Mr X pretended to be Mr Y*. Again, perfectly good English, but do not mix it up with the technical use/mention distinction.

(iii) Philosophers sometimes use the words 'quote' or 'quotation' as a synonym for 'mention' in its technical sense. Things would be *much* better if they did not.

B. Inverted commas: some other uses

(i) Quotation
The most common use of inverted commas is to indicate a **quotation**, e.g.:

'I have fed the cat,' Tom said.

(Inverted commas are often called 'quotation marks' or 'quotes' even when they are not being used in this fashion.) See subsection D below (**direct and indirect speech**). Vallins (1951, pp. 113–125) misguidedly detests inverted commas, but says some very useful things about them.

(ii) Scare-quotes
Inverted commas are often used to indicate that a word is being used in a sense different from its normal sense. Nuclear physicists have a whimsical way of borrowing perfectly ordinary words and giving them perfectly extraordinary senses. They are sometimes kind enough to use scare-quotes to warn their readers, e.g.:

Some electrons have 'charm' and some are 'strange'.

(iii) Quotes of dissociation ('shudder-quotes')
Sometimes, a writer uses inverted commas to indicate that the word he is using is not the word *he* would normally use. This corresponds to

certain indescribable but easily recognized modulations of the voice. Although the term 'shudder-quotes' is well-established, the writer who does this need not be shuddering: he may merely be apologizing, or expressing bashfulness, or being obscurely facetious, e.g.:

> We see the real moral flaw in the outwardly decent man who regards becoming and remaining 'well-off' as the finest thing in life, by considering the quality of national life in a merchant-city, like Carthage, where the 'merchant-prince' is dominant and gives the tone to the whole community, and so on. (A. E. Taylor, 1960, p. 265)

(iv) **Quotes of reversal ('sneer-quotes')**
Inverted commas can also be used to indicate that the writer means the reverse of what he would probably have been taken to mean if he had not used the inverted commas:

Life in the People's Democracies is very different from life in the decadent, fascist West.	Life in the 'People's Democracies' is very different from life in the 'decadent', 'fascist' West.
Himmler was a very good National Socialist.	Himmler was a very 'good' National Socialist.

(v) Do not use inverted commas for merely decorative purposes. If you do, you are likely to distort what you want to say. The fishmonger who put the following sign in his window did not intend to cry 'stinking fish' about his own wares, but that is what he did:

'FRESH'
MULLET

C.   Quotation and context

(i) The context of an extract from a book or other piece of writing is those passages which precede it or follow it. The context of a remark or an event is the setting in which it occurred, the circumstances surrounding it.

(ii) **Out of context:** in the most literal sense, any quotation is, by logical necessity, taken out of context. If you *complain* that something is quoted out of context, you must be prepared to show that the quotation is misleading. If you cannot do this, someone might well suspect your honesty. See also section 1.4(iii) (**say**).

D.   Direct speech and indirect speech; *in propria persona*; *ipsissima verba*; *ipse dixit*; *sic* (Latin)

(i) **Direct speech and indirect speech (*Oratio recta* and *oratio obliqua*).** If someone professes to quote the actual words of a speaker or writer, he is using direct speech or ***oratio recta***. If someone asserts the fact that a speaker said something but does not profess to quote the speaker's actual words, he is using indirect speech or *oratio obliqua* (pronounced awRAHteo obLEEKwa):

Oratio recta	*Oratio obliqua*
Tom said: 'I have fed the cat.'	Tom said that he had fed the cat.

(ii) *In propria persona* (pronounced 'in PROprea perSOna'). Literally: 'in [his] own person'. If I say something *in propria persona*, I am saying it on my own behalf; I am committing myself to what I am saying. If I am reporting what someone else says or might say, I am not speaking *in propria persona*. This is a very important distinction. See also section 1.4(iii) (**say**). The plural form of '*in propria persona*' is '*in propriis personis*' ('in [their] own persons').

(iii) *Ipsissima verba*. Literally: 'his very own words'. This phrase is sometimes used as a synonym for 'direct speech', but, frequently, it is used in the same reproachful fashion as '*ipse dixit*' (see below).

(iv) *Ipse dixit*. Literally: 'He himself has said.' Most often used reproachfully. If Mr X makes unargued but very confident pronouncements on controversial matters, Mr Y might say: 'Mr X thinks his *ipse dixit* is an argument.' If Mr X continually quotes Mr Z and relies too much on Mr Z's authority, Mr Y might say: 'Mr X relies too much on Mr Z's *ipse dixit*.' 'Ah! *Magister dixit*!' ('Ah! The master has spoken') is even more reproachful (and provocative). See section 4.25(vi) (**authority**).

(v) *Sic* (pronounced 'sick'). Latin for 'so' or 'thus'. Frequently inserted in quotations to indicate that the author quoted did indeed use the word indicated. Hence, some have suggested that '*sic*' should be translated as 'Yes, that *is* what the damned fool said', but '*sic*' need not always be so pejorative (and, indeed, one can use '*sic*' about words of one's own choice: 'Yes, that *is* the word I intend. It's not a misprint or a slip.'). For *sic et non*, see section 8.9C.

1.7 TYPE AND TOKEN

(i)

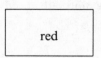

Box A

How many words are there in Box A?
One.

The answer is so obvious that the question sounds silly.

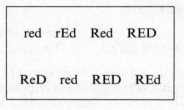

Box B

How many words are there in Box B?

The answer is so non-obvious that the question seems a trick. The answer must, it seems, be either *one* or *eight*. It can hardly be both. And yet there seems to be no clear ground for preferring either answer to the other. If the answerer says 'One', the questioner can object: 'But if you copied the contents of Box B on to a telegram form and presented it at a Post Office, you would be charged for eight words. And you would be most unreasonable if you complained about it.' If the answerer says 'Eight', the questioner can object: 'But if someone said he knew eight English colour-words and rattled off the contents of Box B, you would soon put him in his place.'

(ii) To solve this problem, we need some distinctions. First, we can say that there are eight *inscriptions* (separate bits of writing) in Box B, just as there is one inscription in Box A. Each of the inscriptions in Box B has features which we can use to distinguish it from each of the others. In some cases, the difference is merely one of position. In other cases, there are other differences as well. Each of the inscriptions has features which we can use to classify it with the others: each consists of the same three letters of the Roman alphabet. We call the features which we can use to distinguish each inscription from the others '**token-features**'. We call the features which we can use to classify each inscription with the others '**type-features**'. We say that, in Box B, there are eight word-**tokens** of the one word-**type**. For good introductory treatments of the type/token distinction, see Quine, 1987, pp. 216–219, and Woozley, 1949, pp. 90–91. For a more advanced treatment, see Goddard and Routley, 1966.

1.8   TOKEN-REFLEXIVES

Such expressions as 'I', 'you', 'last Tuesday', etc. A sentence containing such expressions is fully intelligible only if we know the circumstances of its utterance, i.e., they *point back* to the original token-sentence. See section 8.12(iv).

1.9 CONCEPT; SATISFYING A DESCRIPTION; IDEA; PREDICATE; ALIENANS

A. Concept

(i) To have a concept of X is to be able to recognize Xthings, to distinguish them from nonXthings, to be able to compare them with nonXthings. Thus, if we have a concept of X, we can think about Xthings and (usually) talk about them with others. Someone may well have a concept of X without being able to define X. It is possible also to have a concept of X without having any 'mental picture' or 'mental image' of X. See sections 2.5 (**definition**), 5.22H (**phenomenology**), 8.14B (**knowing how and knowing that**), 1.10A(ii) (**universals and particulars**), 5.14 (**unpacking**). Further reading: Lacey, 1976, pp. 34–35; Flew, 1984, p. 69; E. R. Emmet, 1968, Ch. III; Geach, 1971, Ch. V; Manser, 1967.

E. R. Emmet (1968, p. 71) says ' "concept" tends to be a philosopher's word – it might be described in a derogatory way as an example of philosophical jargon'. Not any more, alas! In recent years, the word 'concept' has been adopted by some of the more solemn employees of the media. As a result of their efforts, the word is fast becoming even more ambiguous and confusing than 'idea'. These pompous vandals should be resisted and should certainly not be imitated. A useful rule:

> If it would make sense to say that X is true or that X is false, do not call X **a concept**.

'A new concept' has recently become advertisers' jargon for 'an innovation': 'A new concept in motoring – the Lancia GBXL.' This too is a piece of pompous vandalism which should be resisted.

(ii) A thing X **falls under the concept of** yness IFF (see section 4.1) X is a y. Mr R. J. Hawke falls under the concept of humanity, because he is a human being. He does not fall under the concept of femaleness, because he is not female. If X falls under the concept of yness, then X is an *instance of* yness (i.e., X instantiates yness). See also section 5.2A (**instances**).

(iii) The concept of yness (*or* The concept of y) is **instantiated** IFF there exists at least one thing which is y. The concept of humanity is instantiated because there are some human beings. Each of them is an *instance of* the concept of humanity. If there are no ghosts, the concept of ghost is not instantiated. The concept of a round square cannot be instantiated because the concept of a round square is self-contradictory (section 3.2).

B.   Satisfying a description

A thing, X, satisfies (or 'answers to') a description, 'D', IFF the statement 'X is D' is true. Mrs Thatcher and Mr R. J. Hawke both satisfy the description 'politician'. Mr Hawke satisfies the description 'Australian politician'. Mrs Thatcher fails to satisfy that description.

C.   Idea

Lacey (1976, p. 85) lists nine different meanings of this word and there are more. Clearly, it is a word to be used with caution and should be avoided if its use is likely to be confusing or if something less ambiguous is available. See Lacey, 1976, pp. 85–86; G. J. Warnock, 1975; Quine, 1987, pp. 87–89; Quinton, 1977(c); Flew, 1984, pp. 159–160. See also sections 7.7 (**idealism**) and 1.13A ('**Platonic ideas**').

D.   Predicate

   (i) '**The sky is blue**.' In that statement, *the sky* is the subject. *Blueness* is **predicated of** (i.e., said of) the subject. **The predicate** is '... is blue'. In traditional logic (section 6.24), however, the predicate would be said to be 'blue' rather than '... is blue' and 'is' would be called the **copula** (i.e., *link* between subject, 'the sky', and predicate, 'blue'). With 'to predicate xiousness of Y', cf. 'to characterize Y as xious' (section 6.3). It follows that 'Is existence a predicate?' (section 1.17(ii)) is a rather jerry-built sentence. Better constructed (though less pronounceable) versions would be: 'Is "... exists" a predicate?', 'Can existence be predicated of anything?' (See Moore, 1959, pp. 115–126.) But 'Is existence a predicate?' is traditional and well-established. The practice of **predication** (not to be confused with *prediction*) is the practice of applying predicates. The adjectival form of the word 'predicate' is '**predicative**'.
   (ii) 'Predicative' has another meaning, in which it is contrasted with 'attributive'. An adjective which precedes its noun (e.g., 'blue' in 'A blue car stood in the driveway') is in **the attributive position**. An adjective separated from its noun by a verb (usually a *copula*: 'is', 'are', 'was', etc.) is in the **predicative** position (e.g., 'blue' in 'The sky is blue').

   An adjective is **grammatically predicative** if it can occur only *in the predicative position*. An adjective is **grammatically attributive** if it can occur *only* in the attributive position. Lacey's examples are, respectively, 'well' and 'veritable' (1976, p. 11) (though, nowadays, one sometimes hears the ugly phrase, 'a well person').

   An adjective is **logically attributive** if it is '**substantive-hungry**', i.e., if it cannot be adequately understood unless it is attached to a noun. 'It's big' tells us nothing of a thing's size unless we know what kind of a thing 'it' is. A big cat is a small animal, whereas a black cat is a black animal. Hence 'big' is logically attributive, but 'black' is not. '**Real**' is logically attributive. An object may not be a real duck, but a decoy, while being a real decoy, not a doll. (See J. L. Austin, 1962, pp. 62–67.) There is controversy over 'good'. (See W. D. Hudson, 1983, pp. 335–339; Foot, 1967, pp. 64–82.) There seem to be no logically predicative adjectives.

(iii) It is fashionable to say such things as: 'The Government's policy is predicated on an increasing demand for Australian minerals.' Here, 'is predicated on' means 'assumes' or 'presupposes'. What, I wonder, is wrong with 'assumes' or 'presupposes'?

E.

An adjective, 'xious', is **alienans** with respect to a noun 'Z', IFF saying that something is an xious Z implies either that that thing is not a Z or that it may not be a Z, e.g.: 'imitation leather', 'prickly pear', 'alleged thief'. See also sections 1.16B (**pseudo, quasi**), 1.23(iv) (**potential**).

1.10 UNIVERSAL, UNIVERSE; COSMOS AND CHAOS; NATURE

A.

The word 'universal' has two principal technical senses:

(i) **'Universal' as an adjective**. A **universal proposition** is one which either affirmatively or negatively predicates something of each of the members of a given class, i.e., a proposition of one of the following forms:

Every S is P.

No S is P.

(see section 6.29A(iv)).

(ii) **'Universal' as a noun**. A ripe tomato, a Soviet flag, and an imprudent sunbather of North European origin are all red. Tom, Dick, and Harry are all human. A human being, a goat, and a bacillus are all organic.

In other words, different objects can 'share' features. A specific object is unique (section 1.22A), but it has features which indefinitely many other objects have. The features are called **universals** in contrast with **particulars**, the objects which **instantiate** them (or are the **instances** of those universals. See section 5.2A). The **problem of universals**, i.e., the problem of saying *what* these universals are and *how* they are related to particulars is almost as old as philosophy itself. For brief accounts of the available options, see Lacey, 1976, pp. 227–230; Flew, 1984, p. 360. For a more detailed introduction, see Staniland, 1973. D. M.

Armstrong, 1975 and 1978 are important recent works. See also sections 7.8 (**realism**), 1.15A.III (*in re*).

B.

For **universe of discourse** see section 1.27.

C.   Less technical senses of 'universe' and 'universal'

Some special technical senses of these words are discussed above and elsewhere in this book (see index). But philosophers and logicians, like everyone else, use these words in less technical senses as well.

(i) 'Universal' as an adjective can mean 'with respect to everything' *or* 'with respect to everything of a certain kind'. Thus, **universal scepticism** would be *scepticism about propositions of all kinds*. (For **scepticism**, see section 7.3A.)

A characteristic may be universal *within* a given group or class. Thus, *being Italian* was universal within the class of Popes reigning between 1524 and 1977. (Cf. section 1.19(iv) on **universally accompanying characteristics**. See also section 1.29 on **commonness**.)

(ii) Then there is the word 'universe' in its 'scientific' sense. When we hear a scientist or science journalist talk about 'The Universe', we are usually pretty sure that we know what he is talking about. Sometimes I wonder whether we *do*. 'The universe' is an odd kind of expression. Bertrand Russell once went so far as to say that there is no such thing as the universe and that the word 'universe' is handy but meaningless (Russell, 1957, pp. 50–51). Obviously, that was not one of Russell's better days, but the oddness and the difficulty still remain. We are more likely to talk sense if by 'universe' we mean 'the upper limit of the series: Earth, solar system, galaxy, cluster of galaxies, . . .' (Geach, 1961, p. 112), i.e., 'the **universe** in this [sense] . . . is simply the whole of that reality which is open, at least in principle to scientific observation' (Wicker, 1964, pp. 29–30). If **physicalism** is true, the universe so defined would be all there is, but that is not part of the definition of the word, 'universe'.

The word 'world' sometimes means 'Earth and its atmosphere' and sometimes means 'universe' (e.g., in some arguments for the existence of God (section 8.20)).

D.   Cosmos (Kosmos)

This Greek word is often translated as 'world' or 'universe'. It is related to the verb 'kosmeo' which means 'to set in order', 'to marshal', 'to arrange'. '**Cosmos**' contrasts with '*chaos*'. So, built into the meaning of the word '**cosmos**' is the *faith* or *blik* (section 5.10) that the universe is orderly, that there are regularities to discover, and (very often) that 'the game's not crook'.

If you want to understand what Socrates is on about in *The Apology*, *Crito*, and *Phaedo*, keep remembering the concept of **cosmos**. Etymologically, 'cosmos' is connected with our word 'cosmetic'. The Greeks associated beauty with order. See Vlastos, 1975, Ch. I; Diamandopoulos, 1967. See also sections 1.13A **(forms)**, 7.25A **(cosmology)**.

E. Nature, natural

Raymond Williams says: ' "Nature" is perhaps the most complex word in the language' (1983, p. 219). That might be a little risky, but it would certainly be amongst the top ten. We should be careful about the way we use the words 'nature' and 'natural' and equally careful about the way we use their 'opposites': words like 'unnatural', 'artificial', 'conventional', etc. See R. Williams, 1983, pp. 219–224, and C. S. Lewis, 1960, Ch. II. For **opposites**, see sections 2.6A(v), 10.1B. For **natural laws**, see section 5.12B.

1.11 ABSTRACT AND CONCRETE

(i) These words frequently occur in philosophical discussion, but are seldom given detailed philosophical attention. That is a pity, because they urgently need clarification.

Sometimes, we disagree about whether something is just. Sometimes, we disagree about whether something is political. Some (not all) of those disagreements are quite intractable. I have been told that that is because justice, injustice, and politics are abstractions. True? If you think it is, try to say what it means. I suspect that it is not true that justice and politics are controversial because abstract. Rather, I suspect that it is because they are controversial that we are tempted to fall back on words like 'abstract' as excuses for opting out of the controversy. See section 8.10B **(contestable)**.

(ii) Traditional grammarians use the words 'abstract' and 'concrete' in order to classify nouns other than proper names (section 2.9). The distinction is a useful one. Unfortunately, grammarians have some difficulty in agreeing on a clear account of what the distinction is. I have found it outlined in these different ways:

Concrete nouns	Abstract nouns
(a) Nouns which denote things perceptible by the senses.	(a') Nouns which denote things not perceptible by the senses.
(b) Nouns which denote things which have physical existence.	(b') Nouns which denote things which do not have physical existence.
(c) Nouns which denote a person or an object.	(c') Nouns which denote a quality or state of a person or object.

Quite obviously, these distinctions are not the same, yet each is intended to do the same job. Further, there is a fair amount of agreement on what nouns are concrete and what nouns are abstract. Everyone would agree that 'chair', 'table', and 'cat' are concrete, whereas 'greenness' and 'Marxism' are not. But the distinctions set out above have difficulty in coping with these intuitive identifications. (a') and (b') make greenness into something positively eerie. (c') does not have that fault, but it does not seem to fit very comfortably with nouns like 'Marxism'. I suggest instead:

> A concrete noun is a noun which, in its singular form, denotes or might denote an individual; e.g., 'table', 'chair', 'cat', 'dragon'.

> An abstract noun is a noun which is not concrete (and is not a mere plural of a concrete noun); e.g., 'greenness', 'kindness', 'Marxism'.

Notice the following points:
  (1) This definition implies nothing about the nature of the 'things denoted by' abstract nouns. Indeed, it does not imply that abstract nouns denote (section 2.10B) anything.
  (2) This definition will remain at some distance from crystal-clarity until an account is given of 'individual'. A tentative account is given in section 1.22D.
  (3) This definition is intended to clarify the notion of **concrete noun**, not to provide a clarification of every possible use of 'concrete' (which is multiply ambiguous – see Wuellner, 1956, p. 27).
(iii) Some abstract nouns are pretty clearly the substantival (i.e., noun) forms of adjectives (e.g., 'greenness') or of verbs (e.g., 'knowledge') and it seems reasonable to say that it is the adjectives or verbs that are primary. There are others which do not seem (at least, do not seem obviously) to be like this. Statements containing words like 'greenness' can usually be translated without much difficulty into statements about actual and/or possible green things, and those will be things which are or could be perceptible by the senses. But it has seemed to many philosophers that there are some statements containing abstract nouns which cannot be so translated; e.g., statements about numbers, about propositions (section 1.2), about geometrical points. The number-words, the word 'proposition', and the phrase 'geometrical point' pretty clearly do not denote any sensorily perceptible individuals. The question then arises: 'Do they perhaps denote individuals which are not sensorily perceptible?' This is sometimes called **The Problem of Abstract Entities**. (The answer 'Yes' combined with the definition of 'concrete noun' given above implies that some concrete nouns refer to abstract entities.) Plato's **Theory of Forms** (section 1.13A) is, in part, an attempt to solve this problem. See Sloman, 1977(a); Quinton, 1977(g). See also section 5.24 (**tangible**, etc.).

(iv) **Abstract nouns and philosophical questions**

    'What is knowledge?'   'What is truth?'

How profound! How puzzling! But, if we are more interested in making progress than in wallowing in profundity, we may find it helpful to rephrase the questions, replacing the abstract nouns with other parts of speech:

    'When someone claims to know that something is the case, is he making the same sort of claim as he makes when he claims that he knows how to make an omelette?'

    'Is knowing that the boss is Tom Smith the same sort of thing as knowing Tom Smith?'

    'What makes the claim to know that X is Y legitimate?'

    'What makes the claim to know that X is Y successful and is there a difference?'

    'When someone says that it is true that X is Y, what is he saying about X? What is he saying about the proposition that X is Y?'

Those are not easy questions, but they may be less flummoxing (if less thrilling) than the ones containing the abstract nouns.

1.12   ABSTRACTION

'Abstract' and 'abstraction' come from '*abstractus*', the past participle of the Latin verb '*abstrahere*': 'to draw [something] away or off from [something else].' 'Abstract' and 'abstraction' in all their varied uses preserve this meaning. An *abstract of an essay* is a summary or synopsis, something 'drawn off' from the work as a whole. That anti-hero of a thousand jokes, the absent-minded professor, is in an *abstracted frame of mind*, i.e., his attention is drawn away from his immediate surroundings. *To consider something in the abstract* is to consider it apart from (i.e., metaphorically, to draw it away from) its normal surroundings.

    Similarly, when we notice that two arguments have the same logical form (section 6.23A) even though their topics are quite different, it is natural to say that we are **abstracting**. The same goes for when we notice that a green flag and a green tomato have something in common which neither shares with a red flag or a red tomato, but precisely what this business of abstracting amounts to is a matter of some controversy. See Geach, 1971, pp. 11–44, or the extracts in Hanfling, 1972, pp. 400–416.

1.13   THE THEORY OF FORMS; INNATE; INSTINCT

A.

The Theory of Forms is one of Plato's central theses. The forms, he argues, are entities which are not perceptible by the senses but are perceptible intellectually. (Another way of saying this: The forms are **non-sensible** but **intelligible** or **intellectible**. See section 5.24.) The forms are not dependent on sensorily perceptible objects: instead, those objects are dependent on the forms. The sensorily perceptible world has what order it has because of its relationship to the forms. This awareness is, for the most part, dim and confused. Plato believes that it can be developed by intellectual and moral discipline.

To some extent, the forms correspond to **universal** terms (e.g., 'justice', 'triangularity', 'greenness', etc., see section 1.10A(ii)), but the theory of forms is more than a theory of universals. It is also – amongst other things – a theory about the foundations of morality and a theory which attempts to solve certain problems about change and stability. See Cross and Woozley, 1964, Ch. VIII; Crombie, 1964, Ch. III; Gosling, 1973.

Plato's word is *eidos* (plural: *eidoi*), and the theory was once known as the **Theory of Ideas**, but the word 'idea' usually means something **mind-dependent** (section 1.9C), which is the reverse of Plato's view. 'Ideals' is better, but even that suggests mind-dependence. The word 'forms' is intended to suggest **pattern** and **what gives order to matter**. See section 1.10B (**cosmos**). A Spanish Republican said: 'If there are no Platonic ideals, then what did we fight for?' (Edel, 1963, p. 323). A very good question.

B.

Something (e.g., an ability, a tendency) is **innate** in X IFF it is inborn in X. 'Innate' is not to be confused with 'intrinsic', 'inherent', or 'indelible' (section 1.19 (vi-vii)).

Innate knowledge and **innate ideas** are knowledge or ideas which are not derived from experience but are *inborn*. Most '**innateness**' (or '**innatist**') theories hold that, without such knowledge or ideas, experience would be impossible. Plato's theory of forms (see **A** above) is one such theory. René Descartes (1596–1650) held an 'innateness' theory of a different kind. John Locke (1632–1714) attacked such theories in Book I of his *An Essay Concerning Human Understanding*, holding that the mind begins as a *tabula rasa* (a blank page), and that all its content comes from sense-experience. This empiricist (section 7.12B–C) view was challenged by Gottfried Wilhelm Leibniz (1646–1716) and by Immanuel Kant (1724–1804). For summaries with references, see Copleston, 1959, Ch. IV; 1958, Chs II, XVII; 1960, Chs X, XI, XVII. Karl Popper (1902–) has argued that the theory of inborn *ideas* is absurd, but that there are inborn *expectations* without which experience would be impossible;

i.e., there is innate *knowledge*. (Popper, 1976, pp. 44–53; 1972(a), pp. 42–52; 1972(b): see index to that book.) Recent work in theoretical linguistics (especially by Noam Chomsky) has given new vigour to the debate on innate ideas. See Chomsky, Putnam and Goodman, 1971; Ryle, 1974.

C.

An **instinct** is an innate disposition towards behaviour. A distinction is drawn between **closed** and **open** instincts. The former are such things as the maternal behaviour of rats and the behaviour of the infant cuckoo. These are very detailed and specific patterns of behaviour, unvarying between individual cases, and demonstrably not learnt. An open instinct, on the other hand, cannot be satisfied in behaviour without learning of some kind (e.g., most, perhaps all, human instincts).

The word 'instinct' is often restricted to *closed* instincts – an unfortunate habit, since it can draw attention away from certain possibilities about human beings. 'Instinct' is sometimes used for the *behaviour*, rather than the *disposition* – another bad verbal habit. See Drever, 1977, pp. 139–140; Midgley, 1979, Ch. III; Midgley, 1981, pp. 151–166; Fletcher, 1968.

1.14 SOCRATES AND HIS PHILOSOPHICAL METHODS; INTERLOCUTOR; AUDITOR

A. Socratic questioning

(i) Many of Plato's dialogues show Socrates seeking **an account** or **definition** (*logos*) of **some excellence of character** (e.g., wisdom, temperance, justice, or, the most general of all, virtue). He is usually seeking it from someone who begins by being quite sure that he knows what it is and ends by being not at all sure. The following is a highly schematized version of Socrates's search (page-references are to the Penguin Classics editions. '*LDS*' = '*The Last Days of Socrates*'):

	Steps	Examples
Step 1	The Interlocutor makes an assertion involving the concept, Tness.	Euthyphro's initial remarks about his prosecution of his father. These remarks involve the concept of **piety**. *Euth.* 3E–4E, *LDS* pp. 21–23.
Step 2(a)	Socrates asks the Interlocutor whether he agrees that 'All T things are alike in being T. Every T thing has the characteristic of Tness which enables us to recognize it as being T and	*Euth.* 5C–D, *LDS* p. 24.

	to distinguish it from a non-T thing. Tness is a unitary characteristic (or unitary set of characteristics) common and peculiar to all T things.'	
Step 2(b)	The Interlocutor accepts this.	
Step 3	Socrates says: 'You can distinguish things which are T from things which are non-T, so you know what Tness is. If you know what Tness is, you will be able to tell me what it is. So please tell me.'	*Euth.* 5A–D, *LDS* p. 24.
Step 4(a)	The Interlocutor then gives examples: 'Tness is something like a, b, c, and d; a, b, and c are T.'	
Step 4(b)	Socrates objects that this does not answer his question. He wants to know what the **single thing** Tness is. He does not want a list of many T things.	*Euth.* 5E, 6A–D, *LDS* p. 24; *Meno* 71D–72A.
Step 5(a)	The Interlocutor presents a definition in the form: 'Tness is that which is U, V, W, and X' or 'A thing is a T thing if and only if it is U, V, W, and X.'	*Euth.* 6D–E, *LDS* pp. 25–26; *Meno* 72B–74E.
Step 5(b)	Socrates proceeds to draw inferences from the definition and claims that it leads to unacceptable conclusions. (Much use is made here of *modus tollens*. See section 6.16.)	*Euth.* 7E, *LDS* p. 26.
Step 5(a)'	The Interlocutor puts up another definition.	*Euth.* 7A–9D, *LDS* pp. 26–30.
Step 5(b)'	Socrates treats it as in 5(b).	
	AND SO ON UNTIL:	
Step 6	The dialogue (usually) ends in *aporia* with Socrates saying something to the effect that we really need to do a lot more work on this problem. (For *aporia* see section 6.22(g).)	*Euth.* 15C–16A, *LDS* p. 41; *Lysis* 222E–223B.

For a more detailed account of Socrates's use of the 'What is Tness?' question, see Robinson, 1953, Pt I, especially Ch. V, and Santas, 1979, Ch. IV.

(ii) Step 2(a) has been criticized on the ground that it is not true of all predicates. The objection is that it is not always the case that, whenever there is a predicate 'T', there is always some characteristic (or set of characteristics) common and peculiar to all things correctly said to be T. The concept of Tness may not be *unitary* as Socrates assumes it must be. (See Hospers, 1967, pp. 69–74, especially the quotations from Wittgenstein and Pitcher, pp. 69–70. For '**common and peculiar**', see section 1.29(iii). For '**predicate**', see section 1.9D.)

(iii) Another criticism is that step 3 seems to assume that, unless we can give a definition of a term, we cannot understand it. More generally, someone might object that step 3 assumes that if we understand term 'T', we must have fully articulate knowledge of Tness and that, if we lack that fully articulate knowledge, we know nothing about T at all. Both these assumptions are false. (Geach calls the practice of arguing as if these assumptions are true 'the Socratic fallacy'. See Geach, 1972, pp. 33–35, or Geach, 1976, pp. 38–41. But see also Crombie, 1964, pp. 37–60, and R. F. Holland, 1981.)

B. Socratic ignorance

A follower of Socrates asked the Delphic Oracle whether Socrates was the wisest of men. The Oracle (which liked to keep the customers happy) said he was. Socrates was very surprised, but eventually decided that the Oracle meant that the wisest of men are those who, like Socrates, know that, in respect to wisdom, they are worthless (*Apol.* 23 A–B; *LDS* p. 52).

This attitude of Socrates was a combination of 'the Socratic fallacy' with something much more respectable: devotion to an unachievable but approachable ideal of perfect knowledge, fully articulate, fully understood, and free from any admixture of error, uncertainty, or obscurity. Socratic ignorance is related to *Socratic maieutic* and *Socratic irony* (C and D below).

C. Socratic maieutic

Maieutic is **the art of midwifery**. Socrates said that, while he had no significant ideas of his own, he was an intellectual midwife who helped other people to 'give birth' to their own ideas. See Crombie, 1964, pp. 15–32, 37–60.

D. Socratic irony

This is an odd one. Most reference books say that it refers to Socrates's habit of treating his interlocutor as an expert when he did not believe that he was.

That is not entirely inaccurate, but more needs to be said. Our word 'irony' is derived from the Greek '*eironeia*', current in Socrates's time. Some of his more hostile interlocutors did *accuse* him of *eironeia*. But they did not mean that he was ironical in any modern sense. By ascribing *eironeia* to him, they were accusing him of deceit, of swindling, of (at the very least) slyness.

How *eironeia* lost its pejorative meaning and gave birth to our word 'irony' is something of a mystery. Perhaps Socrates's followers accepted the word 'in a spirit of irony' (our sense) and subtly changed its meaning, rather as members of other groups have defiantly adopted names used as insults by their enemies (e.g., Old Contemptibles, Rats of Tobruk, and Tory Wets (Brewer, 1970, p. 258; Critchley, 1986, p. 77)). W. K. C. Guthrie (1971(a), pp. 122–129) has some very interesting things to say about Socratic irony and Socratic ignorance.

E. The Socratic Problem

If Socrates wrote anything, it failed to survive. All of Plato's dialogues were written after Socrates's execution in 399 BC. This gives rise to what has been called 'The Socratic Problem': How much is the Socrates of the dialogues a faithful representation of the historical Socrates and how much is he a semi-fictional mouthpiece for Plato's own ideas? The problem is complicated by two facts:

   (i) Three of Socrates's contemporaries, Plato, Xenophon, and Aristophanes, wrote works about him which survive. The three versions of Socrates are mutually inconsistent.
   (ii) Plato's version of Socrates is not internally consistent.

The Socratic Problem is an interesting *historical* problem, but it is not a *philosophical* problem. It *can* sometimes be a problem *for* philosophers – when one is trying to speak about an early dialogue and a late dialogue at the same time, for instance – but most of the time, we can treat most of the dialogues as philosophical dramas in which the central character is named 'Socrates'. See Lacey, 1971.

F.

An **interlocutor** is one who takes part in a discussion or conversation. Not a commonly used word, but handy for talking in general terms about (e.g.) the people with whom Socrates argues.

G.

These days, an **auditor** is usually someone who conducts an official examination of account books and (for some mysterious reason) writes his comments in green ink. But the original meaning of 'auditor' is 'hearer' or 'listener' (cf. 'audience'). Thus, A. E. Taylor (1960, p. 174) says that Phaedo is one of the **auditors** of Socrates's last conversation.

1.15   THING; OBJECT

A.I   The indeterminacy of the word 'thing'

It is possible in principle (even if not possible in practice) to set about answering the question 'How many people are there in the world?' But it is not possible in principle to set about answering the question 'How many *things* are there in the world?' A sparrow is a thing and so is each of its feathers, etc. So (perhaps) is its colour, etc. One can count only things of a certain kind, but a thing is not a kind of thing. Thus, 'thing' is a very *indeterminate* word.

Systems of **categories** (section 3.4A) are attempts to list the **conceptually basic** kinds of thing; i.e., those basic to any kind of understanding whatsoever. See also sections 1.17 (**existence**) and 7.23 (**ontology**), and Lacey, 1976, pp. 25–29.

A.II   More specialized uses of 'thing'

(i) **'Thing' as meaning 'individual substance', 'object' or 'particular'.** E.g.: 'Greenness isn't a *thing*, you know.' To talk or think of an abstraction (see section 1.12) as if it were a substance, particular, or object is called **reification** (i.e., 'thing-making', from Latin *'res'*, 'thing', and *'facere'*, 'to make'). See Nisbet, 1982, pp. 257–261.

(ii) **'Thing' as meaning 'material object'.** Hence the label 'reism' (see section 7.9B(ii)), derived from *'res'*. For **material object**, see B(iv) below.

(iii) **'Thing' as distinct from 'person'.** It might be said that a tyrannical employer treats his employees *as things*, i.e., merely as instruments to his own profit. The words 'reify' and 'objectify' are sometimes (unfortunately) used to mean *to treat as a thing rather than as a person*. See Kant, 1948, pp. 63–67; Paton, 1948, pp. 32–33; Acton, 1970; Benn, 1976; Maritain, 1956, pp. 21–90. See also B(iv) below (**object**) and section 1.24 (**person**).

(iv) **'Thing' as distinct from 'sentient, responsive creature'.** Thus, in Judith Wright's poem 'Child with a Dead Animal': 'the creature changed to thing, kindness to dread,/ the live shape chilled, forsaken, left for dead ...' (Wright, 1975, p. 240). For **creature**, see section 8.21B.

(v) **'Thing' as distinct from 'word'.** E.g.: 'The word "Sphinx" has six letters, but it makes no sense to ask how many letters the thing, Sphinx, has.' See also section 1.6A (**use and mention**).

A.III   *in re*

Literally: 'in thing'. This phrase has two principal kinds of use.

(a) In lawyers' Latin, it is pronounced 'in ree' and is to be understood as 'in the matter of'. 'In re Smith v. Jones' at the top of a solicitor's letter means that the letter is about the case of Smith against Jones. This is a piece of lawyers' Latin which is best left to lawyers.

(b) 'In re' occurs also in the terminology of philosophy, especially in scholastic philosophy (section 7.6A). So used, it is pronounced 'in ray'. 'In re' sometimes contrasts with '*in intellectu*' ('in the mind'), the contrast being between actual, extramental existence and 'existence in the mind' or 'as an idea'. In a similar way, 'in re' can be contrasted with 'in spe', literally 'in hope', though the meaning is also widened to 'in claim'. See also section 1.17 (**existence**).

'In re' is used also in talk about the problem of **universals** (section 1.10). An extreme realist, such as Plato, holds that a universal (e.g., blueness) exists extramentally and independently of its instantiations (blue things). In other words, a universal exists *ante rem* (before the thing) and *post rem* (after the thing) and this existence is something independent of whether anyone knows about it.

St Thomas Aquinas, a moderate realist, holds that a universal exists *ante rem* only as an idea in the mind of whoever (God or man) ponders the possibility of its instantiation, *post rem* only as a remembrance of instantiations of it. The only extramental existence it has is *in re* (in the thing, i.e., in its instances). (See Allers, 1955.)

B.   Object

(i) **A quasi-grammatical sense**. If someone has an attitude to someone else or to something, that other person or that thing is *the object of his attitude*. Similarly, if an activity is in some fashion *directed towards* a person or thing, that person or thing is the *object of that activity*. ('Object' here is *not* synonymous with 'objective' or 'outcome sought'.) Thus, an old pop song sings of 'The object of my affection', while J. N. Findlay suggests that we can 'give greater precision to our use of the term "God"' by saying that God is 'the adequate object of religious attitudes' (1963(a), p. 97). See the neat definition in Runes, 1955, p. 217.

(ii) **'Object' and 'thing'**. From 'Jean is the object of Robert's affections', it does NOT follow that Jean is an object. 'Object' can be used in a sense close to some uses of 'thing' (see A above). To treat or think of other people as objects is to treat or think of them without the *respect due to persons* (section 1.24), to treat or think of them as of importance only in so far as they are either obstacles or means to the attainment of one's own desires. (Cf. the phrase 'sex-object'. See R. Baker, 1975.)

An object in the sense of 'Jean is not an object' would normally be something non-human and even perhaps non-living, or at least something *not identified as* human or living: 'In the dim light, I saw an object by the side of the cassia bush.' There is also a tendency to reserve 'object' for comparatively *solid* things. The word seems to fit hailstones and potatoes better than it fits clouds and raindrops.

(iii) **Material object and formal object**. 'Material object' is an ambiguous expression. In the technical vocabulary of scholastic philosophers (section 7.6A), it is contrasted with 'formal object'. The distinction is complex, but a rough idea of it can be given by example:

> Tom, Dick, and Harry are gazing with rapt attention at a huge waterfall. Tom is contemplating it as a thing of beauty and grandeur. Dick is thinking about its geomorphological aspects. Harry is excited about its potentialities as a source of hydro-electric power. Tom, Dick, and Harry are attending to the one **material object**, but each attends to it **under a different aspect**. The **formal objects** of their attention are different. (Cf. Oakeshott, 1962, pp. 207–208.)

See Wuellner, 1956, pp. 82–83. A material object in *this* sense need not be material in the sense of *corporeal* or *non-spiritual*.

(iv) **Material object (Material body)**. The expression is used in a quite different sense by analytical philosophers (section 7.12A). Philosophers writing about perception (section 5.22B) make frequent mention of **material objects** (or **material things** or **material bodies** or **physical things**), but, as J. L. Austin complains, do not always make it quite clear what they are, beyond the assumption that material objects are what the 'ordinary person' thinks he perceives (see section 7.8(ii) (**naive realism**)). The examples tend to be such things as 'chairs, tables, pictures, books, flowers, pens, cigarettes'. Austin points out that such 'moderate-sized specimens of dry goods' are not the only things the ordinary person thinks he perceives and draws up a list including voices, rivers, rainbows, flames, mountains, vapours (1962, pp. 6ff, 106–107 – much of this is directed against theories of A. J. Ayer, who responds in Ayer, 1976, pp. 49–51 and Chs IV, V; Ayer, 1969, pp. 126–148).

Quinton, whose primary concern is not with perception but with ontological (section 7.23) issues, gives a clearer account than most: a material object, he says, is a thing which is normally perceived as spatially continuous. It has a characteristic, definitive shape and, therefore, boundaries which mark it off from other things. It is the sort of thing which can be identified and re-identified. It can be pointed to and counted. Quinton's material objects are 'bounded, individuated, concrete objects'. See Quinton, 1973(a), pp. 3–11, 12–56, 235–251; Quinton, 1975(a). That is admirably clear, but though Quintonian material objects need not be 'moderate-sized', there does still seem to be a certain bias towards 'specimens of dry goods' and flames, voices, etc. seem to be excluded.

(v) Quinton defines a **social object** as 'a group or institution which contains or involves a number of individual human beings, such as a people, a nation, a class, a community, an association, a society ...' (Quinton, 1975(a), p. 1). At first, the terminology might seem strange. One would not ordinarily call the French middle class or the Royal Society *an object* of any kind. But the term 'social object' is meant to contrast with 'material object' as Quinton defines it. See (iv) above.

1.16   REAL; PSEUDO- AND QUASI...

A.   Real

'What is reality?' some philosopher asks himself, presumably because he is puzzled about something (e.g., about what might be meant by asking 'Are colours really in the objects we seem to see them in?' or 'Can we really be certain about anything?'). But his own question is more likely to deepen his puzzlement than to remove it, and, if he is not very careful, he may give himself the impression that reality is some mysterious, fundamental *stuff* out of which everything is made.

That is a typical case of hypnotism-by-abstract-noun (cf. section 1.11), but even if he rephrases his question as 'What is meant by asserting or denying that something is real?', he may remain puzzled. Perhaps his attention is drawn to a case of this kind: Mr X has delusions: he 'hears voices'. These voices are *not real*, unlike the voice of his psychiatrist, Dr Y, who is saying 'Tell me what the voices say to you.'

No philosophical problems there, perhaps, but read on: Mr X decides to deceive Dr Y. Instead of telling what the *real* delusory voices say, he makes something up, so that he is talking not about his *real* delusions, but about *imaginary* delusions. (But what Mr X tells Dr Y is *a real lie*, not just a mistake.) Our philosopher then proceeds to drive himself in the direction of Dr Y's surgery (i) by wondering how anything can be both delusory and real, and (ii) by trying to spot the common property by virtue of which Mr X's delusory voices, Dr Y's voice, and Mr X's lie are *all real*. (And we cannot solve the problem in the fashion of a friend of my student days. Hearing some Deep Thinker ask: 'Will we ever be able to know the nature of reality?', he looked up from his copy of Ayer's *Language, Truth and Logic* and said confidently: 'Reality? There's no such thing.')

Someone worried by these or similar puzzles needs to read Chapter VII of J. L. Austin's *Sense and Sensibilia*. Austin points out that the primary function of 'real' is *negative*, i.e., the word is used to exclude possible ways of being *not* real and the ways of being not real are many and various. Real silk is contrasted with artificial silk. A real oasis is contrasted with a mirage. The word 'real' does not pick out a characteristic common to real oases and real silk. It is **logically attributive** (section 1.9D(ii)). For some criticisms of Austin's account, see Angluin, 1974; Bennett, 1966; Graham, 1977, pp. 173–184.

Austin's account is certainly not the last word and it could do both with some tightening up and with some extension, but it is much better than these critics think it is. See also sections 1.3 (**true**), 1.21B ('**Not quite the same**').

B. Pseudo-...; quasi-...; sort of

'Pseudo' comes from a Greek word meaning 'false'. 'Quasi' in Latin means 'as if'. In English, they are used as prefixes. See *SOED*. To call something **a pseudo-X** is to say that, though it may look like an X or has been classified as an X, it is not an X. To call something **a quasi-X** is to say that, though it is not an X (or sometimes, perhaps, not 'strictly' an X), it is so much like an X or it functions so much as an X does, that, for many purposes, it can be grouped with the Xs or treated as if it were an X. A **quasi-X** is a **virtual X**. 'Pseudo' stresses real unlikeness as distinct from apparent likeness. 'Quasi' stresses real likeness, despite real unlikeness. A **pseudo-X** is a **so-called X**, i.e., something which is improperly described as an X.

Phrases of the 'pseudo-X' type often (though not always) have a derogatory ring, suggesting pretence, or deliberate deceit, or shoddiness. It is important, however, not to use such phrases *merely* as rude noises. If it is *X*s which you are against, then say so: do not berate all Xs as 'pseudo-Xs'. ('Pseudo-X' makes genuine sense only in contrast with 'genuine X'. Cf. A above (**real**).) Most people who complain about 'pseudo-intellectuals' seem actually to dislike all intellectuals, not merely pretended intellectuals. 'So-called' is often misused similarly. ('This so-called "modern" world of today' – a charming phrase I read somewhere.) See also section 1.9E (**alienans**).

A colloquial use of 'sort of' embraces both 'quasi' and 'pseudo'. A **sort of X** is either *an atypical X* or *a near-X non-X*. See Quinton, 1975(c); Fowler, 1968, p. 573.

1.17 EXISTENCE

(i) Existence is not a strange kind of *stuff* – like tooth-paste or mercury, only much more mysterious. Neither is it a strange kind of activity ('something that things do all the time, like breathing, only quieter – ticking over ... in a metaphysical sort of way' – J. L. Austin, 1962, p. 68n). To say 'X exists' is simply to say that there is such a thing as X. To say 'X has existence' is simply to say (in a very clumsy fashion) that X exists, which is simply to say that there is such a thing as X.

I have used the phrase 'simply to say ...' but, in fact, existence-talk is rather complex and there are problems about it. For one thing, there seem *radically different kinds of thing* that can be said to exist. Gilbert Ryle argues that 'exist' has a variety of senses, saying: 'It would be ... a joke to say that there exist prime numbers and Wednesdays and public opinions and navies ...' (1949, p. 23); i.e., the one word cannot 'fit' all the examples while retaining the same meaning.

The question then arises as to whether any one of those senses is *more basic* than the others. Is it the case that statements about (e.g.) Wednesdays and public opinions and navies are misleading versions of statements about individual people and their activities, or about the actual and possible sensations of people, or about fundamental particles, etc.? Urmson, 1956, is relevant to these problems. See also sections 1.15 (**thing, existence in re, in intellectu**), 7.23 (**ontology**); 5.20 (**reductivism**).

(ii) There is also the problem of 'whether existence is a predicate'. (For **predicate**, see section 1.9D.) The sort of issue involved here is brought out by this example:

A	B	C
An applicant should:	An applicant should:	An applicant should:
(i) have a good honours degree,	(i) have a good honours degree;	(i) have a good honours degree,
(ii) be fluent in French and in English,	(ii) be fluent in French and in English,	(ii) be fluent in French and in English,
(iii) be aged between 25 and 35.	(iii) be aged between 25 and 35,	(iii) be aged between 25 and 35,
	(iv) be able to touch-type.	(iv) exist.

Anyone satisfying specification B would also satisfy specification A, but someone could satisfy specification A without satisfying specification B; therefore, specification B contains more than specification A. But, though specification A contains three items and specification C, like specification B, contains four items, anyone who satisfies specification A *logically must* satisfy specification C; therefore, C fails to list any characteristic not listed by specification A.

Existence, therefore, is not a-predicate-like-most-predicates, but it *might* still be a predicate of *some* kind. Those interested in pursuing this further might look at Pears, 1967 and James Thomson, 1967. Prior, 1967(a) deals with this and related problems, but is not light reading. The issues here are relevant to some versions of the ontological argument for the existence of God (see section 8.20A). See also Pontifex and Trethowan, 1953.

(iii) There is a quite different collection of problems which might also be labelled *worries about existence*. These are problems about *whether human life has a purpose or meaning* (and also about *what it means* to wonder whether human life has a purpose or meaning). These problems are obscure but important. For that reason, they need to be treated seriously, and a problem is not treated seriously if logical niceties are ignored. See Halverson, 1976, pts XII, XIII, for a useful introductory treatment. See also Sprigge, 1984. For **existentialism**, see section 7.14.

1.18 CHARACTERIZE, CHARACTERIZATION

To characterize a thing Y as xious is to apply the predicate 'xious' to Y; it is to predicate xiousness of Y (see section 1.9D). But it *need* not be the same as *saying* (i.e., *asserting*) *that Y is xious* (cf. section 1.4(iii)). There is more than one way of characterizing.

Y is characterized **categorically** as xious when someone *asserts* that Y is xious; e.g.: I categorically characterize Primus as a murderer when I say 'Primus is a murderer.'

Y is characterized **hypothetically** (or **conditionally**) as xious when someone asserts a conditional statement in which the predicate 'xious' is applied to Y in the *antecedent* or in the *consequent* (see also section 4.12); e.g.:

> 'If Primus is a murderer, he should be locked up.'
> 'If Primus were a murderer, he would have behaved very differently from the way he did.'

Notice that neither of these hypothetical examples implies that Primus is a murderer. Indeed, the second implies that Primus is NOT a murderer. (That example is what is called a **subjunctive** or **counterfactual conditional**. See section 4.15.)

'Characterized' on its own, however, can usually be interpreted as 'categorically characterized'.

1.19 CHARACTERISTICS

(i)
> 'Greenness is a property of Y.'
> 'Greenness is a quality of Y.'
> 'Greenness is an attribute of Y.'
> 'Greenness is a characteristic of Y.'

Generally, all of these statements would be taken as synonymous, and rightly so. But some philosophers (for perfectly legitimate reasons) have given special technical senses to 'property', 'quality', and 'attribute' (see, e.g., Wuellner, 1956, pp. 10, 99, 103; Runes, 1955, pp. 27, 256, 261; Quine, 1987, pp. 22–24), and some philosophers have given *differing* technical senses to these words. This can be very troublesome. A writer can use one of these words non-technically and be taken to be using it technically, and that can lead to all sorts of misunderstandings. Fortunately, we still have the word 'characteristic'. So far as I know, it has not yet been messed about with technically. (Something thoroughly odd at Runes, 1955, p. 48 does not, I think, count.) It is safe to say: 'Greenness is a characteristic of Y IFF the proposition "Y is green" is true.'

(ii) Xiousness is a **defining characteristic** of things of type y IFF the statement 'There is a thing of type y which is not xious' is self-contradictory;

e.g.: '*Being mammalian* is a defining characteristic of cats.' 'Essential characteristic' is usually synonymous with 'defining characteristic', but see also section 3.5A(iv). For **definition**, see section 2.5.

(iii) Xiousness is a **non-defining but possible characteristic** of things of type y, IFF:

> The statement 'There is a thing of type y which is not xious' is not self-contradictory;
>
> AND
>
> The statement 'There is a thing of type y which is xious' is not self-contradictory.

E.g.: *being ginger* is a possible characteristic of cats. So is *being purple*, though so far as I know, it is not an *actual* characteristic of any cats.

Any individual thing of type y will have those characteristics which are defining characteristics of type y PLUS various characteristics which are non-defining but possible for things of type y. 'Possible' here means *logically possible* (section 3.12A).

(iv) Xiousness is a **universally accompanying characteristic** of things of type y IFF the statement 'There is a thing of type y which is not xious' is not self-contradictory, *but* is false as a matter of fact (see section 3.15). The following statement is not (and never has been) self-contradictory, but there was a time when it was false as a matter of fact: 'There is a psychoanalyst who is not a Central European.' During that time, *being a Central European* was a universally accompanying characteristic of psychoanalysts.

(v) N.B. The following two statements are NOT synonymous:

> 'Greenness is a characteristic of X.'
> 'Greenness is characteristic of X.'

The second statement means that greenness is a *particularly noteworthy* characteristic of X. See also section 3.5B (**integral**).

(vi) A thing or person will have some characteristics which are, *logically speaking*, independent of the existence of anything else. Tom may have inherited his red hair from his ancestors, but, *whether that is true or false*, Tom is still red-haired. Such a characteristic is **an intrinsic characteristic**. But, logically speaking again, Tom can be a brother or a son only by virtue of his relationship to someone who exists or has existed. Such a characteristic is **a relational characteristic**. (N.B. Characteristics of either of these types can also be characteristics of the type dealt with in (ii)–(iv) above.)

(vii) **'Inherent'** is often used much as *'intrinsic'* is, but it is (usually) less strictly defined. The etymology of 'inherent' relates it to 'sticking in' something. In many uses, there is at least a suggestion that what is said to be inherent in X is something which it would be very difficult to remove or change. Sometimes, 'inherent' seems to be used as a synonym for 'essential' in either its technical (subsection (ii) above) or its popular (section 3.5A(iv)) use. 'Innate' (section 1.13B) is sometimes confused with 'inherent'. It should not be. See also section 3.5B (**integral**).

(viii) *per se; per accidens*. Two Latin phrases sometimes used in speaking of different kinds of characteristic. A literal translation of '**per se**' is 'through itself'. 'Y is xious **per se**' means that Y is xious by reason of what Y is in itself, not simply by reason of its relations to other things. '*Per se*' is ambiguous between 'essentially' and 'intrinsically'. '*Per accidens*' contrasts with '*per se*' and has a corresponding ambiguity. 'Y is xious *per accidens*' can mean 'Y happens to be xious', 'Y is contingently xious' or it can mean 'Y is xious simply by reason of its relations to other things and not by reason of what it is in itself.' (See Rolbiecki, 1955.) '**Accidentally**' is sometimes used technically as a synonym of '**contingently**' (i.e., 'non-necessarily'). See also section 3.5A.

1.20   QUALITIES; QUALITY AND QUANTITY

A.

In ordinary speech, to talk of the **quality** of something is usually to talk about how good (or how bad) that thing is. In philosophical talk, the word usually has a different meaning.

  (i) To speak of **the qualities of** a thing is generally to speak of those aspects of it which are grounds for applying predicates to it; e.g., if I say 'Milk is white', I am ascribing the quality of whiteness to milk. But, for reasons given in section 1.19(i), 'characteristic' may be a safer word to use than 'quality'. See section 1.9D (**predicate**).

  (ii) To speak of **a qualitative change** in X is to say that X has become a different kind of thing. If X and Y **are qualitatively the same**, X and Y are things **of the same kind**. (See also section 1.21.) In other words, 'qualitatively' means 'with respect to kind'.

B.

In ordinary talk, **quality** is often contrasted with **quantity** (*how good* as contrasted with *how big* or *how much*). In philosophical talk also, **quality** is often contrasted with **quantity**, but the distinction is rather different: it is the distinction between *what kind* as contrasted with *how big* or *how much*. In some varieties of Marxism, the doctrine that *quantitative changes can become qualitative changes* is regarded as very important. See Lobkovicz, 1973. Note the spelling and pronunciation of 'qualitative' and 'quantitative': each has *four* syllables. For **quality and quantity of proposition**, see section 6.29A (iii–v).

1.21   SAME; 'NOT QUITE'

A.

'Same' can be a tricky little word to handle as there are different kinds of sameness.

(i) **Qualitatively the same and numerically the same**

Mr Primus and Mr Secundus are lunching in a restaurant. 'I'll have the roast lamb,' Mr Primus says to the waitress. 'I'll have the same,' says Mr Secundus.

That is a case of two people wanting the same. But it is not a conflict of interests. The waitress has not been put in the position of an arbitrator who has to decide between two rival claimants. Each wants a thing *of the same kind.* Where two things are *of the same kind,* they are **qualitatively the same**.

But if the police are looking for a man with a red beard and a slight limp, it is not just *any* man with a red beard and a slight limp that they are looking for. 'That's the same man!' in such a case does not mean 'That's *a* man of the same kind': it means 'That man is *the* man who ...' (robbed the bank, or whatever). The sameness here is **numerical** sameness. When one individual is both the individual-who-is-X *and* the-individual-who-is-Y, then the-individual-who-is-X is numerically the same as the-individual-who-is-Y.

(ii) **Identity: qualitative and numerical**

Another way of saying what has just been said is that the-individual-who-is-X is **identical with** the-individual-who-is-Y. But, while this may be precise enough for some purposes, it is not precise enough for all purposes. Two things which are alike in all relevant respects (e.g., the proverbial two peas in a pod) are also sometimes said to be identical. But pea A is *not* identical with pea B in the way in which the Prime Minister of Australia in 1988 and Robert James Lee Hawke of Wills are identical. Pea A is **qualitatively identical** with pea B. The PM of Australia in 1988 and R. J. L. Hawke of Wills are **numerically identical** – '**numerically** identical' because if you are counting people, the PM of Australia in 1988 and R. J. L. Hawke of Wills do not count as two, but as one. The same point is made by the old nursery riddle:

Eliza, Elizabeth, Betsy and Bess,
They went to the woods to find a bird's nest.
They found a nest with five eggs in it.
They took one apiece and left four in it.

(iii) **Contingent identity and necessary identity**
These are two varieties of numerical identity. R. J. L. Hawke is numerically identical with the Prime Minister of Australia in 1988. But the proposition 'R. J. L. Hawke is Prime Minister of Australia in 1988' is **contingent**, not **necessary** (section 3.5); so R. J. L. Hawke is **contingently identical** with the Prime Minister of Australia in 1988. The proposition that Tom's eldest brother is Tom's eldest male sibling is a necessary proposition; so Tom's eldest brother is **necessarily identical** with Tom's eldest male sibling. See also sections 2.10A **(sense and reference)**, 7.9B(iv) **(the identity theory of mind and body)**, and 1.24(iii) **(personal identity)**. See Quine, 1987, pp. 89–92.

(iv) The expression **strict identity** is sometimes met with. But, as it is ambiguous between 'numerical identity' and 'necessary identity', it is one we could well do without.

(v) For **equivalence as a relation between propositions** (i.e., mutual implication), see section 10.3.

(vi) **Material equivalence**. This infelicitous piece of terminology is dealt with in section 6.13.

(vii) **Equivalence by definition**. Two **synonymous** expressions are **equivalent by definition**. ' "X" is equivalent by definition to "Y" ' can be written:

$$\text{'X'} \equiv df \text{ 'Y'}$$

For **synonym** see section 2.6A. For **definition**, see section 2.5. See also section 2.10A on **sense and reference.**

(viii) **Other uses of 'equivalence'**
The word 'equivalence' has, of course, other uses. Should we say that the legislature of Xland is the Xlandic equivalent of the legislature of Yland? Well, we *can*. But, if we want to be really precise, we should not say that unless the Xlandic legislature has precisely the same role in the Xlandic political system as the Ylandic legislature has in the Ylandic political system. If it has not, we would be speaking more accurately if we said *either* that the Xlandic legislature is the Xlandic *counterpart* of the legislature of Yland, *or* that the Xlandic legislature is *analogous to* the Ylandic legislature. See B below (*mutatis mutandis*) and section 8.19A (**analogous**).

(ix) To **equate** X with Y is to say X is *equal to* Y. It is not to compare X with Y, to contrast X with Y, or to reconcile X with Y. It *might* be to *identify* X with Y (see (ii)–(iii) and (viii) above). Cf. section 2.6A(ii) (**synonymous**).

B. **'Not quite the same'**

(i) *Ceteris paribus*. Literally: 'other things being equal.' Less literally: 'provided there are no special circumstances.'

(ii) *Mutatis mutandis*. Literally: 'with those things changed which have to be changed.' Less literally: 'with the necessary changes.' If someone says something about the rules of chess and then says, '*Mutatis mutandis*, the same point can be made about the rules of bridge,' what he means is that *basically* the same point can be made about the rules of bridge, though, because of the differences between the games which are (he hopes) as evident to his audience as to himself, one might have to word it differently.

(iii) **Virtual, veritable**. These must be distinguished. **A virtual X** is something which is not quite an X, but which (perhaps) is so near to being an X that it can, for some purposes, be treated as an X. ('It might as well be an X.') To call something **a veritable X** is to say that it is an X indeed, an X without any doubt at all. See also section 1.16B (**pseudo and quasi**).

1.22   UNIQUE; *SUI GENERIS*; FUNGIBLE; INDIVIDUAL

A.

A thing, X, is **unique** in some respect IFF X, in that respect, is unlike every other thing with which it can be intelligibly compared. N.B.:

(i) To say that something is unique is not necessarily to praise it.

(ii) A unique thing is always unique *in some respect*. In other respects, the thing may not be unique at all.

(iii) In a trivial sense, *everything* is unique. One match is much like any other match from the same box, but match A is numerically distinct from match B (see section 1.21A(ii)); it occupies a different position, and a microscope would reveal other differences. What is worth counting as a uniqueness depends on the topic of investigation.

We are often told that 'unique' does not admit comparison or degree. Certainly 'X is more unique than Y' does not seem to make much sense (though X might be unique in more respects than Y or in some more interesting respect than Y). I am not so sure about *degree*. I have never been able to see what is wrong with 'almost unique', but 'very unique' seems to be nonsense. Do not use 'unique' where 'rare' or 'remarkable' or 'unusual' would do. See Fowler, 1968, p. 665.

B.

To say that something is *sui generis* is to say that it is unique. The literal meaning of the Latin phrase implies that the thing is the only member of its kind. Generally, I think someone who says that something is **sui generis** is not saying literally that the thing cannot in any way be classified with other things. What he is usually doing is protesting against a misleadingly over-simplified classification. See section 5.18 (**heuristic**).

C.

'**Fungible**' is etymologically connected not with 'fungus' but with the Latin 'fungor, functus' in its sense of *performing a function*. If something is fungible, it has no value or significance beyond its function or use. If thing T no longer performs its function as well as it once did, it can easily be discarded and replaced by another specimen of the same kind. If something is fungible, *either* it is not unique in any significant respect *or* any significant uniqueness it has makes it a bad specimen of its kind.

The word 'fungible' is not in common use, but there are certainly jobs for it to do. At least part of the horror most of us feel at the imaginary society of Huxley's *Brave New World* is the fungibility of its inhabitants, especially the 'Deltas' and 'Epsilons' (see the opening paragraphs of Ch. XV). Something of the same revulsion is at the basis of misgivings about genetic engineering, cloning, and other such marvels. See, e.g., Howard and Rifkin, 1980; Goodfield, 1977; O'Donovan, 1984.

D. Individual

A very ordinary, but excruciatingly complicated word. My own attempt at definition goes like this:

> **An individual** is something which

> > may be dissectible, but whose parts or members cannot continue their characteristic function independently of that of which they are parts or members;

> AND

> > can continue to function even if detached from the collective of which it is a member.

Since there are degrees of independence, detachment, and detachability, and degrees to which a thing can continue its characteristic function, there are degrees of individuality. Other accounts (compatible with this one) stress *distinguishability, enumerability, re-identifiability*. Talk of *the individual and society* is common, and often tends to suggest that 'society' is the enemy of 'the individual', which may be at some distance from the whole truth. See R. Williams, 1983, pp. 161–165; Routley and Routley, 1980, pp. 217–259; Quinton, 1975(a); Jouvenel, 1963, pp. 43–66; Koestler, 1970, Chs III, IV; Burnheim, 1978; Strawson, 1959. See also subsections A–C above and section 1.15A (**object**). A different and much thinner sense rests individuality on enumerability (i.e., countability-as-one) alone. In this sense, such problematic entities as *beauty, tennis*, and *the Gothic style of architecture* are all individuals. See Lacey, 1976, pp. 93–94. This thin sense of 'individual' is of no help in elucidating the distinction between abstract and concrete nouns (section 1.11). The *OED*'s entries for 'individual' and its cognates are well worth reading.

1.23   ACTUALITY AND POTENTIALITY (ACT AND POTENCY)

(i) This distinction has had a bad press. Hobbes said that 'potentiality' is 'found only in School-divinity, as a word of art, or rather as a word of craft to amaze and puzzle the laity' (1840, p. 299). Christopher Brennan called it 'a sweet absurdity' (1960, p. 17). A contemporary has said that 'the very notion of potentiality is ... very vague and nefarious [*sic*]' (Werner, 1979, p. 66). Despite these condemnations, the distinction is quite indispensable. (Indeed, Werner unwittingly makes use of it in the same essay.)

(ii)   'Can Joan Sutherland sing the Mad Scene from *Lucia di Lammermoor*?'

'Of course she can. Probably no one can sing it better.'

'Is that so? Well, I happen to know that she has a bad attack of laryngitis and can't even *speak* above a whisper. Do you still say she can sing the Mad Scene?'

Well, what *would* we say? We cannot say 'No' when we know how she sang last week and how (with any luck) she will sing next week. But we cannot say, 'Yes, she can sing' about someone who can scarcely force any sound at all out of her throat. Clearly, we need a distinction, and the distinction between **actuality** and **potentiality** will get us out of trouble. She cannot actually sing now, but she still has the potentiality to sing as she did last week, so, in that sense, she *can* sing the Mad Scene. We must, however, recognize that there are different varieties of potentiality. The vocal potential of a mature but laryngitic Sutherland is a different kind of thing from her vocal potential as a child. And there are different kinds of actuality too. Even a laryngitic Sutherland is actually a singer (particularly when contrasted with someone who cannot stay on key for one bar of 'Happy Birthday to You').

(iii) There are other distinctions that need to be made. In one sense, something is a potential Y IFF it could be made into a Y. In this sense, the Mona Lisa is a potential patch on a tent and any human being (e.g., Mrs Thatcher) is a potential stew for a cannibal feast. That can be called **potentiality in a weak sense**. In a *very* weak sense, Z is a potential actuality IFF the description 'Z' is not self-contradictory. Thus, in a *very* weak sense, I am a potential monarch of the solar system and the Rev. Ian Paisley is a potential Pope. But, if X is something which, under normal circumstances, if not interfered with, would develop into a Y, then X is a potential Y **in the strong sense**.

(iv) It may also be the case that being a potential X in the weak sense is a way of *not* being a Y, but being a potential Y in the strong sense is a way (although not the standard, typical way) of *being* a Y. Certainly, saying that an acorn which has just fallen from the branch is a potential oak seems to have a quite different meaning from saying that an acorn germinated in the soil is a potential oak. ('Potential' (weak sense) is an *alienans* adjective. 'Potential' (strong sense) *may* be non-*alienans*. See section 1.9E.)

(v) Potentiality is certainly a complex and difficult notion, but that is because (like most philosophically interesting notions) it is *all-pervasive*. Without a notion of potentiality, we could have no notion of a predictable future or an intelligible present. (Even so unexciting a concept as that of a bottle of ink embodies beliefs about what can be done with a bottle of ink, how it can be treated, what will happen to it under various circumstances, etc., i.e., the concept has potentiality-beliefs built into it.)

(vi) The actuality/potentiality distinction was first articulated by Aristotle as a way of dealing with certain puzzles about the possibility of change. See Copleston, 1947, pp. 310–314. See also Wuellner, 1956, pp. 3–4, 93–94; Pontifex and Trethowan, 1953, Ch. V.

(vii) The notion of potentiality is of great relevance to controversy about the morality of abortion. See, e.g., M. Cohen, 1974; Feinberg, 1973, 1984; Noonan, 1970; Rachels, 1979, pp. 104–203; Wasserstrom, 1979, pp. 1–74.

1.24   PERSON

A perfectly ordinary and indispensable word. A complex, obscure, and controversial word.

(i) 'Person' is not a synonym (section 2.6A) of 'human being' or of 'man' in its 'species' sense (section 1.25), even though there are sentences in which the words 'man' or 'human being' can be replaced by 'person' without damage to the meaning; e.g.:

> A: A man who throws a custard pie at the Vice-Chancellor shows scant respect for good food.

> B: A person who throws a custard pie at the Vice-Chancellor shows scant respect for good food.

Sentence B says all that would normally be intended by sentence A and says it clearly. But consider the following:

> C: Everyone agrees that all men are mortal.

> D: Everyone agrees that all persons are mortal.

C is true, but D is false: some people believe in God. Further, if someone wonders whether dolphins might be persons, he is not wondering whether they might be human beings.

(ii) Personhood is a controversial concept, but there is a measure of agreement that the traits central to it include the following:

Consciousness of self and of non-selves;

Having interests and aspirations and the capacity of planning and acting to further them;

The capacity to communicate, not merely by means of a fixed and complete system of signals, but by means of an 'open-ended' linguistic system which can embrace an indefinite (virtually infinite) range of messages on an indefinite (virtually infinite) range of topics;

Awareness that some (and only some) non-selves are like oneself in respects such as those listed above.

Respect for persons is a recognition that there are others who have their interests, aspirations, projects, etc. and that, if I have a right to pursue my interests, aspirations, projects, etc., they have an equal right to pursue theirs; i.e., if I am entitled to resent being treated as a mere object (e.g., as an obstacle to be removed or as a means to be exploited) others are entitled to resent my treating them in that fashion. See section 1.15A.II(iii) and references given there. See also section 1.15B (**object**).

For an admirably clear and succinct statement of the notion of respect for persons, see Benn, 1984, p. 141. Much recent work on the concept of a person has been associated with philosophical controversy about abortion, which raises the questions:

Is the foetus a person?

Is the foetus entitled to the respect which persons are entitled to?

Is the foetus *a potential person* (see section 1.23) in a sense which implies that it *is* a person or in a sense which implies that it *is not* a person?

There are also the more general questions:

Is being a human sufficient for being a person?

Is humanhood sufficient to establish a right to respect?

See Feinberg, 1984, pp. 102–172; Downie and Telfer, 1969; R. Young, 1979; Werner, 1979.

(iii) **The problem of personal identity**
What does it mean (and is it true) to say that I am identical with the person who bore the name 'A. W. Sparkes' in 1970? Is bodily continuity necessary/sufficient/necessary-and-sufficient (section 4.16) for personal identity? Is continuity of consciousness necessary/sufficient/necessary-

and-sufficient for personal identity? Is memory neces-
sary/sufficient/necessary-and-sufficient for personal identity? Can a
person survive bodily death? See Vesey, 1974(a), pp. 54–64, and 1974(b);
Hanfling, 1972, pp. 43–87; Parfit, 1971; Geach, 1969, pp. vii–ix, 1–29;
A. Rorty, 1976; Perry, 1975; B. Williams, 1973.

(iv) **Another sense of 'personal identity'**

The previous sub-section concerned what *philosophers* call *the problem
of personal identity*. There is a more popular use of the phrase, as in
'Tom is going through an identity crisis', which, I think, can mean
either or both of the following:

Tom has come to wonder whether certain descriptions of himself
which he has hitherto assumed and regarded as fundamental are
actually true.

Tom is worried over his *autonomy* as an agent, i.e., over whether he
is 'his own man' (or, as they say these days, 'his own person'). This
notion of *autonomy* is closely linked to the notion of *respect for
persons* ((ii) above). See Benn, 1976; Benson, 1983. (See also sections
1.6D(ii) (*in propria persona*); 7.15A (**ego**).)

Identity-talk of this kind can be mere melodramatic piffle (see K.
Hudson, 1977, pp. 115–116), but it does not have to be. How people
see their *identity* (in this sense) is closely related to what social and
socio-political groups[1] they see themselves as members of and how
they see that relation of 'membership', so this kind of *personal* identity
is related to questions of *group* identity. See Kamenka, 1982; W. J.
M. Mackenzie, 1978; Milne, 1968, Ch. VI; Burridge, 1979.

(v) **'Persons' and 'people'**

I have noticed myself writing 'people' a few times above, which is the
ordinary, everyday English plural of 'person', but I wrote 'respect for
persons' which is standard philosophic usage. Philosophers also talk
about whether *persons* can survive bodily death. The apparent oddness
of such talk is, I think, quite valuable. It can draw attention to the fact
that what is being said need not be something applying to human beings
only. It can also draw attention to the fact that the philosopher saying
such things should have some theory about what *a person is*.

Though the philosophic 'persons' may look odd, it is the use of
'people' as the plural of 'person' that is the oddity. Etymologically, the
two words are quite distinct (see *ODEE*).

(vi) **Personhood, personality, character**

Tom's personhood is *the fact that he is a person*, a fact analysable along
some such lines as those suggested in (ii) above. *Tom's personality* is

(roughly) *the kind of person Tom is. Tom's character* is *Tom's personality seen from a moral angle.* See Harré, 1976; Finnis, 1983; Peters, 1973.

1.25   MAN

These days, many people tell us that we should not use the word 'man' in high-level general statements about members of the human species. While I sympathize with the motives behind that advice, I have no intention of following it.

The word 'man' is extraordinarily versatile. In its most common use, it means *adult male human being*, but that is no ground for saying that that is the word's *only* (or, perhaps '*real*') meaning. There is, therefore, no reason for saying that using the word 'man' in its 'species' sense insults women. That complaint would be no more sensible than the complaint that the usage insults adult male human beings by misappropriating the word that 'belongs to them' and making it refer as well to women and children. The word does not 'belong to them'. Consider such usages as 'Masters and men' (obsolescent), 'Officers and men of The Moreton Regiment' (alive and kicking). There is no implication here that the officers are either non-male, or non-adult, or non-human and such a proposition about *masters* would also be obviously preposterous.

There is, of course, such a thing as 'sexism in language' (e.g. the distasteful slang use of the word 'bird'), but it is a mistake to be so keen on tracking it down that one finds it as easily as other would-be reformers find salacity. Mary Anne Warren writes:

> What sort of entity, exactly, has the inalienable rights to life, liberty and the pursuit of happiness? Jefferson attributed these rights to all *men*, and it may or may not be fair to suggest that he intended to attribute them *only* to men. Perhaps he ought to have attributed them to all human beings.
>
> (Warren, 1979, pp. 42–43. Her emphases.)

Jefferson would have replied that, unless Ms Warren has an inadequate grasp of English, she must *know* that he meant all human beings.[2]

The word 'man' in this 'species' sense can be a very equalizing word, drawing attention to the capacities and limitations which we share by virtue of our species-membership, especially the limitations. I first met it when I was very young and was being introduced to that sombre text 'Remember, man, thou art dust and unto dust thou shalt return.' The expositor was a woman and she had no doubt whatsoever that it applied to her. A poem of Judith Wright concerns a child's realization of death:

> The sight you saw had found its home in you;
> it breathes now in your breath,
> sits in your glance. From it those gasping tears fell and will always
>   fall.

They sign you Man, whose very flesh is made
of light's encounter with its answering shade.
　　Take then this bread, this wine; be part of all.

(1975, p. 241)

Setting aside all considerations of metre and rhythm, would anyone say that the substitution of 'human being' or 'person' for 'Man' would leave the meaning of the lines undiminished? Would anyone say that Judith Wright is guilty of sexism? The answer to both questions is 'Yes.' There are people who would say such things. But they do themselves no credit and the language no justice.

　　The real danger in using the word 'man' in high-level generalizations about human beings is not 'sexism'. It is the danger of falsehood or solemn nonsense. The word can tempt people to make wild over-simplifications, what Mary Midgley calls 'cure-all explanations, sweeping theories that man is basically sexual, basically selfish or acquisitive, basically evil or basically good' (1979, p. 57). Talk of 'Man' can obscure the immense complexity within each individual human being and blur the differences between individuals and between groups. It can tempt us into treating something local and temporary as a timeless truth about all members of the species.

　　These are reasons for caution in using 'man' in its 'species' sense, but neither they nor worries about sexism should lead us to abandon it altogether. See also section 1.24 (**person**). For a different view on these (and most other) matters, see Spender, 1980, and C. Miller and K. Swift, 1980. See also R. Williams, 1983, pp. 188–189, 148–151.

1.26   PERSONAL PRONOUNS

A.   'She', 'he', 'his', 'her'

In the 1970s (a bizarre decade in Australia), a Royal Commission was set up 'To inquire into and report upon the family, social, educational, legal and sexual aspects of male and female relationships' (ARCHR, 1977(a), p. ix). The Commissioners given this daunting assignment found something very sinister in the fact that 'There are no singular personal pronouns in English capable of including the male and female gender.' They therefore proposed the abolition of 'he' and 'she' and their replacement with either 'id' or 'hei' or 'se' (ARCHR, 1977(b), pp. 41–42). The suggestion of 'id' is highly infelicitous and offensive: quite apart from its sense in Freudian talk, 'id' is the Latin neuter word corresponding to 'that' (i.e., meaning roughly 'that thing'). I see no advantages in linguistic de-sexing and de-humanization. As to the general point: there are languages which do not distinguish gender in pronouns: e.g., Hungarian and Tok Pisin (Papua New Guinean Pidgin). If you think that makes Hungarian and Melanesian societies less 'sexist' than

Anglophone societies, tell that to a Hungarian or Melanesian woman. It will give her a good laugh.

But, for all that, there *is* a problem about third person pronouns. 'Man' (section 1.25) is a versatile word and its varying uses can be fairly easily distinguished, but 'he' is closely tied to individuals, *male* individuals. 'He' does not have as clear a species-sense as 'man' has (unless used in the same sentence or a neighbouring sentence). We *need* an ungendered personal pronoun, but where do we get it? No one with any sense of the ridiculous could accept the Royal Commission's bizarre linguistic recommendations. Some writers have used 'it' as a personal pronoun, but that is as displeasing as 'id'. Some writers use feminine pronouns in an ungendered sense:

> The self-contained set of *a person's* interests is only a subset of *her* interests...
>
> (Routley and Routley, 1980, p. 255. My emphases.)

But that will not do. If 'his' is jarring, why should 'her' be any more appropriate? And it is so eye-catching as to be distracting, which may not be the case with 'his'. (This use of 'her' also seems just a little *unctuous*: 'And said, "What a good young person am I!" ')

So what should I do if I am tempted to write 'Each student must submit his essay by the due date'? That one is easy. Put it in the plural: 'All students must submit their essays by the due date.' But what if I am tempted to write: 'If a student is unable to submit his essay by the due date, he should contact me as soon as possible'? If that is translated into the plural, some of the sense goes. I need the singular because here I am talking about individual and exceptional circumstances. Dale Spender (1980, p. 149) suggests that we should use ' "they" for sex-indeterminable references'. Following her advice, the sentence should read: 'If a student is unable to submit their essay by the due date, they should contact me as soon as possible', but that, again, destroys the reference to individual and exceptional circumstances. I am afraid we are stuck with 'his or her' and 'he or she' (which can be spelt 's/he').

B. 'My'

This word troubles consciences. There are academics who get lost in extraordinary circumlocutions for fear of saying 'my students' or 'my seminar'. There are clerics who declare their firm intention of never saying 'my parish' or 'my congregation'. Their reason is that 'my' is what the grammar books call *a possessive pronoun* and it is wrong to go on as if other people are your property. I accept both those propositions, but they do not imply that no one should ever say 'my students' or 'my parish'. So-called 'possessive' pronouns are used to indicate ownership, but they are used to indicate other relationships as well ('my boss', 'my enemy', 'my Lord and my God'). If English grammars had followed Latin grammars and talked of the **genitive** case rather than the **possessive** case, we might have been spared much bother.

1.27 UNIVERSE OF DISCOURSE

Those things with which a discussion, argument, narrative, or other piece of discourse (section 1.1) is concerned. As Augustus de Morgan (1806–1871) put it:

> If we remember that in many, perhaps most propositions, the range of thought is much less extensive than the whole universe, commonly so called, we begin to find that the whole range of a subject of discussion is, for the purpose of discussion, what I have called a *universe*, that is to say, a range of ideas which is either expressed or understood as containing the whole matter under discussion.
>
> (Quoted in Stebbing, 1950, p. 55.)

'Universe of discourse' is often abbreviated to 'universe'. For other senses of 'universe', see section 1.10C. See Stebbing, 1950, pp. 55–56; Flew, 1984, p. 361.

1.28 MUTUALLY EXCLUSIVE; COLLECTIVELY EXHAUSTIVE; MUTUALLY EXCLUSIVE AND COLLECTIVELY EXHAUSTIVE

(i) Two classes A and B are **mutually exclusive**, IFF there is nothing which is a member of both classes (e.g., the class of cats and the class of dogs).

(ii) Two classes A and B are **collectively exhaustive** within a given universe (section 1.27) IFF every member of that universe is either a member of class A or a member of class B (e.g., in the universe of adult human beings, the class of men and the class of women are collectively exhaustive).

(iii) Two classes A and B are **mutually-exclusive-and-collectively-exhaustive** within a given universe, IFF every member of that universe is either a member of class A or a member of class B, AND no member of the universe is a member of both.

See also sections 6.11 (**disjunction**), 5.21 (**dichotomy**), 10.1B (**logical opposites**).

1.29 COMMON; PECULIAR; COMMON-AND-PECULIAR

The word 'common' is ambiguous. 'Xiousness is common *amongst* the ys' means that *many* ys are xious. 'Xiousness is common *to* the ys' means that *every* y is xious. 'Common to the ys' is synonymous with 'universal within the class of ys'. In the old and well established terminology discussed below, 'common' has this sense: 'common *to*', not 'common *amongst*'.

The way in which 'peculiar' is used here might seem a little odd, even a little peculiar. The most common use of the word today makes it mean 'odd', 'strange' (usually a puzzling or disturbing kind of oddness or strangeness). But there is an older (and not obsolete) sense of 'peculiar' in which it means *that which belongs exclusively to some specified person, place, thing, or to the members of some specified group* (adapted from *SOED*). This sense of 'peculiar' relates *peculiarity* to *uniqueness* (section 1.22A). 'The koala is peculiar to Australia' means not that the animal treats the country in an odd way but that it has no habitats elsewhere. In this use, *peculiarity* is always *peculiarity to*. It is this second sense of 'peculiar' which I am concerned with here. Please notice that there is only one 'r' in 'peculiar'.

(i) A characteristic Y is **common** to the members of a class A, IFF every member of the class A possesses the characteristic Y.

(ii) A characteristic Y is **peculiar** to the members of a class A, IFF no non-member of the class A possesses the characteristic Y.

(iii) A characteristic Y is **common-and-peculiar** to the members of a class A, IFF every member of the class A possesses the characteristic Y *and* no non-member of the class A possesses the characteristic Y.

For **common noun**, see section 2.9.

2   Meaning

2.1 MEAN, MEANING; MEANINGLESS

(i) These are perfectly commonplace words, yet, as Max Black remarks, 'A little reflection will show "meaning" and its cognates to be one of the most overworked words in the language: it is a very Casanova of a word in its appetite for association' (1972, p. 224). Hospers (1967, pp. 11–12) lists eight different senses. Such words need to be used carefully, especially when we are talking or writing philosophy. Each of the following is sometimes intended when someone says 'p means q':

> 'p implies q'
> 'p suggests that q'
> 'p gives strong support to q'
> 'p can be explained only on the assumption that q'.

(ii) **Theory of meaning** is an important branch of philosophical activity. It 'explores', as Flew's *Dictionary* says very neatly, 'the various aspects of our understanding of words and sentences, and our ability to endow them with a symbolic function' (1984, p. 225). For introductory accounts, see: Lacey, 1976, pp. 122–126; Crystal, 1980, pp. 222–223; Alston, 1964, Ch. I; Black, 1972, Ch. VII; D. E. Cooper, 1973, Ch. II; Quine, 1987, pp. 130–131, 189–192. Parkinson, 1968, is a useful collection of articles. See also sections 2.10B (**connotation, denotation, designation**); 2.2 (**semantics**).

(iii) **Lexicography**. The strict meaning is *writing or compiling a dictionary*. Less strictly, any attempt to discover or to disclose the meanings of words is a **lexicographical** activity.

(iv) If Mr A says that Mr B's remark is **meaningless**, he is saying that Mr B's remark has no meaning. If Mr A thinks he is saying in a very emphatic way that Mr B's remark is false, he is muddled. The word 'meaningful' is often used in a virtually meaningless fashion. See K. Hudson, 1977, p. 154.

The devotees of the **Verifiability Principle** gave the word 'meaningless' a special technical meaning (see section 5.4) but very few people are sure what it was.

2.2   SEMANTICS, SEMIOTICS, SYNTACTICS, PRAGMATICS, SEMANTIC

(i) **Semantics** is the study of signs (including and especially words, phrases, and other verbal signs) and of their relations to what they signify (i.e., the study of *meaning*, in some senses of that promiscuous word – see section 2.1). **Semantics** is one branch of **semiotics** (or **semiosis**), the general study of signs. **Syntactics** is the study of the structure of signs (roughly synonymous with 'grammar'). **Pragmatics** is the study of what is done with signs and with their effects. See Crystal, 1980, pp. 315–318; Alston, 1964: see index, 'semantics', 'signs'.

(ii) **Semantic features/structure** are often contrasted with **syntactic features/structure**. Thus (A) 'Do it for Fred's father', (B) 'Do it for Fred's friend', and (C) 'Do it for Fred's sake' all have a similar syntactic structure, but (A) and (B) have a similarity in semantic structure which they do not have with (C). Cf. section 6.23 (**logical and grammatical form**).

(iii) The distinction between **semantic features** and **pragmatic features** is, at times, so intangible as to vanish, but it does have some point. There are respects in which (E) 'Johann is a Kraut' says precisely the same thing as (D) 'Johann is a German' and there are respects in which it says something very different. The two statements appear to have the same truth-conditions (section 1.3A(ii)). On the other hand, (E), unlike (D), appears to presuppose unfavourable judgements about Johann and his compatriots, and the effects of uttering (E) (especially in Johann's hearing) are likely to be different from those of uttering (D). Consider also:

> (F)   'Johann is a German, but he is not of any European nationality or origin.'
>
> (G)   'Johann is a Kraut, but I admire Johann and Germans generally.'

While (F) is self-contradictory, (G) is not. There is, however, certainly some kind of *inherent logical oddity* about (G). It may be useful to call the respects in which (G) is logically odd and the respects in which (D) differs from (E) **pragmatic features**. (I borrow my examples from D. E. Cooper (1973, pp. 54–61) whose view is rather different.) See section 2.10B (**connotation**) and section 2.4 (**emotive meaning**).

(iv) In journalistic and popular use, 'a semantic issue', 'a semantic difference' have come to mean 'a merely verbal issue', 'a merely verbal difference', 'a distinction without a difference' (see section 2.11). There is no good reason whatsoever for using 'semantic' in this fashion. The difference between 'The house is on fire' and 'The house is not on fire' is semantic, and it usually does matter.

(v) The words 'semantic', 'semantics' are often misused as an excuse for sheer laziness and negligence. At meetings, people who raise questions about the meaning of a proposed resolution will often be rebuked for 'raising merely semantic issues' as if it did not matter at all what the resolution meant. It is noteworthy that a disputant who says that an opponent's point is 'merely semantic' never goes on to say 'so I will adopt your way of speaking'. Such people always stick adamantly to their own original wording. Cf. sections 8.5A–B (**legalistic, pedantry**).

That indicates that more than mere laziness can be involved in this misusage. During an Australian industrial dispute the Transport Workers' Union demanded a clarification as to 'whether the Government has agreed to withdraw, or merely defer, an application to the Arbitration Commission for speedy deregistration of the TWU' (*Sydney Morning Herald*, 27 July 1981, p. 2). The then Prime Minister, Mr Fraser, dismissed this 'as a matter of semantics'. Quite clearly, the difference between undertaking not to do something and undertaking not to do it immediately is not a trivial or merely verbal difference.

2.3   CRITERION

(i) Primus says that pursuing some line of conduct is a good thing to do. Secundus responds with 'How do you define the word "good"?' Primus says: 'Exactly as the *OED* does: "The most general adjective of commendation, implying the existence in a high, or at least satisfactory, degree of characteristic qualities which are either admirable in themselves, or useful for some purpose."' Secundus is unlikely to feel satisfied, but it is his own fault: what he *wants* is information about the standards Primus uses when he applies or refuses to apply the word 'good'. Unfortunately, that is not what he *asks* for. Those standards we can, following R. M. Hare (1952, Ch. VI), call Primus's *criteria for the word 'good'*. See also section 2.11(ii).

(ii) This distinction between **meaning** and **criteria** helps us avoid many muddles. It may well be true that there is nothing common-and-peculiar (see section 1.29) to all crimes except that they are actions forbidden by a law which also prescribes a punishment for those who perform them. From this, some hasty people have drawn the conclusion that 'an action is a crime only because it is defined as such[1] by law' (Buckley, 1976, p. 64) which makes it sound as if there is no good reason why one thing is a crime and another is not. But the conclusion is too hastily drawn and too carelessly expressed. There may be differing reasons why certain differing actions should be forbidden and punishable by law. There may also be no good reason why some actions which are crimes should be crimes, but that question cannot be settled by considering the definition of the word 'crime' (see also Flew, 1975, pp. 91–92).

(iii) The word 'criteria' is plural. One should no more say 'A criteria is ...' than one should say 'A books is ...'.

For a brief exposition of the special role of 'criterion' in the philosophy of Wittgenstein, see Quinton, 1977(h).

2.4   EMOTIVE LANGUAGE AND EMOTIVE MEANING

'Emotive' is often treated as a trendy substitute for 'emotional', but that is to waste a good word.

(i) **Emotive language** is language which either expresses or tends to excite emotion. In recent times, the phrase 'emotive language' has tended to become a piece of emotive language. There is a popular belief that once you have located a piece of emotive language in your opponent's argument, you need argue no further to show that he is wrong and should be ignored. That is a *non sequitur* (section 4.21). See also section 9.4B (**reason and emotion**).

(ii) **Emotive meaning**

'Johann is a German.' (D)
'Johann is a Kraut.' (E)

As remarked above (section 2.2(iii)), there is a sense in which these statements can be said to have the same meaning. There is also a sense in which they can be said to have very different meanings. Although they have the same truth-conditions (e.g., both will be true if Johann was born in Germany of German parents; both will be false if Johann's parents were Ghanaians who named him after the composer of 'The Blue Danube'), (E) expresses a very unfavourable attitude to Johann and his (presumed) compatriots, whereas (D) is neutral. Such cases have led some to distinguish between *factual* (or *descriptive* or *propositional*) meaning and *emotive* meaning:

Emotive meaning is a meaning in which the response (from the hearer's point of view) or the stimulus (from the speaker's point of view) is a range of emotions.

(C. L. Stevenson, 1944, p. 59)

Some (e.g., D. E. Cooper, 1973, pp. 54–61) have argued that this is an inappropriate use of the word 'meaning'. Another difficulty is that, while such a pair of statements as (D) and (E) above make the same central claim about their topic (in this case, Johann), the second invokes not merely emotion, but a whole body of belief about how Germans are likely to behave, which is at least partly as 'factual', 'descriptive', or 'propositional' as (D) (though vastly more complicated and debatable). Thus, if Cooper is right, so-called 'emotive meaning' may be misdescribed by the word 'meaning', and, if I am right, it may be inadequately described by the word 'emotive'. See Alston, 1964, pp. 44–49; Black, 1972, pp. 138–148.

2.5 DEFINE, DEFINITION; DEFINITIONAL FIAT

(i) 'Define' has a great variety of meanings. *SOED* gives eight main senses and a few minor ones as well. Of these, the following correspond best to philosophical usage:

'To set forth the essential nature of'
'To set forth what (a word etc.) means'.

(Some philosophers would say that the former is only a muddled way of expressing the latter.) It is possible to understand a word without being able to define it (section 1.14A(iii)). See Lacey, 1976, pp. 48–49; Geach, 1976, Ch. IX; Robinson, 1954.

(ii) Please do not use 'define' as a fancy substitute for 'call'. An Australian politician (one with ample opportunity to know better) once said:

The Australian community and legislatures have become increasingly aware of and concerned with matters which may be *defined as* matters of private morality and private conscience.

(Whitlam, 1970, p. 4. My emphasis.)

If he had used the word 'called', he would have been speaking more clearly and less pompously. If the simple little monosyllable 'called' seemed insufficiently dignified, he could have said 'characterized as' (section 1.18). See also section 2.3(i).

(iii) **Definitional fiat**

A *fiat* is a decree. (The word is borrowed from Latin in which it means 'let it be done' or 'let it be made'.) If a philosopher, commenting on the work of another says: 'Mr X makes "S is P" true by definitional fiat' what he means is that Mr X has chosen to define words in such a way that, *granted his definitions*, 'S is P' is a necessary truth.

2.6 SYNONYMY AND ANTONYMY; HOMONYMY AND HOMOPHONY

A. Synonym, synonymous, synonymy, synonymity; antonym

(i) If X is **synonymous** with Y, X *has the same meaning as* Y. So, X and Y must be words, phrases, or *symbols* of some other kind. (For **symbol**, see Alston, 1964, Ch. III; Austin, 1979, pp. 117–133.)

(ii) Frequently, 'is synonymous with' is used as if it meant 'always calls to mind', 'is closely associated with', 'is a prime example of'; e.g.:

'Rockefeller is synonymous with money.'

'ITT is synonymous with international capitalism.'

At best, this way of talk is metaphor of a rather wild kind. At worst, it is pretentious muddle. Avoid it when talking philosophy. Confusing words with things of other kinds is one of the most virulent philosophical diseases. Cf. section 1.21A(ix) (**equate**).

(iii) It seems to be a mere matter of taste whether you use 'synonymy' or 'synonymity' as the abstract noun-form, but using them both in the same piece of writing gives a disagreeable impression of carelessness.

(iv) *Perfect* synonymy is rare. It is sometimes alleged that there are only two perfect synonyms in English: 'gorse' and 'furze', though 'under-nourishment' and 'malnutrition' have been nominated as candidates (not to mention 'synonymy' and 'synonymity'). **Meaning** itself (section 2.1) is a rather obscure notion, hence there will be similar obscurities in the notion of synonymy. (Two expressions might be synonymous in most respects yet not interchangeable without oddness.) See D. E. Cooper, 1973, pp. 166–173; Fowler, 1968, pp. 611–613. Professor Quine 'despair[s] of making sense of ... synonymy' but does so in a book which he translated into French and back again into English (Quine, 1970, pp. 67 and xi–xii. See also pp. 3, 8–9).

(v) An **antonym** is 'a term which is the opposite of another, a counter-term' (*SOED*). Thus, 'antonym' is an antonym of 'synonym'. Antonymy is an obscure notion, both for the reasons which make synonymy obscure, and also because the notion of *opposition* which it embodies is very broad. Thus, Nuttall, 1943, gives 'black' as the antonym for 'white', which would not surprise anyone. But is 'black' *the* opposite to 'white'? 'Non-white' is also *an* opposite to 'white' and it clearly has a different meaning from 'black'. See section 10.1B.

B.   Homonymy

The verbs 'deduct' and 'deduce' (section 5.13A) are very different in meaning. The substantival (i.e., noun) form of each is 'deduction'. Should we say that 'deduction' is **ambiguous** (section 2.7)? We *might*, but 'deduction'-from-'deduce' and 'deduction'-from-'deduct' are so very different in meaning and in derivation that it would be clearer to say that here we have two words with the same shape and sound.

I am recommending that the two 'deductions' should be treated as **homonyms**: 'separate words that happen to be identical in form' (Fowler, 1968, p. 248. See also Stebbing, 1950, p. 21). The substantival form is 'homonymy' (stress the second syllable). Homonymy does not always involve identical pronunciations; e.g., 'unionized', in industrial-relations-talk and in physics-talk.

C.

Two words are **homophones** IFF they are different orthographically (i.e., in spelling) and semantically (i.e., in meaning), but identical phonetically (i.e., in sound) (whereas a pair of homonyms are identical orthographically). See Fowler, 1968, p. 248.

English has borrowed from many other languages. As a result, it is particularly rich in homophones. Another result is that English spelling has a rather erratic look. Every second person will tell you that English spelling is absurd and should be made more phonetic. But, granted the large number of homophones, non-phonetic spelling comes in useful. 'There's a buoy floating in the Lake,' you can say, 'I mean b-u-o-y, not b-o-y.' If our spelling were phonetic, it might take much longer to explain what you meant. And, by that time, they might have put out the lifeboats. The substantival form of 'homophone' is 'homophony', pronounced with the stress on the second syllable. Homonymy and homophony are the source of puns, good and bad. They can also be the foundation of very bad arguments. See section 4.24 (*figura dictionis*).

2.7 AMBIGUITY AND VAGUENESS

(i) A word or sentence is **ambiguous** if it can be interpreted in more than one way. See Horner and Horner, 1980, pp. 3–19, 134–142. 'Laszlo is a Hungarian' could be ambiguous. Is it about his national origin or his legal nationality? Contexts can sometimes remove ambiguities.

(ii) To **disambiguate** an expression is to remove its ambiguity, either by recasting it or by stating which sense you intend.

(iii) To *complain* of **vagueness** is to complain that what has been said is, in some relevant dimension, *unacceptably* indeterminate.'

(Flew, 1975, p. 70. My emphases.)

Note the emphasis. It is not always reasonable to complain of indeterminateness. 'Pour in a very little sulphuric acid' might well be objected to as unacceptably indeterminate, because sulphuric acid is dangerous stuff. But if a cookery book says 'Fry the onion in a very little olive oil', we have nothing to complain about. If we know anything about cooking with oil, that is all the precision we need. In a little book professing to teach lecturers how to lecture, I have seen the stern advice that lecturers should never use 'vague words like "some", "most" or "many" '. It would seem to follow from this that, if a lecturer is tempted to say 'Many Athenians resented the Sophists' or 'Most Englishmen in the late sixteenth century were Protestants', he should remain silent until he can produce figures. That does not seem to me to be very sound advice. On both **ambiguity** and **vagueness**, see Flew, 1975, pp. 69–73.

Black, 1949, pp. 23–58, is an interesting study of vagueness. See also sections 2.8 (**obscure**), 8.5B (**pedantry**).

2.8   OBSCURITY (AND SOME WORDS LIKE 'OBSCURE')

A.   Obscure, abstruse, obtuse

Three very useful words, provided they are not confused with one another.

(i) 'Obscure' comes from the Latin '*obscurus*' ('dark'). In contemporary English, 'obscure' and 'obscurity' are most frequently used in connection with *figurative*, rather than *literal* darkness: the 'darkness' of something hard to understand or interpret, or the 'darkness' surrounding someone or something not widely known, rather than the darkness of one of those coffee shops which use subdued lighting to conceal the state of the walls.

Not every vague utterance is obscure: 'I'll call sometime tomorrow' is vague as compared with 'I'll call at five past ten', but it is not obscure. An utterance might be obscure because of ambiguity ('Australian Shares Quiet in London' says the headline. The report concerns the Stock Exchange). But some obscure utterances are neither ambiguous nor vague; e.g.:

> This finitude of the End consists in the circumstance, that, in the process of realising it, the material, which is employed as a means, is only externally subsumed under it and made conformable to it. But, as a matter of fact, the object is the notion implicitly: and thus when the notion, in the shape of the End, is realised in the object, we have but the manifestation of the inner nature of the object itself. Objectivity is thus, as it were, only a covering under which the notion lies concealed.
>
> (Hegel, 1892, p. 351)

For other splendid examples, see Horner and Horner, 1980, pp. 3–19, 134–142. 'An obscure philosopher' is ambiguous between 'a philosopher whose work is hard to understand' and 'a philosopher who is not well known'. For **ambiguity** and **vagueness**, see section 2.7.

(ii) 'Abstruse' comes from a Latin word meaning 'hidden'. It has the sense of *hard to understand because deep and recondite*. An illiterately written, ignorant, muddle-headed article might well be **obscure**, but it would not be **abstruse**.

(iii) 'Obtuse' comes from the Latin word '*obtusus*' ('blunt'). In contemporary English (apart from 'obtuse angle'), it usually means the absence of intellectual 'sharpness', e.g., 'slow on the uptake', 'unobservant', 'stupid'.

B. Obscurantist

'Obscurantist' does not mean the same as 'obscure', neither does 'obscurantism' mean *the habit of talking or writing obscurely*. To be obscurantist is *to oppose inquiry or enlightenment or reform*. Of course, whether something *is* a genuine reform or a genuine instance of enlightenment is one of those things people can disagree about. 'Obscurantist', therefore, is a **contestable** expression. See section 8.10B.

2.9 COMMON NOUNS AND PROPER NOUNS

In this distinction of traditional grammar, 'common' means *shared by many* (cf. section 1.29); 'proper' means *belonging to just one*. The distinction is usually put thus:

A proper noun is used to refer to a particular individual person or thing. A common noun refers to any member of a class.

Thus, 'man', 'city', 'musician' are common nouns. The usual examples given of proper nouns are examples of what common parlance calls (simply) *names*: 'Charles', 'Sydney', 'Engelbert Humperdinck'. But the formula defining **proper noun** fairly obviously does not fit these examples perfectly. There are countless bearers of the name 'Charles'. There is a Sydney in Nova Scotia as well as one in New South Wales. 'Engelbert Humperdinck' names a German composer who died in 1921 and an English pop singer of the 1970s. The definition of proper noun fails to fit *all* the usual examples. It does fit International Standard Book Numbers and the American Social Security Number, but those are not usually regarded as names.

Though 'Charles', 'Sydney', and 'Engelbert Humperdinck' do not conform perfectly to the definition of **proper noun**, they are not common nouns. The members of the class of Charleses share the name 'Charles', but have and need have no properties in common that are not found amongst the members of the classes of Williams, Fredericks, etc. The Carolinity (or 'Charlesness') of the Charleses is *merely* a shared name. The 'man-ness' of men is more complicated; hence dictionaries contain definitions of 'man', but not of 'Charles' (see section 1.10A(ii) on **universals**).

So-called 'proper nouns' can be rendered 'more proper' (as it were) by the addition of descriptive phrases. As we have seen, 'Charles' on its own does not quite do what the grammar books say a proper noun should, but if you add to it 'II, King of England, Scotland, and Ireland', then you have what has been called *a uniquely referring expression*. It picks out one and only one individual. The cataloguers of a great library, faced with a glut of writers called 'David Hume', identified David Hume the philosopher by calling him 'David Hume the historian'.

Various philosophers have adopted and adapted and transmogrified the grammatical notion of the proper noun (or, as they are inclined to call it,

proper *name*). See Searle, 1967; Lacey, 1976, pp. 50, 122–126. Geach (1961, pp. xv, 109–110) argues that the word 'God' 'is not a proper noun but a predicable general term'.

2.10   SENSE AND REFERENCE; CONNOTATION AND DENOTATION

The first of these distinctions is about **proper nouns** or other *uniquely referring expressions*. The second concerns **common nouns** (section 2.9).

A.

'**Sense and reference**' is the usual translation of Gottlob Frege's German phrase '*Sinn und Bedeutung*'. His example is *the morning star and the evening star*. The expressions 'the morning star' and 'the evening star' both refer to the same object, so the morning star is identical with the evening star. (**Identity** is discussed in section 1.21.) Nevertheless, the statement 'The morning star is identical with the evening star' is an informative statement, unlike the trivial tautology (section 3.7) 'The morning star is identical with the morning star.' Further, to discover that the morning star is identical with the evening star is to make a discovery about astronomy: it is not merely to make a discovery about the meaning of a word, as it is when we discover that the morning star is identical with *stella matutina*. To discover *that* is merely to discover the Latin equivalent of an English phrase. The expressions 'the morning star' and 'the evening star' are said, therefore, to have **the same reference**, but **different senses**. Other examples: 'The Prime Minister of Australia in November 1988' and 'The Leader of the Federal Parliamentary Labor Party in November 1988'.

The expressions 'the feast-day of St Patrick' and 'the anniversary of Marx's funeral' quite clearly differ in *sense*, but they have the same *reference*: 17 March.

For introductions to Frege's philosophy see Passmore, 1968(a), pp. 147–155; Dummett, 1984. Lacey, 1976, pp. 122–126 and T. J. Richards, 1978, Ch. XI, are also very helpful.

B.   Connotation and denotation; intension (comprehension) and extension; designation

This is a complicated and somewhat confused area of philosophical terminology. Here, I cannot do more than give very general guidance.

   (i) *Connotation as distinct from denotation*
        The following is an accurate description of the talk of many philosophers: The denotation of a word is all of the individual things which that word can be used to refer to. The connotation of a word is the set

of characteristics a thing must have to be included in the denotation of that word. Thus (if *SOED* is to be believed), the **connotation** of 'snake' is being 'a limbless vertebrate constituting the reptilian order *Ophidia* (characterized by a greatly elongated body, tapering tail, and smooth scaly integument)'. The **denotation** of 'snake' is every creature that is, has, or will have those characteristics.

The same distinction can be drawn by the use of the words 'intension' (instead of 'connotation') and 'extension' (instead of 'denotation'). Please note the spelling of 'intension'.

'Comprehension' has been used as a synonym of 'intension', but that use is now archaic.

Some philosophers, however, use the word 'denotation' (or 'extension') differently. They would say that the denotation of 'snake' is not each and every creature satisfying the definition, but *the class* of all such creatures (which raises lots of lovely questions about the existence and nature of classes, on which, see Flew, 1984, p. 64; Quine, 1987, pp. 22–26; Black, 1975, pp. 85–108).

See Prior, 1967(b), p. 35; Prior, 1967(c); Quinton, 1977(a); Adams, 1967, p. 456; Kretzmann, 1967, p. 394; Brody, 1967, pp. 64, 67.

(ii) **Connotation as distinct from meaning; designation**

Let us suppose that *SOED* has succeeded in giving the *meaning* of the word 'snake'. It is also true that the word 'snake' has other *associations* for most people: snakes are thought of as dangerous, slimy, and revolting. Those characteristics are sometimes called the **connotation** of the word 'snake'. (I borrow the example from Hospers.)

In the first sense of 'connotation', every snake MUST have the characteristics listed when we list the connotation. In this second sense of 'connotation', it is possible that at least some snakes do not have all the characteristics that are listed when we list the connotation. (Not all snakes are dangerous, none are slimy, and whether they are all revolting is a matter of taste.)

Because of this ambiguity and because other words are available, some have proposed that the word 'connotation' be dropped from our vocabulary. 'Associations' can take over the job just discussed and 'intension' can be used as a replacement for 'connotation' as contrasted with 'denotation'. Some use the word 'designation' as a replacement for 'connotation' (e.g., Hospers, 1967, pp. 48–56). Unfortunately, some others use it as a replacement for 'denotation' (e.g., Devitt, 1981). 'Designation', then, is another good word spoilt.

2.11   MERELY VERBAL DISPUTES

(i) Primus, a Queenslander, and Secundus, a Londoner, are trying to remember when some event occurred:

> Primus: 'It happened about tea-time.'
> Secundus: 'Oh no, much later, round about supper-time.'
> Primus: 'But it couldn't have happened so late.'

If each is speaking his native dialect, then there is no genuine disagreement between them, even though they may think there is. In Primus's dialect, 'tea-time' is the time of the evening meal. The Londoner, Secundus, uses 'supper-time' in that sense, whereas Primus thinks of supper as a cup of coffee and a slice of raisin-toast after the theatre. What Secundus calls 'tea', Primus calls 'afternoon tea'. A little bit of informal **lexicography** (section 2.1(iii)) will clear the whole thing up. Their dispute is **merely verbal**, not a genuine dispute at all. Without the lexicography, they may go on disputing hammer-and-tongs, but their opinions on the point at issue do not differ.

Quite obviously, not all disputes over the words to be used are **merely verbal**. If Tertia and Tertius disagree over whether the appropriate word for the thing making the noise outside is 'possum' or 'burglar', their disagreement is straightforwardly factual.

(ii) But there are more complicated cases, neither straightforwardly factual nor pointlessly verbal. If John refers to certain islands as 'the Falklands' and Juan responds with 'Malvinas!', their dispute is most unlikely to be merely verbal, the sort of thing that can be settled by someone pointing out that the linguistic habits of the speakers' native communities differ. That particular difference rests on differences of a more substantial and intractable kind. See section 2.2 (**semantic**).

The case of the cat, Montrose, in Iris Murdoch's *The Nice and the Good* is similar. The rather terrifying children in Montrose's household are constantly inventing tests of his intelligence, but the question is never resolved because the children 'were always ready to return to first principles and discuss whether cooperation with the human race was a sign of intelligence at all' (Murdoch, 1968, p. 15). The children's disagreement is not over the *meaning* of the phrase 'intelligent cat'. They disagree over the *criteria* for the application of that phrase. See sections 2.1, 2.3.

3 Nonsense, necessity, and possibility

3.1 SELF-REFUTING, SELF-REFUTATION

A statement is **self-refuting** IFF *either* its meaning *or* the manner or medium of its utterance is *sufficient* to show that it is false.

People sometimes say 'Every rule has an exception.' If by 'rule', they mean 'universal affirmative statement', what they say is self-refuting *by its own meaning* (since *it* is a universal affirmative statement). On the other hand, 'I cannot utter a single sentence in English' is self-refuting if spoken or written in English, but not if translated into some other language. 'I cannot speak' is self-refuting if spoken, but not if written. (In these examples, it is the *medium* of the utterance which is significant.) If a man says 'I am not losing my temper', he may or may not be telling the truth, but, in some cases, the *manner* in which he says it may be conclusive evidence that he *is* losing his temper. For something solid on self-refutation, see Passmore, 1961, Ch. IV. See also section 5.8 (**self-fulfilling, self-frustrating, self-stultifying**).

3.2 SELF-CONTRADICTORY, SELF-CONTRADICTION

A **self-contradictory** statement is one which is internally inconsistent and, therefore, *on logical grounds*, cannot be true. If a statement is self-contradictory its **negation** is **analytically true** (see section 3.6). If a statement is self-contradictory, all statements **equivalent** to it are self-contradictory (see section 10.3).

'Black cats are not black.' (A)
'There are round squares.' (B)
'Cats eat nothing but grass.' (C)

(A) and (B) are internally inconsistent. (C) is inconsistent with something outside itself (namely: the behaviour of cats). It is, however, quite consistent in itself.

Self-contradiction is one variety of **self-refutation**, but not all **self-refuting** statements are self-contradictory. If Primus says, 'I do not exist,' he has quite clearly said something which is false and no ordinary falsehood either. But he has not uttered a self-contradiction. The statement 'Primus does not exist' is equivalent to his statement and it is not self-contradictory. The statement 'Primus exists' is the negation of Primus's statement, but it is not an analytic truth. See section 7.13B (*cogito ergo sum*).

3.3   NONSENSE AND ABSURDITY

(i) The exclamation '**Nonsense!**' is a term of emphatic rejection which is often used in response to preposterously false statements, like the examples in section 3.2. But, in the **strict** sense of the word, nonsense *cannot* be true and *cannot* be *false* because it is without meaning (section 2.1): **non-sense**.

'The gostak distims the doshes.' That has the syntactic structure (section 2.2) of an English indicative sentence (section 1.5), but it cannot be a statement because its key 'words' (or 'verbiform components') lack meaning. The point is not that there are no gostaks, but that there are no linguistic rules for classifying something as a gostak or for excluding it from that class (and the same goes for distimmings and doshes). Thus, 'gostak' differs from 'mermaid'. There are no mermaids, but 'mermaid' is a perfectly intelligible English word. 'The mermaid kissed the Minister' is not nonsense (in the strict sense). It is merely false.

'If anyone kissed the Minister, it was not a mermaid' would be true. 'There are no round squares' is *necessarily* true, but 'The gostak does not distim the doshes' is every bit as nonsensical as the original sentence. Cf. sections 6.23 (**logical and grammatical form**) and 3.4B (**category mistake**). For the strange phrase, 'a nonsense', see P. Howard, 1978, pp. 119–121. The sentence 'about' the gostak is borrowed from Ogden and Richards (1956, p. 46), who borrowed it from A. Ingraham.

(ii) '**Absurd**' (like '**Nonsense!**') is sometimes used as a more intense version of 'false', especially in order to reject a proposition on highly general and/or well-known and well-established grounds. If someone says: 'My cat is ill', what he says *may* be false, but only an examination of the animal will tell. If he says: 'My cat understands differential calculus', his statement is **absurd** because it conflicts with very well-known and well-established general propositions about the intellectual capacities of cats and the intellectual complexity of differential calculus. In other words, the statement is rejected as an assertion of an **empirical impossibility** (section 3.12A(ii)).

'Absurd' is also a suitable word to use when rejecting a statement on the ground that it is **self-contradictory**, i.e., on the ground that it asserts a *logical impossibility* (section 3.12A(i)). When geometrical propositions are rejected as **absurd**, they are rejected on that ground.

'Absurd' is used also of syntactically statement-like utterances (section 2.2 (ii)) which cannot be true or false because they are non-sensical, including those sometimes said to involve **category mistakes** (section 3.4B). For **reduction to absurdity**, see section 8.8C.

The word 'absurd' (or, to be precise, '*absurde*') is also used by various French philosophers and dramatists as a reaction to their startling discovery that all human beings are mortal and that, even when alive, no one gets everything he wants. See T. Nagel, 1971. See also section 7.14 (**existentialism**).

3.4 CATEGORIES AND CATEGORY MISTAKES

A. Categories

(i) Aristotle (384–322 BC) used this term to apply to **basic kinds of predication** (section 1.9D(i)). The sentence frame 'Socrates is ...' can be completed not merely in many different ways, but in several different *kinds* of ways. If we fill the gap with

'human', we ascribe membership of a *kind*;
'exophthalmic', we ascribe a *quality*;
'five feet seven inches tall', we ascribe *quantity* (or *size*);
'older than Plato', we ascribe a *relation*;
'in Athens', we ascribe *spatial location* (*place*);
'[a man who lived] in the fifth century BC', we ascribe *temporal location* (*time*);
'talking', we ascribe an *activity*;
'accused of impiety', we ascribe *something undergone*.

(ii) Kant (1725–1804) used the term 'category' for what he regarded as the basic ways in which a human mind has to think about experience if experience is to be intelligible. In Kant's view, there are four basic categories, each of which is divided into three sub-categories:

Quantity	*Quality*	*Relation*	*Modality*
Unity	Reality	Inherence and subsistence	Possibility or impossibility
Plurality	Negation	Cause and effect	Existence or nonexistence
Totality	Limitation	Reciprocity	Necessity or contingency

(iii) Although Kant is concerned with classifying *judgments* (or *propositions*) and Aristotle is concerned with classifying *predicates* (*one element* of judgments or propositions), each is concerned to identify a set of basic, necessary, sense-making conceptual equipment. This sense of the word has persisted in philosophical (and, to some extent, in anthropological) talk. Cf. **epistemological framework**, see section 5.11(i)).

Not every kind or class or sort is a category. If categories are kinds, classes, or sorts, they are very special *fundamental* kinds, classes, or sorts. Please do not, in philosophical talk or any other kind of talk, use the word 'category' as a fancy-dress substitute for 'kind', 'class', or 'sort'. It is said that a certain Cabinet Minister once sent back the draft of a speech with the notation: 'More big words, please.' 'Category' as a fancy-dress substitute for 'kind', etc., should be left to such as he. See Fowler, 1968, p. 80.

(iv) The adjectival form of 'category' in this sense (or these senses) is 'categorial', not 'categorical', for which see section 4.11.

See Lacey, 1976, pp. 25–29; Ryle, 1975; Copleston, 1960, Ch. XII; Bird, 1962.

B.   Category mistake

Gilbert Ryle (1900–1976) used a notion of **category** similar to that of Aristotle in an attempt to distinguish different ways in which sentences could go wrong and to distinguish (some forms of) nonsense (section 3.3) from falsity. I insert that parenthesis because, when Ryle speaks of nonsense, he is concerned with sentences which:

(1) pass ordinary grammatical (or **syntactic** (section 2.2)) criteria (i.e., are not random strings of words)

and

(2) are made up entirely of genuine words, not things like 'The gostak distims the doshes' (section 3.3(i)).

The point can oe brought out by considering examples:

'A Sao biscuit is square.'   (A)
'My left eye is square.'   (B)
'Virtue is square.'   (C)

Let us assume that all three sentences are in standard, everyday English (i.e., we set aside obsolescent slang and geometrical scruples). We can say, then, that sentence (A), if used assertively, is used to make a true statement, and that sentence (B), if used assertively, is used to make a false statement.

Sentence (C), however, differs from sentence (B), because, if I deny the statement made with sentence (B), you can intelligibly ask me 'Then what shape is it?' and an intelligible reply is possible. The same question asked about virtue cannot be so treated. Whatever virtue is, it is not the sort of thing that can have a shape of any kind. Ryle diagnoses the error as *a category mistake*: the syntactic combination of items from logically uncombinable categories. (Not every philosopher agrees. See, e.g., Passmore, 1961, Ch. VII; Prior, 1954.) See also Lacey, 1976, pp. 26–29; Ryle, 1938; Ryle, 1949, pp. 15–18; Ryle, 1954, Ch. I; Strawson, 1970. For a particularly charming category mistake, see W. H. Auden's poem 'Some Say That Love's a Little Boy' (Auden, 1977, pp. 230–231).

3.5 NECESSITY; INTEGRAL

A. Necessity

(i) **Necessary propositions and contingent propositions**

A proposition is necessarily true IFF no possible circumstance could have made it false. A proposition is necessarily false IFF no possible circumstance could have made it true. (The expression 'necessary proposition' is often used as a contraction for 'necessarily true proposition'.)

A proposition is contingent IFF circumstances are possible which could have made it false.

(ii) **Necessary truth and necessary falsehood**

A self-contradiction is necessarily false. The negation of a self-contradiction is necessarily true. That is *logically* *necessary* truth and *logically* *necessary* falsehood. Whether there are other kinds of necessary truth is a matter of some controversy.

Scientific laws are, on certain views, *statements of physical (or empirical) necessity*, but not everyone would agree. See D. M. Armstrong, 1979, 1983.

(iii) **Logically necessary propositions and logically contingent propositions**

A proposition is logically necessary IFF its denial is self-contradictory. Thus, if the proposition -p is self-contradictory the proposition p is logically necessary. ('-p' means 'It is false that p'.)

A proposition p is logically contingent, IFF neither p nor -p is self-contradictory.

(iv) **Non-technical uses of 'necessary' and 'essential'**

In the technical senses, there cannot be degrees of necessity or essentiality. If being female is essential (i.e., a necessary condition) for being a cow, then no non-female is a cow. If cats are essentially furry, then the natural existence of a non-furry cat is impossible ('natural' because no one would argue that shearing a cat would turn it into a non-cat).

There are popular uses, however, which allow for degree and qualification. 'Is your journey really necessary?' means something like 'Would the disadvantages or loss of advantages resulting from your not taking your journey so seriously outweigh the advantages that not taking your journey would be wrong or irrational?' (No wonder the designers of a certain Second World War poster preferred the phrase 'really necessary'!) 'Essential' is used in much the same way. Necessity and essentiality in non-technical senses tend to be related to *the achieving of purposes*. In the technical senses, they tend to be related to *the structure of concepts*.

The popular use of 'necessarily true' is, I think, invariably *negative*:

Primus: 'Summer time is shark time.'
Secundus: 'Not necessarily.'

Here, 'not necessarily' means 'not invariably', 'not always', 'not universally', 'there are exceptions to your generalization'.

Primus: 'Richard III had the Princes in the Tower murdered.'
Secundus: 'That's not necessarily true.'

Here, Secundus's remark means something like 'Be a bit more cautious. The evidence is far from conclusive.' There is nothing wrong with these popular uses of 'necessary', 'essential', and 'necessarily true', but they need to be distinguished from the technical senses.

B.

If X is a part of Y, X is an **integral** part of Y, IFF *either* X's ceasing to function as a part of Y would destroy Y; *or* X's ceasing to function as a part of Y would severely damage Y.

See also section 1.19 (**characteristics**).

3.6 ANALYTIC PROPOSITIONS AND SYNTHETIC PROPOSITIONS

A proposition is **analytic** IFF its truth-value is determined by its meaning alone. A proposition is **synthetic** IFF its truth-value is not determined by its meaning alone (see also section 7.12A, note).

'A triangle has three sides' is analytically true.
'A triangle has four sides' is analytically false.
'The emblem of the YMCA is a triangle' is synthetic.

Logically necessary truths are analytically true. Self-contradictions are logically necessary falsehoods, analytic falsehoods.

'Analytic proposition' as defined above covers both analytic truths and analytic falsehoods. 'Analytic proposition' is, however, commonly used as an abbreviation of 'analytically true proposition'. When 'analytic proposition' is used in that sense, the usual contrasting term is 'self-contradiction'. See Lacey, 1976, pp. 5–7; Flew, 1984, p. 12.

The analytic/synthetic distinction has been attacked by Quine (1953(b)) and defended by Grice and Strawson (1956). Many philosophers are uneasy about it, but most of them see no way of doing without it. Munsat, 1971, is a useful collection of essays.

3.7 TAUTOLOGY

'Tautology' is often used as a synonym for 'analytic truth'. It has, however, a more specialized meaning: a compound propositional form, any substitution-instance of which must be true (see sections 6.9, 6.4). By extension, a sub-stitution-instance of such a propositional form is also called a **tautology**. Thus, any substitution-instance of 'Not both p and -p' is true, so it is a tautology. A substitution-instance of a tautology is a logically necessary truth.

A propositional form, any substitution-instance of which must be false, is **tautologically false**; e.g., 'Both p and -p'. A substitution-instance of a tautologically false propositional form is a logically necessary falsehood.

Outside philosophy, the word 'tautology' is often used to mean *an utterance containing repetition* or *pleonasm* (see section 3.18(iii)). Please keep this use *outside* philosophy.

3.8 EMPIRICAL PROPOSITIONS AND NON-EMPIRICAL PROPOSITIONS

The question whether an empirical proposition is true or false is settled (if it can be settled) by observing facts (other than facts about the meaning of the symbols in which the proposition is expressed – see section 5.3). Thus many philosophers would say that the proposition that $2 + 2 = 4$ is non-empirical because to settle whether it is true or false, we need not go beyond an understanding of the meaning of arithmetical symbols. On the other hand, the proposition that cigarette smoking is a danger to health is empirical because its truth-value depends on facts external to the symbolism in which it is expressed. Some philosophers would maintain that the proposition that $2 + 2 = 4$ is non-empirical, but that its truth is not merely a matter of the meanings of its component symbols. See Gorovitz *et al.*, 1979, Ch. VI; Hospers, 1967, pp. 182–193.

3.9 *A PRIORI* PROPOSITIONS AND *A POSTERIORI* PROPOSITIONS

Pronunciation: AypryOReye, AyposteereeOReye.

A proposition is an *a priori* proposition IFF it can be known to be true or false independently of observation and experience. A proposition is an *a posteriori* proposition IFF it can be known to be true or false only on the basis of observation and experience.

Empirical propositions are *a posteriori*. Analytic propositions are *a priori*. Whether there are any synthetic *a priori* propositions is a matter of some controversy. See Flew, 1984, p. 16; Lacey, 1976, pp. 8–10; Gorovitz *et al.*, 1979, Ch. VI.

3.10　SELF-EVIDENT, SELF-EVIDENCE

SOED says: '**Self-evident**, Evident of itself without proof; axiomatic'. That seems close to the way the term is used in philosophical discourse. *Unless* a proposition contains *within itself* sufficient grounds to show that it is true, then it is *not* self-evident. A self-evident proposition must be a proposition whose truth can be established independently of observation, testimony, or memory.

But can we say that ALL propositions of this type are self-evident? On this point, there are differences in verbal habit amongst philosophers. Some would say that any proposition whose truth can be established independently of observation, testimony, or memory is self-evident. Others would add the qualification that its truth must also be immediately obvious to the average rational person.

On the first interpretation, both $(2+3=5)$ and some monstrous piece of differential calculus would be self-evident, because both are logically necessary. On the second interpretation, $(2+3=5)$ would be self-evident, but the piece of differential calculus would not be, because the average rational person cannot see at a glance that it is true. (See Geach, 1976, Ch. XV.) The difference is not a difference in opinion, merely a difference in the way words are used, but it can create confusion. See sections 5.2B (**evidence**), 3.9 (*a priori* and *a posteriori*), 8.12(iii) (**demonstratively true**), and 5.25 (**intuition**). See also Quine and Ullian, 1978, Ch. IV.

3.11　LOGICAL STATUS

If we are concerned about the logical status of a proposition, we are concerned with whether it is analytic, or synthetic, or self-contradictory, whether it is a logically necessary truth, or a logically necessary falsehood, or a logically contingent proposition.

3.12　POSSIBILITY, IMPOSSIBILITY; FEASIBILITY; VIABILITY

The notion of possibility (at least as it plays a part in philosophical talk) is best **explicated negatively**; i.e., we can get a better grasp of a proposition of the type 'Y is xically possible', if we reformulate it as 'Y is not xically impossible' or 'There are no xical reasons for saying that Y is impossible' or 'There are no xical reasons for rejecting the proposition that there is a Y.'

A.　Logical possibility; empirical possibility; technical possibility, etc.

(i)　Logical possibility and logical impossibility

Formula A:
'It is logically impossible that p.'

Formula B:
    'It is logically possible that p.'

Formula A can be used to reject a proposition. It is correctly used when
the proposition in the 'p' place is one which *can be correctly judged
false on logical grounds alone*; i.e., when the proposition in the 'p' place
is *one which is false by virtue of its meaning*; i.e., **self-contradictory**; when
it cannot be asserted without internal inconsistency, and also when
what is in the 'p' place is a nonsensical pseudo-proposition (see sections
1.2; 3.3). Here are three substitution-instances of Formula A:

Substitution-instance A(i):
'It is logically impossible that there is a round square.'

Substitution-instance A(ii):
'It is logically impossible that pelicans eat fish.'

Substitution-instance A(iii):
'It is logically impossible that a human being could jump ten thousand
feet into the air by his own unaided muscular effort.'

Instance A(i) is true because the description 'round square' is self-
contradictory. Instance A(ii) is false. Pelicans *do* eat fish and that
implies that it is false that they cannot. (*Ab esse ad posse consequentia
valet.*[1]) But instance A(iii) is also false. Instance A(iii), like the two
other instances, is a proposition about a proposition. The proposition
which A(iii) is about is:

'A human being can jump ten thousand feet into the air by his own
    unaided muscular effort.'

If that proposition should be rejected, the rejection cannot be made on
logical grounds alone. It cannot be rejected as nonsense (like 'The
gostak distims the doshes'), and it cannot be rejected as self-contradictory (like 'Tom drew a round square on the blackboard'). Hence,
it would be false to call such a leap a *logical* impossibility. It is a **logical
possibility**. By calling it that, all we are saying is that it cannot be
rejected on logical grounds alone. There may well be other grounds for
rejecting it. (There *are* other grounds for rejecting it.)

'It is logically possible that p' does not mean 'Logic gives us grounds
for thinking that p may be true.' All it means is 'Logic alone does not
give us grounds for saying that p is false.' To confuse logical possibility
with other kinds of possibility can produce all sorts of other confusions.
See Malcolm, 1942, section III.

(ii) **Empirical possibility and empirical impossibility**

> *Formula C:*
> 'It is empirically impossible that p.'

> *Formula D:*
> 'It is empirically possible that p.'

Norman Malcolm (1942) uses the phrase 'empirical possibility' to cover all forms of possibility other than logical possibility. A narrower use is convenient. In this narrower use, Formula D means that we cannot deny p on the basis of scientific laws alone (for **scientific laws**, see section 5.12). On these grounds, we can reject the possibility of the Great Leap Upward described in sub-section (i) and get:

> *Substitution-instance B(ii):*
> 'It is empirically impossible that a human being could jump ten thousand feet into the air by his own unaided muscular effort.'

Notice that empirical possibility is as *negative* a notion as logical possibility. To say that something is empirically possible is merely to say that it is not excluded by scientific laws. There may well be other reasons for rejecting it or for saying that it is impossible. Another point to notice:

To say that S is a scientific law is to say (amongst other things) that S is true and that S is an open universal statement (see section 6.30). It follows that if, at one time, something is empirically possible or impossible, then the same is true of it at any time.

Empirical possibility and empirical impossibility do not change. Our **beliefs** about what is empirically possible and empirically impossible *do* change.

(iii) **Technological (or technical) possibility and technological (or technical) impossibility**

To say that something is technologically possible is to say that the knowledge, skills, and procedures are available to make it or do it. The empirical possibility of the computer was discovered by Charles Babbage in 1822. But it was not *then* a technological possibility because techniques for making the parts were not available until much later.

(iv) **Logical relations amongst different types of possibility statements**

'X is logically possible' is in the relation of **subimplication** to 'X is empirically possible' and 'X is empirically possible' is in the relation of **superimplication** to 'X is logically possible.' The same pattern holds between 'X is logically possible' and 'X is technologically possible' and between 'X is empirically possible' and 'X is technologically possible' (for **logical relations**, see section 10.3).

(v) **Other types of possibility**

Philosophers sometimes talk as if there were only three types of possibility: Logical, Empirical, and Technological. But that cannot be true.

There is nothing technologically impossible about the idea of delivering my lectures by radio without getting out of bed. But it is impossible for other reasons: I could not afford the apparatus and the University authorities would disapprove. So it is **impossible in practice**. See B below.

B. Theoretically possible, practically possible; possible in principle; possible in practice

These are not different *kinds of* possibility from those just discussed. They are merely a different (and less precise) *way of talking about* possibility.

  (i) 'X is **theoretically possible**' is an ambiguous remark. If a philosopher says it, he *probably* means '**logically** possible' (see A above). If a scientist says it, he *may* mean '**empirically** possible'. But he may even mean that X is *technologically* possible (see A(iii) above). 'X is theoretically possible' may be a way of saying that the knowledge, skills, and procedures are there for making or doing X, while not committing oneself to saying that there is nothing standing in the way of making or doing X (see A(v) above).

 (ii) In this third sense 'theoretically possible' is contrasted with 'practically possible'. If X is not theoretically possible, it is not practically possible either. If X is theoretically possible, it may be practically possible or it may not. If X is practically possible, it is theoretically possible (cf. A(v) above).

   X is practically possible IFF there is nothing to prevent X from being made or done.

(iii) 'Practically possible' in that sense is synonymous with 'possible in practice'. In colloquial speech 'practically' sometimes means 'almost': e.g., 'Practically no one voted for Tom.' Try not to follow this colloquial use. It is confusing and sometimes confused.

C.

'**Possible in principle**' is synonymous with 'theoretically possible' and, like it, can be ambiguous. In the days before the American and Soviet space programmes, a standard example of a proposition whose verification (see section 5.1) was 'possible in principle, but not in practice' was 'There are mountains on the other side of the moon.'

D.

'**Feasible**' is not synonymous with 'possible'. It has a narrower meaning. If X is feasible, then it is possible *to make* X or *to do* X. It follows that 'feasible' should not be treated as an elegant substitute for 'plausible' or 'credible' (for which, see section 8.17).

E.

'**Viable**' is not a fancy synonym for 'good', 'satisfactory', 'true', or 'sound'. 'Viable' means 'able to survive'. It is an important term in medical ethics. See P. Ramsey, 1978, index.

3.13   CONSISTENCY AND INCONSISTENCY

Several senses need to be distinguished.
  (i) **Consistency as self-consistency**
      A statement, narrative, etc., is self-consistent IFF it is not self-con-
      tradictory (see section 3.2). In this sense, 'His story is inconsistent'
      means that it is inconsistent *with itself*, i.e., that it contains self-con-
      tradictions, logical impossibilities. 'His story is consistent' means that
      it is logically possible (see section 3.12A) for his story to be true.
 (ii) **Consistency with ...**
      Tom's story is consistent with Dick's story IFF they are mutually
      compatible; i.e., IFF they can both be true, IFF their conjunction is
      not self-contradictory. 'Tom's story is consistent with Dick's story' is
      sometimes abbreviated to 'Tom's story and Dick's story are consistent.'
      A statement is inconsistent with the facts if it is a factual statement (see
      section 3.15(i)) which is false. See section 1.3A(ii) (**truth-conditions**).
(iii) '... is consistent with ...' has a special use in the talk of forensic (see
      section 8.4C) pathologists. 'The injuries of the deceased are consistent
      with his having been struck on the head with a candlestick.' In the
      logician's sense of 'consistent', they are also consistent with suffering
      from tinea, or with being a retired health inspector, or with the truth
      that Kuwait produces oil, or with the falsehood that it does not, but
      the pathologist means something stronger than that. Saying that the
      injuries are consistent with a hypothesis seems to be a way of saying
      that they give support to that hypothesis without going so far as saying
      that they establish it.
          The pathologist's sense of '... is consistent with ...' appears to be
      similar to 'cohere' as that word is used by some philosophers: a group
      of propositions is coherent if they are *mutually supporting*. If five people
      who have never met testify independently to having seen a puce Rolls
      Royce in Rankin Drive on Wednesday, their testimonies are coherent
      in this sense (though it is possible that they are all wrong). See Hospers,
      1967, pp. 116–117. It is possible, in this sense of 'consistent', to speak
      of *degrees of consistency*. *The Newcastle Herald*, 13 January 1984 (p. 4)
      reports a Judge as saying:

'The silence of the media at the time would appear to be more consistent with Mr Sinclair not making, than with him making, any such complaint to the media.'

'Logicians' consistency', however, is an all-or-none affair. Two propositions are either consistent with each other or they are not, and there is no more or less about it.

(iv) People are said to be consistent to the extent that their opinions or professed opinions do not conflict with one another, to the extent that their actions seem to reveal a coherent set of values, to the extent that their actions and professions are in harmony. Given our capacity to be wrong, it is not clear that this consistency must be a virtue. See also sections 9.6 (**hypocrisy**, etc.), 4.28 (***argumentum ad hominem***).

3.14   LOGICAL

This word has several different senses.

  (i) In ordinary speech, it sometimes means *rational* ('It's only logical to take an umbrella with you when the weather is rainy').

 (ii) 'Logical' can also mean *in accord with the principles of logic*. (The distinction between *truth* and *validity* is relevant here. An argument might be **logical** in this sense but have preposterous premises and conclusion. See section 4.10.)

(iii) Another meaning is *of, like, or pertaining to logic* as 'the theoretical study of the forms and principles of argument' (Flew, 1975, p. 21). Notice that:

To call something 'logical' in sense (i) is to *endorse* it;

To call something 'logical' in sense (ii) is to *endorse it at least partially*;

To call something 'logical' in sense (iii) is not to endorse it at all. In this sense, we can speak of **logical fallacies** without self-contradiction.

Senses (i) and (ii) correspond to the non-technical and technical senses of 'valid argument' (see section 4.9).

See Geach, 1976, pp. vii-viii; Flew, 1975, Ch. I; Strawson, 1952(a), Ch. VIII; Quine, 1987, pp. 63–67. See also section 6.26.

3.15   FACTUAL

This is a tricky and ambiguous word because it is used to draw a number of quite different distinctions.

  (i) It may be used in contrast with the word 'logical'. The connexion between *being a king* and *being a monarch* is a **logical** connexion, because the proposition that *Frederick is a king but not a monarch* is self-contradictory.

The connexion between *drinking an entire bottle of whisky in one session* and *being intoxicated* is a **factual** connexion, because the proposition that *Frederick has done this without being intoxicated* is **not self-contradictory** (though it would certainly be **false**). In such contexts, 'factual' is a near-synonym of '**causal**' (see section 3.16). 'Factual *proposition*', on the other hand, is better understood as a synonym of '**synthetic proposition**' (see sections 3.6, 3.8).

(ii) The word 'factual' may be used in contrast with the word 'fictional'. Statements about the career of Mr Pickwick are fictional. Statements about the career of Charles II are factual. 'Mr Pickwick was sued for breach of promise' is a fictional (and true) statement. 'Charles II was beheaded' is a factual (and false) statement.

(iii) The word 'factual' may be used in contrast to the word 'evaluative'. Some would say that the statement: 'Brutus killed Caesar' is purely **factual** because whether we agree with it depends solely on whether we believe that certain events occurred and does not depend on any moral judgment about those events. The same philosophers would contrast that statement with the statement: 'Brutus treacherously murdered Caesar', which (they would say), is **partly factual** and **partly evaluative**, since whether we would agree with it depends in part on our moral judgments about the events reported. See also sections 9.2 (**value-judgment**), 9.4A (**fact/value**).

There are other contrasts involving the word 'factual' and other problems concerning the word 'fact'. See Lacey, 1976, pp. 67–68; Herbst, 1956; Lucas, 1958. **Fact** 'is not so simple a concept as it appears to be in its four-lettered innocence' (Urmson, 1956, p. 145).

In philosophical talk, the words 'factual' and 'non-factual' are NEVER used as synonyms of the words 'true' and 'false'. A statement can be both factual and false. The word 'factual' is used to indicate that a **question** is a factual one, rather than a question of some other kind. Whether the wearing of motorcycle helmets is likely to prevent more injuries than they cause is a factual question. Whether the wearing of motorcycle helmets should be compelled by law is (at least partly) an *evaluative* question. The philosophical use of the words 'fact' and 'factual' should suggest the phrase 'It is a matter of fact *whether* ...' rather than the phrase 'It is a matter of fact *that* ...'

Further, as philosophers usually use the words, 'It is a matter of fact whether p' is an assertion about how, *in principle*, the truth-value of p *could* be determined, not an assertion that the truth-value of p *can*, *in practice* be determined. In other words, the contrast is NOT with 'It is a matter of opinion whether p.' (On **in principle** and **in practice** see section 3.12C. For **counterfactual**, see section 4.15.)

3.16   CAUSAL; NEXUS

A.

'Causal' means *of, like, or pertaining to the cause-effect relation (i.e., to causation).* 'Causal' is frequently misread and misprinted as 'casual', a rather unfortunate error. 'There is a causal link between smoking and cancer' sounds alarming. 'There is a casual link between smoking and cancer' sounds almost reassuring.

The notion of cause is both fundamental and familiar. It is also one of the most complex notions, and one of the least understood. For brief, introductory treatments, see Lacey, 1976, pp. 29–32; Flew, 1984, pp. 58–59; Goddard, 1977, Ch. I; R. Taylor, 1967. Mackie, 1974, is likely to remain a most important work on the topic. An extract will be found in Honderich and Burnyeat, 1979, pp. 381–416. See also sections 3.17 (**causal consequence**); 9.8 (**double effect**).

B.

One of the Latin meanings of '**nexus**' is 'a tying up, binding together, fastening, joining, interlacing, entwining, clasping' (C. T. Lewis, 1889, p. 668) – in other words, *an act of or case of* tying up, etc. But the meaning which has passed into English is 'a bond or link; a means of connexion' (*SOED*) *SOED*'s examples are:

> Cash Payment . . . the universal sole nexus of man to man.
>
> (Carlyle)
> *Causal nexus*, the necessary connexion between cause and effect.

One occasionally finds 'nexus' used to mean not the bond or the link, but those things which are bound or linked, e.g.:

> indeed, it is a multi-relational nexus of different factors that comprises what [sociologists] understand by a culture.
>
> (D. Emmet, 1966, p. 92)

But, for the sake of clarity, it would be better not to use 'nexus' in this sense. 'Complex' would be better.

3.17   CONSEQUENCE

(i) **Logical consequence**: the consequences (i.e., *logical* consequences) of a *proposition* p are those propositions which are *implied by* p (see section 4.2). See section 4.21 (*non sequitur*).

(ii) **Causal consequence**: the consequences (i.e., *causal* consequences) of an *event* or *state of affairs* E are those other **events or states of affairs** which occur as a result of E. See also section 3.16. **Consequence** must not be confused with **consequent** (see section 4.12(i)).

3.18   PLATITUDE; TRUISM; PLEONASM

(i) J. I. M. Stewart's character, Gavin Mogridge (Stewart, 1974–78) says things like 'We must put first things first. Otherwise, we might get them in the wrong order.' That corresponds well with *SOED*'s definition of **platitude**: 'a flat, dull, or commonplace remark or statement; especially one uttered with an air of importance.' But we should be cautious about using the word dismissively. Sometimes, it is used to dismiss a proposition on the quite inadequate ground that many people have asserted it, and the flattest of platitudes may express truths which we are in danger of overlooking, e.g., 'You are not getting any younger', or Butler's 'idiosyncrasy platitude'. See section 5.18 (**heuristic**). See also D. Emmet, 1962.

(ii) To call something a **truism** is not to say merely that it is true; a truism is an *obvious* truth. Uttering a truism is sometimes pointless, but not always. What is obvious to you may not be obvious to me (see Flew, 1975, p. 73). A **logical truism** is an *analytic truth*. See sections 3.6, 3.7.

(iii) **Pleonasm** is the practice of using more words than are necessary, especially by way of repetition. Sometimes, pleonasm may be legitimately used for emphasis (e.g., 'I saw it, with my own eyes, I saw the yeti'), but, more often, it is mere woolliness which we could do without, e.g.: 'looking back in hindsight', 'the elementary rudiments', 'over-exaggerated', 'superfluous and redundant'.

Pleonasm is sometimes called **tautology**, but, as that word has a different meaning in philosophical talk (see section 3.7), 'pleonasm' or 'redundancy' is preferable. See Fowler, 1968, pp. 455–456, 615–616; Horner and Horner, 1980, pp. 48–55, 151–152; E. Partridge, 1973, pp. 325–327, 344–345.

4   Inferring, implying, arguing, and 'if'

4.1   IFF

In philosophical writing, 'IFF' is a useful abbreviation for 'if and only if'. In philosophical speech, 'IFF' is pronounced as 'if and only if'. (The more usual abbreviation is 'iff', but, as that can be mistaken for a misprinted or miswritten 'if', 'IFF' is preferable.)

4.2   INFER, INFERENCE; IMPLY, IMPLICATION

1. **Inferring** is something done by arguers and thinkers (see section 4.3).
2. In a **valid inference**, the conclusion is **implied by** the premisses (see sections 4.3, 4.4, 4.9).
3. One proposition may **imply** or **be implied by** another. No proposition infers or can infer anything (see section 4.4).
4. People are sometimes said to imply things, but it might be better if they were not (see section 4.3).

4.3   INFER, INFERENCE

(i) To **infer** is to **draw a conclusion**.

    I infer a proposition p from a proposition q when I assert p on the basis of q. I infer a proposition p from a fact F when I assert p on the basis of the existence or occurrence of F. I infer a proposition p from a proposition q when I note that anyone who asserts q is committed to assent to p.

    (A)   From the proposition that Socrates is a man and the proposition that all men are mortal, I infer that Socrates is mortal.

    (B)   From the fact that the canary is nowhere to be seen and the fact that bloodstained yellow feathers are scattered about, I infer that a cat has eaten him.

    (C)   Tom asserts that he was in Geelong last Tuesday at 12.00 noon. From that, Dick infers that Tom could not have been seen lunching in Newcastle on Tuesday. But as Dick saw Tom lunching in Newcastle on Tuesday, he knows that Tom is not telling the truth.

In (A) and (B), the speakers commit themselves to the truth of what they infer. In (C), Dick brings out a proposition implicit in Tom's assertion. Dick is not committed to that proposition. In fact, he has reason for denying it and, therefore, for denying Tom's assertion also.

(ii) The word 'inference' has what is called '**process-product ambiguity**', i.e., it is used to refer both to the *process* (or, more accurately, *activity*) of drawing a conclusion and to the *product* of that activity, i.e., the conclusion itself.

> (D) ('**Process**') The inference from 'At least one poet is Swiss' to 'At least one Swiss is a poet' is a valid immediate inference (see section 6.29A(xiii), note).
>
> (E) ('**Product**') 'At least one Swiss is a poet' was the inference which I drew from 'At least one poet is Swiss.'

(iii) '**Infer**' is sometimes used as a synonym for 'assert indirectly', 'hint', 'give reason to assert', 'imply', 'indicate', etc.

> (F) When he said: 'I see you are working hard' in that nasty tone of voice, he was inferring that I was loafing.
>
> (G) The canary cannot be found and there are a lot of bloodstained yellow feathers scattered about. This infers that a cat has eaten him.
>
> (H) 'Jack and Jill went up the hill' infers that Jack went up the hill.

This usage is well-entrenched and is of some antiquity. It even has Milton on its side:

> (J) 'Consider first that Great or Bright infers not Excellence.'
> (*Paradise Lost* VIII.90–91. See also IX.285–286.)

But, despite that, the usage blurs some important distinctions. It should be scrupulously avoided in philosophical talk and it is simply a nuisance in any kind of talk.

4.4   IMPLY AND IMPLICATION; ENTAIL AND ENTAILMENT

A.

(i) In the technical vocabulary of philosophy, **implication** is a *relation between propositions*. A proposition p implies q IFF it would be *self-contradictory* (see section 3.2) to assert p and deny q.

(K)   'This figure is a rectangle' (K^1) implies 'This is a plane figure'
(K^2), but K^2 does not imply K^1.

It is part of the definition of **implication** that *a true proposition cannot
imply a false* (α). It is also part of that definition that *a false proposition
CAN imply a true* (β). Those two points are vital. Most people have no
difficulty in accepting (α), but, somehow or other, (β) tends to get stuck
in the immune system. There are, however, plenty of examples to show
that it is true:

(L)   'Mrs Thatcher is a Socialist politician' (L^1) is false, but it implies
'Mrs Thatcher is a politician' (L^2) which is true.

(ii) One common use of 'imply' makes it synonymous with '*give reason to
assert*' or '*indicate*'. Thus, the utterer of (B) in section 4.3 might say
instead:

(M)   The fact that the canary is nowhere to be seen (M^1) and the
fact that bloodstained yellow feathers are scattered about (M^2)
imply that a cat has eaten him (M^3).

But the relation of ((M^1) & (M^2)) to (M^3) is quite different from the
relation of (K^1) to (K^2) or of (L^1) to (L^2). There would be *no self-
contradiction* in accepting ((M^1) & (M^2)) and denying (M^3). To accept
(K^1) while denying (K^2) or to accept (L^1) while denying (L^2) would be
self-contradictory.

The use of 'imply' as a synonym for 'give reason to assert' is fairly
well-entrenched, but it should be *avoided* in philosophical talk, because
it smudges a very important distinction: that between inferences whose
premisses, if true, guarantee the truth of the conclusion and those whose
premisses, if true, merely give good reason for accepting the conclusion.
See sections 4.18 (**paradoxes of validity**) and 8.12 (**demonstrative and
non-demonstrative argument**).

(iii) **Another non-technical sense of 'imply': Implication, not as a relation
between propositions, but as something people do**
In this sense, **implying a proposition** is *asserting it indirectly* (cf. section
4.5A on **innuendo**). One way of doing this is by stating an *elliptical* (or
truncated) argument:

Tom: 'Either Dick knows nothing about poisons or he was trying
to kill me. And Dick is the author of a standard text-book
on toxicology.'
Harry: 'Tom is implying that Dick tried to kill him.'

A proposition or judgment may also be implied (in *this* sense) by
emphasis, choice of words, gesture, etc. This sense of 'imply' is less
bothersome than sense (ii) above. Nevertheless, it is best avoided in
philosophical talk if there is any risk of confusion with sense (i). (On

conversational implicature, see Fogelin, 1978, pp. 3–31; Grice, 1975; Jackson, 1987, Ch. V.)

(iv) In ordinary speech we sometimes use the word 'implication' as a near-synonym for 'involvement'. The involvement is that of a person in a situation, usually criminal or improper:

> The Chairman was dismissed because of his implication in suspect financial deals.

But 'implication' used with this sense is not the substantival (i.e., noun) form of the verb 'imply'. It is the substantival form of the verb 'implicate'. The connexion between 'imply'/'implication' and 'implicate'/'implication' is remote. Both are derived from the Latin verb *implicare*, the literal meaning of which is 'to enfold, to wrap up'. There is more than one way in which something can be metaphorically wrapped up in something else. See section 2.6B (**homonymy**). ('Implicate' and 'implicature' have been given a technical meaning by H. P. Grice. See references in (iii) above.)

B.   Entail, entailment

Roughly speaking, 'entail' is synonymous with 'imply'. For something less rough, see Lacey, 1976, pp. 90–91.

4.5   INNUENDO; *SUGGESTIO FALSI, SUPPRESSIO VERI*

A.

(i) From the Latin '*innuere*' = 'to nod', 'to give a sign', 'to intimate', 'to hint'. In medieval Latin, 'innuendo' was used to introduce a parenthetical clarification; i.e., it was used as synonymous with 'that is to say', 'meaning thereby', or 'i.e.'.

In the law of defamation, innuendo is that part of an indictment or a pleading which seeks to connect the words complained of with the plaintiff or to bring out their defamatory meaning, e.g., 'The defendant said "If I heard him [meaning thereby the plaintiff] say that today is Wednesday, I would check with the calendar" [meaning thereby that the plaintiff is thoroughly untrustworthy].' The phrases in square brackets are, in the legal sense, **innuendoes**. See Mozley and Whiteley, 1977, p. 173; Osborn, 1976, p. 179.

(ii) Outside technical legal talk, an innuendo is a *hint*, usually of an unpleasant or derogatory (though sometimes of a sexual) nature. Some journalists are particularly good at innuendo, managing to say or suggest very derogatory things without falling foul of the law of defamation. Were I to quote an actual example, I would be struck down by two writs, one from the newspaper and one from its victim. The following example is imaginary:

> Henry Primus was convicted of fraud in 1960 and sentenced to thirty-five years' imprisonment. In a controversial decision, the then Minister for Prisons, Mr Joseph Secundus, released Primus after he had served only five years. (Mr Secundus is now facing charges of conspiring corruptly to release two other prisoners.)
>
> After his release, Primus was involved in various commercial undertakings, including some in which he was in partnership with Mr Thomas Tertius. (Mr Tertius is one of the people with whom Mr Secundus is alleged to have conspired.)

'Innuendo' is similar both in sound and in meaning to 'insinuation', hence the portmanteau word,[1] 'insinuendo'. Both Room (1979, pp. 72–73) and *OED*, 1989, disapprove of 'insinuendo'. I suppose they are right, but it seems almost a pity.

Innuendo is a form of *implication* in a *popular* sense of that word, but please do not call it 'inferring'. See sections 4.2–4.4 (**imply** and **infer**).

B. *Suggestio falsi; suppressio veri*

(i) *Suggestio falsi*. Literally: 'suggestion of the false'. I doubt whether *CODCE*'s definition could be bettered:

> Positive misrepresentation not involving direct lie but going beyond concealment of the truth.

Suppose Mr X has accused Mr Y of conspiring with Mr Z. Mr Y replies in scornful and indignant tones: 'I have never spoken so much as a word to Mr Z. I have never even met him. I wouldn't know him if I bumped into him. I don't know whether he is tall or short, bearded or clean-shaven. I have never heard his voice. If I am not even acquainted with Mr Z, I could not possibly have conspired with him.' Mr Y's final assertion is, I suspect, a necessary truth. (That depends on the criteria for *being acquainted with*.) Let us also suppose that his other assertions are true (contingently). They are all consistent with the proposition that Mr Y and Mr Z have been conspiring by mail. If that proposition is true, Mr Y's reply to Mr X is a *suggestio falsi*. Ignorant and pretentious journalists call this sort of thing 'semantics', but they should not be imitated. See section 2.2.

(ii) *Suppressio veri*. Literally: 'suppression of the true'. In practice, the line between *suppressio veri* and *suggestio falsi* is often so thin as not to be there at all. As with *suggestio falsi*, *Concise Oxford*'s definition is crisp and clear:

Suppression of truth, misrepresentation by concealment of facts that ought to be made known.

Crisp and clear, but is it quite accurate? If the Gestapo are after you and ask me where you are and I give them some misleading reply, have I concealed facts that *ought* to be made known?

(iii) Whether **suggestio falsi** and **suppressio veri** always or ever amount to **lying** and under what conditions (if any) they are morally justified are controversial topics. Each involves what is called *mental reservation* or *mental restriction*: the form of words expresses what the speaker believes to be the case, but could also be taken to express another meaning. The speaker *mentally* restricts his meaning to the former but leaves the hearer the task of working it out for himself; i.e., the speaker **equivocates**. See W. D. Hughes, 1966(a), (b); Knox, 1953, pp. 146–147; Schulhof, 1915; Bok, 1980.

4.6   ARGUE, ARGUMENT

There are several different, though related, senses of 'argument':
  (i) A piece of discourse consisting of one proposition (the **conclusion**) and one or more other propositions (the **premiss** or **premisses**) which are put forward as reasons for assenting to the conclusion. (Strictly speaking, if the arguer is arguing not that some position is true but that some action should be done, he is arguing not to a conclusion, but to a **recommendation** or **prescription**.)
 (ii) An interchange between two or more people involving disagreement or non-agreement and the giving of reasons. (Sometimes called **dialectical argument**.)
(iii) An **altercation**, e.g., 'Three men were taken to hospital and four were charged with a variety of offences after an argument in a hotel.'

In philosophical discourse, senses (i) and (ii) are common but sense (iii) is rare. An argument (sense (ii)) will contain several arguments (sense (i)). An argument (sense (iii)) may contain nothing but an exchange of insults. Some arguments (sense (ii)) can – sadly – degenerate into arguments (sense (iii)). Please note that there is only one 'e' in the word 'argument'. See Geach, 1976, Chs I, IV; T. J. Richards, 1978, Chs I–III; Passmore, 1969; Fogelin, 1978, Ch. II. For **validity**, see sections 4.9–4.10.

4.7   TRANSITION-MARKERS[2]

There are various words which indicate that an **argumentative transition** is being made; i.e., they indicate that the speaker is putting forward some propositions as **support for** another proposition. They indicate that he is **arguing from premisses** to a conclusion or a recommendation. By a quirk of the language, however, most of these words have other uses as well, so they are not all absolutely infallible signs that the text they occur in is argumentative. (And not all arguments contain such marker-words.)

(a) **Three little words: 'because', 'because', and 'because'**

(i) It would be easy enough to prove beyond reasonable doubt that Sir Edmund Hillary climbed Everest. There are photographs, documents, witnesses, the unanimous testimony of those in a position to know. It is, of course, possible that he did not and that there has been an immense conspiracy to deceive the world, but that is a **merely logical possibility** (see section 3.12A) and is considerably less probable than the proposition that the evidence is genuine. (Keeping such a conspiracy secret would be much more difficult than climbing Everest.)

We might summarize the available evidence into a few neat sentences. Should anyone demand to know why we think Hillary climbed Everest, we can trot out those neat sentences preceded by 'because'. If we wanted to, we might re-formulate the argument, textbook style:

[Sentence 1]
[Sentence 2]
[Sentence 3]

Therefore, Hillary climbed Everest.

The propositions expressed in sentences 1, 2, and 3 would be put forward as **reasons for believing that** Hillary climbed Everest. In the first, conversational formulation of the argument, 'because' introduces those reasons. In the second, textbook-style formulation, 'therefore' introduces the conclusion drawn from them.

(ii) When Hillary was asked why he climbed Everest, he made the famous reply, 'Because it's there.' Was he using the word 'because' as it is used above? If he were, then he would be putting forward the presence of Everest as a reason for believing that he had climbed it:

Everest was there

Therefore, Hillary climbed it.

But that would be a dreadful argument. The mountain was there long before he was even thought of. Someone who argued like that would be too muddle-headed to climb a step-ladder successfully. 'Because' in Hillary's reply has a different sense from 'because' in the conversational argument of (i) above. Hillary is not giving a **reason for believing** that he climbed Everest. He is giving **his reason for acting** as he did (Paul Thom's example).

(iii) Things are complicated a little by the fact that *sometimes* (not always, e.g.: 'I lent him the money because I was a gullible fool and was impressed by his story') when we use 'because' in its reason-for-action sense, we are arguing that what we did was right, or reasonable, or appropriate, or excusable, but in such cases, the conclusion of our argument is not the proposition that we performed the action, but the proposition that we acted rightly, or reasonably, or appropriately, or excusably. Thus if Hillary's reply is interpreted as an argument, it should be spelt out NOT as:

Everest was there

Therefore, Hillary climbed it,

but as

Everest was there

Therefore, Hillary acted appropriately in climbing it.

(iv) There is yet another sense of 'because'. The electric jug refuses to work when Primus and Secundus want a cup of tea. Primus says 'It doesn't work because some goat switched it on when there wasn't enough water to cover the element.' He is not offering a reason for believing that the jug does not work. He and Secundus know that already. What he is doing is asserting that one event happened as the result of another. This is the **explanatory** 'because'.

(v)   There is, however, a complication similar to that noted in (iii).

Suppose Primus and Secundus are travelling in a light aircraft. Secundus suddenly leaps out of the aircraft. He has no parachute. Primus draws the conclusion that Secundus is or will soon be dead.

Here Primus has reasoned as follows:

Secundus has leapt out of the aircraft without a parachute.
[Various general propositions about gravity and about what happens to unsupported human bodies falling from great heights at great speeds.]

Therefore, Secundus is dead.

In other words, the proposition that an event has occurred together with our general knowledge of what-causes-what can provide grounds for asserting another proposition that another event has occurred. Hence, if Primus later says, 'Secundus is dead', and someone asks, 'How do you know?', he can reply, 'Because he jumped out of a plane without a parachute.' There, Primus is arguing, but if he is asked, 'How did Secundus die?' and he replies, 'Because he jumped out of a plane without a parachute,' he is not arguing but asserting that one event happened as a consequence of another, i.e., a **causal connection** (see section 3.17). He is **explaining**.

The 'because' dealt with in (i) is *the argumentative* (reason-for-belief) *'because'*. (ii) and (iii) discuss *the reason-for-action 'because'*. That dealt with in (iv) and (v) is the *explanatory 'because'*.

(b) **'Therefore'** is usually argumentative, though it can be used in an explanatory fashion (e.g., 'I stood in his way; therefore he struck me').

(c) **'Because' and 'therefore'**

'Because' in its argumentative sense is related to 'therefore', but they do not have the same meaning. 'Because' precedes premisses and may follow a conclusion. 'Therefore' follows premisses and precedes (or, sometimes, is placed within) a conclusion:

'Socrates is mortal because he is a man, and all men are mortal.'

'Because Socrates is a man and all men are mortal, Socrates is mortal.'

'All men are mortal and Socrates is a man; therefore Socrates is mortal.'

'All men are mortal and Socrates is a man. Socrates is, therefore, mortal.'

'A, because B' implies 'B, therefore A' and *vice versa*. 'Because' is a **premiss-marker**. 'Therefore' is a **conclusion-marker**.

(d) **'Since'**

Since his Majesty went into the field, I have seen her rise from her bed, throw her nightgown upon her, unlock her closet, take forth paper, fold it, write upon't, read it, afterwards seal it, and again return to bed; yet all this while in a most fast sleep.

> (Shakespeare, *Macbeth*, Act V, scene 1)

And *since* to look at things in bloom,
Fifty springs are little room,
About the woodlands I will go
To see the cherry hung with snow.

> (A. E. Housman, 1939, p. 11)

Since Socrates is mortal and all men are mortal, it follows that Socrates is mortal.

Only the third of these uses 'since' in an argumentative sense. In the first, it marks the beginning of a stretch of time. In the second, it states a reason for action. Argumentative 'since' is virtually synonymous with argumentative 'because'.

(e) **'Hence'**

Before I go hence, and be no more

It is so with men generally, and hence we assume it to be so with you.

> (*SOED*'s examples)

In both cases, 'hence' can be paraphrased as 'from this', but only in the latter is it argumentative (i.e., 'from this premiss' rather than 'from this place'). Argumentative 'hence' is virtually synonymous with argumentative 'therefore'.

(f) **'So'** can be used as an argumentative marker:

'All men are mortal and Socrates is a man, so Socrates is mortal.'

But it also has a very large number of other uses. The *Shorter Oxford* takes almost two closely-printed columns to list them.

(g) **'It follows that ...'** To say this amounts to saying 'The statement I am about to make is *shown to be true* by the statement(s) I have just made.' That is to make a very strong claim, which should not be made negligently or as a bluff. See also section 4.21 (**non sequitur**).

(h) **'Ergo'** is Latin for 'therefore'. (The symbol '∴' is derived from a contraction of 'ergo' used by mediaeval scribes.) In English, 'ergo' is sometimes used to emphasize the 'neatness' of an argument, but is more often used ironically to emphasize that the argument being quoted is a *non sequitur* (section 4.21).

(j) **'Q.E.D.'** *'Quod erat demonstrandum'* is Latin for 'which is what needed to be proved', the traditional crow of victory written below the conclusion of a geometrical theorem.

(k) **'Must'**

If someone argues: 'Every man is mortal and Socrates is a man. Socrates must be mortal', his conclusion is not 'Socrates must be mortal', but 'Socrates is mortal'. 'Must', here, is a conclusion-marker.

See also Fisher, 1988, Ch. II; Ryle, 1950.

4.8   PREMISSES, PREMISES

Those statements which are used to support a conclusion may be called either 'premisses' or 'premises'. There is no difference in pronunciation: the final syllable is pronounced as is that of 'promises'. 'PremisEEZ' is bogus gentility. 'Premises' is more common, but 'premisses' avoids any confusion with 'premises' in the everyday sense (roughly: *a building and/or enclosed land*) or in the closely related legal sense (see Mozley and Whiteley, 1977, p. 250). See also section 2.6B, C (**homonymy** and **homophony**).

The homonymy of 'premises' inspired the Rev. Sydney Smith (1771–1845) to produce one of his most pleasantly outrageous puns. Walking down a narrow lane, he noticed two women shouting insults from opposite windows. 'They will never agree,' he said, 'because they argue from different premises' (Pearson, 1948, p. 304).

4.9   VALID, VALIDITY

(i) *Propositions* or *statements* are *true* or *false*. *Arguments, inferences, pieces of reasoning* are **valid** or **invalid** (see also section 4.10). In philosophical talk, 'valid argument' has a strict technical meaning:

An argument is valid IFF its premises, taken conjointly, *imply* its conclusion.

Because of the way in which 'implication' is defined (see section 4.4), we can express this as:

An argument is valid IFF the affirmation of its premises and the denial of its conclusion conjoined together make a self-contradictory statement.

An **invalid argument**, then, is one whose premises, taken conjointly, do not imply the conclusion. If an argument is invalid, it would not be self-contradictory to affirm the premises and deny the conclusion.

(ii) It is worth emphasizing that, in the technical language of philosophy, that is *all* that 'valid argument' and 'invalid argument' mean. A valid argument might consist of utterly silly premises and conclusion:

All persons with purple hair are surgeons.
Mr R. J. Hawke has purple hair.

Therefore, Mr R. J. Hawke is a surgeon.

Drivel, but a valid argument because the premises taken conjointly imply the conclusion. In non-philosophical talk, 'valid argument' has a different and more laudatory sense. *CODCE* says that a valid argument is one which is 'sound, defensible, well-grounded'. In this sense, that example would *not* be valid.

There is nothing wrong with such talk, but it should be avoided when talking philosophy. Every skilled activity has its technical terms and, very often, those terms are words which are used rather differently in everyday speech. A physicist uses the word 'weight' in one way when he is talking physics and in a different way when he is talking about his physique.

(iii) In the technical sense, an argument may be valid, but NOT 'sound, defensible, well-grounded', and an argument may be 'sound, defensible, well-grounded', but invalid. The following argument is invalid in the technical sense, but any reasonable person would have to agree that it is 'sound, defensible, well-grounded':

A period of darkness has occurred in the Lake Macquarie area once in every twenty-four hours for an indefinitely long period in the past.

There have been no relevant recent reports of aberrant astronomical phenomena.

Therefore, a period of darkness can be expected to occur in the Lake Macquarie area once in the next twenty-four hours.

An argument can be invalid but *strong*. An argument can be valid but *weak*. There are valid arguments which are bad arguments. There are good arguments which are invalid. See sections 4.18, 4.19A, 5.13 (**strength**, etc.; **induction**).

(iv) It is worth noting that, in formal logic and in other branches of philosophy, the term 'valid' can apply *either* to an argument as a whole *or* to the transition from premisses to conclusion. Thus:

'A valid argument.'
'A validly drawn conclusion.'

The following uses of the term 'valid' should be avoided, although the second of them is a little more intelligible than the first:

'A valid premiss.'
'A valid conclusion.'

(v) **Valid schema**: see section 6.4(ii).

(vi) There are a number of non-philosophical uses of the word 'valid' with which we are all familiar and which are perfectly clear. For instance, a *valid season ticket*, a *valid vote*, a *valid statute* are things which satisfy certain rules or conventions and, therefore, can function as we expect season tickets, votes, and statutes to function. Notice that in none of these examples is 'valid' a synonym of 'true'. Season tickets, votes, and statutes are not things which can be true (or false, for that matter).

Do not use the word 'valid' as a fancy-dress synonym for 'true'. Do not use the word 'valid' as a mere general term of commendation. The word 'good' is quite useful. Generally, I would say that to use 'valid' as a synonym for either 'true' or 'good' is to combine sloppiness with pomposity – two things we can well do without, in philosophy and elsewhere.

4.10   TRUTH AND VALIDITY

As observed in section 4.9:

(i) arguments are valid or invalid, their component statements (i.e., premisses and conclusion) are true or false;

(ii) a valid argument may have component statements which are false.

Because of the definitions of **validity** and **implication**, the following combinations are possible in a valid argument:

| truth in the premisses | falsity in the premisses | falsity in the premisses |
| true conclusion | false conclusion | true conclusion |

The one combination IMPOSSIBLE in a valid argument is:

all premisses true
false conclusion

Such an argument is invalid.

4.11   CATEGORICAL

 (i) If you **categorically deny** an accusation, you are saying that the accu-
    sation is *completely* false; your denial is *unconditional, unrestricted,
    unqualified, absolute*. See also section 7.19 (**absolutely**).
 (ii) The technical use of 'categorical' in logic is similar to this, although it
    is not the case that a categorical proposition is always 'stronger' than
    a non-categorical counterpart. ('Must' makes a stronger claim than 'is'.
    For this sense of 'stronger', see section 4.19B.)

    A **categorical proposition** simply asserts that something is the case
    (e.g., 'That's a poinsettia'). It does not say that something is the case
    if some condition is satisfied (i.e., it is not like 'If it's a poinsettia, the
    petals will be red') and it does not modify or qualify the assertion,
    either by strengthening it or weakening it (i.e., it is not like 'That's
    probably a poinsettia' or 'That must be a poinsettia').

    A categorical proposition is perhaps best defined as one which is
    neither conditional (section 4.12) *nor* modal (section 6.28(ii)).

    E.g.:

Categorical	Non-categorical
'Every cat is mammalian.'	'If anything is a cat, it is mammalian.' (Conditional)
	'Cats must be mammalian.' (Modal)

    See Kelley, 1988, Ch. VIII.
 (iii) **Categorical syllogism**: see section 6.28(i).
 (iv) Do not confuse 'categorical' with 'categorial' (see section 3.4A(iv))
 (v) For **categorical imperative**, see section 9.10.

4.12   CONDITIONAL PROPOSITIONS

 (i) A conditional proposition has the form 'If p then q.' (Substitutions for
    p and *q* can be affirmative or negative.) The **consequent** (literally, 'the
    follower') or *apodosis* is the proposition in the *q* place. The **antecedent**
    ('the goer-in-front') or *protasis* occupies the *p* place. 'If it rains, the
    streets are wet' is a conditional proposition. Its antecedent is 'It rains'
    (i.e., 'Raining occurs'). The consequent is 'The streets are wet.' *Conse-
    quent* must not be confused with *consequence* (see section 3.17)
 (ii) To assert a conditional proposition is to assert that something is the
    case on condition that something else is the case; e.g.:

If our Vice-Chancellor committed the Jack-the-Ripper murders, he must be over a hundred years old.

Unless interest rates come down, the position of the average salary-earner will continue to deteriorate.

Tom will donate $500 provided that three other people undertake to do the same.

(iii) Conditional propositions have the form 'If p then q', but, as the above examples show, the 'then' is dispensable and other words can sometimes do an 'if'-like job. Not all utterances containing the word 'if' are conditional propositions:

If it rained last night, the grass will be wet this morning.   (A)
If you're hungry, there's a pot of spaghetti on the stove.   (B)

(A) is a conditional. It asserts a relation of dependence between the weather last night and the state of the grass this morning: something will be true of the latter if something else is true of the former. Someone who utters (B) would be very surprised if he were interpreted as saying that the other person's hunger is some sort of condition of there being a pot of spaghetti on the stove.

A proposition is not a genuine conditional proposition unless it implies its **contrapositive**. Putting it another way: a proposition of the 'if p then q' type is a conditional proposition only if it implies a proposition of the 'if -q then -p' type.

(A) implies: 'If the grass is not wet this morning, then it did not rain last night.' (B) does *not* imply: 'If there is no pot of spaghetti on the stove, then you are not hungry.' Within a genuine conditional, neither antecedent nor consequent is asserted, but (B) *does* assert its 'consequent' (which is *not* a genuine consequent).

(iv) If a philosopher says something about **a conditional**, he means *a conditional proposition*. Conditionals are sometimes called **hypotheticals**, but that way of talk should be avoided, because it could suggest that all conditionals are mere assumptions-for-the-sake-of-argument. (For **hypothetical question**, see section 1.2B(iii).)

See Aune, 1967; Geach, 1976, Ch. XVIII; Lacey, 1976, pp. 35–37; Ryle, 1950; Jackson, 1987 (not introductory).

4.13   IMPLICATIVE AND NON-IMPLICATIVE CONDITIONALS

(i) A statement of the form 'If p then q' is an **implicative conditional** IFF it asserts that p (the antecedent) *implies* q (the consequent) (for 'imply' see sections 4.2, 4.4A).

If a geometrical figure is a square, it is four-sided.   (C)

If it's Thursday night, most of the shops will be open.   (D)

Each has the form 'If p then q', but there is an important difference in their **logical status** (section 3.11). The relationship between antecedent and consequent in (C) is *a matter of logic*: the antecedent implies the consequent. (C) is true by virtue of the meanings of its component symbols alone. (D) is different. The relationship between its antecedent and consequent is a **matter of fact**, rather than of logic (section 3.15). The antecedent does not imply the consequent. (D), if true, is true, not by virtue of the meanings of its component symbols alone, but by virtue of facts about the habits of shopkeepers.

(ii) **Rebutting an alleged implicative conditional**

If someone is a woman, she is female.   (E)

If John is a bachelor, he is an ummarried male.   (F)

When a conditional is implicative, it asserts that the antecedent implies the consequent. If someone alleges that a conditional is implicative, his contention is refuted if it can be shown that denying the consequent and asserting the antecedent is not self-contradictory.

(E) and (F) cannot be so refuted because they are true, but if someone were to assert either of the following as implicative conditionals, it would be possible to refute him in one of those ways:

If anything is a cat, it is furry.   (G)

If Dai is a Welshman, he has a good singing voice.   (H)

Even if Dai is both Welsh and possessed of a good singing voice, there is nothing self-contradictory in the notion of a Welshman with a poor voice. (G) might seem trickier. Someone might plausibly maintain that furriness is part of the definition of the word 'cat', so that a non-furry cat is (logically) like a triangle with more or fewer than three sides. He might refer us to *CODCE*, which is certainly on his side. But then we refer him to *The Complete Cat Encyclopaedia*, 1972, pp. 260–261. There, one reads of a variety of cat known as 'sphinx' which is not furry – which is, indeed, almost hairless. In other words, we claim to produce a **counterinstance** (see section 5.2A(ii)).

If he is stubborn, our objector may still say 'It's not a cat, because it can't be. You might call it a cat, and you might call a grasshopper an elephant. But that makes no difference to the conceptual point that the grasshopper does not have features which any creature MUST have if it is to be an instance of the concept of an elephant.'

Despite all that, the creature is like a standard cat in all matters but the absence of fur; it is descended from standard cats; it can mate successfully with standard cats, etc. That being so, denying that the poor thing is a cat seems to do greater violence to our system of concepts than admitting that it is a cat. So the sphinx *is* a counterinstance to (G).

Similarly with (H), if we produce any Welshman with a poor singing voice, we show that the proposition 'Dai is a Welshman' does not imply 'Dai has a good singing voice' (cf. Flew, 1975, Ch. III).

(iii) **Causal conditionals**

Someone might assert one or more of these:

If glass is thrown against a brick wall, it will break.
If you go on teasing the cat, he'll scratch you.
If acid is dropped on to blue litmus, the litmus turns red.

Even if these are true, there is no self-contradiction in the notions of *glass surviving such a shock*, a *thoroughly teased but non-scratching cat*, or *acid and litmus shocking us by disobeying the textbooks*. Thus, the connections asserted in the examples are not implicative relations between propositions but are **causal** connexions between events or states of affairs (see also section 3.16A).

(iv) **Non-implicative, non-causal conditionals: statements of regular correlation**.

If it's Tuesday, Professor Quartus will be lecturing.   (J)

If so, then (within whatever spatio-temporal frame is being presupposed), there will be a regular connexion between the occurrence of a Tuesday and Professor Quartus lecturing. But the antecedent does not imply the consequent (the notion of a *Quartus's-lecture-less Tuesday* is not self-contradictory). Neither does it seem plausible to assert that its being Tuesday *causes* Quartus to lecture (as inhaling pepper causes him to sneeze). There is a **regular correlation** between the state of affairs, *the day being Tuesday*, and the state of affairs, *Quartus lecturing*. That correlation can probably be *explained* in terms of decisions by Quartus's department, Quartus's contract, his sense of duty or enlightened self-interest, etc. But (J) says none of this, so we would do best to treat J as merely an assertion that, within the relevant spatio-temporal frame, it is never the case that it is Tuesday and Quartus is not lecturing.

If it's 10.00 p.m. in Newcastle, it's 9.30 p.m. in Adelaide.   (K)

The state of affairs picked out by the antecedent does not *cause* the state of affairs picked out by the consequent. Antecedent does not *imply* consequent. The correlation of states of affairs could, I expect, be accounted for partly in terms of astronomy, and partly in terms of acts of parliament. Unfortunately, I know little of that, but even if I knew nothing of it, I could still understand example (K). That seems to indicate that here we have another statement of a regular correlation, so regular that the occurrence of the antecedent situation is sufficient evidence that the consequent situation occurs.

> If a person smokes cigarettes, he risks contracting cancer of the lung. (L)

Most scientists agree that that statement is true. Most *also* agree that it expresses a causal connexion. But those are *two* points, not just one. Almost certainly, the connexion is causal, but it would not be self-contradictory to accept (L) and deny that the connexion is causal. At one time, H. J. Eysenck argued that *proneness to cigarette smoking* and *proneness to contracting lung cancer* are both caused by something else. If Eysenck is wrong, we cannot show him to be wrong merely from the meaning of (L); we need to refer to statistics, experimental data, pathological investigations, etc. (i.e., to **facts** – see section 3.15). As a discussion of the physiological effects of smoking, Eysenck, 1965, is long out of date, but it is full of interesting remarks on the difficulties involved in establishing causal connexions and the importance of not treating the existence of a correlation of variables as sufficient evidence of a cause-and-effect relationship between them.

(v) **Non-implicative, non-causal connexions: statements of legal connexion**

> If an Australian is 18, he is entitled to vote. (M)
> If an Australian is 18, he is obliged to vote. (N)
> Unless an American has turned 30, he is not eligible for election to the Senate. (O)
> If Tom is a Seventh Day Adventist, he is forbidden to eat pork. (P)
> If a student passes Philosophy I, he can enrol for a second-year philosophy subject. (Q)

All these examples concern *obligation*, or *entitlement*, or *permission*, and this is directly indicated within the statements. (That is so even of (Q) since there is a well-established use of 'can' making it synonymous, not with 'is able to', but with 'is permitted to'.) Antecedent does not imply consequent (there is nothing self-contradictory in the notion of a vote-less Australian 18-year-old). Neither is the connexion causal. Antecedent and consequent are connected by virtue of some legal system or other system of regulation. We can say, for short, that examples (M)–(Q) are **statements of legal connexion**. For further reading, see the list at the end of section 4.12.

4.14 'MATERIAL CONDITIONALITY'

A conditional of any kind is false if its antecedent is true and its consequent is false. In other words, the *minimum* commitment for anyone who makes an assertion of the form (If p then q) is that it is not the case that p is true and q is false. This minimum commitment can be symbolized as (-(p & -q)). This aspect of conditionals has led logicians to formulate the notion of **material conditionality**.

> A proposition p is a **material condition** for a proposition q IFF it is not the case that p is true and q is false.

If we use the symbol ($\supset$) ('hook' or 'horseshoe') to symbolize material conditionality, we can say:

> (p $\supset$ q) is a compound proposition (see sections 6.8–6.9) which is true IFF it is not the case that p is true and q is false.

It follows that a material conditional (p $\supset$ q) is true in any of the following circumstances:

> p true & q true
> p false & q true
> p false & q false

So (p $\supset$ q) is true whenever p is false. Obviously, when someone makes an 'If p then q' assertion, he almost always means a lot more than (p $\supset$ q), so (p $\supset$ q) should be pronounced 'p hook q' or 'p horseshoe q', not 'If p then q'. Sometimes the symbol ($\rightarrow$) is used instead of ($\supset$). This is unfortunate because the arrow is sometimes used to symbolize implication in the sense defined in section 4.4.

Let 'S' denote the proposition that Gadaffi is the Mayor of Jerusalem. Let 'T' denote the proposition that $5 + 2 = 7$. S is false and T is true, so the material conditional (S $\supset$ T) is true. Some logicians would say: 'Therefore S **materially implies** T'. That is an utterly perverse misuse of the word 'imply'. It is equally perverse to pretend that (S $\supset$ T) means the same as (If S then T).

If p implies q, p 'materially implies' q. But from 'p "materially implies" q', we cannot draw the conclusion that p implies q. For **material equivalence**, see section 6.13.

4.15   SUBJUNCTIVE CONDITIONALS

> If Hitler had invaded Britain in 1940, he would have conquered the whole country.   (A)

Hitler did not invade Britain in 1940 and he did not conquer it. If (A) were treated as a material conditional (see section 4.14), that would be enough to make it true, but, if the following pieces of tomfoolery are treated as material conditionals, they also are true:

If Queen Anne is dead, $2+2=4$.   (B)

If St Augustine wrote *Fanny Hill*, Canberra is the capital of Australia.   (C)

If Hitler had killed himself in 1938, he would have conquered all of Britain in 1940.   (D)

Pretty clearly, someone who asserts, denies, or ponders (A) does not assert that, deny that, or ponder whether it is true as (B), (C), and (D) are true. (A), if true, is not true merely because its antecedent is false. (A) is a **subjunctive conditional**, i.e.:

> a conditional which implies or suggests that the antecedent is false or leaves open the possibility of the antecedent being false,

and

> which, if true, asserts some kind of real connexion between the state of affairs described in the antecedent and that described in the antecedent.

Subjunctive conditionals are sometimes called: *contrary-to-fact conditionals, counterfactual conditionals, contrafactual conditionals, unfulfilled conditionals.* There are important affinities between subjunctive conditionals and **hypothetical questions** (see section 1.2B(iii)). N.B.: 'Counterfactual' does NOT mean 'false'. See Flew, 1984, pp. 70–71; Geach, 1976, Ch. XVIII; Lacey, 1976, pp. 35–37; Walters, 1967(a); Jackson, 1987, Ch. IV.

4.16   SUFFICIENT CONDITION; NECESSARY CONDITION; NECESSARY-AND-SUFFICIENT CONDITION

(i) X is a **sufficient condition** for Y, IFF *X and non Y is an impossibility* (see section 3.12). E.g., *being a king* is *sufficient* for *being male* as is *combustion* for *the presence of oxygen.*

(ii) X is a **necessary condition** for Y, IFF *Y but nonX is an impossibility.* E.g., *being male* is necessary for *being a king* as is *the presence of oxygen* for *combustion.*

(iii) X is a **necessary-and-sufficient condition** for Y, IFF *X but nonY* and *Y but nonX* are both impossibilities. E.g., *being a male monarch ranking immediately below an emperor* is necessary-and-sufficient for *being a king*, as is *being a rectangular plane figure with four equal sides* for *being a square.*

(iv) **Alternative ways of expressing these conditions**
E.g.,

X is a sufficient condition for Y	If X then Y Whenever X then Y
X is a necessary condition for Y	Unless X, then nonY Y only if X
X is a necessary-and-sufficient condition for Y	If X then Y, and if nonX then nonY
	X if and only if Y
	X IFF Y

Above, I have discussed necessary (etc.) conditions in terms of *states of affairs*. They can be discussed also in terms of the truth-values of propositions: the truth of p is a necessary condition for the truth of q, IFF (If -p then -q).

(v) **Logical relations** (see section 10.3) **between condition-statements**
The relation between (If p then q) and (If -q then -p) is equivalence (**transposition** – see section 6.18) hence (X is a sufficient condition for Y) and (Y is a necessary condition for X) are also equivalent to each other.

(p IFF q) and (q IFF p) are equivalent to each other, hence (X is a necessary-and-sufficient condition for Y) is equivalent to (Y is a necessary-and-sufficient condition for X).

(p IFF q) implies (If p then q) which does not imply (p IFF q), hence the relation of (p IFF q) to (If p then q) is superimplication and the relation of (If p then q) to (p IFF q) is subimplication. The same pattern holds between (X is a necessary-and-sufficient condition for Y) and (X is a sufficient condition for Y) etc., etc.

(vi) If rain last night is a sufficient condition for wet grass this morning, wet grass this morning is a necessary condition for rain last night – which does not mean that the wetness of grass this morning had any part in causing last night's rain. If there is any possibility that 'condition for' might be confusing, say 'indication of' instead.

(vii) **Negating** (see section 6.12) **statements of necessary (etc.) conditions**
Many logic books say that a statement of the form (If p then q) is false IFF p is true and q is false. That is not true. It confuses conditionals with so-called 'material conditionals' (sections 4.14, 4.15). Denying that the truth of p is a sufficient condition for the truth of q is not saying (p & -q). It is saying that (p & -q) is a possibility.

Condition-statement	Negation
X is a sufficient condition for Y.	X and nonY is a possibility.
X is a necessary condition for Y.	Y and nonX is a possibility.

| X is a necessary-and-sufficient condition for Y. | At least one of X and Y is possible without the other. |

4.17 'IFS', REGULAR AND IRREGULAR

> If you gamble all your money away, you will not be able to pay the rent.   (A)
>
> If it's an emu, it's a wingless bird.   (B)

Each has the form (If p then q) and each is a non-problematic assertion that something (mentioned in the antecedent, the 'pthing') is a **sufficient condition** for something else (mentioned in the consequent, the 'qthing'). Each leaves open the possibility that something other than the pthing could also be a sufficient condition for the qthing, i.e., neither asserts that its pthing is a **necessary condition** for its qthing. Let us, however, look at some conditionals which are not so well-behaved.

In ordinary talk, 'if' often does duty for 'if and only if' ('IFF') and for 'only if'. That is particularly so in promises and resolutions:

> If I finish writing my essay by midnight on Saturday, I'll go to the beach on Sunday.   (C)
>
> Yes, you can watch television tonight – if you finish your homework first.   (D)

Grammatically, each looks like a statement of a sufficient condition, but, as a matter of linguistic fact, utterers of either intend something else. The (C)-utterer (at least, if he is speaking to himself) is stating a necessary condition. The (D)-utterer lays down a necessary-and-sufficient condition (a combination threat and promise):

> I'll go to the beach on Sunday only if I finish writing my essay by midnight on Saturday.   (C')
>
> You can watch television tonight, if (but only if) you finish your homework first.   (D')

'I'll believe it when I see it', taken literally, says that *seeing it* would be a sufficient condition for *believing it*, but what is *intended* is necessity-and-sufficiency. These little loosenesses of ordinary talk are seldom troublesome. Context and tone of voice often remove the misleading impression which the bare words might create. Indeed, they often remove it so thoroughly that we are not aware of the possibility of a problem. It is important, though, to remember the distinctions which ordinary if-talk tends to blur. A young philosopher was once appointed to a temporary lectureship and was told by his professor that, if he obtained his Ph.D. within three years, his appointment would be made permanent. Later, he discovered that his professor, an eminent logician, believed that he had thereby given fair warning that, if the Ph.D. were *not* obtained within three years, the appointment would *not* be made permanent.

4.18   PARADOXES OF IMPLICATION AND VALIDITY; VALIDITY, FORMAL SOUNDNESS, STRENGTH

A.

In a **logical paradox**, an apparently unacceptable conclusion is derived from apparently acceptable premises by means of apparently acceptable reasoning (see, e.g., Sainsbury, 1988; Quine, 1976, pp. 1–18; see also section 6.22(g) (*aporia*)). The definitions of **implication** and **validity** imply propositions which look very odd indeed. Here are the definitions:

(1) An argument is valid IFF its premiss(es) imply its conclusion.
(2) A statement implies another statement IFF it is self-contradictory to affirm the former statement and deny the latter statement.

THEREFORE:
(3) Since it is self-contradictory to deny a necessarily true statement, any statement whatever implies a necessarily true statement.
(4) Since it is self-contradictory to affirm a self-contradictory statement, a self-contradictory statement implies every other statement.
(5) Since it is self-contradictory to affirm and deny the same statement, any statement implies itself.

All that being so, examples A–E below are true statements and examples F–L are valid arguments:

'My left ear is itchy' implies that $2 + 2 = 4$.   (A)

'Reagan won the 1984 election' implies that $2 + 2 = 4$.   (B)

'Reagan lost the 1984 election' implies that $2 + 2 = 4$.   (C)

'$2 + 2 = 5$' implies that Reagan won the 1984 election.   (D)

'$2 + 2 = 5$' implies that Reagan lost the 1984 election.   (E)

My left ear is itchy (F)
∴ $2 + 2 = 4$

Reagan won the 1984 election (G)
∴ $2 + 2 = 4$

Reagan lost the 1984 election (H)
∴ $2 + 2 = 4$

$2 + 2 = 5$ (J)
∴   Reagan won the 1984 election.

$2 + 2 = 5$ (K)
∴   Reagan lost the 1984 election.

Reagan is a socialist (L)

∴ Reagan is a socialist

Students usually find the above rather depressing. (A)–(E), the implication-statements, seem bad enough, but (F)–(L), the arguments, seem insane. We can, however, draw the fangs of these paradoxes by distinguishing between: **valid** argument, **formally sound** argument, and **strong** argument.

B. Validity, formal soundness, strength

An argument is **valid** IFF its premiss(es) imply its conclusion.

An argument is **formally sound** IFF it has non-self-contradictory premisses which, if true, understood, and accepted, would provide someone who previously did not accept the conclusion with absolutely conclusive grounds for accepting it.

In general, an argument is not **strong** *unless* its premisses are true (a necessary, not a sufficient condition). Such an argument is strong to the extent that it is *cogent*, i.e., to the extent that it provides good reasons for accepting its thesis (i.e., its conclusion) and for rejecting theses incompatible with it. **Strength** admits of degree, i.e., an argument may be *fairly strong, rather strong, very strong*. Validity and formal soundness do not admit of degree.

Examples (F)–(L) are valid, but neither formally sound nor strong. The example in section 4.9(ii) is valid and formally sound, but totally devoid of strength. That in section 4.9(iii) is neither valid nor formally sound, but is very strong. See also section 4.21 (**non sequitur**).

These 'paradoxes' are troublesome only if we forget the distinction between the technical and popular senses of 'valid argument', treating it as a term of unrestricted commendation. See section 4.9. See also Hamblin, 1970, Ch. VII.

4.19 ARGUMENTS, GOOD AND BAD; STRENGTH OF ARGUMENT AND STRENGTH OF ASSERTION

A. Arguments, good and bad

The more extreme Sophists (section 7.3E) would have said that an argument is good IFF it achieves what the arguer wants. The more extreme formal logicians would say that an argument is good IFF its premisses imply its conclusion (see also section 4.20(iv)). Somewhere between these two extremes lies sanity.

A good argument is a strong argument (and strength admits of degree) (see section 4.18B). When we consider argument as something intended to *persuade*, another dimension of argumentative goodness emerges: the premisses should not merely be true, but should be intelligible to and accept-able by the intended audience. See also section 8.8 (**proof**).

B.   Strength of argument and strength of assertion

   (i) Calling an argument strong is not the same as saying 'It convinces me and ought to convince you', but it is a *limited* endorsement, roughly equivalent to 'That's a case to be answered.' Cf. sections 8.10A, 9.12B (**arguable; prima facie case**).
   (ii) To call an assertion **strong** is *not* to endorse it, but to say that it *claims a lot*. Thus, an *open universal proposition* is stronger than a *closed universal proposition* (see section 6.30) and a claim of the form 'Every S is P' is stronger than one of the form 'At least one S is P.' Stronger assertions are *riskier* than weaker assertions.

4.20   FALLACY

   (i) **A fallacy is *not* a false proposition**, but a fault in argument. A fallacious argument is one which fails to give the required support to its conclusion for reasons *other than falsity in the premisses*. The required support is not there even if the premisses are true.
   (ii) A **formal** fallacy (sometimes called **deductive fallacy** or **logical fallacy** (see sections 5.13A, 3.14) is an *invalid* type of argument, a type of argument in which the premisses fail to give *deductive* support to the conclusion because they do not *imply* it (see section 4.4). In other words, it is possible for the conclusion to be false, even if the premisses are true. See Flew, 1975, pp. 26–30; Hamblin, 1970, Chs VI, VII.
   (iii) An **informal** fallacy is a type of argument which would fail to support its conclusion, even if the premisses are true and even if they imply the conclusion. See sections 4.23–4.30, 6.26. See also Walton, 1987.
   (iv) A **deductivist** (see section 5.13A(v)) might agree that there are informal fallacies, but he would insist that a deductively invalid argument is *thoroughly* invalid (in even the popular sense – see section 4.9) and can give *no support whatsoever* to its conclusion. That is true of many deductively invalid arguments, but, if we go all the way with the deductivist, we must reject all inductive arguments (see sections 4.9(iii), 5.13B) and agree that we have no rational basis for our opinion that walking out of a fiftieth-storey window is unlikely to be good for us (something quite seriously asserted by Feyerabend, 1978, pp. 221–222).
   (v) In popular talk, 'fallacy' often means *a widely held false belief*, specially one which is taken so much for granted that it 'goes without saying'. Philosophers and even logicians sometimes come close to talking this way. See, e.g., section 1.14A(iii) (**the Socratic fallacy**). A fallacy in this sense works something like a rule for getting from premisses to

conclusion, so there is a certain similarity to 'fallacy' in the technical sense (but see Frankena, 1952, p. 103).

4.21 NON SEQUITUR

The literal translation of this Latin phrase is 'It does not follow' (see section 3.17 on **consequence** and section 4.7(g)). If the conclusion of an argument does not follow from the premisses, that argument is a **non sequitur**. A *fallacious argument* (see section 4.20) is a **non sequitur**. 'Does not follow from' is, however, ambiguous. It can mean either 'is not implied by' or 'would not be supported by those premisses even if they are true'. Any proposition implies itself (see section 4.4), so 'Tom is the rightful Emperor of China' implies 'Tom is the rightful Emperor of China.' But suppose Tom says: 'I will give you an argument why you should acknowledge my claim: I am the rightful Emperor of China, because I am the rightful Emperor of China.' His argument is valid in the technical sense, but it gives no support whatsoever to his claim (see section 4.23). On the other hand, an argument might fall short of validity and yet give overwhelming reason for accepting its conclusion. '**Non sequitur**' would be a quite inappropriate label for such an argument. See also section 4.18B (**strong and weak arguments**).

4.22 ELLIPTICAL ARGUMENT; ENTHYMEME; TRUNCATED ARGUMENT

Three synonymous expressions meaning *an argument which is not fully stated*, e.g.,

'*Of course* Socrates is mortal. He's a *man* isn't he?'

The arguer has stated his conclusion ('Socrates is mortal') and one of his premisses ('Socrates is a man'). He has not, however, stated his other premiss ('All men are mortal'), **leaving it to be understood** by the audience. He has **tacitly assumed that premiss**. It is **implicit in** his presentation of the argument. A premiss treated this way is sometimes called **a suppressed premiss**. In section 4.4A(iii), there is an example of an argument with a **suppressed conclusion**.

Taken strictly literally, an elliptical argument is not valid. To supply the appropriate premiss which makes it valid is to **validify** the argument. The supplied premiss is the **validator**. See Stove, 1982, pp. 66–68.

The phrase 'elliptical argument' should not be confused with 'circular argument' (i.e., an argument in which the conclusion is argued for from itself – see section 4.23(ii)). The confusion arises because, in geometry, an ellipse is a sort of squashed circle. The word as used by logicians is *not* derived from the word as used by geometers (or vice versa). Both uses are derived from a Greek word meaning 'a coming short'. (If that sets you wondering why a geometrical ellipse is a coming short, see the *SOED*.)

4.23   BEGGING THE QUESTION (*PETITIO PRINCIPII*)

(i) This is one of many unsatisfactory ways of arguing. The Latin phrase can be translated as 'asking for the first thing'. Neither that nor 'begging the question' is transparently clear.

When Primus is trying to persuade Secundus to accept a conclusion, the conclusion *is the thing in question* (or, for short, *the question* – cf. 'the question before the meeting', meaning 'the motion under consideration'). The conclusion (that which Primus is arguing for, that which he hopes to *end* by establishing) is likely to be the proposition with which the argument *began*: Primus makes an assertion; Secundus expresses doubt or dissent; Primus tries to give reasons for accepting his assertion. In other words, Primus's thesis is *the first thing* of the argument. Primus will try to argue from premisses which Secundus accepts:

> Primus: 'You do agree that all men are mortal, don't you?'
> Secundus: 'Yes.'
> Primus: 'You do agree that Socrates is a man, don't you?'
> Secundus: 'Yes.'
> Primus: 'Then, you must agree that Socrates is mortal.'

The premisses are things which Primus *asks Secundus to grant*. If Primus smuggles in the conclusion as one of his premisses, then he is asking (or begging) Secundus to grant the thing in question, the thing which began the argument. He is **begging the question**, committing a *petitio principii*. See Sparkes, 1965.

(ii) Begging the question is also called **arguing in a circle, circular argument** (i.e., instead of advancing from premisses to something else which is a conclusion, the arguer tries to move from the conclusion to the conclusion). Sometimes, however, 'arguing in a circle' is used colloquially to describe a situation in which two disputants continually come back to the same point of disagreement. That, while most frustrating, need not involve fallacy. **Begging the question**, however, is a fallacy (of an informal kind). (See section 4.20. See also Jackson, 1987, Ch. VI – not elementary.)

(iii) An arguer begs the question when he treats the matter under dispute as if it were common ground. It is rare for anyone to perpetrate arguments as transparently question-begging as this:

> This is a genuine diamond because it is a genuine diamond.   (A)

But sometimes, we find examples like these:

> To allow man an unbounded freedom of speech must always be, on the whole, advantageous to the State; for it is highly conducive to

the interests of the community that each individual should enjoy a liberty, perfectly unlimited, of expressing his sentiments. (B)

(Collected by the nineteenth-century logician,
Richard Whately. Quoted, Jepson, 1948, p. 199.)

People should be allowed to buy liquor on Sundays because they have a right to buy liquor on Sundays. (C)

In (B), the premiss ('it is highly conducive . . .', etc.) is a mere paraphrase of the conclusion. The premiss in (C) ('they have a right . . .') is not a mere paraphrase of the conclusion. If, however, no more is said about the foundation of the alleged right, the premiss is just as problematical as the conclusion and for the same reasons.

Any proposition implies itself, so *petitio* arguments are valid arguments in the technical sense of that phrase, but are logically unsatisfactory. See sections 4.9, 4.10, 4.18. Some have been worried by the fear that all valid arguments beg the question. See Anschutz, 1968, pp. 67–83; McCloskey, 1971, pp. 22–28; Ryan, 1974, pp. 70–74; Hamblin, 1970, index entry 'Begging the question'.

(iv) The expression 'beg the question' used in this sense has been with us for a very long time. So far as I know, it first appeared in the sixteenth century as a literal translation of the Latin, '*petitio principii*', which is a literal translation of the Greek phrase used by Aristotle. So we can trace the ancestry of 'beg the question' right back to the beginning of Logic as a systematic study in the West. Over the past fifteen years, however, it has become fashionable to treat 'beg the question' as if it were a synonym of 'raise the question', or 'prompt the question' or 'provoke the question':

Frequent elections beg the question how ungovernable we have become.

(ABC current affairs broadcast, 1974)

There is no good reason for this innovation. I suspect that people who talk like this have the vague feeling that 'beg the question' sounds more impressive than 'raise the question' and that they are much more interested in sounding impressive than in making sense. The two expressions 'beg the question' and 'raise the question' have quite distinct (and very useful) jobs to do. Linguistic innovations are worthwhile only when they enhance intelligibility. This one would have the opposite effect. To speak of a question as *begging for a certain (or certain kind of) answer* (e.g., Popper, 1972(a), p. 25) is not silly, but the point can be made much more clearly. See sections 1.2B(iv), (v) (**leading question; fallacy of complex question**). (Cf. Flew, 1975, p. 68.)

4.24   *FIGURA DICTIONIS* (ARGUMENT BY PUN)

The literal translation of the Latin is 'figure of speech', but as that means something else, the Latin is best left as it is. *Figura dictionis* is a fallacy (see section 4.20). Someone commits it when he overlooks (inadvertently or otherwise) the ambiguity or homonyny of a word and moves from the premiss that S is P in one sense of 'P' to the conclusion that S is P in a different sense of 'P':

> Every party is a gathering for enjoyment.
> The ALP [i.e. Australian Labor Party] is a party.

Therefore, the ALP is a gathering for enjoyment.

Outside a logic lecture, you are not likely to meet an argument so blatantly fallacious. But there are more sophisticated sophistries based on the same logical error. See section 9.5C.

Because arguing in this fashion involves using a word in two different senses, it is sometimes called **the fallacy of equivocation** or **argument by pun**. The syllogistic (see section 6.28) version of *figura dictionis* is sometimes called '**the fallacy of four terms**' (or '*quaternio terminorum*'). See the 'party' example above. Superficially, it seems to have, like any well-behaved syllogism, three and only three terms: 'party', 'gathering for enjoyment', 'and 'the ALP'. But, as 'party' is used in two different senses, there are four terms in the argument.

4.25   *IGNORATIO ELENCHI*

'*Ignoratio elenchi*' is an old technical term for a family of faults in argument. It can be translated as 'missing the point', 'ignoring the issue', 'arguing for the wrong thing', 'fallacy of irrelevance', etc., etc. An *ignoratio elenchi* is a **red herring** (Brewer, 1970, p. 528).

  (i) E.g., if Primus says that Secundus's argument is hackneyed, or perfectly predictable, or unoriginal, or old-fashioned, he may well be right, but that does not refute Secundus's argument.
 (ii) Similarly: Primus may assert a proposition. Secundus does not agree with the proposition, but, instead of arguing against what Primus says, he pretends that Primus has said something else which is easier to demolish (**the straw man** – see section 4.26).
(iii) **The personal attack** and *argumentum ad hominem*. See section 4.28.
 (iv) *Tu quoque* ('You too!'). See section 4.27.
  (v) *Argumentum ad misericordiam* (appeal to pity)

> 'Members of the jury. Today is the accused's twenty-first birthday. Could you bear to give a young man a verdict of guilty, a bad name, and a prison sentence as a twenty-first birthday present?'

What is the underlying assumption? That it is impossible (or even unlikely) that someone whose trial ends on his twenty-first birthday should be guilty as charged? Obviously silly. Even a more serious biographical fact about the accused (e.g., that he is poor or that his childhood was deprived) might be irrelevant to the question of his guilt or innocence.

On the other hand, what is irrelevant to the question of the guilt or innocence of the accused might be very relevant to *the question of sentence*. In some other cases, unfortunate biographical facts about the accused might be relevant to questions about his motives and intentions, about provocation, etc., and, hence, might be relevant to the question of *what* (if anything) he is guilty of, e.g., murder or manslaughter.

Although the following story is not an instance of *argumentum ad misericordiam* (*argumentum ad pulchritudinem*, perhaps – '*pulchritudo*' meaning 'beauty'), it would be a pity to leave it out:

> Phryne, the mistress and model of the ancient Athenian sculptor, Praxiteles, was (like Socrates) charged with impiety. Unlike Socrates, she was acquitted, perhaps because, being a woman, she was not allowed to conduct her own defence, which was entrusted to one Hyperides. He persuaded the jury that she was not guilty by ripping her chiton off and exclaiming: 'Can such beauty be guilty?'

(vi) Many **appeals to authority** are not fallacious. The fact that an eminent cardiologist comes to some conclusion about a patient's heart *does not imply* that the conclusion is true, but it is nevertheless a good reason for taking it seriously. Unlike a test-cricketer endorsing a breakfast cereal as nutritious, the cardiologist is speaking in his field of expertise. See Shaw, 1981, Ch. XVI; J. D. MacKenzie, 1988.

(vii) *Argumentum ad populum* (literally: **appeal to the people**; less literally: **appeal to widespread opinion**, or **appeal to fashion**).
'Forty million Frenchmen can't be wrong.' Of course they can, and the fact that most people, or all people, hold an opinion is not sufficient to prove that it is true. Arguments beginning 'In this day and age' are almost always mere appeals to fashion and quite spurious as arguments. On the other hand, the fact that very many people hold an opinion provides some reason for not dismissing it out of hand, for examining it carefully, etc. Cf. (vi) above.

(viii) *Argumentum ad baculum*
Literally, 'appeal to the stick'. The term is used for the kind of 'argument' which relies on *threat* (e.g., a Mafia offer-which-you-cannot-refuse), but also for 'argument' which relies on table-banging and similar sound and fury (see section 8.4A (**rhetoric**)). Thus, it is related to the equally spurious 'argument' which relies on flattery or on a 'sincere' manner (?*Argumentum Reaganosum*?).

See Flew, 1975, Ch. VII; Stebbing, 1939, Ch. XIII; Geach, 1976, pp. 26–31; Passmore, 1969, pp. 43–53; Hamblin, 1970, Ch. IV.

4.26   STRAW MAN

(i)
The Aunt Sally or **Straw Man**, something set up solely for the purpose of knocking it down or destroying it. Political scientists are prone to this usually rather pointless form of activity. Assertions which no one but an idiot would dream of making are patiently denied or disproved.

(Spann, 1966, p. 6)

Not just political scientists do this, but everyone who yields to the temptation to score a victory without actually fighting. At the same time, it is important to remember that thoroughness in investigation is not a vice and that the testing of unlikely hypotheses can be illuminating. Cf. section 8.5B (**pedantry**). Spann, however, is (quite rightly) complaining about people who put most of their energies into refuting (see section 8.11) the *easily* refutable.

(ii) That is bad enough, but it does not amount to misrepresentation. That occurs when someone has a real opponent and, instead of arguing against what that real opponent says, pretends that he has said something which is much easier to demolish, e.g., Primus denies that everyone is selfish; Secundus attacks him for saying that no one is selfish. See also Flew, 1975, pp. 40–42.

This style of arguing is a variety of *ignoratio elenchi* (see section 4.25). It is also a variety of either sheer muddle-headedness or sheer dishonesty. (For the derivation of the phrases 'Aunt Sally' and 'Straw Man', see Brewer, 1970, pp. 59–60, and *CODCE*, 1976, p. 1138.) A logician's *straw man* is not to be confused with a lawyer's *man of straw* (someone too impecunious to be worth suing).

4.27   *TU QUOQUE*

'*Tu quoque*' is the Latin for 'You too'. Suppose Primus accuses Secundus of **xifying** (see section 6.3). There are different ways in which someone can defend himself against an accusation:

He can offer arguments in an attempt to show that he did not do it.

He can admit that he did it, but argue that there was nothing wrong with doing it.

He can admit that he did it and that he should not have, but argue that there were extenuating circumstances.

Instead of using one of these defences, Secundus says: 'You are a fine one to talk. You xified last Wednesday' or 'You have done such-and-such which is just as bad as xifying.' When Secundus does that he has made a *tu quoque* **move**.

The *tu quoque* move is often a version of *ignoratio elenchi* (see section 4.25). Even if Secundus's counter-allegation is true, that is in no way inconsistent with Primus's allegation; neither would it show that xification by Secundus would be justifiable, or that there are circumstances which would extenuate Secundus's guilt. Secundus may succeed in embarrassing Primus into silence or in diverting attention from himself to Primus, but he has said nothing relevant to the accusation against himself. If Secundus is, in effect, arguing:

'Primus has done the same sort of thing as he accuses me of doing,
Therefore,
either I am not guilty *or* I should be let off lightly,'

then Secundus has produced an enormous **non sequitur** (see section 4.21).

A *tu quoque* move may well be of that type, and, if so, it is fallacious. But there are circumstances in which a *tu quoque* move may not be an *ignoratio elenchi* but a misleadingly phrased attempt to do something else.

The person who makes the ***tu quoque*** may be wanting to say: 'You have done the same thing. If you think it was all right for you to do it, why do you think it was wrong for me to do it?'; OR, he may be wanting to say: 'You have done the same sort of thing. If you think you deserve compassion and forbearance, why do you refuse compassion and forbearance to me?'

Either of these would be a legitimate (though not decisive) move. So *tu quoque* can be a rather complicated business. Whether justified or not, *tu quoque* is a form of ***argumentum ad hominem*** (see next section).

4.28   *ARGUMENTUM AD HOMINEM*

'**Ad hominem**' is Latin for 'to a/the man' (in the sense *member of the human species* – see section 1.25). An ***argumentum ad hominem*** is an argument concerning not the issue under discussion, but one's opponent – in other words, directed to the man rather than *ad rem* (to the thing). Three rather different kinds of thing go by this label.

(i) Suppose Primus makes an assertion or puts forward an argument. His opponent, Secundus, does not argue against Primus's assertion or argument. Instead Secundus makes a *personal attack* on Primus.

Most of the time this is quite fallacious, a variety of ***ignoratio elenchi*** (see section 4.25), the fallacy of **irrelevance** (see section 10.7). Suppose Primus has put forward some views concerning taxation. Secundus strongly dissents from Primus's views. 'Primus,' he says, 'is a bottle-nosed Baptist with a bad driving record. Let's not take any notice of him.' That is not a good argument. It does not say anything to show that Primus is wrong about taxation (even if, indeed, he is a bottle-nosed Baptist with a bad driving record).

(ii) But not all *ad hominem* moves are illegitimate. Suppose someone reports seeing a ghost or a flying saucer. If he has a long record as a pathological liar or a practical joker, then it would be relevant to raise these matters. Notice, however, *why* it is relevant: it is relevant because the question is *whether we should accept his testimony (or at least take it seriously)*.

The following is NOT a good argument, even if the premisses are true:

'Primus says he saw a flying saucer over Belmont.
But Primus likes to play practical jokes.
Therefore,
There was no flying saucer over Belmont.'

But provided the premisses are true, the following *is* a good argument:

'Primus says he saw a flying saucer over Belmont.
But Primus likes to play practical jokes.
Therefore,
It would not be wise to accept Primus's story if it has no support but Primus's word.'

Again, suppose Primus and Secundus are opposing candidates in a council election. In his campaign, Primus argues continually for a new and radical approach to kerbing and guttering. Secundus says not a word about kerbing and guttering. Instead, *he* argues continually that Primus is lazy, inefficient, and generally untrustworthy. Obviously, Secundus has not shown that Primus is wrong about kerbing and guttering. But that is not the only question at issue. Another very important question is *who should be voted for*? (cf. section 4.25(vi)). For more on *ad hominem* and similar moves, see T. J. Richards, 1978, pp. 38–43.

(iii) A quite different sort of thing from either of the above is sometimes called **argumentum ad hominem**:

Primus contends that X is Y. Secundus objects that certain other views which Primus holds imply that X is *not* Y.

Some logicians maintain that this is fallacious: Secundus, they say, even if right, has not shown that X is not Y. The most he has shown is that Primus is inconsistent. Certainly, if Secundus thinks he has shown that X is not Y, he is mistaken. But why MUST he think that? And, if he does not think or say that, where is the fallacy? He is arguing *with Primus*, not with someone else, and if he shows that Primus needs to do a bit more thinking about the point at issue, he has shown something quite relevant. See Geach, 1976, Ch. VI.

4.29   SPECIAL PLEADING

As a term used in assessing arguments (it has a different meaning in the history of English law – see Mozley and Whiteley, 1977, p. 320), **special pleading** is argument which distorts the facts by being one-sided: it recites all the **pros** and disregards all the **cons** (or *vice versa* – see section 8.9B) or it bases a conclusion about all Xs on premisses which are true of only some kinds of X.

The term is sometimes found used in a way which suggests that the user regards it as a rather learned way of saying 'bad argument'. Sometimes it seems to be used as if it meant *argument that might look good but isn't* (i.e., it is confused with **specious argument** – see section 8.18B). Sometimes it is used to mean *argument in support of a special interest* (i.e., '**sectional**' interest – as we all know, sectional interests are very wicked unless they happen to be the interests of sections we approve of). These three uses are pretentious **mis**uses which should be left to those who get a cheap thrill out of using words which they do not understand.

4.30   FALLACY OF PSEUDO-REFUTING DESCRIPTION

This is Flew's title for the logical error of 'trying to refute a view merely by classifying it in some irrelevant way' (1975, pp. 65–67). 'That's just what I'd expect a Christian / or Marxist / or Atheist / or . . . / to say' may well be true, but it is not in itself an argument against what it is a comment on.

Another version of the same error occurs when an arguer uses a word appropriate to an *excessive* or *faulty* case of X for any case of X which he happens to find unwelcome or inconvenient. See sections 8.5B (**pedantry**), 7.2A (**dogmatist**). The fallacy of pseudo-refuting description is a species of **question-begging** (see section 4.23).

5 Investigating

5.1 VERIFY, FALSIFY, CONFIRM, CORROBORATE, DISCONFIRM

(i) To **verify** a proposition is to show conclusively that it is true. A proposition is **verifiable** IFF it is possible to test it in a way which would conclusively show it to be true if it were true. (So a proposition could be *both* false *and* verifiable.) For the important distinction between **verifiability in practice** and **in principle**, see section 3.12B, C. For the **verifiability principle**, see section 5.4.

Please note the spelling: 'verify', 'verification, verifiable', not 'varify', etc. The meanings of these words are related to *truth* (Latin: *veritas*), not to *variety*.

(ii) To **falsify** a proposition is to show conclusively that it is false. A proposition is **falsifiable** IFF it is possible to test it in a way which would conclusively show it to be false if it were false. (So a proposition could be *both* true *and* falsifiable.)

Please notice that this technical use of 'falsify' differs considerably from the non-technical use. Outside philosophy, 'to falsify a theory' would mean *to fake a theory*. In philosophical talk, it means *to show a theory to be false*. See also section 5.4.

(iii) The word '**confirm**' is hard to pin down. It has a variety of senses and many writers have a way of sliding from one to the other without noticing. The best one can say briefly is that something confirms a proposition when it supports it or makes it more probable. There can be evidence supporting false propositions so a false proposition can be confirmed. See Lacey, 1976, pp. 37–41; Kneale, 1949, pp. 110–113; Chalmers, 1982, Chs IV–VI; Quine and Ullian, 1978, Ch. VIII.

(iv) A proposition is **corroborated** IFF:

(a) it is subjected to a test which could falsify it; and
(b) that test does not falsify it.

(So a false proposition could be corroborated.) See Flew, 1975, Ch. III;

Popper, 1959, Ch. X; Hooker, 1987, Ch. III; Putnam, 1979.

(v) **'Disconfirm'**: a technical word, but, alas, used inconsistently. Some use it as a synonym of 'falsify'. That is a sad misuse, because we need a word which will enable us to talk about a circumstance which does *not* falsify a hypothesis, but which *counts against it*. Let the hypothesis be 'Tom is very fond of chamber music.' Acceptance of that hypothesis *would lead us to expect* Tom to attend chamber music concerts regularly. Suppose, however, that he rarely, if ever, attends. That does not **falsify** the hypothesis, but it *counts against* the hypothesis *unless* someone can explain it in a manner consistent with the hypothesis (e.g., Tom cannot afford the tickets; he has to work at the usual time of concerts, etc.). It would be helpful if we could say 'and, therefore, the fact that Tom does not regularly attend the concerts **disconfirms** the hypothesis that he is very fond of chamber music', but, as things are, we cannot say that with clarity unless we also give a careful account of what we mean by 'disconfirm'.

5.2 INSTANCES; EVIDENCE

A. Instances

(i) **Confirming instance**: a confirming instance for a proposition of the form 'Every S is P' is an S which is P. Notice that a confirming instance for such a proposition *does **not** prove* that the proposition is true. For 'S', substitute 'cat'; for 'P' substitute 'black'.

(ii) **Counterinstance**: a counterinstance for a proposition of the form 'Every S is P' is an S which is non-P. Notice that a counterinstance for such a proposition *disproves* that proposition. For 'S' substitute 'cat'; for 'P' substitute 'black'.

Not every kind of proposition is disproved by a single counterinstance. Take the proposition: 'Smoking causes serious pulmonary and cardiovascular disease and shortens the life-span.' A counterinstance to this could be someone who smoked heavily and was healthy all his adult life, survived into vigorous old age, and finally died at the age of 97. There has been at least one such person: the philosopher, Bertrand Russell. That, however, does not disprove the proposition about the effects of smoking which is not an assertion about every smoker, but a statement of probability.

(iii) **Falsifying instance**: a falsifying instance for a proposition is an instance which shows that the proposition is false. Cf. **counterinstance** above.

(iv) **Refuting instance**: synonymous with 'falsifying instance'. For 'refute' see section 8.11A. See Flew, 1975, Chs II–III. See also section 1.3A(iii) **(truth-claims)**.

(v) **Substitution instance**: see section 6.4.

(vi) **Disconfirming instance**: see section 5.1(v).
(vii) **Instantiation**: see section 1.9A(iii).

B. Evidence

(i) In contemporary English (outside legal talk), 'evidence' means facts or factual propositions supporting (though not necessarily establishing) another factual proposition (see sections 3.15, 3.6). Pythagoras's theorem can be proved, but, as it is not a factual proposition, there is no evidence for it (or against it).

A **non-cognitivist** (see section 8.14A(ii)) would deny that there can be evidence for or against a moral judgment, precept, or principle, and even many cognitivists would prefer to speak of *grounds, reasons*, or *support* and restrict talk of **evidence** to the 'ordinarily' factual. See section 9.4A (**fact and value**).

(ii) This, however, is not the only meaning 'evidence' has had. Contemporary usage separates it from the adjective 'evident', but, originally, 'evidence' meant, in the *SOED*'s words, '*The quality or condition of being evident; evidentness*'. As applied to propositions, the word meant something like *plausibility, credibility, probability*. Hume (1711–1776) uses the term in this fashion. See Hume, 1975, pp. 110–111 (*ECHU* sec. x pt 1). Cf. **self-evident** (see section 3.10). (The kind of pen which we call a *highliter* is known to Italians as an *evidenziatoro*.)

(iii) The legal concept of evidence is complex (and of great philosophical interest). Only the barest outline is possible here. In the thinnest sense of the word, evidence is whatever is sworn to and placed before the court. In a less thin sense, it is what is sworn to and relevant, or what is sworn to, relevant, and admissible under the rules of evidence.

Circumstantial evidence is contrasted with **direct** evidence. The distinction, as stated in legal works of reference, is somewhat obscure, but examples make it tolerably clear. Direct evidence that Primus shot Secundus dead would be either evidence of someone who saw it (i.e., someone quite literally an *eye-witness*) or a confession by Primus. *All other* evidence would be circumstantial (testimony of those who heard the shot and saw Primus running, fingerprints, powder-burns, Primus's wallet dropped at the scene, etc.). Thus, the popular notion that circumstantial evidence must be unreliable is a mistake. (And sometimes what is given as direct evidence turns out to be erroneous, e.g., cases of mistaken identification and false confession.)

Hearsay evidence. If the question is whether event X occurred and witness Mr A testifies not that he witnessed the event, but that Mr B said that it had occurred, then Mr A's evidence is hearsay. Even in the law, hearsay evidence is not always inadmissible. See Mozley and Whiteley, 1977, pp. 125, 60, 104, 156–157; Baalman, 1979, pp. 48–54. See also section 9.12B (**prima facie** case); section 5.25 (**intuition**).

5.3 SETTLING THE TRUTH-VALUE OF AN EMPIRICAL PROPOSITION (see section 3.8)

(i) There are some propositions whose truth-value can be conclusively settled as true or false by observation (provided that reliable perceptions (see section 5.22B) are possible). Suppose the proposition is 'There is a five feet tall mermaid sitting on the edge of the kitchen table.' In that case, we go and have a look. If we see her there, we have determined the truth-value as true. If we do not see her there, we have determined the truth-value as false. That is the appropriate **decision-procedure** for such a proposition. In other words, provided we can assume that our perceptions are reliable, that proposition is both **verifiable** and **falsifiable** (see section 5.1).

(ii) There are some propositions whose truth-value, if they are true, can be conclusively settled as true, but cannot be conclusively settled as false (even if they are false). 'There are mermaids' would be conclusively shown to be true if someone produced a genuine mermaid. It cannot, however, be conclusively shown to be false. Mermaids may be elusive. (That is not the same as saying that there is no reason for believing the proposition to be false. See section 5.15.) In other words, provided we can assume that our perceptions are reliable, the proposition 'There are mermaids' is **verifiable** but it is not **falsifiable**.

(iii) There are some propositions whose truth-value can be conclusively settled as false, if they are false, but cannot be conclusively settled as true, even if they are true. 'Every crow is black' would be shown to be false by one non-black crow. But there is no comparable observation which would show the proposition to be true, because it ranges over all the crows there ever were or ever will be. See section 6.30.

(iv) There are some propositions which look as if they are empirical, but cannot be conclusively settled as either true or false. What could falsify or verify 'Every metal has a solvent' or (more alarmingly) 'Every event has a cause'? (See section 5.10.)

5.4 THE VERIFIABILITY PRINCIPLE; FALSIFIABILITY AND VERIFIABILITY

A. The Verifiability Principle

The **Verifiability** (or **Verification**) **Principle** was the central tenet of the philosophical movement known as **Logical Positivism** (see section 7.12E). That principle was believed to be the criterion for distinguishing sense from nonsense. Formulating the criterion proved somewhat difficult. The original formulation was: 'The meaning of a statement is its method of verification', but that, though neat, has no very obvious meaning itself.

The Logical Positivists believed that the only meaningful (i.e. genuine) propositions are either **tautologies** (see section 3.7) or **verifiable, empirical** propositions (see sections 3.8, 5.3) and that any purported proposition which falls outside these classes is a nonsensical pseudo-proposition. The problem was to arrive at a formulation of the Principle which would eliminate as meaningless what the Logical Positivists wanted to eliminate (e.g., religion and **metaphysics** (see section 7.22A)) while leaving intact the things which the Logical Positivists approved of (e.g., science, mathematics, and logic). But **scientific laws** (see section 5.12C) and **open universal propositions** generally (see section 6.30) proved an insuperable obstacle. (So did the Verifiability Principle itself because, however it is formulated, it is difficult to see how it can be either a tautology or empirically verifiable.)

See K. Campbell, 1976, pp. 14–19; D. E. Cooper, 1973, pp. 45–53; Urmson, 1975(b); Ayer, 1946, Ch. I. Ayer's earliest book, *Language, Truth and Logic* (first ed., 1936) is an enthusiastic exposition of Logical Positivism. Wisdom, 1953, pp. 229–247, is a sort of elegy for old Positivist certainties. For brief statements of Ayer's later views, see Ayer, 1946, pp. 5–16 and 1959, pp. 10–17.

B.   Falsifiability and Verifiability

K. R. Popper lays great stress on **falsifiability** (see sections 5.1–5.3) and has been thought by some to be offering either a revised version of or a rival to the Verifiability Principle. But the Verifiability Principle is intended to be a criterion of *meaningfulness*. Popper presents falsifiability as a criterion for demarcating scientific propositions from non-scientific propositions. He does not take the view that only scientific propositions are meaningful and has many times disclaimed any interest in a criterion for meaningfulness. See, e.g., Popper, 1976 (consult its index under 'falsification', 'meaning', and 'verification'); Chalmers, 1982. See also section 5.13B.

5.5   HYPOTHESIS; CONJECTURE; ASSUMPTION; DATA; THEORY AND PRACTICE

A.

(i) A **hypothesis** is a proposition put forward for investigation and testing. Tom's hypothesis may or may not be one of Tom's beliefs. See Quine and Ullian, 1978, Ch. VI. A 'hypothetical' (i.e., conditional) proposition (see sections 4.12–4.17) need not be a hypothesis. A hypothesis (e.g., 'Let us consider the hypothesis that the butler did it') need not be a 'hypothetical' proposition. See also sections 1.18 (**hypothetical characterization**), 1.2B(iii) (**hypothetical question**). On **hypothetical argument**, see Hamblin, 1970, pp. 233–246.

(ii) *ex hypothesi*. Literally 'from the hypothesis'. If someone says that a proposition is *ex hypothesi* false, he is saying that it is inconsistent with the hypothesis he is working with.

B.

Conjectures are (uncontroversially) *guesses*. The word is sometimes used interchangeably with '**hypothesis**' (see Popper, 1972(a), pp. 33–59), but whether hypotheses are merely guesses is a controversial matter. See Stove, 1982.

C. Assume, assumption

(i) 'Assumption' can mean much the same as 'hypothesis'; i.e., 'assumption for the sake of argument': a proposition put forward, not as true, but in order to see what follows from it and (perhaps) how it accords with the facts. See also section 8.8C (**indirect proof and** *reductio ad absurdum*).

(ii) 'Assumption' can also mean *presupposition*: a (probably unstated, even perhaps unrecognized) basis of an assertion.

People sometimes talk as if it were irrational or improper to assume anything: sometimes one hears 'Mr X's view is based on assumptions' said in a tone which suggests that the speaker thinks he has wholly or partly discredited Mr X's view simply by saying that.

That is muddled. There is *no* proposition which assumes the truth of no other proposition. Even the unexciting little proposition that $2 + 2 = 4$ makes some assumptions about the meanings of arithmetical symbols and about Heaven knows what horrendous propositions concerning the foundations of mathematics. If the only rational thinkers are those who make no assumptions, then the only rational thinkers are beings which never think at all. Which is absurd. If you think that someone has made an *unwarranted* assumption or a *controversial* assumption, then say so. But also say why you think so. Do not mistake 'There are assumptions here' for an argument against either the assumptions or the thesis which rests on them. It is all a little like the business of a quotation being 'out of context'. See section 1.6C.

(iii) *per absurdum; per impossibile*. These Latin phrases are sometimes used to signal certain kinds of assumption-for-the-sake-of-argument.

(a) The nearest one can get to an intelligible literal translation of '*per absurdum*' is 'by means of something absurd', which is not very illuminating. The phrase is used in this way:

'If proposition p, *per absurdum*, were true, proposition q would be true' means 'Proposition p is absurd and so cannot be true, but if it could be true and were true, proposition q would also be true.'

(b) '*per impossibile*' is used in this fashion:

'If situation X, *per impossibile*, occurred, then situation Y could also occur', means 'Situation X is impossible, but, if it were not and if it occurred, then situation Y could also occur.'

See also sections 3.3(ii) (**absurd**), 8.8C (*reductio ad absurdum*).

(iv) '**Data**' is a borrowing from Latin. Its literal meaning is 'given things', and so it is *plural*. In Latin, the singular form is 'datum'. This is sometimes met with in English, though, as Fowler says (1968, p. 119), 'one of the data' is more common. To treat something as a datum is to treat it as a fact, as something indisputably there from which inferences may be drawn and/or which needs to be accounted for. Sometimes 'given' (or, more pretentiously, the French word '*donnée*') is used as a synonym for '**datum**'. Merely treating something as a **datum** does not *make* it a **datum**. See also section 3.15 (**fact**). Pronounce as 'dayta', 'daytum'. Please do not say 'This is a data' or 'The data is ...' For **sense-datum**, see section 5.22F. (The *given* is that which can be *taken for granted*.)

D. Theory, theoretical

(i) In colloquial talk, 'X's theory' usually means 'X's **hypothesis**' (see A above) – a proposition put forward by X, but not established. Hence, the distinction between **theory and fact**. To talk of 'mere theory' (in this sense) is reasonable if the point is that the proposition has not been established, but people often move (quite absurdly) from that to the proposition that there is something *wrong* with propounding hypotheses. See O'Neil, 1969.

(ii) In most philosophical talk, 'X's theory' means approximately the same as 'X's *thesis*': an opinion which X puts forward, which he elaborates, which he is prepared to argue for. Often, any sort of thesis or opinion is dignified with the title 'theory', so that 'X's theory' becomes approximately synonymous with 'X's view', but that smudges a useful distinction. It is better to reserve the word 'theory' for *systematic, comprehensive* attempts to solve problems. (See D. E. Cooper, 1973, pp. 42, 45.)

Notice that to call something 'a theory' in this sense is not to say anything derogatory about it: it is not to say that it is false, or inadequately supported, or 'based on assumptions' (whatever that means – see C above). See also section 7.2D (**ideology**).

(iii) Another philosophical use of the word 'theory' is in such phrases as 'theory of knowledge', 'decision theory', etc. – labels for different branches of philosophy, rather than for specific theses or specific systematic, comprehensive accounts.

(iv) For **scientific theory**, see section 5.12D.

E. Theory and practice

(i) A quite ancient classification divides human skills and endeavours into **theoretical** and **practical**, the theoretical being concerned primarily with *the discovery of truth*, the practical being concerned primarily with *making and doing* (see Maritain, 1930, Pt Two, Ch. I). Notice that there is no suggestion in such a classification *that the theoretical is inferior to the practical*. Indeed, such a view would amount to saying that truth does not matter. Often, however, people *do* use the word 'theoretical' as a term of rebuke and 'practical' as a term of praise. What does this amount to?

Sometimes, the complaint is a justified one against people who burble on in grand dogmatic style without bothering to take a good hard look at the relevant facts. The complaint may be justified, but this is an unfortunate use of the term 'theory' (see D(i) above). There is always a great deal of ill-informed, confident waffle to protest against, but the 'Practical, good. Theoretical, bad' way of talk is, all too often, mere self-satisfied praise of prejudiced ignorance. Careful, critical study of a subject is not a disqualification from holding an opinion on it, but that bizarre view is often what lies behind the sneering use of the word 'theorist'. Cf. section 8.7 on '**academic**'.

(ii) But preferring 'the practical' to 'the merely theoretical' is not always the expression of self-satisfied block-headedness. Sometimes, the point that lies behind such talk is that there are some matters that can only be adequately understood after one has had experience of doing them or of observing them very closely. And this is a very reasonable point. (It is just as true of such etherial pursuits as philosophy as it is of growing cabbages or building houses.)

– A very reasonable point, but a very obscurely expressed one, because it is *not* the case that (e.g.) the newly graduated doctor or engineer is 'very strong on theory but weak on practice'. Since *understanding* his subject involves being able *to do it* and to deal with the unexpected complications of actual situations, his understanding of **the theory** is still weak, no matter how many High Distinctions or Alphas he got in his exams. Give him time. And, even before he begins his professional career, he knows a lot more about his subject than the complacently ignorant oaf dealt with in E(i) above. The point may be made in terms of **necessary conditions** (see section 4.16):

Practical experience may be a necessary condition for expertise, but that does *not* imply that 'theory' (i.e., academic study) is not *also* a necessary condition for expertise.

(iii) Journalists sometimes use 'theory' to mean 'hope', 'expectation', 'intention'. Do not imitate them.

5.6   VACUITY

Literally: 'emptiness'. This word has two quite distinct uses in philosophical talk:

(i) A hypothesis is **rendered vacuous** by re-interpreting it so that no evidence can count against it. Flew quotes a Black Power Leader, Stokely Carmichael, as asserting that the world is divided between exploiting whites and exploited non-whites. When someone objected: 'What about Castro and Guevara?', Mr Carmichael replied: 'I don't consider them white.' An assertion about people of a certain skin colour is protected against **falsification** (see section 5.1) by re-interpreting the term 'white man' so that the *only* 'real' white men are white men who behave as the original assertion maintained that *every* white man behaved. That way of protecting a hypothesis from falsification, Flew says, inflicts on it **The Death of a Thousand Qualifications**. One might also say that a hypothesis can be Too True to be Good. See also sec. 5.7 (**prediction**). See Flew, 1975, Ch. III.

(ii) The other use of 'vacuity', 'vacuous' is connected with the notion of **empty terms**, for which see sections 6.29A(ix), 6.31.

5.7   PREDICTION

(i) To predict is, etymologically, to 'say before', i.e., to assert that something will happen. 'Thomas Beverley . . . predicted the end of the world for 1697. He was still alive in 1698, and wrote a book to prove that the world *had* come to an end without anybody noticing it' (Hill, 1958, p. 329). That is a rather noteworthy case of making a prediction suffer The Death of a Thousand Qualifications (see section 5.6). A genuine prediction needs to be something which could, in principle, fail to come true (i.e., be **falsified** – see section 5.1). It needs to be incompatible with some describable state of affairs. 'Tomorrow, there will either be rain or there will not' is grammatically in the future tense, but it fails to be a genuine prediction. Similarly, if predictions can be 'made true' by retroactive gerrymandering in the style of Mr Beverley, there is no point in making them or in listening to them. As Popper remarks, 'It is a typical soothsayer's trick to predict things so vaguely that the predictions can hardly fail: that they become irrefutable' (1972(a), p. 37).

(ii) It is probably worthwhile to distinguish **predictions** from **warnings**. A weather *forecast* is, obviously enough, a prediction or a set of predictions, yet it might contain the phrase 'possible late thunderstorms'. The non-occurrence of a late thunderstorm will not falsify that proposition, yet it does not seem to be **vacuous**, like 'There will either be a late thunderstorm or there will not.' The difference, I think, is that, though 'possible late thunderstorm' is not falsifiable by future evidence, it is

criticizable in the light of present evidence and it does provide guidance. If the meteorologists simply say it to be on the safe side, they are playing the fool. If, however, they have data which, while not making an unqualified prediction rational, do indicate that it would be rational to take precautions, then what they say is reasonable *as a warning*. The possibility needs to be more than a 'merely logical' possibility (see section 3.12A). See also section 5.8 (**self-frustrating and self-fulfilling predictions**); Ryle, 1971(b), pp. 373–380.

5.8   SELF-FULFILLING; SELF-FRUSTRATING; SELF-STULTIFYING

Self-contradiction and other forms of self-refutation are discussed in sections 3.1–3.2.

'Self-fulfilling' and 'self-frustrating' are applied to predictions and to some utterances of a non-propositional type (see sections 1.2, 1.5). A **self-fulfilling** prediction (or prophecy) is one the utterance of which (given the circumstances) is sufficient for or is largely instrumental in bringing about the event predicted. A tutor says to a student: 'You will fail.' This prediction upsets the student so much that he gives up trying and fails. The prediction has fulfilled itself. The same tutor (obviously not a very nice man) tells a second student that he will fail. This student is tougher than the first one. He says to himself: 'Oh, will I? Well I'll just show the old swine.' He works very hard and passes quite creditably. The prediction has **frustrated** (or **stultified**) itself. (See Cranston, 1953, pp. 160–172.)

A self-frustrating (or self-stultifying) *request* or piece of *advice* is one the utterance of which produces a result contrary to the intention (or to the ostensible intention) of the utterer.

> 'Whatever you do, don't throw me into the briar patch,' Br'er Rabbit says pleadingly to his enemy, Br'er Fox. Br'er Fox, of course, throws him into the briar patch.

> 'Don't be so self-conscious,' bland, secure Primus says to self-conscious, awkward Secundus. The result is that Secundus becomes much more self-conscious and awkward.

I said 'contrary to the intention (or to the ostensible intention)', i.e., to the intention expressed in the words uttered, because it is possible for people to make requests or give advice with the intention of producing a contrary result. Br'er Rabbit, as we all know, was a perfect Machiavellian and the briar patch was just where he wanted to be. And, although there is no shortage of stupid, well-meaning people, we nevertheless do well to suspect the motives of those who advise self-conscious or nervous people not to be self-conscious or nervous.

Some have wondered whether the publication of opinion polls about voting intentions has an effect on voting intentions, especially in countries without compulsory voting. ('Since my side's going to win anyway, I might as well go fishing instead of voting.' 'The poll says my side's going to lose, so I'd better vote.') Michael Frayn points out that the study of nuclear particles would become immeasurably more complicated if the particles were able to read books on particle theory and modify their behaviour as a result (Frayn, 1974, section 65).

There can also be self-frustrating policies and attitudes. Dr Grimstone, the headmaster in *Vice Versa*, declares to his pupils: 'I'll establish a spirit of trustful happiness and unmurmuring content in this school, if I have to flog every boy in it for as long as I can stand over him!' (T. A. Guthrie, 1917, p. 54). 'Self-frustrating' and 'self-stultifying' are roughly synonymous with the much more voguish 'counterproductive'.

5.9   *WELTANSCHAUUNG*, WORLDVIEW

Both expressions are used, the English one being a translation of the German (though 'world-outlook' might be a shade more accurate). A *Weltanschauung* is a general view of the universe and of human life and destiny, i.e., the sort of thing which is popularly called 'a philosophy', even though what philosophers (especially Anglophone philosophers) do is sometimes remote from such 'Meaning-of-life stuff' as a former colleague of mine used to call it. See also section 7.2D (**ideology**).

5.10   BLIK

(i) A term introduced by R. M. Hare (1955) and presumably (though not very appropriately) derived from the German '*Blick*' which means 'glance'. A blik may well be a *Weltanschauung* as defined above. The important features of a blik are that (1) it is unfalsifiable in that it is not possible to specify a single possibility which would refute it; (2) it is not vacuous or tautological; (3) it is a belief which structures many other beliefs of its holder.

A belief that the universe is orderly and, in principle, intelligible is a blik, and so is the belief that the universe is absurd or a mere chance bundle of events. The causal principle, i.e., the proposition that every event has a cause, is a blik. It seems to be neither vacuous nor tautological, but it is not falsifiable either. (What would an uncaused event be like? How would you distinguish it from an event with an undiscovered cause?) Indeed, the causal principle bears some embarrassing resemblances to the belief (found by anthropologists in many parts of the world) that, for every human death, there is a human killer. You and I (I suppose) accept the former and reject the latter, but just as a denier of the causal principle would be unable to make much headway in argument with us, we would find similar difficulty in arguing against the belief that, for every death, there is a human killer.

It is in terms of blik that we decide what kind of thing is evidence for what kind of proposition. Our blik determines what count as basic facts: hence, the argumentative futility of saying 'Science works. Sorcery doesn't' to someone who regards sorcery as one of the hard facts of reality.

(ii) To hold a blik is to hold a belief which is unfalsifiable because it is not possible to specify precisely what observation or experience would refute it. (Belief and disbelief in Divine Providence are, in this respect, on precisely the same footing.) It is, nevertheless, possible to adopt or abandon a blik rationally. The relevant question is: 'How well does this blik accommodate experience?' There is no algorithm (see section 5.18) for answering that question, but if it cannot be answered rationally, no question can be answered rationally.

Specifically on blik: see Flew, 1955(a); Hare, 1955; B. Mitchell, 1955; Flew, 1955(b); Crombie, 1955; Butterfield, 1977; Sparkes, 1979; Mohanty, 1988.

On rationality: see Winch, 1958; B. R. Wilson, 1970; Trigg, 1973.

5.11 PARADIGM, PARADIGMATIC

The original meaning of the word 'paradigm' seems to be 'pattern' or (roughly) 'example'. I insert the qualification '(roughly)', as not every example of something can be said to be paradigmatic.

If X is a paradigmatic example of Y, then EITHER X is an *exemplary, ideal (or near ideal)* example of Y, OR X is a *typical* example of Y. When F. P. Ramsey (1931, p. 263n.) called Russell's Theory of Descriptions 'that paradigm of philosophy', he was using the word in its first sense (cf. section 5.16, **ideal type**; see M. Tanner, 1964, pp. 64–65). When a language-teacher says that 'The house is big' is a paradigm of a simple English subject-predicate sentence, the word is being used in its second sense. 'Paradigm' has acquired two senses in philosophy and related disciplines:

(i) One sense is derived from Kuhn (1970), who sees the normal condition of a science as one in which scientists accept certain assumptions about what the scope of that science is, about what sort of thing is a problem for that science, about what sort of thing is to count as evidence, about the methods to be used in dealing with problems, about the sort of thing which is to count as a solution to those problems. Kuhn calls this framework of assumptions a **paradigm**. More generally, a Kuhnian paradigm is the basic set of assumptions in the light of which a person or group attempts to understand events and the world. (It is this sort of thing which anthropologists and sociologists have in mind when they speak of *epistemological frameworks*. See also sections 3.4A (**categories**), 7.24 (**epistemology**).) The connexion between the Kuhnian sense of 'paradigm' and what I have called the original sense is that Kuhn sees the basic assumptions of a science as being taught by drawing attention to standard examples of 'good research' which the beginner is urged to emulate.

Kuhn's theory of science is more complex and more controversial than I have indicated. For discussions of it and its relation to other theories, see Vesey, 1974(a), Ch. IX, and Chalmers, 1982, Chs VIII and IX. These are introductory treatments. For more advanced discussions, see Ryan, 1972; Lakatos and Musgrave, 1970.

(ii) In the second philosophical use, 'paradigm' simply means 'standard case'. It is closely related to a type of argument used by some of the people known as 'linguistic philosophers' (see section 7.12F). A **paradigm case argument** has this general structure:

  1. The description '*d*' has a **standard correct use** in our language.
  2. This correct use can be exemplified by saying 'X, Y, and Z are ds.'
  3. X, Y, and Z do exist and are, therefore, paradigm ds.
  4. Therefore, any theory which denies the existence of ds must be rejected either as false or as nonsensical, since it involves either mistake about the facts or a misuse of the expression *d*.

Thus (in a classical example – see Stebbing, 1937, pp. 48–54) if someone denies the existence of solid objects, we can draw his attention to tables on which one can pound one's fist, walls which one cannot walk through, etc., and then say: 'If you deny that these things are solid, what can you possibly mean by "solid"?' (See also papers by Mates and Cavell in Chappell, 1964.)

Paradigm cases can, at the least, present an argument which needs to be answered, but they are not as powerful as many linguistic philosophers have assumed. Everything depends on the truth of step 2 in the outline given above. *Are* X, Y, and Z *genuine* ds? A loyal Nepali may well point to his King as an example of an incarnation of the god, Vishnu, but that is unlikely to persuade the average westerner that Hindu gods exist. See Lacey, 1976, pp. 152–153; Quinton, 1977(e); D. E. Cooper, 1973, pp. 61–65.

5.12 LAWS

A. Prescriptive/descriptive

(i) 'Law' is a very ambiguous word. One important distinction is that between **prescriptive** (or **normative**) law and **descriptive** (or **scientific**) law. **Prescriptive** law sets out what is to be done and what is not. Some examples are the Ten Commandments, the Australian Constitution, Acts of Parliament, the University of Newcastle's regulations governing the BA degree. When people think of prescriptive law in general, they tend to think of **penal law** (imperatives addressed to everyone in the relevant jurisdiction, prescribing or, more usually, proscribing behaviour of a specified kind, and threatening punishment for non-compliance), but that is only part of a legal system. Other kinds of law set out the ways in which certain significant acts are to be done, and the only 'penalty' for non-compliance is failure to do what one set out to do (e.g., make a will, transfer title of ownership, cast a valid vote, etc.). See Dworkin, 1977, pp. 1–9; Golding, 1975, Chs I–II; Hart, 1961; Watson, 1977.

(ii) Prescriptive laws can be (and often are) broken or otherwise not complied with. They do not, because of that, cease to be laws. 'Breaches' of an *alleged de*scriptive law refute it and show it *not to be a descriptive law*. Very roughly, a descriptive law has the form: 'If an A-event occurs, it will be followed by a B-event.' If we observe a case of an A-event not followed by a B-event, then we do not say 'Lo, a breach of a descriptive law.' We say 'There's a falsifying instance [see section 5.2A(iii)] to that alleged law. It's not a law at all.'

(iii) A genuine descriptive law might well describe not what actually *is* the case but what *would* be the case if something else which *is not* the case *were* the case.

(iv) There are, however, certain law-like propositions, which, though not precisely true, have had a long history in science and which are still 'useful'. Some of these are still referred to as 'X's law' (e.g. Boyle's Law in physics, Bode's Law in astronomy). Perhaps we can call them *honorary laws*. What has happened here is that a phrase originally intended as a *description* has become a *proper noun* (see section 2.9) which names, even though it no longer describes accurately. There are other cases of the same linguistic phenomenon, e.g. the Demilitarized Zone in Vietnam which was still called that, even when it had become one of the most militarized pieces of land on earth. See N. Smart, 1969, pp. 33–37; Benn and Peters, 1959, pp. 15–18.

B. Natural law; law of nature

(i) Two synonymous and equally ambiguous expressions. Sometimes, they are used in the same sense as 'descriptive law', 'scientific law', or 'law of science'.

(ii) In *philosophy of law*, the phrase 'natural law theory' is often used to refer to any theory which (in some way or other) maintains that there is an important connection between law and morals. Sometimes, 'natural law theory' seems to be used as the logical opposite (see section 10.1B) of '*legal positivism*' but as 'legal positivism' itself is a somewhat vague term, that scarcely clarifies matters. All legal positivists would agree that 'The existence of law is one thing, its merit or demerit is another' (John Austin (1790–1859), 1954, p. 184). All 'natural lawyers' would say that it is possible for an alleged law to be so 'demeritorious' that it is not a genuine law. Both those propositions allow for a wide range of positions, and it is not always easy to distinguish temperate legal positivists from temperate 'natural lawyers'. See Golding, 1975, Ch. II; Hart, 1958, 1961; Fuller, 1971, pp. 157–167, and 1969; d'Entrèves, 1952.

(iii) **Natural law as a theory of ethics**

'A natural law theory of ethics' may mean many things. It may mean any kind of 'objectivist'[1] theory – i.e., any theory which maintains that questions of right and wrong are not *merely* a matter for human decision. To use the phrase 'natural law theory of ethics' so loosely is unacceptable. The expression 'natural law theory of ethics' should be confined to theories based on the notion of natural good purposes in things which it is the duty of human beings to respect. Today, the most vigorous kind of natural law thinking is that influenced by the work of St Thomas Aquinas (1225–1274).

Maritain, 1954, pp. 76–85[2], and Pieper, 1957(a) are readable modern presentations of the theory. Pieper, 1957(b), pp. 51–75, gives a lucid statement of the metaphysical and religious background of the theory. Evans, 1965, is a collection of critical looks from *inside* the tradition. D. J. O'Connor, 1967 is a critical look from *outside*. See also W. D. Hudson, 1983, pp. 333–370. (Notice that Natural Law theory of the Thomist type is not *primarily* a philosophy of **law**. *Primarily* it is a philosophy of *morals* which *contains* a philosophy of law.) See section 9.4A (**fact and value**).

C.   Scientific laws; laws of science

I am here using the expressions 'scientific laws' and 'laws of science' as synonymous with each other and with 'descriptive laws'. There is some controversy about the concept of a scientific law, but there would be widespread (though not universal) agreement that a scientific law has these characteristics:

A scientific law
  (i) is a statement, not a command; a description not a prescription (see A above).
 (ii) is a universal statement, not a particular statement (see section 6.30).
(iii) is an open universal statement, not a closed universal statement (see section 6.30).
 (iv) is an open universal statement, not naming any specified individual person, time, place, or object.
  (v) is lacking in existential import (see section 6.31). (Thus we can have laws about non-existent things such as frictionless bodies. The non-existence of such things is not a refutation. Only an actually existing counterinstance would be a refutation.)

 (vi) is true ('false scientific law' is a self-contradictory phrase).
(vii) is something which can be denied without self-contradiction, i.e., is synthetic (see section 3.6).
(viii) is falsifiable (see section 5.1).
 (ix) implies counterfactuals (see section 4.15).
  (x) if a non-ultimate law, is deducible from a law or laws of wider scope.
 (xi) if an ultimate law, is recognizable as ultimate by the number and variety of laws deducible from it (for **deducible**, see section 5.13A).

All that may sound a little complicated. Indeed, it is over-simplified and some of it is very problematical. See Walters, 1967(b); Hempel, 1966, Ch. V; Quine and Ullian, 1978, Chs VII–VIII; D. M. Armstrong, 1979, 1983.

D.   Scientific laws and scientific theories

A distinction is often drawn between scientific **laws** and scientific **theories**. Putting it very roughly, a law makes reference only to *observable* entities, whereas a theory is a statement of wider scope which implies two or more laws and which makes reference to *unobservable entities* (e.g., *electrons, space-curvature, electro-magnetic waves, etc.*).

The distinction is more complicated than that. There is also some controversy about whether it is a genuine distinction or not and, if it is genuine, how hard and fast it is. This use of 'scientific theory' can be confusing as the same phrase is often used to mean the same as 'scientific hypothesis'. See section 5.5. As sub-section A above indicates, 'scientific law' is not always used as this distinction would require (and some would say that there is little reason why it should be). See Hesse, 1967; Hempel, 1966, Ch. VI; Chalmers, 1982, Chs VII–VIII.

E.   Laws and law-like statements

If someone says that statement S is a law (in the sense of **descriptive law** – see A above), he is *endorsing* statement S. That is to say:

'Statement S is a scientific law' implies that statement S is true.

If, on the other hand, he wants to say that statement S has all the **intrinsic** characteristics (see section 1.19(vi)) of a scientific law, but he does not want to commit himself to the truth of S, what he should say is: 'Statement S is a law-like statement.' If the analysis of C above is acceptable, to say that S is law-like commits you to saying that S has characteristics (i)–(v) and (vii)–(xi). It does not commit you either to asserting or denying that S has characteristic (vi).

5.13   DEDUCTION AND INDUCTION

A.   Deduction, deductive, deduce, deducible, deductivism

(i) In detective stories, 'deduction' usually seems to mean: *observing things which few other people observe and drawing important and surprising conclusions from those observations*. Sherlock Holmes is forever talking about his 'deductive powers' in this sense.

(ii) In philosophy these words are used differently. If a philosopher claims to have deduced conclusion r from premisses p and q,

> he is saying that he has *inferred* r from p and q;

> he is claiming that p and q *imply* r (i.e., he is claiming that, if someone affirmed both p and q, but denied r, that person would be asserting a self-contradiction).

In other words, r is deducible from p and q together IFF (p&q) implies r. (For **imply** and **infer** see sections 4.2–4.4. For '&', see section 6.10. Cf. section 8.12(v) (**derivable, demonstrable**).)

(iii) In English, there are *two* words 'deduction' with two quite different meanings. See section 2.6.

(iv) **Deductive reasoning**. In deductive reasoning, the conclusion is presented as being *implied by* the premisses (i.e., on the ground that to hold the premisses and to deny the conclusion would be *self-contradictory* – see section 3.2). In non-deductive reasoning, the premisses are presented as supporting, but not implying the conclusion.

(v) **Deductivism** is the opinion that an argument can be satisfactory *only if* its premisses *imply* its conclusion. See (ii) above. Deductivism is one source of *the problem of induction* (B(iii) below) and has given rise to worries about evaluative reasoning (section 9.4A). See Stove, 1982, Ch. IV.

B.   Induction, inductivism, 'The' Problem of Induction

(i) 'Induction' is a word with a vast variety of meanings, as a glance at the *OED* will reveal. Unfortunately, even as a philosophical term, it is by no means as clear and unambiguous as one would like.

    (a) In one sense, 'inductive reasoning' is used to mean *reasoning which does not profess to be deductive* (in the philosophical sense – see A(ii) above).

    (b) In another sense, 'inductive reasoning' means reasoning from premisses about *some* things of a certain kind to conclusions about *all* the things of that kind.

Those are only two of the senses the word has, but they are the two most common in philosophical talk.

(ii) **Induction and inductivism (inductionism)**

Students are sometimes rather startled when they come across philosophers (most notably Sir Karl Popper) who appear to deny the existence of induction. What these philosophers are doing is denying the **inductivist view** of science. One can deny the inductivist view of science without affirming that induction has no place in science, but that distinction is often not drawn. See below. See also Lacey, 1976, pp. 94–97; Hempel, 1966, Ch. II; Quine and Ullian, 1978, Ch. VII.

One very influential view of the nature of scientific inference is that put forward by Francis Bacon (1561–1626) and John Stuart Mill (1806–1873), a view often labelled **inductivism** or **inductionism**. This view says that the scientist arrives at laws and theories by moving from premises which are reports of individual observations and experiments to universal conclusions (i.e., laws and theories). Although many philosophers and scientists have agreed with this view of science, it has been denied by others, notably William Whewell (1794–1866) and Sir Karl Popper (1902–). See (iv) below.

(iii) **'The' Problem of Induction** is 'the' problem of justifying one or more of the following:

induction in the first sense distinguished in (i) above;

induction in the second sense distinguished in (i) above;

scientific method as described by the inductivists (see (ii) above).

Those are, in fact, three problems, but they have an important common feature: all these types of induction seem to involve drawing a conclusion which is wider in scope than its premises (i.e., the reasoning seems to be invalid – see section 4.9). The question then arises: 'How can it be rational to reason in this way? And, if it is not rational, what becomes of science and of most of our ordinary beliefs about the world?' See Harré, 1960, Ch. V; Ayer, 1956, pp. 71–75; Goddard, 1977, Ch. II; Chalmers, 1982, Chs I, II; Stove, 1978. Swinburne, 1974, is a good collection of essays with a helpful introduction.

(iv) **Hypothetico-deductive method**

Sir Karl Popper and others have denied the inductivist view of science. Popper contends that scientific reasoning typically works by setting up a conjecture or hypothesis (see section 5.5), deducing conclusions from it, and testing whether those conclusions are true. If the conclusions are false, the hypothesis is false (*modus tollens* – see section 6.16). That procedure of hypothesis, deduction, and empirical test is what Popper calls **the hypothetico-deductive method** or the method of **conjecture and refutation**. Popper maintains that though a hypothesis can be shown to be false by this method, there is no way of showing it to be true or even of showing that it is probably true.

If true, this solves (or, perhaps, *dissolves*) at least one version of the problem of induction. If the Problem of Induction is 'How can we prove a scientific theory?' Popper's answer is that there is no problem. We *cannot* prove a scientific theory and we should not try to. We can, however, subject a scientific theory to severe tests. (See Popper, 1983, pp. 101–180; Lacey, 1976, pp. 37–41.)

Even with that accepted, some awkward questions arise, e.g.:

Is this the whole story or only part of it? Does induction play no part at all in scientific investigation?

Can the findings of science be called **knowledge** (see section 8.14B)? When, if ever, are we entitled to say that they are true?

Popper's views have come under heavy attack in recent years. See, e.g., Hooker, 1987, Ch. III; Stove, 1978, 1982; Chalmers, 1982.

5.14   EXPLANATION; EXPLICATION; PRECISIFICATION; UNPACKING

(i) We talk of explaining *an event*. We also talk of explaining a *poem* or a *philosophical theory*. To explain an event is *to say why it happened*. To explain a poem or a philosophical theory is *to say what it means, to make it intelligible*.

Since these two kinds of 'explanation' are so different (and since the former kind is both heterogeneous enough and controversial enough on its own), I suggest that – at least when we are talking philosophically – we should talk about **explicating** a poem or a philosophical theory, rather than *explaining* it.

(ii) 'Why did that window break?' asked by a policeman in the course of his duties requires one kind of answer. Asked by a physicist in the course of his duties, it requires an answer of a quite different kind. That is a sample of the heterogeneity of the notion of *explaining an event*. There is controversy over whether historical explanation is of the same type as explanation in physics and over whether **teleological explanation** (see (iii) below) is a satisfactory form of explanation.

Further reading: Sloman, 1977(b); Lacey, 1976, pp. 64–66; Kim, 1967; Weingartner, 1967; Shapere, 1967; Donnellan, 1967; Edwards, 1967; D. M. Taylor, 1970; Ryan, 1973; Quine and Ullian, 1978, Ch. IX.

(iii) A *teleological explanation* of some phenomenon is an explanation of it in terms of *function, purpose* or *intention* (see section 7.18A). For more discussion of explanations of this kind (or: of these *kinds*) and their relation to explanations of other kinds, see Swinburne, 1970, pp. 53–57; White, 1968; C. Taylor, 1964; Sprigge, 1971; Montefiore, 1971.

(iv) 'Explication' is sometimes used for the *activity of making a hitherto imprecise notion more precise*. (See Lacey, 1976, p. 66.) For this, the word **'precisification'** is preferable. When one is not trying to render a notion more precise but merely trying to bring out its full force, the metaphor of '**unpacking**' is useful. See section 9.13B (**implicit, explicit**).

5.15   OCKHAM'S (OR OCCAM'S) RAZOR

A principle (or, perhaps, family of principles) of investigation associated with the mediaeval English philosopher and theologian, William of Ockham (*circa* 1285–1349). The general point is that one should not make an assertion without good reason and that one should not assume the existence of something unnecessarily. Here are three formulations of Ockham's Razor. (The first, which is the best known, does not seem to have been used by Ockham himself):

1. Entia non sunt multiplicanda praeter necessitatem.

1. Entities must not be multiplied without necessity.

2. Pluritas non est ponenda praeter necessitatem.

2. Plurality is not to be posited[3] without necessity.

3. Frustra fit per plura quod potest fieri per pauciora.

3. It is a waste of time to explain something by more assumptions if it can be explained by fewer.

Here are some more recent formulations:

4. Do not postulate the existence of anything unless you have to.
5. Choose the simplest hypothesis compatible with the facts.
6. 'Desire to dream of no more things in heaven and earth than need be' (Quine, 1970, p. 3).

Ockham's Razor is also known as the 'principle of economy' or the 'principle of parsimony'.

In my undergraduate days, I once quoted formulation 1 to a very eminent British philosopher. Without the least hesitation, he replied: 'Well *I* say: "The more the merrier."' That is going a little far, but it is also possible to wield Ockham's Razor in too Sweeney-Toddish a fashion. 'Entia non sunt multiplicanda praeter necessitatem' is a good maxim, but so also is 'Entia non sunt subtrahenda praeter necessitatem' ('Entities are not to be subtracted without necessity').

Further reading: Quine and Ullian, 1978, Chs V–VIII; Boehner, 1957, pp. xvi–xxiii; Moody, 1967; Dunbar, 1980; Holsinger, 1981; Dunbar, 1981.

5.16   IDEAL TYPES

The term 'ideal types' was introduced by the German sociologist, Max Weber (1864–1920). An ideal type (sometimes called 'pure type') is a **theoretical construct**, i.e., a concept which is not exactly instantiated in the world but may be useful in the endeavour to understand the world. There are no perfectly straight lines to be met with in the world; nevertheless, a geometry employing the concept is useful in coping with the world. There is no one whose motivations are purely economic, but the concept of 'economic man' can be of use in the endeavour to understand the behaviour of actual people.

The word 'ideal' here is not a term of praise or commendation: the complete sadist is as much an ideal type as the complete philanthropist. 'Ideal' here means *thought up, constructed in thought*, and contrasts with 'real' in its sense of 'instantiated in the world'. See Knopfelmacher, 1968, pp. 149–152; Andreski, 1970; Watkins, 1973. See also section 5.11 (**paradigm**).

(As someone has said, 'Economic man may be a useful theoretical construct, but you wouldn't want your sister to marry one.' For critiques of *economic man*, see Bensusan-Butt, 1978; Nurick, 1989.)

5.17 METHOD, METHODOLOGY, METHODICAL, METHODOLOGICAL

'Methodology' means **the study of** method. There are people who seem to think that it is a learned way of saying 'method' which is simply silly. See Fowler, 1968, pp. 342–343 (long variants) and 344–346 (love of the long word). But 'methodical', in contemporary English, usually means *orderly, systematic, according to plan*, etc. So 'methodical' is not the right word for *of, like, or pertaining to method*. 'Methodological' is better suited to that job. For the same reason 'methodological' should be used if one means *as part of a method*. Descartes used 'feigned' or 'hyperbolical' doubt as a method of investigation. Such doubt was not ordinary doubt, but **methodological doubt**. See also sections 7.13B (**Cartesian doubt**), 5.18 (**heuristic**).

5.18 HEURISTIC, ALGORITHM

(i) Something is **heuristic** to the extent that it stimulates or directs investigation. An **algorithm** is a procedure consisting of a finite set of steps which, if correctly applied, will inevitably solve a problem or obtain a correct result. Anyone correctly applying the same algorithm to the same task will obtain the same result. By contrast, a heuristic procedure is an investigative procedure which guarantees neither success nor unanimity, but may well be informative and illuminating.

That may sound as if algorithms are superior to heuristic procedures. The truth is that algorithms are applicable in mathematics but in very little else. See Flew, 1984, pp. 10, 147; R. E. Young, Becker, and Pike, 1970, pp. 119–163; Jouvenel, 1963, pp. 204–212.

(ii) A **heuristic pretence** is a false assumption treated as if true for the limited purpose of guiding an investigation. More particularly, it can be a false assumption which the investigator knowingly makes *about himself* for the limited purpose of guiding an investigation. Thus, Descartes's **feigned doubt** (see sections 5.17, 7.13B) was a heuristic pretence. A customs officer who asks himself 'If I were a smuggler, what would I be likely to do if ...' is doing the same sort of thing, as is a literary scholar who says 'If I had been used, all my life, to seeing *The Two Noble Kinsmen* included in volumes of Shakespeare's complete works, would I have any reason for doubting its authenticity?'

(iii) An utterance may be uninformative as a **statement** (see section 1.2), but highly significant **heuristically**. A good example is the 'idiosyncrasy platitude' of Joseph Butler (1692–1752): 'Everything is what it is, and not another thing' (1949, p. 23). That may sound as empty as Antony's 'description' of the crocodile:

> It is shaped ... like itself, and it is as broad as it hath breadth; it is just so high as it is, and moves with it own organs. It lives by that which nourisheth it ... [is] of it own colour ... and the tears of it are wet.
>
> *(Antony and Cleopatra*, Act II sc. 7)

W. K. Frankena, for instance, complains that Butler's remark 'is a tautology [see section 3.7] and should be expanded as follows: "Everything is what it is and not another thing, unless it is another thing, and even then it is what it is"' (1952, p. 110). But that is to miss Butler's point. He is protesting against the 'nothing but' habit of mind, an over-readiness to ignore differences and to insist that everything is 'really' the same. He is not trying to give us information; he is telling us to attend to differences and peculiarities and not merely to similarities. As a statement, his remark says almost nothing. As a heuristic imperative (see section 1.5), it is full of life. See Wisdom, 1953, pp. 248–282; Frayn, 1974, sections 65–66, 119, 141–144. See also section 5.20 (**reductionism**).

5.19 PROCRUSTES AND THE PLATYPUS

A. Procrustes, Procrustean bed

(i) According to Greek mythology, Procrustes was a robber who terrorized ancient Attica. He had a particularly disagreeable way of making sure that his guests fitted the bed in the guest-room: he either stretched them on a rack or abridged them with an axe. Sir Arthur Eddington alleged that, in addition, he carefully measured them the next morning 'and wrote a learned paper "On the Uniformity of Stature of Travellers" for the Anthropological Society of Attica' (1939, p. 109). See also Ardley, 1950, Chs I–IV.

(ii) Traditional logicians are given to Procrusteanism. Having committed themselves to the opinion that there are four and only four forms of proposition (viz.: 'All Ss are P', 'Some Ss are P', 'No Ss are P', 'Some Ss are not P' – see section 6.24), they are then faced with the fact that people say things which seem a little different; e.g., things of the forms

'Most Ss are P' and 'A few Ss are P'. They deal with this by saying that such utterances *really* say no more and no less than 'Some Ss are P', that the differences are 'merely verbal' or 'merely rhetorical'. This implies that the following propositions are equivalent:

> 'Some Irishmen are Protestants.'
> 'A few Irishmen are Protestants.'
> 'Most Irishmen are Protestants.'

Since the first of this trio is clearly true and the third is clearly false, being a full-blooded traditional logician requires an extraordinary talent for pulling the wool over one's own eyes.

B.   The slaughter-all-platypuses fallacy

A variety of Procrusteanism. Someone commits this fallacy when he denies or ignores the well-established or probable existence of Xs on the ground that Xs will not fit comfortably into his favourite system of classification.

5.20   REDUCTIVISM (REDUCTIONISM)

A reductivist project is one which sets out to show that things of the more complex and/or more puzzling kind, X, are, in reality, things (or complexes of things) of the (allegedly) simpler and less puzzling kind Y; i.e., it sets out to reduce Xs to Ys. Some examples are:

psychological egoism (the doctrine that all human motivation is selfish – see section 7.15D)

the Marxist doctrine of **ideology** (which alleges that art, religion, philosophy, etc., are merely expressions of class interests (see section 7.2D))

doctrines which would like to show that all truths are expressible in the language of (e.g.) physics

doctrines which maintain that physical objects are merely 'permanent possibilities of sensation' (J. S. Mill), or that 'selves' are merely 'bundles of perceptions' (Hume)

Russell's **logical atomism** which maintained that the ultimate realities are 'atomic' facts (i.e., facts which cannot be divided into further facts), composed of **sense data** (see sections 5.22F, 7.12C; see also Urmson, 1956)

It would, therefore, be a bad mistake to assume that reductivists are a party of people who agree on a body of doctrine. One can be reductivist about some things, non-reductivist about others. Reists (like Quinton) regard material objects as the basic entities, so they believe that 'social objects' are nothing but their individual human members, but they deny that human beings are nothing but complexes of impressions (see section 7.9B).

Reductivisms can be classified (roughly) as **unmasking** (i.e., **eliminativist**) or as **revisionary**. An unmasking reductivism alleges that things generally regarded as Xs are not Xs at all, that they are *nothing but* Ys, which are generally regarded as nonXs, and that therefore the belief that there are Xs is radically wrong. At the other extreme, a reductivism could maintain that the common-sense everyday view of Xs is wrong only in so far as it is not consistently conjoinable (see section 6.10(i)) with the explanation that Xs are compositions of Ys or special cases of Ys. Such a theory could maintain that ordinary X-talk need involve no falsity, but is incompletely revealing of relevant truths. Some theories labellable as **reist** or as **scientific realist** come close to being of this thoroughly revisionist kind (see sections 7.8(i), 7.9B).

Eliminative (i.e., *unmasking*) reductivisms are sometimes called **nothing-butteries** because of their supporters' addition to the phrase 'nothing but'.

5.21 DISJUNCTION AND DICHOTOMY

(i) I do not know (and would very much like to know) how the word 'disjunction'[4] acquired the sense which it has as a technical term in logic. Etymologically, it is related to *separating, dividing, severing, dismembering, disuniting*. But, as a technical term, its associations are with less drastic notions: *alternative possibilities, choice*. And, of course, possible choices are not always opposed to one another or mutually exclusive. Hence, we have the notions of *non-exclusive (or inclusive) disjunction* and *exclusive disjunction*. See section 6.11.

(ii) The word 'dichotomy', however, stays closer in meaning to its etymology: *a cutting in two* (and one can have *trichotomies, tetrachotomies*, etc. as well). In logic, **dichotomy** is a division of a class of things into two sub-classes of things, which do not overlap and which, together, include all members of the wider class. The following is a time-honoured example:

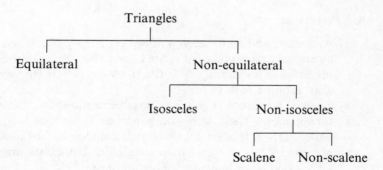

In other words, a dichotomy is a division of a class into two mutually exclusive and collectively exhaustive sub-classes (see section 1.28). A dichotomy can be expressed in a proposition which is an exclusive disjunction: 'A triangle is either equilateral or non-equilateral.' Cf. section 10.1B (**logical opposites**).

(iii) A **false dichotomy** is a division which, though treated as a dichotomy, either:

> fails to be mutually exclusive;

or

> fails to be collectively exhaustive;

or

> fails to be mutually exclusive and fails to be collectively exhaustive.

> See Routley and Routley, 1980, pp. 250–259. See also sections 7.15C and 9.4B.

(iv) 'Dichotomy' is frequently misused by those who like big words and do not worry much about their meaning (beautifully mocked by Peter De Vries, 1961, p. 189). I have heard the word used as if it were a synonym for 'conflict' or even 'problem' (perhaps a confusion with 'dilemma' – see section 6.22).

5.22　APPEARANCE AND REALITY

A.

For **reality**, see section 1.16.

B.　Perception

(i) Awareness and apprehension of objects, events, etc., especially *sensory* awareness and apprehension. See Lacey, 1976, pp. 154–156; Flew, 1984, pp. 264–265; Goddard, 1977, Ch. III; Vesey, 1971; Hamlyn, 1961. See also section 1.15B(iv).

(ii) There is a current vogue for using 'perception' as a fancy substitute for 'opinion'. There seems no good reason for following this vogue, particularly as it often goes along with muddle and/or trickery. 'In my perception, X is Y,' says Mr Noodle, giving himself the impression that he has said something *much* more authoritative than 'I think that X is Y.' 'If someone believes he is sick,' Professor Doodle declares, 'then, in his own perception, he really is sick,' not noticing that all he has said is 'If someone believes he is sick, he believes he is sick.'

C. The senses

Traditionally, there are *five* (ordinary) *senses*: sight, smell, taste, hearing, and touch. The expression 'sixth sense' has been used for less 'ordinary' forms of immediate awareness (ranging from 'second sight' to such better attested phenomena as subliminal perception and realizing-that-something's-been-changed-but-not-knowing-what). 'Touch', however, is ambiguous between (i) an action (typically with the hand) and the species of sensations thereby produced, and (ii) a much larger range of bodily sensations other than visual, olfactory, gustatory, or auditory (feeling hot or cold, pain, awareness of movement (kinaesthesia), etc., etc.). It is convenient to distinguish these from tactual sensations of type (i) and (for most purposes) to lump them together under '*somaesthesia*' (or '*somaesthesis*'), i.e., 'body-sensing'. This lumping-together is, however, a matter of convenience and sometimes further distinctions are required. D. M. Armstrong, 1962, is a detailed philosophical study of somaesthesia. (According to legend, the title of this book, *Bodily Sensations*, once led to the temporary seizure of a copy by an officer of Her Majesty's Customs.)

Philosophers have a bad habit of saying 'the senses', 'sense-perception', or 'perception' and thinking of vision only. This and other besetting sins are suitably rebuked by J. L. Austin (1962). The English words derived from Latin '*sensus*' and '*sentire*' make up a large and ill-assorted family. See C. S. Lewis, 1960, Ch. VI; R. Williams, 1983, pp. 280–283. See also section 5.23 (**feel**).

D. Phenomenon, phenomena, phenomenal

The word 'phenomenon' is singular. 'Phenomena' is plural. To say 'a phenomena' is as bad as saying 'a tables'.

There is a well-established ordinary use according to which something is called 'a phenomenon' only if it is, in some way, startling, out-of-the-way, or noteworthy. Scientists, however, have the habit of using the word 'phenomenon' to refer to any event or process (however commonplace) that might call for explanation: 'the phenomenon of water boiling', 'the physical phenomena associated with ageing', etc. Sometimes scientists (and, more often, people who would like to sound like scientists) say 'phenomenon' when the simple old monosyllable 'thing' would do the job better. See section 8.5C (**sciolism**).

The Greek word *phainomenon* means *appearance* and this meaning is preserved in philosophical talk. The phenomena are *what is apparent to the senses*, which may or may not be 'how things really are'. Immanuel Kant (1724–1803) distinguished **the phenomenal world** from the *world-as-it-is-in-itself* (the *world of reality* or the **noumenal world**). (See Kraushaar, 1955; Körner, 1975.) Thus, in Kantian talk, we have the following contrasting terms:

'phenomenon'   'noumenon'
'phenomena'   'noumena'
'phenomenal'   'noumenal'

See also **F** below (**sense-data**).

E.   Saving the phenomena

'To save the phenomena' (or 'To save the appearances') is the literal trans-lation of a Greek phrase embodying two rules of investigative method:

(i) A hypothesis should account for all known relevant facts;

AND

(ii) If your hypothesis about how things *are* is at variance with how things *seem to be*, then you have a problem which you need to solve.

Someone might complain that this phrase begs the question (see section 4.23) too much in favour of the phenomena. *May* it not be that at least some things are radically 'not what they seem'? *Must* the phenomena always be 'saved'? The objection is reasonable, but one must not forget the circumstances in which the phrase originated. The dominant philosophico-scientific schools of the pre-Socratic period were the Herakleitians and the Parmenidians. Each started from plausible-looking premisses and proceeded by valid-looking reasoning. The Herakleitians reached the conclusion that reality must be nothing but flux, change, heterogeneity, and that any impression of per-manence or fixity, any persistence of objects or selves must be illusory. 'You can't step into the same river twice,' said Herakleitos. 'You can't even step into it once,' said his follower, Kratylos. The Parmenidians came to a different conclusion. Their finding was that reality must be unitary, uniform, un-changing, undifferentiated, and that any impression of change, variety, or plurality must be illusory. All there could be was The One. The Many could not exist.

In such an intellectual climate, the phenomena needed all the help they could get. See A. H. Armstrong, 1965, Ch. II; J. Burnet, 1964, Ch. III; A. E. Taylor, 1960, p. 198; W. K. C. Guthrie, 1950(a), Ch. III. See also sections 4.18A (**paradox**) and 6.22(g) (*aporia*).

F.   Sense-data

A sense-datum is (or is alleged by some to be) what is immediately given to us by sense (i.e., by sight, touch, smell, taste, hearing, somaesthesia). Those who talk this way usually hold that sense-data are not identical with the material objects (see section 1.15B(iv)) of which they may seem to be appear-ances and that they would not exist if they were not sensed. Thus, 'sense-data' is a more 'theory-laden' word than 'phenomena'. See Lacey, 1976, pp. 195–197; G. J. Warnock, 1967(b).

The most influential **sense-datum theorists** are H. H. Price (1899–1984), G. E. Moore (1873–1958), and A. J. Ayer (1910–1989). Ayer, 1976, Chs IV–V, is a useful introduction to sense-datum thinking. Critics have argued that there is no need to postulate sense-data (see D. M. Armstrong, 1961; J. L. Austin, 1962). Ayer (1969, pp. 126–148) defends the theory against Austin's attack. Jackson, 1977, has stimulated much recent discussion of sense-datum theory. For **'datum'**, **'data'**, see section 5.5C(iv).

G. Phenomenalism

A phenomenalist view is one which maintains:

   (i) that we can only know appearances (**phenomena**)

   AND

   (ii) that we need not postulate an unknowable world of 'reality' (**noumena**) lying 'beyond' or 'under' those appearances.

(That is the generally accepted meaning of the word 'phenomenalism' these days, but it has also been used to include views which assert (i) and deny (ii).) See Lacey, 1976, pp. 157–158; Quinton, 1975(b); Ayer, 1954, pp. 125–166; Vesey, 1971, Chs IV–VI.

H. Phenomenology

'In its broadest meaning,' says Marvin Farber, 'the term phenomenology signifies a descriptive philosophy of experience' (1975, p. 216). Tillich (1953, p. 118) characterizes the phenomenological approach by saying that its aim is:

> ... to describe 'meanings', disregarding, for the time being, the question of the reality to which they refer. The significance of this methodological approach lies in its demand that the meaning of a notion must be clarified and circumscribed before its validity can be determined.

The point is that, before we can decide whether (e.g.) miracles are possible, we need to be clear on what a belief in miracles amounts to. That is not simply a matter of rattling off a definition, since definitions (at least of non-technical terms) are, at best, accurate abridgements of discourse and at worst may give a distorted and inaccurate view of discourse. (A user of a term may give a definition of it which does not reflect his usage of it at all.) To stay with the *miracles* example, a phenomenological approach would require a careful, descriptive approach to *miracle-discourse* (i.e., scriptures, stories, prayers, etc.), not mere reference to the systematizations of philosophers and theologians (even ones who believe in miracles). Only *after* that kind of investigation would it be possible to come to a reasonable conclusion as to whether miracles are possible or not. In more general terms:

> We need to know *what the concept is* before we can come to a conclusion *about its instantiation.* (See section 1.9A(iii).)

The word 'phenomenology' is usually associated with certain Continental philosophers, especially with Edmund Husserl (1859–1938). But the Anglophone 'Ordinary Language philosophers' (see section 7.12F) use a phenomenological approach when they attempt (in Ryle's words) 'to determine the logical geography of concepts'. As Austin says, 'Certainly ... ordinary language is *not* the last word: in principle it can everywhere be supplemented and improved upon and superseded. Only remember, it *is* the *first* word' (1979, p. 185). See also Farber, 1940, 1975; Luckmann, 1978; Ryle, 1971(a), pp. 167–196, 215–224.

5.23   FEEL

> 'That's a great deal to make one word mean,' Alice said in a thoughtful tone.
> 'When I make a word do a lot of work like that,' said Humpty Dumpty, 'I always pay it extra.'
> 'Oh!' said Alice. She was too much puzzled to make any other remark.
> (Lewis Carroll, *Through the Looking Glass*, Ch. VI, 1974, p. 194)

The word 'feel' certainly deserves a substantial over-award payment. Lacey (1976, p. 68) takes a paragraph of sixteen lines to list different types of object that the verb 'feel' can take, many of which involve giving 'feel' different senses. Such a versatile word can be dangerous. One can slip from one sense to another without noticing it and draw all sorts of odd conclusions from what is nothing more than an unintentional pun. Obviously, it would be absurd to suggest that anyone drop the word 'feel' from his vocabulary, but it is a word to be Handled With Care. In particular, 'feel' should not be used where 'say', 'assert', 'maintain', 'think', or 'argue' will do. To say 'Plato feels the forms provide ultimate explanations' makes an argued theory sound like a mere hunch. See section 5.22C (**the senses**).

5.24   SENSIBLE, INTELLIGIBLE, INTELLECTIBLE;   TANGIBLE; PALPABLE

(i) **Sensible, intelligible**: The most frequent popular senses of these words are, respectively, 'rational' and 'understandable'. A more technical sense of 'sensible' is 'perceptible or apprehensible by the senses'. A corresponding sense of 'intelligible' is 'perceptible or apprehensible by the intellect' or 'perceptible or apprehensible ONLY by the intellect'. Sometimes, 'intellectible' is used instead of 'intelligible'. See section 1.13A (**theory of forms**) and section 5.25 (**intuition**).

(ii) 'Tangible' literally means 'capable of being touched'. It is used frequently as a synonym for 'concrete' (see section 1.11). Sometimes, something (a theory, a proposal, etc.) is said to be tangible to the extent that all of its details are available for consideration (the etymology is alive and kicking here via the metaphor of 'getting a grasp of').

(iii) **Palpable**: 'tangible' (in varying senses); readily perceptible; obvious.
See also section 8.17 (**credible, plausible**).

5.25 INTUITION, INTUITIVE, INTUITIONISM

(i) These words come from the Latin '*intueri*': 'to look at', 'to observe', 'to gaze at', 'to give attention to'. The English derivatives are typically concerned with *intellectual* seeing rather than with *optical* seeing: seeing the point or the joke or the force of the argument, rather than seeing the cat or the milk-bottle (though, in Immanuel Kant's philosophy, the word 'intuition' is used with reference to the purely sensory element in our relation to sensible objects and this has influenced the usage of some Anglophone philosophers).

One element of optical seeing is its apparent *directness*:

Primus: 'How do you know he caught the bus?'
Secundus: 'I was there. I saw him. That's how.'

Secundus here claims to know that an event occurred by virtue of a direct acquaintance with it. He is not relying on testimony. He is not reasoning on the basis of evidence that it occurred. Indeed, he has *no* evidence, except 'the evidence of his own eyes', and, as J. L. Austin says, 'the point of this trope is exactly that it does *not* illustrate *the ordinary* use of "evidence" – that I *don't* have evidence in *the ordinary* sense' (1962, pp. 115–116n).

Another element of optical seeing is the rather obvious one that it is *optical* – obvious, but not entirely trivial. You and I may be having precisely the same optical experiences: we are in the same place at the same time and our eyesights are equally good. All of a sudden, your expression changes and you exclaim 'Ohh! I *see*!' You have 'seen' what it 'adds up to,' the significance of it. But there I stand, unenlightened and gormless, *optically* seeing precisely what you are seeing, but, in the sense of your exclamation, *not* seeing at all.

In philosophical parlance, the word 'intuition' does not have one unvarying meaning. Sometimes, the emphasis is on the directness which intellectual seeing seems to have in common with optical seeing. Sometimes, the emphasis is on its differences from optical seeing, i.e., on the point that one can see something, without seeing its significance. On some occasions when the second element is stressed, the first disappears altogether. There are occasions when the two elements are equally stressed or when both are there but in different degrees.

So, when a philosopher talks about intuition, we need to take a very close look at what he says. We should also be cautious about dismissing such talk. In ordinary talk, the word 'intuition' is *sometimes* used by people who want to give a special status to their hunches, which *may* be worth listening to, but can be based on irrelevant quirks of the unconscious ('I just *know* that fellow's a crook. It's something about him. I can't put my finger on it, but it's *there*', says someone, not realizing that the 'something' is a facial resemblance to Captain Hook in a production of *Peter Pan* thirty years earlier). Another use of 'intuition' in ordinary speech is for talk about alleged extraordinary and inexplicable powers held by the very few.

'Intuition' in these senses has little to do with the opinions of philosophers who would accept the title 'intuitionist', but, to read some of their philosophical enemies, you would not think so. Critics of *ethical* intuitionism frequently ridicule the notion of intellectual seeing as 'mysterious' or (strong language, this) 'mystical'. The intuitionists, however, are not professing to describe some strange and unusual experience (as a genuine mystic does), but to give an account of quite ordinary experience. It may be that they have misdescribed that experience; but one does not establish that by throwing the words 'mysterious' and 'mystical' about. It also seems (*prima facie*, anyway) that the intuitionists get *some* support from such unmysterious and unmystical ways of talk as 'I see what you are getting at', 'I saw then that it just wouldn't do', etc. See Hospers, 1967, pp. 136–139; Pole, 1961, Ch. I; Quine and Ullian, 1978, Ch. VII.

(ii) **Ethical intuitionists** (e.g. Richard Price, G. E. Moore, H. A. Prichard, Sir David Ross, H. J. McCloskey) place a great deal of emphasis on the sort of 'intellectual seeing' just talked about, but they give it an extra twist, by taking the view that there are *ethical properties* of acts, states of affairs, etc., existing over and above the non-ethical properties of those acts, states of affairs, etc. These properties are said to be *non-natural* in the sense that they are not perceptible by the senses, but are intellectible (see section 5.24). See W. D. Hudson, 1967; Strawson, 1952(a); Lucas, 1971.

In insisting that the criterion for morally correct action is, in this sense, *non-natural*, ethical intuitionists reject all theories which are *naturalistic* in the sense that they treat some empirically observable feature of the real world as the moral criterion. See Kemp, 1970; G. J. Warnock, 1967(a), Ch. VI; Midgley, 1979, Ch. IX; W. D. Hudson, 1983, Ch. VII.

The term 'ethical intuitionism' is sometimes given to ethical theories which take the view that there are several distinct moral duties or values which are equally basic and therefore not reducible to one another or to anything else. This kind of view and the view outlined above are not identical, but are frequently combined. See Findlay, 1970.

(iii) **Mathematical intuitionism; intuitionist logic**
The clearest, best-informed, and most helpful thing I can say about these two topics is: see Flew, 1984, pp. 178–179, and Lacey, 1976, p. 102.

(iv) **'Intuition' and 'intuitive' in a 'thin' sense; counter-intuitive**
The words 'intuition' and 'intuitive' also have philosophical senses not laden with any of the various doctrines outlined above. If a philosopher says 'My intuition is that X is Y', he is usually saying (i) that he believes that X is Y, and (ii) that, though this belief is not necessarily a mere hunch or gut-feeling, it is a belief held in advance of special and close investigation of the precise issue; i.e., he is pretty sure that X is Y, but he is not closing off the possibility that it is not.

'It seems intuitive that X is Y' is usually (despite the 'seems') a little less modest and 'personal'. It is usually the assertion that, on the basis of available general information, there is a reasonable presumption in favour of the proposition that X is Y and that the onus of proof (see section 8.9A) is on the person who wants to deny that X is Y. To say that it seems intuitive that X is Y is to say that the proposition 'X is not Y' is **counter-intuitive**.

5.26 ANTHROPOMORPHISM

The word is derived from two Greek words: *'anthropos'* = 'man' (species sense – see section 1.25) and *'morphe'* = 'shape' or 'form'.

There are (at least) two different ways of **proceeding anthropomorphically**. One is to discourse of (see section 1.1) something non-human on the analogy (see section 8.19) of human beings. The other way is to discourse of something non-human in a way which attributes to it characteristics which *only* a human being can possess.

'Anthropomorphism', then, can be a term of reproach (or, at least, of heavy qualification). It does *not* follow that every attribution to a non-human being of a characteristic possessed by human beings is to be dismissed as **anthropomorphic**. In some respects, human beings and other animals have the same *'morphe'* and the extent of that sharing may be an open question. See Midgley, 1979, pp. 344–351.

If one describes the behaviour of apes in terms more usually applied to human beings, one is guilty of anthropomorphism and of being *very* unscientific. If one describes the behaviour of human beings in terms more usually applied to apes, one may well be Desmond Morris and a celebrity. See Koestler, 1970, pp. 30–33, on the **ratomorphism** of behaviourist (see section 7.11) psychologists.

'Anthropomorphic' should not be confused with '**anthropocentric**'. The two words are alike, in meaning as in shape, but there are differences. An anthropocentric theory, outlook, etc., is one which treats the human species as the central fact about the universe (*CODCE*, 1976, p. 40) and measures everything else in terms of the (presumed) interests of the human species. The distinguished biologist, Sir Macfarlane Burnet, says such things as these: 'the numberless experiments which have been devised by nature', 'Nature has gone to extraordinary pains ... to ensure that pure-line strains can never develop' (1978, pp. 45, 52; see also pp. 9, 14, 15, 19, 62, 121, 211). To talk that way is to treat nature **anthropomorphically** (even perhaps **theomorphically**[5]), but it is compatible with the very non-anthropocentric view that mankind is just one species amongst others and of no special importance.

5.27   ANECDOTE, ANECDOTAL

An anecdote, as the *OED* says, is 'the narrative of a detached incident, or of a single event, told as being in itself interesting or striking'. The words 'anecdote' and 'anecdotal' are often used as terms of reproach by those who find it convenient to pretend that nothing really happens outside laboratories – a superstitious and unscientific pretence, if ever there was one. (A remark heard on Australian radio in June 1989: 'Some of these stories are anecdotal.')

Sometimes, a more serious thought may lie behind the reproachful use of these words: perhaps the objection is that the anecdote complained of is (for some special reason) unreliable as evidence. Perhaps the objection is a warning that a hypothesis is not adequately supported merely by quoting *confirming instances* (see sections 5.2, 4.29). But, if it is something like this that the objector is getting at, he would be speaking more clearly if he said so explicitly. I know of people who believe (i) that anecdotal evidence is very, very bad, and (ii) that *oral history* is very, very good. How do they do it? It's easy! On the history of the word 'anecdote', see Sutherland, 1977, pp. v–x.

5.28   PARAMETER

'Parameter' is a technical term used in various scientific enterprises. Uvarov and Chapman (1971, p. 280) give two senses. Philip Howard (1980, pp. 77–78) lists seven. In geometry, for instance, if two variables x and y are each expressed in terms of a third variable, t, so that they are functions of t, the equations expressing that are called **parametric equations** and t is called **a parameter**. In experimental sciences, a parameter is a variable which can be held constant while the effects of other variables are examined.

When the word 'parameter' is used in its native scientific settings it is usually clear enough to those reasonably well-informed about the science in question. Unfortunately, it has become a favourite of those who like to add what they think is a little scientific flavouring to their own unscientific utterances. Sometimes, it seems to mean 'limit'; sometimes, it seems to mean 'basic assumption'; sometimes it is difficult to tell what – if anything – it means. Here, for instance, is a quotation from a book written by a member of the Canberra Press Gallery:

... the Cairns paper was fully endorsed as defining budget parameters.

(Kelly, 1976, p. 67)

There is nothing wrong with the words 'limit' and 'basic assumption'. There is nothing wrong with the word 'parameter' *in its native scientific settings.* Outside those settings, it becomes pretentious mumbo-jumbo, mere sciolistic nattering (for **sciolism**, see section 8.5C). In some of these silly misuses, there seems to be some confusion with *perimeter*, the outer boundary of a geometrical figure. A sciolist, therefore, is the sort of person who cannot tell a perimeter from a parameter. See also K. Hudson, 1977, pp. 177–178; Room, 1979, p. 100; J. O'Connor, 1956, sections 329, 23.

5.29   CONSPIRACY AND PARANOIA

A.   Conspiracy theory

Etymologically, a conspiracy is a 'breathing together', but the term has come to be restricted to 'breathings together' with unlawful intent or at least intent which would be gravely deleterious to someone. Conspiracies do occur and not every theory that a conspiracy has occurred or is occurring should be written off as false, absurd, or neurotic. But 'conspiracy theory' is (with good reason) a pejorative phrase. It follows that not every theory that a conspiracy has occurred or is occurring is a conspiracy theory.

The conspiracy theory of society is the view that the way to explain a social phenomenon, especially an undesirable one (e.g., a war, a depression, an epidemic, the unpopularity of a government supported by the speaker) is to identify the individuals or groups who have planned to bring the phenomenon about because they hope to profit by it. Such a view, as Karl Popper says (see references below), overlooks the fact that social action typically has many unpredicted, unintended, and unwanted consequences, so that social phenomena may occur without anyone having planned or desired them. The main logical fault of the conspiracy theory is that it unwarrantedly rules out possible explanations, insisting that explaining a phenomenon *must* consist in identifying its designers. The conspiracy theory is a special case of a more general error, the view that human intention necessarily governs results (e.g., Primus puts forward a proposal. Secundus objects that adopting the proposal could have undesirable effects. Primus replies, 'Oh, but I don't *intend* that to happen,' and believes that he has disposed of the objection. Primus is confusing himself with God. See section 8.21A (**creation**)).

In its most pathological form, conspiracy theory insists not merely that there *must* be *a* band of conspirators behind a social phenomenon, but that it *must* be a *specific* band of conspirators (e.g., The Jews, The Jesuits, The CIA, The Communists, The Bankers, etc.). For the holder of such a view, anything can be confirming evidence and nothing can be disconfirming evidence. See also section 6.29C (**McCarthyism**). See Popper, 1966, Ch. XIV (reprinted in Popper, 1983, pp. 345–356); Popper, 1972(a), Chs IV, XVI. See also Burns, 1977; Hofstadter, 1967, pp. 3–40.

B.   Paranoia, paranoiac, paranoid

These are three terms from the technical vocabulary of psychiatry. They are often used carelessly and cruelly by ignorant people. **Paranoia** is a serious psychotic disorder, marked by systematized and persistent delusions of persecution or grandeur. The delusions are strongly defended by the sufferer, not merely in the sense that he argues for them, but also in the sense that he allows no evidence or absence of evidence to count against them and interprets virtually everything as evidence for them. The delusions tend to make it impossible for the sufferer (the **paranoiac**) to enter into normal personal and social relationships. See *LDPP*, 1984, pp. 532–533; Allport, 1958, pp. 394–397; Brooker, 1972.

To call someone **paranoid** is to say that, while he *may* not be paranoiac, there are aspects of his thought and behaviour which strongly resemble those of a paranoiac. To speak of 'Mr X's paranoia' is to imply that Mr X is suffering from a very serious mental disorder. To say that Mr X is paranoid is, at the very least, to say that he is deeply irrational and shows tendencies toward that very serious mental disorder. To use these words merely to 'write off' someone who holds suspicions which you do not share is a cruel and dishonest piece of verbal bullying. It is also worth remembering that while there can be paranoiac and paranoid delusions, there can also be paranoiac and paranoid realities (e.g., those imposed by totalitarian regimes and by some family tyrants).

5.30   THE

(i) Used in front of a singular name or description the definite article 'the' suggests that there is only one of whatever it is, or only one at any one time, or only one within a presupposed context, and usually the suggestion is correct:

> 'The Brisbane River'
> 'The Lord Mayor of London'
> 'The refrigerator'

Sometimes, however, the suggestion is false. We can take some such uses in our stride: 'The Great Barrier Reef is endangered by the crown-of-thorns starfish.' That gives us no trouble, even though its two 'the's work quite differently. We are not likely to think that there is one single individual creature – a marine counterpart of Macavity the Mystery Cat – which is doing all that endangering.

But there are occasions when we are misled. We say 'the distinction between public and private' and assume that there is just one distinction. It can take quite an effort of imagination to grasp the simple point that the distinction between public and private companies is quite different from that between public and private property (see Benn and Gaus, 1983).

That use of 'the' is stylistically convenient and it would be next to impossible to do without it. If we keep our wits about us, it will not mislead us. (The old one about the chicken and the egg gets a little of its flavour from the ambiguity of 'the'.)

(ii) In talk about arguments for the existence of God, philosophers and others talk about '*the* cosmological argument', '*the* ontological argument', etc. But there is not just one cosmological argument or one ontological argument. These are *styles of* argument, and an objection which demolishes one ontological argument may not be successful against another. See section 8.20.

6 Symbols; basic propositional forms; basic argumental forms

6.1 THE GREEK ALPHABET

Mathematicians, logicians, and philosophers often use Greek letters as symbols. There are also some books (e.g., A. E. Taylor, 1960) which print Greek words in Greek letters. So it is useful for a student to have some knowledge of the Greek alphabet.

Capital	Lower-case	Name	English transliteration
A	α	alpha	a
B	β	beta	b
Γ	γ	gamma	g
Δ	δ	delta	d
E	ε	epsilon	e (short)
Z	ζ	zeta	z
H	η	eta	e (long)
Θ	θ	theta	th
I	ι	iota	i
K	κ	kappa	k **or** c
Λ	λ	lambda	l
M	μ	mu	m
N	ν	nu	n
Ξ	ξ	xi	x
O	o	omicron	o
Π	π	pi	p
P	ρ	rho	r
Σ	σ (at end of words: ς)	sigma	s
T	τ	tau	t
Y	υ	upsilon	u **or** y
Φ	φ	phi	ph
X	χ	chi **or** khi	kh **or** ch
Ψ	ψ	psi	ps
Ω	ω	omega	o

In English speech, the names of the letters are usually pronounced as if they were English words (e.g., one says 'beeta', not 'bayta'). The 'ch' in 'chi' is always pronounced like the 'ch' in 'Christian', not like the 'ch' in 'chicken'. 'Epsilon', 'omicron', and 'upsilon' are pronounced with the stress on the second syllable. With 'omega', the stress is put on the first syllable.

6.2 PLACE-HOLDERS AND SIGNIFIERS

A. Place-holders and propositional logic

(i) As noted in section 1.2, the relationships of *sentence* to *proposition* and *numeral* to *number* are similar and equally obscure. In the present section, I shall use the words 'number' and 'proposition'. I do this purely as a matter of convenience and with no intention of begging any metalogical (see section 7.22B) questions. Anyone who wishes to replace 'number' with 'numeral' and 'proposition' with 'sentence' can do so with my blessing. The point of the present section does not depend on the differences in metalogical doctrine hinted at by those verbal preferences. (See also section 6.7.)

(ii) In algebra, small letters are used as **place-holding expressions** for numbers. In a formula like

$$(x\,(y+z)) = (xy+xz),$$

the letters stand for no specific numbers. Rather, *any* numbers whatsoever can be substituted for them, provided that the substitution is consistent. In a similar way, propositional logic uses small letters as place-holders for simple propositions (see section 6.8). Consider the following:

The gatling's jammed and the Colonel's dead.

The sheep's in the meadow and the cow's in the corn.

Today, the dollar declined on the exchange market and interest rates increased sharply.

These are very different in *matter* (or *content*), but each has the same **structure** (or **form** – see section 6.23): each is a **two-component (or two-member) conjunction** (see section 6.10); i.e.:

each can be broken down into two less complex propositions

and

each is true if and only if both its less complex component propositions are true.

A more succinct way of making that point is this: 'Each has the form (p & q).' In that formula, neither letter stands for any actual proposition. Rather, any proposition can be substituted for 'p' and any other proposition can be substituted for 'q'. The formula (p & q) depicts the form of (but does not symbolize the meaning of) *any* two component conjunction.

B.   Signifiers (or symbolizers or proposition-denoters)

If we wanted to symbolize briefly one or more of those conjunctions discussed above, we could use capital letters, each of which symbolized one component. Capital letters so used can be called **symbolizers** (or **signifiers**, or **proposition-denoters**).

Our first step is to draw up a 'dictionary' or 'glossary' which assigns a meaning to each capital letter:

Dictionary

C   The gatling's jammed.
D   The Colonel's dead.
E   The sheep's in the meadow.
F   The cow's in the corn.
G   Today, the dollar declined on the exchange market.
H   Today, interest rates increased.

That enables us to symbolize the conjunctions thus:

C & D
E & F
G & H

For the duration of a piece of analysis, a capital letter so used has a definite significance. The small letters in such formulae as (p & q) have no definite meaning. They are (as it were) sophisticated blanks. The capital letters are symbols which symbolize *something*. The small letters are symbols, but they do not symbolize anything. See also section 6.7.

6.3   PLACE-HOLDERS AND 'IMPURE' SYMBOLS

In philosophy, we are often concerned with very general principles, so place-holding expressions (or things like them) are often useful. Greek letters are often used this way, as are certain names (e.g., 'Tom', 'Dick', and 'Harry'). The Latin ordinal number-words from 'first' to 'tenth' are also useful as *proper-name-substitutes*: 'Primus', 'Secundus', 'Tertius', 'Quartus', 'Quintus', 'Sextus', 'Septimus', 'Octavius', 'Nonus', 'Decimus'. I find it convenient to use 'xify' as a general substitute for *verbs of action*, 'xious' and 'xical' for adjectives, and 'Xland' and 'Yland' for names of countries.

Frequently, however, these symbols are 'impure'; e.g., 'Primus' etc. waver between being names of fictional persons and being place-holders replaceable by actual names. Usually, this ambiguity gives no trouble. See also section 6.7.

6.4   SUBSTITUTION-INSTANCE; SCHEMA

(i) When words or signifiers (see section 6.2B) are substituted for place-holders (see section 6.2A), the resultant formula is a **substitution-instance** of the original formula. Thus, 'The gatling's jammed and the Colonel's dead' and 'The sheep's in the meadow and the cow's in the corn' are substitution-instances of (p & q). A formula containing place-holders is a *schema*. The plural of 'schema' is 'schemata'.

(ii) A **necessity-schema** is a schema, every substitution-instance of which is either true by logical necessity (see section 3.5A(ii)) or false by logical necessity. A **necessity-schema** of the first type is a **necessary-truth-schema** (e.g., (p v -p)). One of the second type is a **necessary-falsehood-schema** (e.g., (p & -p)).

A schema whose substitution-instances *may* be true or false (i.e., are *logically contingent* – see section 3.5A(iii)) is a **contingency-schema** (e.g., (p & q)).

The expression 'valid schema' is more frequently used (and neater) than 'necessary-truth-schema', but 'necessary-truth-schema' is preferable. 'Valid schema' can lead to confusion with **validity of arguments** (see section 4.9) and has a nasty smell of deductivism (see sections 5.13A, B) about it. See section 6.7.

6.5   LOGICAL OPERATORS, TRUTH-FUNCTIONAL OPERATORS; SCOPE; WELL-FORMED AND ILL-FORMED

(i) An expression by means of which we can construct a proposition out of one or more other propositions is a **logical operator**. If one places the phrase 'I believe that ...' in front of the proposition 'The sheep's in the meadow', the result is a new proposition 'I believe that the sheep's in the meadow.' If, instead, we add the operator 'It is not true that ...', we get the new proposition 'It is not true that the sheep's in the meadow.' The constructed propositions are called **compounds** (see sections 6.8–6.14).

The truth-value (see section 1.3A(i)) of 'It is not true that the sheep's in the meadow' depends on the truth-value of 'The sheep's in the meadow', hence 'It is not true that ...' is called a **truth-functional logical operator** (for **'truth-functional'** see section 6.8). The truth-value of 'I believe that the sheep's in the meadow' is not dependent on the truth-value of 'The sheep's in the meadow', hence 'I believe that ...' is a **non-truth-functional logical operator**.

The expressions 'v', '-', '&', '⊃', '≢', etc., are **truth-functional logical operators**. See sections 6.8–6.14.

Truth-functional logical operators are sometimes called *truth-functional* **connectives** or *truth-functional* **constants**. They retain the same meaning in every instance of their use (hence '*constant*') and are (with the exception of '-' – see section 6.12) used to connect propositions together (hence, '*connective*'), to make truth-functional compounds (hence '*truth-functional*'). See section 6.6.

(ii) The **scope** of an operator is those parts of a compound which are governed by it. Thus, the scope of 'It is not true that' in 'It is not true that the sheep's in the meadow' is 'The sheep's in the meadow.' In 'The sheep's in the meadow and the cow's in the corn', the operator is 'and' (approximately – see section 6.14(i)). The propositions 'The sheep's in the meadow' and 'The cow's in the corn' are the propositions within its scope. We can make the point more generally by the use of symbols. In a proposition of the form (-p), the scope of the operator is (p). In a proposition of the form (p & q), the two simple propositions (p), (q) are the propositions within the scope of the operator.

(iii) In the following formula, it is not possible to say what is in the scope of what:

-p & q v r

What is being negated? Is it simply (p) or is it (p & q)? And there are other possibilities. For similar reasons, it is not possible to say what comes within the scope of the ampersand (&) or the vel (v). Such an ambiguous formula is said to be **not well-formed** or an **ill-formed formula**. To remove such ambiguities, curved brackets are used; e.g.:

-p & (q v r)
-(p & q) v r
-(p & (q v r))
-((p & q) v r)

Those are unambiguous formulae, **well-formed formulae** (or *wffs*, pronounced 'woofs' or 'wifs', for short). In the first, the negation of p is conjoined with the disjunction of (q) and (r). The second says that either the conjunction of (p) and (q) is false or (r) is true. The third says that it is not true that *both* (p) and the disjunction of (q) and (r) are true. The fourth says that neither (p & q) nor r is true.

The scope of (-) is whatever expression, bracketed or unbracketed, immediately follows it. Each of the other truth-functional operators has within its scope the expressions (compound or simple) which immediately precede and immediately follow it. For more information, see Flew, 1984, pp. 74, 212–213; Prior, 1962, Ch. I; Basson and O'Connor, 1959, pp. 37–40. See also sections 6.2A(i) and 6.7.

6.6 CONSTANTS AND VARIABLES

Constants (i.e., *operators*) are contrasted with **variables**. A variable is an expression which can be replaced by an indefinite range of expressions. Thus in (p & q) the ampersand is a logical constant but 'p' and 'q' are variables because an indefinite range of propositions can be substituted for them. The only restriction is that, within the same formula or system of formulae, all occurrences of one variable should be replaced by the same proposition on any one occasion on which substitutions are made within that formula or system of formulae. 'p' and 'q' in that formula are *propositional* variables. In 'All S are P', 'S' and 'P' are *term* variables (for **terms**, see section 6.29A(ii)). See sections 6.2A(i) and 6.7.

6.7 VARIABLES AND SCHEMATIC LETTERS

It will be objected that in sections 6.2–6.6, I have not taken proper account of Quine's distinction between *variables* and *schematic letters*. That is true. The reason is that I do not think that that distinction can be introduced without a detailed exposition of Quine's philosophy of logic. That cannot be done in the space available. Those who wish to follow the matter up should read Quine, 1970. I find it consoling that Quine himself, in a recent book intended for the general reader, discusses variables, but nimbly evades any mention of schematic letters (Quine, 1987 – see index). The issue of Quine's distinction is important for formal logic, but informal logic (see section 6.26) can operate with a simpler distinction between **constants, place-holders**, and **signifiers** (see sections 6.2–6.6).

6.8 COMPOUND; SIMPLE; TRUTH-FUNCTIONAL COMPOUNDS

(i) A proposition/statement is **compound** IFF it has other propositions as *components*.

'Tom believes that Stalin was a CIA agent.'   (A)
'It is a cold night and we have no oil for the stove.'   (B)

Since it is *not* the case that assertion of a compound proposition/statement *always* involves assertion of its components, it is misleading to say that such a compound is composed of statements. See sections 4.12(ii), 1.2.

(ii) A proposition/statement is **simple** IFF it has no other propositions as components.

'Stalin was a CIA agent.'   (C)
'It is a cold night.'   (D)
'We have no oil for the stove.'   (E)

'Simple' here contrasts with 'compound', not with 'difficult'.

(iii) A compound is **truth-functional** IFF its *truth-value* (see section 1.3A(i)) is completely dependent on the truth-value of its component propositions together with the meaning of the connective(s). Thus, (B) is truth-functional because if either of its components is false, (B) is also false. (A) is NOT truth-functional because it could be true even if Stalin was not a CIA agent and it could be false even if Stalin was a CIA agent.

(iv) **Some types of truth-functional compound:**
Conjunction (section 6.10); disjunction (section 6.11); negation (section 6.12); 'material conditionality' and 'material equivalence' (sections 4.14, 6.13).

6.9   COMPONENT, CONSTITUENT

The **component** (or **constituent**) simple (see section 6.8) propositions of a *compound proposition* are the simple propositions contained within that compound proposition; e.g.:

Compound proposition	*Component simple propositions*
1. Roses are red and violets are blue.	Roses are red. Violets are blue.
2. If he touched the glass, his fingerprints will be on it.	He touched the glass. His fingerprints are on the glass.
3. He did not touch the glass.	He touched the glass.

Notice that a compound proposition does not always *assert* its component propositions; hence, while it is appropriate to call the compound proposition *a compound **statement***, it may be misleading or simply false to talk of *its* component *statements*.

In an argument, a conclusion is asserted on the basis of propositions which are also asserted. In other words, the premisses and conclusion are the *component statements* of the argument. The *component simple propositions* of an argument are those simple propositions contained within its premisses and conclusion. The component simple propositions of an argument are not always identical with the component statements of that argument; e.g.:

> If there were such a book, it would be listed in the British Museum catalogue.
> It is not listed in the British Museum Catalogue.

∴   There is no such book.

The component simple propositions of this argument are:

There is such a book.
The book is listed in the British Museum catalogue.

Both propositions are denied in the argument.

For the very different notion of components and constituents of *facts*, see Urmson, 1956, Ch. II.

6.10 CONJUNCTION

(i) A conjunction is a truth-functional compound which is true IFF *all* its component propositions are true.

Example (B) in section 6.8(i) above is a conjunction with two components. A two-component conjunction is often symbolized as follows:

p & q

The components of a conjunction are its *conjuncts*. Each is **conjoined with** the other(s). The *truth-conditions* (see section 1.3A(ii)) for (p & q) are: the truth of p *and* the truth of q. The connective symbol '&' is known as **ampersand**. p and q are **consistently conjoinable** IFF (p & q) is not self-contradictory.

(ii) NB. In traditional grammar, the word 'conjunction' is used with a different meaning. A grammarian's conjunction is a *word* whose function is to link other words or to link sentences; e.g., 'and', 'but', 'either ... or ...', 'if', 'although', 'because'. A logician's conjunction is a *compound proposition* which is true if and only if all of its components are true.

6.11 DISJUNCTION

(i) A **non-exclusive disjunction** is a truth-functional compound which is true IFF *at least one* of its component propositions is true.

'Either Tom or John will meet Harry at the station.'   (F)

(F) would be *true* in *any* of the following circumstances:

Tom (but not John) meets Harry at the station.
John (but not Tom) meets Harry at the station.
Tom and John meet Harry at the station.

(F) would be false *only* in the following circumstance:

Neither Tom nor John meets Harry at the station.

A two-component disjunction is often symbolized as follows:

p ∨ q

Truth-condition for (p ∨ q): The truth of *at least one of* p and q. Non-exclusive disjunction is sometimes called '**inclusive disjunction**'. The connective symbol 'v' is known as *vel* or as *wedge*.

(ii) An **exclusive disjunction** is a truth-functional compound which is true IFF *only one* of its disjuncts is true. In terms of the symbolism used in sections 6.10–6.12 a two-component exclusive disjunction is symbolized as follows:

(p ∨ q) & -(p & q)

Sometimes (e.g., Basson and O'Connor, 1959, p. 31) a two-component exclusive disjunction is symbolized as:

p ∧ q

Sometimes (e.g., T. J. Richards, 1978, pp. 83–84), a two-component exclusive disjunction is symbolized as:

p ≢ q

Truth conditions for an exclusive disjunction whose components are p and q: The truth of *only one of* p and q.

The symbol ' ∧ ' is known as *aut* (pronounced like 'out') or as *inverted wedge*. The symbol ≢ is known as *crossed tribar*. (Unfortunately, there is yet another notation in which the inverted wedge is the symbol for conjunction. See Hodges, 1977, pp. 93–95.)

(iii) **Disjuncts**. The components of a disjunction are its **disjuncts**.

(iv) Disjunction stirs strange passions. Take a statement like 'John is either hard-working or very clever' (Shaw's example). Clearly, it is false if John is neither hard-working nor very clever. Clearly also, it is true if John is hard-working but not very clever or if he is very clever but not hard-working. But what if he is *both* hard-working *and* very clever? Is the statement true then?

That question, put to a group of non-logicians, will usually elicit very confident but divergent responses. Some will say that, *of course*, the statement is true and others will say that, *of course*, it is false. Eventually a spirit of compromise will prevail and people will agree that it depends on what you mean by 'or'. That compromise is embodied in the distinction between *non-exclusive* (or *inclusive*) *disjunction* and *exclusive disjunction*.

But, though this is a distinction which the logicians have made, most of them are lukewarm about exclusive disjunction. They maintain that genuine examples are not easily found. There are certainly disjunctive statements, only one of whose components can be true; e.g.:

'He is either alive or dead.'
'Either George or Charles Edward is the lawful monarch.'
'He either flew all the way to Sydney or took a train.'
'Jean is Prime Minister or Leader of the Opposition.'

But, they say, the mutual exclusiveness of the alternatives can be accounted for by the meanings of *the disjuncts*, not of 'or'. That is true, but there is nothing in the meaning of the words 'Weetabix' and 'Cornflakes' that implies that you cannot have both cereals, nor is there anything in the words 'eggs' and 'sausages' to make it impossible to eat both at the one meal. But, if you look at the menus produced by motels which offer you a breakfast, cost included in the charge for accommodation, you will find that they crawl with such disjunctions. The clearest way of talking about this is to say that the motel folk are using 'or' *exclusively* as distinct from using it inclusively (non-exclusively). Such a sense of 'or' is (I suspect) more often found in orders and offers and statements reporting them than in other kinds of statements.

Many logicians recognize that such exclusively disjunctive statements do occur, but say that they can be catered for without a special symbol. In logic, we can make use of a device which we use in ordinary English:

'Either p or q, *but not both*.'

That can be symbolized as:

(p v q) & -(p & q)

That being so, (they say) there is no need for ' ∧ ' or ' ≢ ' (inverted wedge or crossed tribar).

I have no objection to that when it applies to the sort of task most logicians are involved in; i.e., the building of formal systems akin to those of mathematics. Such systems are of great interest in themselves and frequently cast light on fundamental philosophical problems. But, if one is concerned with everyday arguments (as most logicians are not), there is a role for a special symbol for exclusive disjunction. People *do* assert exclusive disjunctions, *tacitly* (sometimes *unconsciously*) ruling out the possibility of more than one disjunct being true. We would distort such utterances by representing them *as if* their utterers had *explicitly* ruled out that possibility. See Shaw, 1981, Ch. IV. See also section 5.21 (**disjunction and dichotomy**).

6.12   NEGATION

(i) A negation is a truth-functional compound which is true IFF its component proposition is false.

'It is false that Stalin was a CIA agent.'   (G)

'Stalin was not a CIA agent.'   (H)

The component proposition within each of these propositions is 'Stalin was a CIA agent.' Examples (G) and (H) are true IFF that component proposition is false. (Hence, they are two ways of saying the same thing.)

Negation is often symbolized as follows:

-p

Truth condition for (-p): the falsehood of p.

The symbol '-' is known as *dash*.

(ii) Do not confuse the logician's '-' (dash or negation sign) with the '$-$' (minus sign) of arithmetic and algebra. In algebra $(-(x+y))=(-x+-y)$, so you might be tempted to think that the logical formula (-(p & q)) means the same as (-p & -q), but that is not the case. (-(p & q)) means 'It is false that both p and q are true' which means not 'Both p and q are false', but 'At least one of p and q are false', i.e. (-p v -q). (For 'p', read 'Britain is a monarchy.' For 'q', read 'The USA is a monarchy.')

It was once customary to use the sign '~' (known as *tilde*) as the sign for negation. But few typewriters can manage '~', whereas most can manage '-'.

(iii) It may be objected that in calling a negation *a compound*, logicians are doing violence to the English language. 'Compound' (unlike 'truth-functional') is borrowed directly from ordinary English, according to which a compound is something made up of two or more ingredients. Disjunction and conjunction fit this nicely: a compound of at least two propositions ('ingredients') bonded together by the appropriate connective (see sections 6.5–6.11). It is possible, however, for a negation to have only one component. It is a strange compound that has only one 'ingredient' and a strange connective that connects something with nothing else.

I sympathize with the complaint, but I do not think that anything can be done about it.

6.13   'MATERIAL IMPLICATION'; 'MATERIAL EQUIVALENCE'

(i) 'Material implication' (or 'material conditionality') is discussed (with well-merited disrespect) in section 4.14. 'Material equivalence', though less pernicious, is equally perverse. It is not to be confused with *equivalence* (see section 10.3). Two propositions are equivalent IFF each implies the other. Two propositions are materially equivalent IFF they have the same truth-value (see section 1.3A(i)). 'Brisbane is the capital of Queensland' and 'Gold is not soluble in water' are *not* equivalent propositions, but, as they are both true, they are *materially* equivalent. Similarly, the two false propositions, 'Brisbane is the capital of Victoria' and 'Gold is soluble in water' are also materially equivalent. In Russellian notation (see section 6.15), 'p is materially equivalent to q' is symbolized as:

p ≡ q (p tribar q)

The safest way to read this is: 'p and q have the same truth-value.'

(ii) A 'material conditional' is a truth-functional formula. Genuine conditionals assert some kind of *connection* between the *situations* posited in antecedent and consequent (e.g.: 'If it rains, the streets will be wet'). A 'material conditional' merely asserts that it is not the case that the antecedent is true and the consequent is false (e.g.: 'If Hitler dropped dead in 1938, he gave a victory speech from the balcony of Buckingham Palace in 1942'). It follows that genuine conditionals are not truth-conditional and that 'truth-functional (or material) conditionals' are not genuine conditionals.

'Material implication' is the Darien scheme, the Edsel car of modern logic.

6.14 TRUTH-FUNCTIONAL CONNECTIVES AND ENGLISH WORDS; COMMUTABILITY

(i) In sections 4.11 and 6.13, I have given reasons for not reading ('p ⊃ q') or (p → q) as (If p then q). It is also advisable to read (p & q) and (p v q) as (p ampersand q) and (p vel q), *not* as (p and q) and (p or q). The reason is that, though these logical symbols correspond to some uses of 'and' and 'or', they do not correspond to all of them. 'Jack and Jill went up the hill' is truth-functional and its 'and' corresponds to the ampersand as defined in section 6.10, but 'Jack and Jill are engaged' is not truth-functional and its 'and' does not correspond to the ampersand so defined. 'Or' is far more complicated than the vel or crossed tribar (see section 6.11); e.g., 'The Bishop is a Ruritanian spy – or so I have been told', 'The platypus, or ornithorhyncus, is indigenous to Australia.'

Some uses of 'but' can be translated by '&', but usually with some loss. 'He is a philosopher and an honest man' and 'He is a philosopher but an honest man' can both be treated as having the form (p & q), but they are not identical in meaning. See Strawson, 1952(b), pp. 56–58; T. J. Richards, 1978, Chs VII, XV.

(ii) Disjunction and conjunction are *commutable*, which means that the order in which their components are placed does not matter: (p v q) says the same as (q v p); (p & q) is an exact equivalent of (q & p). But

'He leapt into his saddle and rode away' is not an accurate equivalent of 'He rode away and leapt into his saddle.'

6.15   SYSTEMS OF NOTATION

(i) **Russellian notation**

The best-known system of symbols for the representation of propositions and arguments is one derived from that used by Bertrand Russell and A. N. Whitehead in their *Principia Mathematica* (first edition, 1910–1913), which was itself derived from a notation devised by Giuseppe Peano (hence the system is sometimes called '*Peano-Russell*'). Russell himself made a number of changes to the notation in later works and some changes have been made by other writers. The notation eventually reached a standard form which can be found briefly outlined in Copi, 1978, Chs VIII, X, or Copi, 1979, Ch. II.

(ii) **Modified Russellian notation**

Russellian notation has been the system most commonly used by English-speaking logicians in this century. More recently however a modified system has been developed, which is more convenient because all the symbols can be typed (if you have a sufficiently sophisticated typewriter). For an outline, see Lemmon, 1965, Chs I and III.

(iii) **Polish notation**

There is a quite different system of notation designed by the Polish logician, Jan Łukasiewicz. Polish notation does the same jobs as Russellian notation, but it does them rather differently. The most striking difference is that Łukasiewicz found a way of doing without brackets or equivalent punctuation marks. For reasons obvious to any English-speaking person and even more obvious to any Pole who lives in an English-speaking country, this notation is known as 'Polish notation' rather than as 'Łukasiewicz notation'. For a very brief outline and comparison with Russellian notation, see Hughes and Londey, 1965, pp. 368–370.

(iv) The following table indicates the manner in which the three systems represent the basic truth-functions:

	Russellian	*Modified Russellian*	*Polish*
Negation	$\sim p$	-p	Np
Conjunction	p·q	p&q	Kpq
Disjunction (non-exclusive)	p v q	p v q	Apq
Disjunction (exclusive)	no symbol (see section 6.11)	p≢q	Jpq
Material implication	p⊃q	p→q	Cpq
Material equivalence	p≡q	p↔q	Epq

The arrow and double arrow have other uses as well. Some writers use (→) as a symbol for *strict* implication (i.e., implication as defined in sections 4.2, 4.4) and (↔) as a symbol for *strict* equivalence (i.e., mutual strict implication – see section 10.3). For an example of the symbols being used in this fashion, see Hamblin, 1966, *passim*.

In **structure diagrams** of the type devised by J. L. Mackie, (→) is used not as an operator for the construction of compound statements but as a sign of the transition between premisses and conclusions (i.e., as a symbol for 'therefore'). (See, e.g., Stove, 1973, pp. 30–32, 44–45; Stove, 1982, Ch. IV.)

6.16 MODUS PONENS; MODUS TOLLENS

Two valid forms of argument. **Modus ponens** consists of:

A conditional (see section 4.12) premiss.
A categorical (see section 4.11) premiss which *affirms* the antecedent of the conditional premiss.
A categorical conclusion, which affirms the consequent of the conditional premiss.

That is to say, a **modus ponens** argument has this logical form:

If p then q	If something is the case, something else is the case.
	AND
p	The first-mentioned thing is the case.
∴q	∴ The second-mentioned thing is the case.
Example:	'If it rains, Tom won't go shopping today. It is raining.

Therefore, Tom won't go shopping today.'

Modus tollens consists of:

A conditional premiss.
A categorical premiss, which *negates* the *consequent* of the conditional premiss.
A categorical conclusion, which *negates* the *antecedent* of the conditional premiss.

That is to say, a **modus tollens** argument has this logical form:

If p then q	If something is the case, then something else will be the case.
	AND
-q	That something else is not the case.
∴-p	∴ The first-mentioned something isn't the case.

Example:

'If Tom is an entirely reliable source of information about himself, he won't go shopping today.
Tom has gone shopping today.
<hr>
Therefore, Tom is not an entirely reliable source of information about himself.'

'Modus ponens' literally means 'the putting (or placing) style'. 'Modus tollens' literally means 'the taking away style'. See Flew, 1975, Ch. II; Shaw, 1981, Ch. III.

6.17   FALLACIOUS RELATIVES OF MODUS PONENS AND MODUS TOLLENS

Modus ponens and **tollens** are valid, but they have some illegitimate, **fallacious** (see section 4.20) relatives.

(i) **Fallacy of denying the antecedent**

Any argument of the following form commits this fallacy:

If p then q
-p
<hr>
∴ -q

Example:

If it rains, then the streets will be wet.
It has not rained.
<hr>
Therefore, the streets will not be wet.

(If this were valid, it would be logically impossible to wet the streets by hosing them. For the meaning of '-p', see section 6.12 on **negation**.)

(ii) **Fallacy of affirming the consequent**

An argument of the following form commits this fallacy:

If p then q
q
<hr>
∴ p

Example:

If it rains, then the streets will be wet.
The streets are wet.
<hr>
Therefore, it has rained.

See also section 5.1 on **confirmation** and **corroboration** and section 6.19 (**transposition fallacies**).

(iii) The names of these two fallacies are a little misleading. There is *nothing* fallacious about denying the antecedent of a conditional proposition.

What is fallacious is to use this denial as a premiss to 'prove' the falsity of the consequent. There is *nothing* fallacious about affirming the consequent of a conditional proposition. *What is fallacious* is to use this affirmation as a premiss to 'prove' the truth of the antecedent. So the two names are shorthand: 'Fallacy of denying the antecedent' is shorthand for 'Fallacy of denying the antecedent and, on that basis, denying the consequent.' 'Fallacy of affirming the consequent' is shorthand for 'Fallacy of affirming the consequent and, on that basis, affirming the antecedent.' See Flew, 1975, Ch. II; Shaw, 1981, Ch. III.

6.18 TRANSPOSITION

The Rule of Transposition states that: A proposition of the form (If p then q) is equivalent to (If -q then -p); e.g.:

'If it has been raining, then the streets will be wet', is equivalent to 'If the streets are not wet, then it has not been raining.'

Since that equivalence (i.e., mutual implication) holds, arguments of the following forms are valid:

If p then q	If -q then -p
∴ If -q then -p	∴ If p then q

Transposition is sometimes called **contraposition**. (If -q then -p) is the **contrapositive** of (If p then q). (This is related to, but not identical with contraposition in the traditional (see section 6.24) doctrine of immediate inference. See D. Mitchell, 1964, pp. 33–40.)

6.19 TRANSPOSITION (OR CONTRAPOSITION) FALLACIES

(i) The fallacy of **spurious transposition** is committed when someone argues thus:

> If p then q
> ∴ If q then p

Example:

> If Tom is a politician, then Tom is a human being.
> ∴ If Tom is a human being, then Tom is a politician.

(ii) The fallacy of **non-transposition** is committed when someone argues thus:

> If p then q
> ∴ If -p then -q

Example:　　　　　　　If Tom is a politician, then Tom is a human being.

∴　If Tom is not a politician, then Tom is not a human being.

6.20　DISJUNCTIVE SYLLOGISM

(a) In a disjunctive syllogism, one premiss is a disjunction and the other is a simple proposition (see sections 6.11, 6.8); e.g.:

'Either Tom stole the pearls or Dick stole the pearls.
Tom did not steal the pearls.

Therefore, Dick stole the pearls.'

(b) That is valid, but the following is valid ONLY IF the disjunctive premiss is an *exclusive disjunction*:

'Either Tom stole the pearls or Dick stole the pearls.
Dick stole the pearls.

Therefore, Tom did not steal the pearls.'

(c) The following are valid argument forms:

pvq	pvq	p≢q	p≢q	p≢q	p≢q
-p	-q	-p	-q	p	q
∴q	∴p	∴q	∴p	∴-q	∴-p

(d) The following are invalid argument forms (disjunctive fallacies):

pvq	pvq
p	q
∴-q	∴-p

(e) **Challenging a valid disjunctive syllogism**
The following is a valid argument:

'He is either drunk or under the influence of some other drug.
He is not drunk.

Therefore, he is under the influence of some other drug.'

A challenger might object on one of the following grounds:

(i)   The categorical premiss is false (i.e., the man is drunk).

(ii) The disjunctive premiss is false (i.e., the man is neither drunk nor under the influence of some other drug).

(iii) The disjunctive premiss *may* be true, but does not state all relevant possibilities and is, therefore, not known to be true.

If the challenger raises objection (iii), but not objection (i), he might say that the syllogism should read:

> 'He is either drunk or under the influence of some other drug or suffering from concussion or very tired.
> He is not drunk.
> _____
>
> Therefore, he is either under the influence of some other drug, or suffering from concussion or very tired.'

The challenger's syllogism has the form:

p v q v r v s
-p
_____
∴.q v r v s

6.21   CONDITIONAL SYLLOGISM (OR CHAIN ARGUMENT)

An argument whose premisses and conclusion are all conditional statements (see section 4.12). In a valid conditional syllogism, the antecedent of the conclusion is the antecedent of the first premiss and the consequent of the conclusion is the consequent of the final premiss. The simplest possible conditional syllogism has the form:

> If p then q
> If q then r
> _____
> Therefore, if p then r

E.g.:

> 'If it has rained, the streets are wet.
> If the streets are wet, they will be slippery.
> _____
> Therefore, if it has rained, the streets will be slippery.'

Argument of this kind is often called 'hypothetical syllogism', but, for reasons given in section 4.12, 'conditional syllogism' is a better label.

6.22　DILEMMA

A dilemma has two premisses: one is a conjunction of conditionals; the other is a disjunction involving either the antecedents or the consequents of those conditionals. There are four recognized valid types of dilemma:

(a) Simple constructive dilemma
(b) Complex constructive dilemma
(c) Simple destructive dilemma
(d) Complex destructive dilemma.

The 'constructives' are developed from *modus ponens*. The 'destructives' are developed from *modus tollens* (see section 6.17). 'Complexes' conclude with a disjunction. 'Simples' conclude either with a simple proposition or with the negation of one.

(a) **Simple constructive dilemma**

$$(\text{If } p \text{ then } q) \ \& \ (\text{If } r \text{ then } q)$$
$$\underline{p \lor r}$$
$$\therefore \quad q$$

Example:　If the University Council takes that decision, I will not resign, and if the University Council does not take that decision, I will not resign.
Either the Council will take that decision or it will not.

Therefore, I will not resign.

(Declaration of a well-known Australian logician during a controversy at his university. Strictly speaking, this is a dilemmatic *declaration*, rather than a dilemmatic *argument*, but it deserves to be in print.)

(b) **Complex constructive dilemma**

$$(\text{If } p \text{ then } q) \ \& \ (\text{If } r \text{ then } s)$$
$$\underline{p \lor r}$$
$$\therefore \quad q \lor s$$

Example:　If he spoke sincerely, he is a fool, and if he spoke insincerely, he is a rogue.
Either he spoke sincerely or insincerely.

Therefore, he is either a fool or a rogue.

(c) **Simple destructive dilemma**

$$(\text{If } p \text{ then } q) \ \& \ (\text{If } p \text{ then } r)$$
$$\underline{-q \lor -r}$$
$$\therefore \quad -p$$

Example:　If he were efficient, he would have sent

us a message, and if he were efficient, he would have organized a communications system that works.

Either he has not sent us a message or he has not arranged a communications system that works.

Therefore, he is not efficient.

(d) **Complex destructive dilemma**

(If p then q) & (If r then s)

-q v -s

∴   -p v -r

Example: If the Minister were aware of the existence of the document, he would have resigned. If the journalist were well-informed, he would know about the Minister's resignation.

Either the Minister has not resigned or the journalist does not know about the Minister's resignation.

Therefore, either the Minister is not aware of the existence of the document or the journalist is not well-informed.

(e) Those are valid dilemmatic forms. Invalid ones are also possible. They embody either the fallacy of *affirming the consequent* or the fallacy of *denying the antecedent* (see section 6.17).

There are also objections which can sometimes be used against *valid* dilemmas. These all involve questioning the adequacy of the premisses. They are discussed by logicians in a rather odd terminology. To begin with, the disjunctive premiss is called the **horns of the dilemma**, the notion being that the arguer is trying to impale his opponent on those horns. The opponent may, however, object that the disjunctive premiss does not cover all relevant alternatives. If the opponent makes this objection, he is trying **to escape between the horns of the dilemma**. If the opponent denies the truth of the premiss which is a conjunction of conditionals, he is **taking the dilemma by the horns**. If the opponent replies with another dilemma, the conclusion of which is inconsistent with the conclusion of the arguer's dilemma, he is trying to **rebut** the arguer's dilemma.

(f) In ordinary speech, someone who is in a situation which presents him with a choice between two unpalatable alternatives is said to be *in a dilemma* (e.g., 'Damned if you do and damned if you don't'). That is quite legitimate, but there is no point in using the word 'dilemma' merely as a 'learned' substitute for the words 'problem' or 'predicament'. It is fashionable (but not very clever) to use the title of a silly and sadistic but immensely successful novel as a substitute for the word 'dilemma' in its popular sense.

(g) An **aporia** is a situation in which there seem to be equally compelling reasons for asserting p and for denying p. The adjectival form of 'aporia' is '**aporetic**'. For an example, see section 9.6A (**akrasia**). See also section 4.18A (**paradox**).

(h) For more about dilemmatic arguments, see M. R. Cohen and Nagel, 1934, pp. 105–109.

6.23   LOGICAL FORM; GRAMMATICAL FORM; LOGICAL ANALOGY

A.   Logical form

This is a controversial and obscure, but very important notion. Consider these two arguments:

| Every Greek is human. | Every Dominican is a Roman Catholic. |
Socrates is a Greek.	Thomas Aquinas is a Dominican.
Therefore, Socrates is human.	Therefore, Thomas Aquinas is a Roman Catholic.

There are obvious differences between these two arguments. But there are only slightly less obvious similarities. Each argument says that:

> Every [something] is [a something else].
> [Someone] is [a something].
> _____
> Therefore, [Someone] is [a something else].

It is this kind of combination of difference and similarity that philosophers have in mind when they talk about the distinction between *the form* (or *structure*) of an argument or proposition and its *content* (or *matter*). See Flew, 1975, Ch. I, especially pp. 23–26. For something more advanced, see Strawson, 1952(b), Ch. II, Pt 2; Prior, 1962, Ch. I. See also section 6.2A.

B.   Logical form and grammatical form

Logical form and grammatical form do not always coincide. The point is made in a passage in Lewis Carroll's *Through the Looking Glass*:

> 'Who did you pass on the road?' the King [said] . . .
> 'Nobody,' said the Messenger.
> 'Quite right,' said the King: 'this young lady saw him too. So of course Nobody walks slower than you.'

'I do my best,' the Messenger said in a sullen tone. 'I'm sure nobody walks much faster than I do!'

'He can't do that,' said the King, 'or else he'd have been here first.'

(1974, p. 203)

There are three statements here containing the word 'nobody':

'I passed nobody on the road.'
'Nobody walks slower than you do.'
'Nobody walks much faster than I do.'

With these we can compare:

'I passed Jim on the road.'	'I passed Jack on the road.'
'Jack walks slower than you do.'	'Jim walks slower than you do.'
'Jim walks much faster than I do.'	'Jack walks much faster than I do.'

There are similarities between all three sets of statements, but the 'nobody' statements do not resemble the 'Jim' statements or the 'Jack' statements in the way that the 'Jim' statements and the 'Jack' statements resemble each other. The similarities in *verbal structure* mislead the King into thinking that there is a *similar pattern of implications*. The second 'Jim' statement is equivalent to 'There is someone, namely Jim, who walks slower than you do.' The second 'Jack' statement is equivalent to 'There is someone, namely Jack, who walks slower than you do.' And the King wrongly thinks that, therefore, the second 'nobody' statement is equivalent to 'There is someone, namely Nobody, who walks much faster than I do.' It is similarities and differences of those kinds that philosophers are getting at when they distinguish **logical form** from **grammatical form**.

The example is, of course, fantastic. But people have sometimes thought that because we can talk both of *the movement of a fieldsman* and of *the movement of time*, it must therefore make sense to talk of time moving backwards or sideways or with velocity. Some have thought that the word 'nothing' must refer to a strange and rather sinister *something*. There have been similar bothers about **reality** (see section 1.16A) and **existence** (see section 1.17). See also sections 1.26B (**possessive pronouns**), 1.2B(ii) (**rhetorical question**). See Heath, 1967; Ryle, 1932; Findlay, 1963(b); J. J. C. Smart, 1956.

C. Logical analogy

Suppose you have an argument:

p
<u>q</u>
∴ r

If the argument is valid (see section 4.9), the following combinations of truth-values (see section 1.3A) are possible:

p	q	r
true	true	true
true	false	true
true	false	false
false	true	true
false	true	false
false	false	true
false	false	false

If the argument is valid, the one combination of truth-values which is IMPOSSIBLE is:

p	q	r
true	true	false

It follows that an argument can be shown to be invalid if one can construct another argument with the same form in which *true* premises lead to a *false* conclusion. This is known as **refutation by logical analogy** (or more colloquially, as the **'you-might-as-well-say' counter**). (Logical analogy is not to be confused with **argument from analogy** which is something quite different – see section 8.19B.)

What one is saying in using logical analogy is 'If *that*'s a good argument, so is *this*, but *this* is obviously not a good argument', e.g.:

Primus: 'Admirers of Adolf Hitler are racists. Very few Australians are admirers of Adolf Hitler. Therefore, very few Australians are racists.'

Secundus: 'If that's a good argument, so is this: "Protestants reject the authority of the Pope. Very few Russians are Protestants. Therefore, very few Russians reject the authority of the Pope."'

If Primus thinks there is nothing wrong with the proposition that very few Russians reject the authority of the Pope, or if he thinks the premises in Secundus's analogue are false, Secundus's objection will be lost on him. Primus will have failed to *prove his point to* Secundus. See section 8.8A.

Refutation by logical analogy is a form of **quasi-reductio** (see section 8.8 C). See Flew, 1975, pp. 23–26; Geach, 1976, Chs IV, VI.

6.24   TRADITIONAL LOGIC

Traditional logic is sometimes called 'Aristotelian logic', but that is a misdescription, because it is very different in several important respects from the logic of Aristotle. The central theses of traditional logic are as follows:

(i) All propositions can be represented as categorical subject-predicate propositions (see sections 1.2A(v), 4.11).
(ii) Any proposition can be represented as having one of these four forms:

All S is P	(Universal affirmative)
No S is P	(Universal negative)
Some S is P	(Particular affirmative)
Some S is not P	(Particular negative)

(These are sometimes known respectively as the *A*, *E*, *I*, and *O* forms, 'E' and 'O' being the vowels in Latin '*nego*', 'I deny' and 'A' and 'I' being the first two vowels in '*affirmo*', 'I affirm'.)
(iii) Any argument for a conclusion can be represented as a categorical syllogism (see section 6.28). Some traditional logicians, however, regard disjunctive syllogisms as an exception to this.
(iv) No proposition is in logical form unless all its terms are 'real' (see section 6.29A(ix)).

Traditional logic is called 'traditional logic' for two reasons:
(1) because it has been taught for a long time;
(2) in order to distinguish it from **symbolic logic** (sometimes called 'modern logic') (see section 6.25).

The leading exponent of traditional logic in Australia was John Anderson (1893–1962). Most of his writings on logic are unfortunately still unpublished, but there are several papers on logical topics in Anderson, 1962. His logic is discussed by A. J. Baker, 1986, Ch. VI. Luce, 1958, gives a brief introductory exposition of the traditional system. See also Prior, 1967(b); Sinclair, 1951; D. Mitchell, 1964. Geach, 1972, pp. 44–61, attacks it vigorously – even violently. Prior, 1962, Pt II, gives a version of traditional logic which is more Aristotelian than the traditional versions of traditional logic are. See section 5.19A (**Procrustes**).

6.25 SYMBOLIC LOGIC

Logicians have always used symbols in their study of arguments because their interest is in underlying principles rather than in the subject-matter of arguments. (See section 6.23 on **logical form**.) So even traditional logic (see section 6.24) is 'symbolic' to some extent, but what is called 'symbolic logic' carries the symbolizing process much further. Rather as algebra uses letters instead of numerals, the different branches of symbolic logic use letters instead of sentences and instead of terms and words referring to classes and their members. There are three main branches of symbolic logic:

Propositional calculus concerns truth-functions of unanalysed simple propositions (see sections 6.5–6.15).

Predicate calculus concerns the internal structure of propositions and the relations between propositions with different internal structures.

Class calculus concerns the relations between classes and between classes and their members.

For an introduction to symbolic logic, see Copi, 1978, Chs VIII–X.

6.26   LOGIC, FORMAL AND INFORMAL

Logic is the study of relations of commitment, compatibility and incompatibility between propositions, and analogous relations between such non-propositional discourse-elements as imperatives and questions. Most attention has been given to propositional logic, though imperative and erotetic logics (see sections 1.5, 1.2B(i)) have not been entirely neglected. Logic is especially concerned with *argument* and with relations of *support* between *premisses* and *conclusions* (see sections 4.6, 4.8).

The starting point of logic is such familiar activities as conversing, arguing, wondering, enquiring, etc. (in short, thinking and talking). It can, however, be developed in different directions. One legitimate way of doing logic (and one with impressive achievements) concentrates on *implication* and *validity* as strictly defined (see sections 4.4, 4.9). This is called **formal logic**, because of its exclusive focus on *logical form* and its lack of interest in *content* or *matter* (see section 6.23). Formal logic is **deductive** logic (see section 5.13). It has affinities with mathematics.

Informal logic treats the familiar activities of arguing, wondering, enquiring, etc., not merely as its *starting point*, but as its *subject matter*. The informal logician adopts and adapts those techniques of formal logic which are likely to be useful, but makes no attempt to build a formal system. Informal logic, then, *might* be called 'applied logic' in contrast to the 'purity' of formal logic, but that way of talk obscures the fact that informal logicians have had to develop some techniques of their own for the critical analysis of arguments in **'natural language'** (as contrasted with the **artificial languages** of mathematics and formal logic). This century has been one of the great ages of formal logic, but those very achievements have revealed the need for a different approach to the critical analysis of 'natural-language' arguments. A good, quick way of getting a feel of the difference is to read one chapter of Prior, 1962 and one of Fisher, 1988. Informal logic does not ignore **deductive** (or **demonstrative**) support, but it is concerned with other forms of support as well (see sections 5.13, 8.12, 4.19B).

6.27 THE 'LAWS OF THOUGHT'

These are principles, traditionally regarded as fundamental to rational think-ing. I have used scare-quotes (1) because there is some controversy about one of them, and (2) because some people have been puzzled as to what sense the word 'law' can have here. (For **law**, see section 5.12; for **scare-quotes**, see section 1.6B(ii).)

These principles can be expressed either as principles about **predicates** (see section 1.9D) or as principles about **propositions** (see section 1.2A). In the following formulations, the letter 'A' is a *place-holding expression* for any predicate and the letter 'p' is a *place-holding expression* for any proposition (see section 6.2).

Law of Non-Contradiction

No statement can be both true and false; i.e.: -(p & -p).

Nothing can be both A and nonA.

Law of Identity

If any statement is true, it is true; i.e.: p implies p.

Whatever is A is A.

Law of Excluded Middle

Any statement is either true or false; i.e.: p v -p.

Everything is either A or nonA.

For some obscure reason, the Law of Non-Contradiction is sometimes called '**the Law of Contradiction**'. For the significance of the symbols '-', '&', and 'v', see sections 6.10–6.12. See Copi, 1978, pp. 4–5, 306–308; Angell, 1964, pp. 79–85; Flew, 1984, pp. 46, 115.

The controversial law is the Law of Excluded Middle. It looks obvious enough, but there are some tricky cases. In one of 'Michael Innes's' detective stories, someone knocks on a front door and asks the butler: 'Is Mr Tytherton at home?' The butler replies: 'Yes and no, sir.' On being asked to explain that strange utterance, he says that Mr Tytherton is in the house, but is unable to receive visitors because he has been shot dead (Stewart, 1978, p. 12).

It looks, in other words, as if the statement 'Mr Tytherton is at home' may be neither true nor false (or, at least, that, even with all relevant facts in our possession, we may be uncertain as to its truth-value (for **truth-value** see section 1.3A)). Similarly, *must* it be true that someone is *either* bald *or* non-bald? (think of a few examples; see Flew, 1975, p. 71); and what about 'The King of France in 1989 has a beard'? Is that either true or false? If Tom's only contact with Thai territory was half an hour in the transit lounge at Bangkok, can he honestly answer 'Yes' or 'No' to the question 'Have you ever been in Thailand?'? See Quine, 1987, pp. 55–57; Lacey, 1976, p. 63; Cohen and Nagel, 1934, pp. 181–187; N. Cooper, 1978.

(The Bangkok example is not as troublesome as it might seem. The proposition 'Tom has been in Thailand' is true, but it so barely satisfies the truth-conditions that the answer 'yes' without amplification would be misleading. Whether all bothersome cases can be so dealt with is another matter.)

6.28   SYLLOGISM, SYLLOGISTIC

(i) **Categorical syllogism**

A categorical syllogism is an argument, valid or invalid, in which a conclusion is drawn from two categorical (see section 4.11) premisses. Typically, each of these three propositions asserts that things of one kind also belong to another kind; e.g.:

> 'All human beings are mortal.
> All Greeks are human beings.
>
> Therefore, all Greeks are mortal.'

It is also possible to have a syllogism in which one of the premisses and the conclusion allot an *individual* person or thing to a kind; e.g.:

> 'All human beings are mortal.
> Socrates is a human being.
>
> Therefore, Socrates is mortal.'

To *put an argument into syllogistic form* is to *express it as a syllogism*. Categorical syllogisms are often simply called **syllogisms** and if the word 'syllogism' is used without qualification, it is usually safe to assume that **categorical syllogism** is meant. See Lacey, 1976, pp. 211–213; Flew, 1984, pp. 346–347.

(ii) **Modal syllogism**

A modal proposition is one which asserts that something is necessarily the case, possibly the case, etc. A modal syllogism is one which has at least one modal proposition as a premiss; e.g.:

> 'It is a necessary truth that cats are mammalian.
> Bartholomew is a cat.
>
> Therefore, Bartholomew is mammalian.'

See Lacey, 1976, pp. 132–136; Flew, 1984, p. 235.

(iii) **Syllogistic argument and non-syllogistic argument**

Here are two arguments which, in *some* respects, come to much the same thing:

Argument A	*Argument B*
'All human beings are mortal. Socrates is a human being.	'If Socrates is a human being, Socrates is mortal. Socrates is a human being.
Therefore, Socrates is mortal.'	Therefore, Socrates is mortal.'

They are not, however, identical: Argument A is a categorical syllogism, whereas Argument B is a *modus ponens* argument. Both arguments are valid, but, because of that difference, there is a difference in the ways in which validity can be shown. The component statements of Argument A (i.e., its premisses and conclusion) are also its component simple propositions; i.e., none of its component statements is a compound. The first premiss of Argument B is, however, a compound. The component *statements* of Argument B are, of course, its premisses and conclusion, but its component *simple propositions* are 'Socrates is a human being' and 'Socrates is mortal' (see section 6.9). Representing these as 'Y' and 'Z' respectively, we can symbolize the argument as:

If Y then Z.
Y
_____
∴Z

If we represent the component simple propositions of Argument A by S, T, and V respectively, we symbolize the argument as:

S
T
_____
∴V

Fairly obviously, the validity of Argument B is brought out by the symbolization, whereas the validity of Argument A is disguised by it. This difference is sometimes marked by calling arguments of the Argument A type **syllogistic arguments** or **syllogisms** and calling arguments of the Argument B type **non-syllogistic arguments**. These terms are defined as follows:

A syllogistic argument is one whose logical form or structure (see section 6.23) depends on the internal logical form or structure of its component simple propositions.

A non-syllogistic or truth-functional argument is one whose logical form or structure does not depend on the internal logical form or structure of its component simple propositions.

All that, while not madly exciting, is tolerably clear. Unfortunately, there are non-syllogistic argument-forms which logicians habitually refer to as *disjunctive syllogism* and *hypothetical syllogism* (see sections 6.20, 6.21). The habit is so deeply entrenched that all we can do is put up with it and remember that logicians are human. Non-syllogistic arguments are sometimes called 'truth-functional arguments', but that is a misnomer: it involves the error of treating all conditionals as truth-functional (see sections 6.8, 6.13).

6.29　STRUCTURE AND RULES OF THE TRADITIONAL SYLLOGISM; SOME SYLLOGISTIC FALLACIES

A.　Structure

(i) The traditional categorical syllogism consists of three propositions, all in subject-predicate form: two premises and a conclusion; e.g.:

> All human beings are mortal.
> All Greeks are human beings.

Therefore, all Greeks are mortal.

(ii) The subjects and predicates of the component propositions of the syllogism are the *terms* of the syllogism. The part of the verb 'to be' ('is', 'are') linking the subject and the predicate is known as the *copula*.

(iii) The words 'all' (or 'every'), 'no', 'some', and 'some ... not ...' indicate the *quality* and *quantity* of a proposition. These are sometimes called *quantifiers*, but *quanto-qualifiers* would be clearer.

(iv) A proposition which makes an assertion, either affirmative or negative, about all the members of the class of things referred to by the subject term is *universal in quantity*; e.g.:

> 'All Greeks are mortal.'
> 'No cows are carnivorous.'

(v) A proposition which makes an assertion, either affirmative or negative, about only some of the members of the class of things referred to by the subject term is *particular in quantity*; e.g.:

> 'Some Greeks are philosophers.'
> 'Some Greeks are not philosophers.'

(vi) Expressions of the form 'Some Xs' are treated as synonymous with expressions of the form 'At least one X'. Hence, 'Some Greeks are philosophers' is compatible (see section 10.2) with 'All Greeks are philosophers.'

(vii) A proposition which *affirms* that every member or some members of a class have a specified characteristic is *affirmative in quality*.

(viii) A proposition which *denies* that every member or some members of a class have a specified characteristic is *negative in quality*. (For the **four forms**, see section 6.24(ii).)

(ix) According to traditional logicians, all terms in a syllogism must be '*real*'. What this means is:

> (1) A term should occur in a syllogism only if it is assumed (see section 5.5C) that there are instances (see section 5.2A) corresponding to it.

AND

(2) A term should occur in a syllogism only if there are (or, perhaps, can be) instances NOT corresponding to it.

The second condition rules out such terms as 'beings', 'things' (see section 1.15), and 'existents'. The first condition rules out such terms as 'mermaids', unless we are prepared to assume that there are such things as mermaids. If that is too much to swallow, 'No mermaids wear spectacles' must be rephrased as 'No women are both fishtailed and bespectacled' (or, I suppose, 'No fish are both womantopped and bespectacled').

(x) A valid syllogism contains three and only three *terms* (i.e., the total number of different subjects and predicates in premisses and conclusion is three).

(xi) The term which is the predicate of the conclusion is called the **major term**.

(xii) The term which is the subject of the conclusion is called the **minor term**.

(xiii) The term which does not appear in the conclusion is called the **middle term**.[1]

(xiv) The premiss containing the major term is called the **major premiss**.

(xv) The premiss containing the minor term is called the **minor premiss**.

(xvi) A syllogism is to be arranged as follows:

> Major premiss
> Minor premiss
> ----
> ∴Conclusion

(xvii) A term immediately preceded by 'all' (or 'every'), 'no', or 'not' is said to be **distributed**. The predicate of any negative proposition is *distributed*. Other terms are said to be *undistributed*. For **fallacies of distribution**, see C below. (The concept of *distribution* is highly controversial. See Hamblin, 1970, pp. 195–196; Geach, 1962, Ch. I, and 1972, pp. 53–66; Quine, 1964. But this is the sort of philosophy which is For Mature Audiences Only.)

B. Rules of the syllogism

The following rules are designed to eliminate all *invalid syllogisms* (i.e., syllogisms of a form which would allow a false conclusion to be drawn from true premisses):

(1) The syllogism must have three and only three terms. Each must appear in two different positions.

(2) The middle term must be distributed at least once.

(3) A term which is distributed in the conclusion must be distributed in the premisses.

(4) No conclusion can be drawn from two negative premisses.

(5)   No conclusion can be drawn from two particular premisses.

(6)   If either premiss is negative, the conclusion must be negative.
See also Angell, 1964, Ch. II.

C.   Syllogistic fallacies

Syllogistic fallacies are breaches of the rules listed in (B).

  (i)   Breach of rule 1: **Fallacy of** Four Terms. See section 4.24.

 (ii)   Breach of rule 2: **Fallacy of** Undistributed Middle; e.g.:

> All fascists oppose Communism.
> All members of the Liberal Party oppose Communism.

Therefore, All members of the Liberal Party are Fascists.

This fallacy is a very common one. Flew (1975, pp. 25–26) says that, during the heyday of Senator Joseph McCarthy and the Committee on Un-American Activities, some called it '*The Un-American Fallacy*' because of the Senator's habit of labelling people as Communists because they held some views which Communists also held. Perhaps '**The McCarthyite Fallacy**' would be a suitable permanent label, provided that we remember that McCarthyism is not a vice peculiar to the Right.

(iii)   Breach of rule 3: **Fallacy of Illicit Process of the Major Term OR Fallacy of Illicit Process of the Minor Term (Illicit Major** or **Illicit Minor).**

The fallacy committed depends on *which* term distributed in the conclusion is undistributed in the premisses.

Example of Illicit Major:

> All ordinary men are fallible.
> Some scientists are not ordinary men.

Therefore, Some scientists are not fallible.

Example of Illicit Minor:

> All scientists are intelligent.
> No scientists are literary critics.

Therefore, No intelligent people are literary critics.

(iv)   Breach of rule 4: **Fallacy of Two Negative Premisses** (or **Fallacy of Exclusive Premisses**); e.g.:

> No Quakers are militarists.
> No Quakers are Anglicans.

Therefore, Some Anglicans are militarists.

 (v)   Breach of rule 5: **Fallacy of Two Particular Premisses**; e.g.:

Some socialists are pacifists.
Some Quakers are pacifists.

Therefore, Some Quakers are socialists.

(vi) Breach of rule 6: **Fallacy of Affirmative Conclusion, Negative Premiss**;
e.g.:

No freshwater fish are marine animals.
Some crustaceans are freshwater fish.

Therefore, Some marine animals are crustaceans.

D.

Fairly obviously, no one who has not studied logic is going to be very
impressed if you tell him that he has left his middle undistributed or performed
an illicit process of his major term. For this reason, the technique of **logical
analogy** is very important. See section 6.23C.

6.30   OPEN UNIVERSAL PROPOSITIONS AND CLOSED UNIVERSAL PROPOSITIONS

(i) The phrase 'universal proposition' is defined in section 1.10. There is
an important distinction between

universal propositions which either affirmatively or negatively predicate something of each of the members of an **open class**

and

universal propositions which either affirmatively or negatively predicate something of each of the members of a **closed class**.

A closed class has a finite number of members which can, in principle,
be enumerated. Thus, if I am standing in front of an aviary and I say
'Every bird in that aviary has black plumage,' I am talking about the
members of a closed class: there is a definite number of birds in the
aviary. We could give each of the birds a name and enumerate all the
members of the class (e.g., if there are five birds and we name them
Adam, Barbara, Claire, Dominic, and Edward, I could say: 'Every bird
in that aviary has black plumage, or to spell the matter out, Adam and
Barbara and Claire and Dominic and Edward all have black plumage').
But if I say 'Every raven has black plumage,' I am not talking about
the members of a closed class. The class *is not one whose members are
in principle enumerable*: I am talking about ravens who are dead, ravens
who are living, and ravens who are to be hatched; i.e., I am talking
about the members of an *open class*.

(ii) Notice a difference in the degree of 'risk' involved in the two propositions. Provided I have correctly observed each of the birds in the aviary and correctly described each of them, then I can be quite sure that my proposition is true. I might even say that I have proof of it, in a strict sense of 'proof' (see section 8.8). But no amount of careful observation can *prove* a proposition about all the members of an open class. No matter how careful I am, I cannot observe *correctly* each of the members of an open class, for the very good reason that I cannot *observe* each of the members of an open class. My assertion about the ravens ranges over all time and space. My assertion about the birds in the aviary ranges over a limited sector of time and space.

Granted accuracy of observation (an important proviso), a closed universal proposition can be verified. An open universal proposition cannot be *verified*, but it CAN be *falsified* (see section 5.1). *Any* observation of *any* non-black raven at *any* time or *any* place would refute my assertion about ravens. On the other hand, my assertion about the birds in the aviary applies only so long as (i) the membership of the class is unchanged and (ii) the character of each of the members of the class is unchanged.

If you show that I have overlooked a sulphur-crested cockatoo which is in the aviary with the five birds I have enumerated, then you have refuted my assertion. But if, after my assertion, you put a sulphur-crested cockatoo into the cage, or if one of the birds unaccountably turns green, my assertion is not refuted: it no longer applies. Thus there is a difference in *tense* between an open universal proposition and a closed universal proposition:

A closed universal proposition is in the **simple present tense**.

An open universal proposition is in the **timeless present tense**.

See also N. Smart, 1969, pp. 33–34 (paras 2.24–2.25), and Woozley, 1949, p. 94; Quine and Ullian, 1978, Ch. VIII.

6.31   EXISTENTIAL IMPORT

If (and only if) a proposition implies that something exists, then it has existential import. 'Implies' here has its strict technical sense. In other words, proposition p has existential import IFF there is some proposition of the form ' ... exists / existed / will exist' which *must* be true if p is true. 'Shakespeare was a dramatist' has existential import, because if it is true, 'Shakespeare existed' must also be true. Similarly, a proposition of the form 'Some poets are English' implies the existence of at least one poet. ('Some' is sometimes called an **existential quantifier** in contrast to the **universal** quantifier, 'All' or 'Every'.)

On the other hand, a proposition of the form 'Nothing is both an X and a non-Y' or 'If anything is an X, it is also a Y' can be true even if there is nothing corresponding to its terms. The proposition, therefore, lacks existential import. (For 'an X', read 'a dragon'. For 'a Y', read 'a fire-breathing serpent'.) If there is nothing corresponding to a term, that term is said to be *vacuous* or *empty*. Traditional logicians (see section 6.24) insist that a proposition can figure in a syllogism (see section 6.29) only if its terms are non-vacuous or non-empty. Symbolic logicians, on the other hand, insist that universal propositions have no existential import. In other words, they interpret 'All fowls have feathers' as 'Nothing is both a fowl and non-feathered' and 'No fowls read *The Herald*' as 'Nothing is both a fowl and a reader of *The Herald.*' Those propositions would be true if there were no fowls, no feathers, and no *Herald*. On this interpretation of universal statements, if there are no dragons, then 'All dragons breathe fire' and 'No dragons breathe fire' are both true.

There are actually good reasons why symbolic logicians should treat universal propositions in this seemingly perverse fashion. (See Shaw, 1981, pp. 146–149.) It is, nevertheless, true that none of us would regard a childless man who says 'All of my children are mathematical geniuses' as a teller of the truth. Existential import has *nothing* to do with existentialism, for which see section 7.14. For **ontological commitment**, see section 7.23.

7   Of isms, ists, and ologies

7.1   ISMS; ...IST AND ...ISTIC; ANGLOPHONE, FRANCOPHONE

A.   Isms and ists

Most 'ism' words denote bodies of doctrine, 'schools of thought', movements, parties, factions, etc. Some 'ism' words concern traits of character, physical or psychological syndromes, 'ways of living' ('heroism', 'cretinism', 'barbarism'). Others, says the *SOED* (rather desperately), are nouns 'of action, naming the process, or the completed action, or its result' ('aphorism', 'baptism', 'syllogism'). Most of the 'ism' words dealt with below are of the first type. Some 'isms' are discussed elsewhere. See the index entry, 'Philosophical movements'.

'Ism' words are often ambiguous (see especially sections 7.7 and 7.8 on **idealism** and **realism**) and, even when not ambiguous, present standing temptations to over-simplification. Philosophers rarely belong to disciplined, virtually unanimous movements. There *are*, of course, identifiable movements, but there is usually a great deal of variety and dissent within them. Philosophical ism-terms are useful and non-misleading *only* if that is remembered – hence the pejorative adjective 'ismistical' sometimes used to characterize those introductions to philosophy which discuss problems in terms of what '*the* empiricist', '*the* rationalist', '*the* idealist', etc., have to say about them. See Ryle, 1971(b), pp. 153–169.

B.   ...ist and ...istic

For some odd reason, the '...istic' form of an 'ist' adjective often (though not always) has a pejorative ring. 'Realistic' is not pejorative, but a socialist would never call his own ideas socialistic unless he was doing a parody of his opponents. Cf. section 9.7B (**casuist, casuistic**). See R. Williams, 1983, pp. 173–174.

C. Anglophone, Francophone

These two odd-looking words were originally introduced to distinguish those African countries which use English as an official language from those which use French. They can be more generally useful. Not all who do philosophy in English are English and, sometimes, an attempt is made to recognize this fact by talking about 'Anglo-Saxon philosophy'. But 'Anglo-Saxon' is an offensively inappropriate term to apply to Scots like Hume and Anderson and to British subjects with names like *Popper, Wittgenstein,* and *Waismann.*

7.2 DOGMA; DOCTRINE; DOCTRINAIRE; IDEOLOGY

A. Dogma, dogmatic, dogmatist

'Dogma' is derived not from the Latin '*docere*' ('to teach') but from the Greek '*dokein*' ('to be acceptable'), so (it has been said) 'dogmas are the tenets on which a school or party are agreed' (Waugh, 1962, pp. 202–203).

Quite so. But, as such tenets are sometimes put forward intolerantly and without argument, the words 'dogma', 'dogmatic', 'dogmatist' have also acquired derogatory senses. It does not follow that, because something is a **dogma** in the *neutral* sense outlined by Waugh, it must also be **a dogma** in the *derogatory* sense. Some philosophers of a **sceptical** (see section 7.3A) tendency have a habit of calling all non-sceptics **dogmatists** or **dogmatic philosophers**. But that is a question-begging habit (see section 4.23). Sceptics need to *prove* that non-sceptics are wrong and applying a label is not the same as a proof. 'Non-sceptic' is an appropriate term for a non-sceptic. See section 4.30 (**fallacy of pseudo-refuting description**).

B. Doctrine, doctrinal

A doctrine is *a teaching, a thesis, a proposition which someone or some group of people professes and maintains.* 'Doctrinal' is the adjectival form of 'doctrine'. Pronounce it either as 'dokTRYnel' or as 'DOKtrinel'. Please note the spelling: 'doctrine', not 'doctorine'. For **theory**, see section 5.5D.

C. Doctrinaire

'Doctrinal' means 'Of, like or pertaining to doctrine'. Raymond Williams (1983, pp. 108–109) seems to suggest that 'doctrinaire' is *nothing but* a derogatory version of 'doctrinal'; i.e., if your doctrine differs from mine, 'doctrinal' is the word I use for mine and 'doctrinaire' is the word I use for yours (with a sneer).

'Doctrinaire' *is* derogatory, but things are not quite as simple as Williams says. To say that Mr X is doctrinaire is not *merely* to say that Mr X holds mistaken doctrines; it is to say EITHER that Mr X holds doctrines regardless of arguments or evidence to the contrary OR that Mr X seeks to impose or apply those doctrines regardless of the consequences. (Thus one could hold *true* doctrines and still be doctrinaire.) So 'doctrinaire' is not merely a derogatory version of 'doctrinal'. Cf. section 7.7 (**idealist**) and D below (**ideological**).

D. Ideology, ideological

The first thing to say about these dreadful (or, perhaps, sadly mistreated) words is negative: *'Ideology' is not a mere fancy substitute for 'opinion', 'belief', 'attitude', 'theory'*. In the most general meaning of the word, an ideology is a system or cluster of norms and propositions (usually of a very general or high-level kind; e.g., on the nature and destiny of man) which functions as a justification for a way of life, system of social organization, programme of action, etc. Cf. section 5.9 (**worldview, *Weltanschauung***).

The ideological can be contrasted with **the pragmatic** or **the practical**. Primus and Secundus are rival candidates for office. The conflict between them may be merely a matter of who is more likely to do a job (conceived of by both in virtually identical terms) with optimum efficiency. On the other hand, the conflict between Primus and Secundus may be a conflict between two views of how society should be organized, two views of what the goals of society should be, two views of what sort of creature man is and what sort of place the universe is. To the extent that a conflict is of the first type, to that extent it is pragmatic or practical. To the extent that a conflict is of the second type, to that extent it is ideological.

The ideological can also be contrasted with **matters of material interest**. Primus and Secundus may be in conflict merely because each wants the same thing and satisfying the desire of one means the disappointment of the other. (The thing may be anything from a lollipop to global hegemony.) On the other hand, they may be in conflict because each holds a different worldview. To the extent that a conflict is of the first type, it is a conflict of material interests. To the extent that a conflict is of the second type, to that extent it is ideological.

'Ideological' sometimes has a pejorative ring:

(1) It can be used to complain of an *excessive* stress on the highly general and theoretical and a neglect of the pragmatic and of matters of material interest. The complaint may be either a complaint about *impracticality* or a complaint about *fanaticism* (or both). (Cf. sections 7.7 (**idealist**) and C above.)

(2) The other pejorative use focuses on the function of justifying ways of life, forms of social organization, etc. 'Merely ideological' is used as an accusation that a theory (or doctrine, or value, or ...) is a mere **rationalization**. It is held, not because there are or seem to be good reasons for believing it to be satisfactory, but because it gives support to certain material interests or forms of social organization. See section 10.7 (**relevant**).

The latter use is often found in the discourse of Marxists, though it is not restricted to them. See R. Williams, 1983, pp.153–157; Christenson *et al.*, 1972; Nisbet, 1982, pp. 179–183; Plamenatz, 1970; Marx, 1963, pp. 17–43, 67–101, 169–174; Singer, 1980; Seliger, 1976.

7.3 SCEPTICS; AGNOSTICS; SOLIPSISTS; NIHILISTS; SOPHISTS

A. Sceptic, sceptical, scepticism

The Greek word '*skeptikos*' originally meant *enquirer*, but it soon acquired the additional sense of *doubter*. In technical philosophical usage, a **sceptic** is usually one who *denies the possibility of knowledge*, either in general (a logically awkward position to take – see section 3.1 on **self-refutation**) or in some particular area (e.g., someone might be a sceptic about knowledge of other minds, or knowledge about the past, or the senses, etc.). See Ayer, 1956, Ch. II; Chipman, 1977; Unger, 1976.

To deny the possibility of knowledge either generally or in some particular area is to take an **epistemic** or **epistemological** (see section 7.24) position, a position of **epistemic scepticism**. Notice that the epistemic sceptic does not question the notion of **truth**. Rather, he tends to take it for granted. His arguments are usually for the conclusion that we have no clear way of telling *which* of two incompatible propositions *is* true; e.g., 'Either I am dreaming or I am not dreaming, but I have no way of deciding which.' The epistemic sceptic's challenge is not: 'Is there any truth?' or '*What* is truth?' but '*Which* are truths?'

There is a far more radical kind of scepticism: a scepticism which maintains *either* that the notion of truth does not make sense, *or* that a proposition is true IFF some group of people or some individual person think it is true, etc. This kind of scepticism can be called **alethic scepticism**. (The Greek for 'truth' is '*aletheia*'.) Alethic scepticism *is* radical and it is very dramatic-sounding. It does, however, run into some logical difficulties (e.g., 'There are no real truths.' 'Really? Are you sure?' 'Of coure, it's obviously true.'). See a very elegant little argument by Alasdair MacIntyre (1964, p. 512, col. 2, paragraph beginning: 'If I hold that truth is subjectivity . . .'). See also section 1.3B **(truth)**.

Sometimes, someone who is not prepared to take propositions for granted is called **sceptical**. It would be more appropriate to call such a person **critical** (section 8.1A). Scepticism needs also to be distinguished from **fallibilism**. A sceptic maintains that no claim to know that p is the case is justifiable unless p is established beyond any possibility of doubt. A fallibilist maintains that proof beyond reasonable doubt is sufficient, and that, therefore, even the most reasonable knowledge-claims are subject to the possibility of revision. See Flew, 1984, p. 119. See also section 8.7 **(academic)**.

B.   Agnosticism

The **gnostics** of the first two centuries AD claimed to have received a special revelation which gave them knowledge (*gnosis*) of God and ultimate truth. T. H. Huxley (1825–1895) coined the word '**agnosticism**' as a label for the contention that knowledge of God and ultimate truth is impossible. The 'a-' here means 'not' or 'without' as in 'apolitical'. See Dockrill, 1971(a), 1971(b).

C.   Solipsism

(i)   '*Solus*' is Latin for 'alone': '*Ipse*' is Latin for 'himself'. A **solipsist** is someone who believes that he alone exists. Solipsists are rather rare creatures (and, if solipsism is true, they are very rare indeed). Solipsism is less important as a *theory* than it is as a *challenge*. The epistemic sceptic does not assert that solipsism is *true* (if he did, he would cease to be a sceptic), but he does want to know what reasons there are for saying that solipsism is *not* true. It is also sometimes argued that a theory which holds that the immediate objects of experience are *ideas* or *sense-data*, or some other 'mind-dependent' thing implies solipsism and is therefore false. See Flew, 1984, p. 330; Rollins, 1967.

(ii)   Scepticism about (or even denial of) the existence of *other minds* is a marginally less *outré* form of solipsism: 'How can I know that there are any other conscious beings, that what seem to be conscious beings are not all automata?' Philosophers of **behaviourist** (see section 7.11) outlook often end up in that mess. See Ayer, 1954, Ch. VIII; J. L. Austin, 1979, pp. 76–116; Wisdom, 1965.

(iii)   'Are there any solipsists in this department?' a philosopher visiting an Australian university once asked one of his hosts. 'No theoretical ones, but several practical ones,' was the reply. 'Egomism' is a rare synonym of 'solipsism'.

D.   Nihilism

'*Nihil*' is Latin for 'nothing' so a nihilist would seem to be a **nothingist**. But that is not very illuminating. The word 'nihilism' is used in two rather different senses today:

(i)   It is sometimes used to mean the state of mind in which nothing whatsoever seems to matter or to be of any value at all. That, I think, is more of a pathological condition than a theory. But to say that is not to say that people who take a nihilist view can just be written off as 'sick'.

(ii)   'Nihilism' (or 'moral nihilism') is sometimes used as a family name for theories which deny or doubt that moral standards – ANY moral standards – have rational foundations. (This attitude is sometimes called **moral scepticism**.)

For two different views on this, see Bambrough, 1979, and Mackie, 1977. See also Macquarrie, 1973, pp. 31–33, 55–57, 206–219; Gibbs, 1976, Ch. VIII. **Nothing** and **nobody** are discussed in section 6.23B. For 'nihilism' as a political term, see Scruton, 1983, p. 324.

E. Sophists

The Greek word is '*sophistes*', literally 'practitioner of wisdom'. In the latter half of the fifth century BC, it was used to refer to the professional itinerant teachers, so numerous at that time. They were a mixed lot. Most professed to teach *rhetoric*, the art of public speaking and persuasion (see section 8.4A). That art can be used with a scrupulous regard for truth and it can be used quite unscrupulously. Not all Sophists were scrupulous. Not all were unscrupulous. Some were simply clever charlatans. Some were serious enquirers. Many had a tendency towards epistemic and/or moral scepticism (see sections A and D above). Even those who did not seemed, in the eyes of many, to be very subversive, nihilistic characters, simply because they had a habit of asking awkward questions. See Copleston, 1947, Ch. XII; W. K. C. Guthrie, 1950(a), Ch. IV, and 1971(b), which is a very thorough study of the Sophists.

The Sophists acquired the reputation of being too clever by half, of being able to produce clever-looking arguments for any proposition whatsoever, and of tying honest people in intellectual knots either for profit or just for fun. Hence, 'sophistry' or 'sophism' can mean *a convincing looking but logically unsound argument*, or *a specious argument* (see section 8.18B), and the word 'sophist' can mean something very much like *intellectual crook*. See also section 8.17(iii) (**plausible**). 'Sophism' can also mean *paradoxical argument* (see section 4.18A). For *sophismata* as a topic of mediaeval logic, see Hamblin, 1970, Chs II, III.

7.4 PLATONIC, PLATONISM, PLATONIST; ARISTOTELIAN

A.

(a) In philosophical talk, '**Platonic**' usually means *of, like, or pertaining to Plato and/or his work*. The popular meaning of 'non-sexual' (in such phrases as 'Platonic love') is derived from a rather hazy understanding of Plato's dialogue, *The Symposium*.

(b) **Platonism**
   (i) Plato's philosophy in general. See Flew, 1984, pp. 268–272.
   (ii) That part of Plato's philosophy which asserts the independent existence of certain abstract entities (see sections 1.10A(ii), 1.11(iii), 1.13A).
   (iii) A general tradition of philosophy which developed from Plato's philosophy and which tends to agree with Plato and to dissent from Aristotle on various important points. (See Copleston, 1947, pp. 260–262; A. H. Armstrong, 1961, and 1965 – see index; Merlan, 1975.)

(iv) All theories which assert the independent existence of any abstract entities, however different some of these theories may be from Plato's. See Flew, 1984, pp. 223–224; Quinton, 1977(f).

(c) **Platonist**
  (i) A follower of Plato.
  (ii) Someone who specializes in the study of Plato (whether or not he agrees with him).
  (iii) Anyone who holds a theory of the independent existence of abstract entities (see section 1.11(iii)).

B.   Aristotelian; peripatetic

(a) **Aristotelian, Aristotelean**
Of, like, or pertaining to the work of the Greek philosopher, Aristotle (384–322 BC). Either spelling is acceptable, though (outside the United States) 'Aristotelian' has a slight edge over 'Aristotelean'. For a brief outline of Aristotle's philosophy, see Ackrill, 1975, or Copleston, 1947, Pt IV.

(b) **Peripatetic**
'*Peripatetikos*' is the Greek for 'having the habit of walking about'. According to one story, Aristotle had the habit of walking up and down while lecturing or conducting a discussion. According to another story, the place where he taught, the Lyceum, was also called *the Peripatos* or *covered walk*. Either way, the **peripatetic philosophy** is Aristotle's philosophy and the **peripatetics** are his followers, particularly the ancient ones.

7.5   CYNICISM; STOICISM

A.   Cynicism

The original **cynic** was Diogenes who flourished in the fourth century BC (and was probably influenced by Antisthenes, one of the companions of Socrates). The modern sense of 'cynic' is 'one disposed to deny and sneer at the sincerity and goodness of human motives and actions' (*SOED*). Diogenes was disposed to sneer at most things, but 'cynic' is derived from the Greek for 'dog' and Diogenes was nicknamed *the dog* because of his alarming interpretation of the imperative 'Follow nature'. The ideal of Diogenes and his followers was *self-sufficiency* which they interpreted as entailing the rejection of all convention. They did not, however, withdraw from society. They were too fond of defying convention to want to do it without a shocked audience.

If **philosophy** is a matter of critical, argumentative investigation of ideas, then cynicism was hardly a philosophy at all. Diogenes and his followers made lots of rude noises but they showed no great interest in investigation and no great skill in argument. They were **critical** only in the sense that they continually disapproved. (For **criticism** and **argument** see sections 8.1A, 4.6.) Cynicism was a **philosophy** only in the semi-slang sense of *way of life, attitude to life*. For more information, see Finley, 1972, pp. 88–98, and Kidd, 1975(a), (c), (d).

B.   Stoicism

Stoicism began a little later than Cynicism, being founded by Zeno of Citium at the end of the fourth century BC. Like the Cynics, the Stoics advocated '*following nature*' and *self-sufficiency*, but were considerably more reflective and theoretical. Self-sufficiency was a matter of putting no reliance in what was beyond human control. Happiness was primarily a matter of having the correct attitude of mind, of knowing what was to be feared and what was not, and of accepting the cosmos (see section 1.10D) as a rational (if not fully intelligible) system.

There is an obvious connexion between these beliefs and the modern use of the word 'stoical' to mean (roughly) *self-controlled and unworried by misfortune*. Oddly enough, this is the first thing that comes to many people's minds when they hear the word 'philosophical'. The same people often expect professional philosophers to be particularly good at maintaining such an attitude. That expectation is frequently disappointed. Stoicism was more than a mere 'way of life' and some of the Stoics made important contributions to the development of logic. See Kidd, 1975(b); Kneale and Kneale, 1962, Ch. III; R. G. Tanner, 1982; K. Campbell, 1985. 'Stoic' is pronounced 'sto-ik'.

7.6   SCHOLASTIC PHILOSOPHY; SCHOLASTICISM; THOMISM; NEO-THOMISM

A.   Scholastic philosophy, scholasticism

 (i) These labels are applied to mediaeval European philosophy. The mediaeval European philosophers are sometimes called *the schoolmen*. See Wuellner, 1956, p. 112; Copleston, 1972.

 (ii) The labels also have a narrower use in which they are applied to the philosophy of St Augustine, St Thomas Aquinas, and their followers. In this sense, one can speak of *twentieth-century scholasticism* (e.g. the work of Etienne Gilson and Jacques Maritain).

(iii) Mediaeval philosophy, like anything else, had its bad periods. Because of this and because of the work of various not-too-scrupulous propagandists, the word 'scholasticism' is sometimes used as a term of reproach. In this pejorative sense, to accuse someone of scholasticism is to accuse him of a concern with spurious problems, of indulging in hair-splitting and spurious subtlety and various similar faults.

To suppose that such faults characterized the whole of mediaeval philosophy is like judging English poetry on the basis of singing commercials.

B.   Thomism

The philosophy of St Thomas Aquinas (1225–1274). For brief discussions of St Thomas's life and thought, see Gilby, 1975; Copleston, 1950, Chs XXXI–XLI; Kenny, 1980. The first syllable of Thomism rhymes with 'home', not with 'bomb'. The 'h' is pronounced as in 'Thomas'. A **Thomist** (or **Thomistic**) doctrine is one put forward by St Thomas Aquinas (or sometimes a doctrine based on what he put forward). To call someone a **Thomist** is to say that he is a follower of St Thomas. In most library catalogues, entries for books by and about St Thomas will be found under 'T', not under 'A', as 'Aquinas' is not a surname but a description (the Thomas who comes from Aquino, as distinct from other Thomases). Every now and then, I read a student's essay in which reference is made to 'Sir Thomas Aquinas'. Thomas's name would be an adornment to any Royal Honours List, but it has never appeared in one. He was not a knight. If you don't like calling him 'St', just call him 'Thomas Aquinas'. See also sections 5.12B (**natural law**), 8.20–8.21 (**creation; existence of God**).

C.   Neo-Thomism

'Neo-Thomist' sometimes simply means 'a modern Thomist'. But sometimes it can also mean a person who, though basically a Thomist, is engaged in the enterprise of bringing St Thomas up to date. See Hawkins, 1975; Pieper, 1957(b), pp. 77–112. Jacques Maritain, a distinguished modern follower of St Thomas, has some rather irritable things to say about the word 'Neo-Thomism' (Maritain, 1958, pp. 15–23).

7.7   IDEALISM

(i) A very obscure word. Popular senses of the word relate it to **ideals**, i.e., *standards, norms*, etc. Philosophic senses relate it to **ideas**, but, as 'idea' is an extremely ambiguous word (see section 1.9C), philosophic talk about 'idealism' can fall short of that crystalline clarity which many regard as a philosophic ideal.

(ii) In non-philosophic talk, saying that someone is an idealist may mean one (or more) of the following:

that he has high ideals;

that he endeavours to follow his ideals, to put them into practice, to **realize** them (in the sense of making them real);

that he endeavours to realize his ideals regardless of the consequences such an endeavour might have;

that he has a readiness to assume that ideals are realized.

Thus, calling someone an **idealist** (in the popular sense of an *ideal-ist*) may or may not be complimentary. See sections 7.2C, D (**doctrinaire, ideological**).

(iii) In philosophic talk, 'an idealist' means 'an *idea-ist*', which, as remarked above, does not pin the word down very firmly. An idealist may be someone who holds that reality (i.e., whatever exists) is, in *some* way, spiritual or mental or non-material, or dependent for its existence on being perceived by a mind. The word is also used to characterize positions which stress the interconnectedness and/or interdependence of all existing things. Sometimes, 'idealist' is primarily a contrast-drawing word: a position may be said to be idealist because it rejects some form of **realism** or some form of **materialism** (thus, some Marxists have a way of labelling all non-Marxist philosophers as idealists). 'Realism' and 'materialism' are themselves highly ambiguous terms (see sections 7.8, 7.9). Thus, a doctrine which is idealist from one point of view may be non-idealist or even anti-idealist from another. 'Idealism' (like most 'ism' words) is messy and should be handled with care. See Quinton, 1977(d); Ewing, 1975; R. Williams, 1983, pp. 152–153; Sprigge, 1984, pp. 56–76.

7.8   REALISM, REALIST

(i) These are perfectly dreadful words which should be used with great caution (cf. **idealism**, section 7.7).

A realist theory of **universals** (see section 1.10A(ii)) is one which (like Plato's theory of forms – see section 1.13A) holds that universals exist (in some way or other) independently of human beings and are not to be identified with concepts, words, or linguistic conventions. (See Wuellner, 1956, p. 105.)

A realist theory of **perception** holds that what is perceived exists independently of being perceived. (See Lacey, 1976, pp. 154–156.)

A realist theory of **science** (i.e., a **scientific realism**) holds that the unobservable entities mentioned in scientific theories are (if the theories are true) objects which exist independently of the theories and are not mere useful fictions. (See Hesse, 1967. See also section 5.12D.)

Et cetera, et cetera.

Quite clearly, one can be a realist on one of these matters and a non-realist on another. Plato's theory of forms makes him a realist with respect to universals (indeed, makes him an *extreme* realist), but, since the forms are non-material, intellectible entities of which material objects are mere manifestations, the theory of forms also makes him **an idealist** (see section 7.7). See Hirst, 1967; Devitt, 1984, pp. 11–122; Lacey, 1976, pp. 180–181, 154–156; R. Williams, 1983, pp. 257–262;

Putnam, 1976; L. Stevenson, 1983; R. Walker, 1983.

(ii) **Naive realism**

In everyday speech, to say that someone is a **realist** is often to praise him, while calling him 'naive' is usually the reverse. That being so, 'naive realist' might sound highly paradoxical. Actually, it is neither praise nor blame. **Naive realism** is the view that we perceive objects directly and as they are. I have even heard quite sophisticated philosophers describe *themselves* as naive realists. See sections 1.15B(iv), 1.16A (**material object, real**).

(iii) **'Australian realism'**

Andersonianism (see section 7.12G) has recently been given that title (A. J. Baker, 1986). Not every Australian philosopher who regards himself as a realist is delighted.

7.9 MATERIALISM

Another grossly ambiguous word.

A. Vulgar materialism

A person whose only or ruling interests are money, power, physical comfort and pleasure, and worldly success might be called a **materialist**, someone with **a materialistic outlook**, etc. Materialism, in this sense, is a matter of interests, goals, values, 'attitudes to life', etc.: **vulgar materialism**. There are, however, other senses of the word and someone who is a materialist in one of those other senses need not be a vulgar materialist. Indeed, a vulgar materialist would probably reject all philosophy as a silly waste of time and a materialist in one of the philosophic senses of the word would reject such vulgar materialism as anti-intellectual. Unfortunately, some controversialists confuse philosophical materialism with vulgar materialism, talking as if rejection of the latter necessitated rejection of the former. Such confusion may be honest or dishonest, but, either way, is highly regrettable. See Stebbing, 1948, Ch. II.

B. Philosophical materialism

As Flew remarks, it is easier to say what philosophical materialists deny than what they positively assert (1984, pp. 222–223). They deny the existence of such things as Plato's forms (see section 1.13A), gods and spirits, minds except as entirely dependent on brains-and-nervous-systems, etc. That does not imply that philosophical materialists are rather vague or 'merely negative'; what it implies is that there are many different ways of being a philosophical materialist. (Lycan and Pappas (1972, pp. 149–151) give neat and helpful characterizations of some ways of being materialist about the mind.) The following are amongst the more important materialisms:

(i) **Atomist materialism**

The doctrine that the basic constituents of reality are fundamental material particles. All that is and all that happens consists of arrangements and rearrangements of such particles. Such theories were developed by some of the ancient Greeks, the first atomist probably being Leucippus of Miletus who flourished in the mid-fifth century BC. Modern atomism began in the seventeenth century as an attempt to make the physics of Galileo a complete theory of reality. Hobbes (1588–1679), La Mettrie (1705–1751), and Holbach (1723–1789) are exponents of this form of philosophy.

Contemporary physics is, of course, immensely more complicated than the physics of Galileo. Atomism, however, has its counterpart in **physicalist** ontologies (for **ontology**, see section 7.23). Briefly and crudely, a physicalist ontology is one which maintains that reality as studied by the physicist is all the reality there is. It is, however, not easy to arrive at a non-controversial characterization of reality-as-studied-by-the-physicist. (There is (or was) a kind of physicalism which rests on adherence to Verificationism (see section 5.4; Acton, 1975). Few who now call themselves physicalists would be happy if tarred with that brush.)

On **atomism**, see Flew, 1984, p. 30; J. Burnet, 1964, pp. 76–81, 157–164. On **physicalism**, see D. M. Armstrong, 1980, pp. 149–165.

(ii) **Reism** is the doctrine that 'the fundamental constituents of the world are material bodies in space and time' and that, therefore 'essences can be interpreted in terms of language and behaviour, experiences as states of the brain, the theoretical entities of science as material bodies or as constructions out of them, and values in terms of the responses of sensitive organisms' (Quinton, 1973(a), pp. 10–11). For **material body** see section 1.15B(iv).[1]

(iii) **Eliminativist materialism**

If you find someone saying things which imply that 'There is no such thing as consciousness; people only think there is', then you have encountered an eliminativist materialist. See R. Rorty, 1970; Quine, 1976, Chs XXI, XXII, and 1987, pp. 132–134; Cornman, 1968; D. M. Armstrong, 1980, pp. 55–67; Popper, 1983 – see index ('consciousness'). See also section 5.20 (**reductivism**).

(iv) **The identity theory of mind (central state materialism)**

The doctrine that there are mental events and that they are identical with states of the brain and the nervous system. On this theory, talk in terms of thoughts, feelings, etc., and talk in terms of states of the brain and the nervous system describe the same things, but are not identical in meaning. (Cf. section 2.10A on **sense and reference** and section 1.21A(iii) on **contingent identity**.) The leading exponents of this theory are Australians (D. M. Armstrong and J. J. C. Smart) and it is jocularly called *The Australian Heresy*. See D. M. Armstrong, 1980, pp. 1–67; K. Campbell, 1970, Ch. V; Borst, 1970. The identity theory is a **revisionist** reductivism (section 5.20).

(v) **Historical (or economic) materialism** is the Marxist doctrine that human history and human thought (including religion, philosophy, art, etc.) are the product of **material processes and conditions** (i.e., the way in which economic production, distribution, and exchange are organized). See Marx, 1963, pp. 67–81, and 1973, especially Ch. VI; Mills, 1963, Chs I–VI; Acton, 1955.

(vi) **Dialectical materialism** is a development of historical materialism for which Marx's friend, Friedrich Engels is chiefly responsible. See Doniela, 1974; Gregor, 1965, Ch. II; Hook, 1955; Kharin, 1981. See also section 10.3 (**contradiction**).

In contemporary Anglophone philosophical parlance, 'materialism' is usually short for 'psychological materialism' (see (iii) and (iv) above). An opponent of such materialism will almost certainly be (or be accused of being) a **psychological dualist** of some kind (see section 7.10).

7.10   DUALISM, DUALIST

A.   General

To take a **dualist** view of X is to take the view that X is composed of two fundamentally distinct elements. To take a dualist view of X and Y is to take the view that X and Y are fundamentally two distinct things. Thus, to take a dualist view of *knowledge and belief* is to regard them as two quite distinct 'acts of the mind' (as opposed to regarding knowledge as belief which is 'successful' in a special kind of way – see section 8.13A, 8.14A on Ryle's important distinction between **achievement words** and **task words**). Plato's theory of the intelligible world of the forms and the sensible world of particulars may be described as a **dualist view** of reality (see sections 1.13A, 7.4A). Descartes's view of **substance** is also dualistic: substance is either **extended** or **thinking**, and the two are radically different. See Copleston, 1958, Ch. IV; Vesey, 1974(a), Chs VI–VII; Sprigge, 1984, pp. 13–33.

B.   Dualism, monism, pluralism

Quinton, 1977(b), lists five kinds of dualism, and that is a selection. Where a **dualist**-about-X asserts that X is composed of *two* fundamentally distinct elements, a **monist** asserts that X fundamentally consists of just one element, and a **pluralist** says that they are both wrong: X consists of elements of things of many kinds. (According to Professor Michael Tooley, a philosophical sexist maintains that there are six and only six basic kinds of thing.)

In politico-social theory, 'pluralism' has a variety of meanings:

'Pluralism' can mean the condition of a society in which there is no single power elite, so that power is shared and rotated amongst varying groups.

'Pluralism' can mean the condition of a society in which no single worldview is dominant and in which the existence of a variety of opinions and ways of life is not merely tolerated but accepted as desirable.

'Pluralism' can mean the belief that one or both of the above are desirable.

('Plural society', however, is a much broader term than 'pluralist society'.

It covers not merely societies of the kind sketched above, but also such ruinously 'two-nation' societies as Northern Ireland, South Africa, and Lebanon.)

C. Psychological dualism

More often than not, when a philosopher writes 'dualism', he means **psychological dualism, dualism about the psychophysical constitution of human beings, dualism about mind and body**.

Those three 'expansions' of the term 'dualism' are synonymous, but there is an ambiguity about 'dualism' in this sense:

(1) A dualist theory may be any theory which denies that the mental can be reduced to the physical (see section 5.20); i.e., any theory which asserts that any attempt to give an account in purely physical terms of what it is to be a human person must be incomplete and unsatisfactory. (See Shaffer, 1968, Chs III–IV.)

(2) 'Psychological dualism' can also mean any theory which asserts not just that mind and body are distinct, but also that a human being considered as a psychophysical thing is really two things, a mind (or soul) *and* a body, and that the mind (or soul) is to be identified as the human person, the body being, as it were, a mere container or instrument. Thus, St Augustine (354–430) described man as 'a rational soul using a mortal and earthly body' and as 'a certain substance participating in reason and fitted for ruling a body' (quoted, Copleston, 1955, pp. 151–152). Plato is a dualist in this sense (see his dialogue, *Phaedo*) and Descartes is generally regarded as one also (which he is most of the time, but see *Meditation VI* (Descartes, 1954, p. 117, or 1986, pp. 134–135)).

Notice that a theory which is **dualist in sense (2)** must also be **dualist in sense (1)**, but a theory which is **dualist in sense (1)** need not also be **dualist in sense (2)**. Sense (1) is *of wider scope* than sense (2). Thus, **Thomists** (see section 7.6B) would admit to having a dualist theory of mind in sense (1), but would deny having a dualist theory of mind in sense (2). See Copleston, 1955, Ch. IV.

For pleasant cartoon versions of various mind-body 'isms', see R. Taylor, 1974, p. 19. Vesey, 1964, and Flew, 1964, are collections of readings on the mind-body problem covering several centuries and many more philosophical outlooks.

7.11 BEHAVIOURISM

A theory or method which aims at understanding psychological functioning solely in terms of observable behaviour. Behaviourism comes in different *strengths* (see section 4.19B on **strength of assertion**).

Metaphysical behaviourism claims that observable behaviour is all the psychological functioning that there is. There is no such thing as consciousness and thinking is nothing but movements of the larynx which are, in principle (see section 3.12C), observable. The best known behaviourists of this extreme type are J. B. Watson (1878–1958) and B. F. Skinner (1904–). F. P. Ramsey said that to adopt such a theory is to 'feign anaesthesia'. See Koestler, 1970, Ch. I. See also sections 7.3C (**solipsism**), 9.13A (**overt, inner**).

Methodological behaviourism makes no pronouncement on the question of the existence of consciousness, but claims that observable behaviour is all that a scientific psychology needs to study, or, indeed, *can* study and remain scientific.

Analytical (or **conceptual** or **logical**) **behaviourism** claims that psychological concepts can all be analysed in terms of observable behaviour alone and that that analysis gives the meaning of such concepts.

Some influential recent philosophers, such as Gilbert Ryle (1900–1976) and Ludwig Wittgenstein (1889–1951) have denied that the mental and the physical are mutually exclusive and insisted that (in Wittgenstein's words) 'inner processes stand in need of outward criteria'. Whether this amounts to a behaviouristic approach and, if so, *how* behaviourist it is, is a matter of some controversy. See Pitcher, 1968, pp. 231–383; Wood and Pitcher, 1971, pp. 17–180.

7.12 ANALYTICAL PHILOSOPHY, EMPIRICISM, ETC.

A.

(i) The term '**analytical philosophy**' covers a wide variety of philosophical movements and tendencies, chiefly Anglophone in origin, though not exclusively; e.g., the **Logical Positivists** of the **Vienna Circle** (see E below) would be counted as analytical philosophers.

'Analytical' comes from a Greek word meaning 'taking apart'. It is contrasted with '**synthetical**', which is connected with 'putting together'. The philosophers called *analytical* tend to distrust attempts to construct large-scale theories of 'reality as a whole'. They think not in terms of one big problem, but in terms of many problems, some of them significantly related, some not related in any significant way at all. Analytical philosophers often put a great deal of emphasis on the task of **critically elucidating** already existing ideas and beliefs (e.g., those already existing in the sciences, or in religion, or everyday beliefs about the world – see section 5.14(iv) (**unpacking**)). They have (at the least) a tendency toward **empiricism** (see B below).

(ii) Most analytical philosophers would warmly endorse Wittgenstein's remark that 'Philosophy is not a body of doctrine but an activity' (Wittgenstein, 1974, p. 25: *TLP* 4.112) and, like Socrates, would be unhappy if they were expected to be Wise Men with a ready (though profound) answer to all questions. Thus, analytical philosophers have a tendency to stress the *unfinished, incomplete* nature of philosophy. 'I dreamt,' J. L. Austin says, 'a line that would make a motto for a sober philosophy: *Neither a be-all nor an end-all be*' (1979, p. 271n.).

(iii) The ancient Greek poet, Archilochus, wrote that 'The fox knows many things, but the hedgehog knows one big thing.' What he meant is not at all certain, but Sir Isaiah Berlin (1963, pp. 1–3) has used the line as the basis for a rough-and-ready classification of thinkers. In these terms, analytical philosophers are *foxes* and synthetical philosophers are *hedgehogs*. (Amongst the synthetical philosophers, I would put Spinoza, Leibniz, the Marxists, most Existentialists, and many Thomists.)

(iv) Because of the technical senses of 'analytic' and 'synthetic' (see section 3.6), the phrases 'analytical philosophy' and 'synthetical philosophy' are preferable to 'analytic philosophy' and 'synthetic philosophy'.[2] See Klemke, 1983; Nerlich, 1964.

B. Empiricism

The word 'empiricism' has no connexion with the word 'empire'. It is derived from the Greek word '*empirikoi*', the name of an ancient school of physicians who claimed that all their rules of practice were derived *from experience alone*. To say that a philosopher is an empiricist is to say that he places particular emphasis on experience, observation, and perception in his account of knowledge and belief. Fairly obviously, there can be different types and degrees of empiricism (see Hamlyn, 1967). J. S. Mill, a standard example of empiricism, used the word as a term of reproach. See Anschutz, 1968, pp. 59–67.

C. British empiricism (classical empiricism)

The three 'classical' British empiricists are John Locke (1643–1714), George Berkeley (1685–1753), and David Hume (1711–1776). Two other very important ones are John Stuart Mill (1806–1873) and Bertrand Russell (1872–1970).

They deny doctrines of innate ideas and/or innate knowledge (see section 1.13B) and tend to regard experience as basically *passive*. We receive *impressions* or *sense-data* passively and our active role is simply to combine these basic experiences together into more complex ideas. Thus the British empiricists take an *atomist, reductionist* view of our notions of objects. Any such notion can be *analysed without remainder* (i.e., without anything being left out), or *reduced* into a set of direct, basic sense-experiences; e.g., one's concept of a table can be analysed into a set of visual and tactile experiences (see section 5.20). Sometimes, British empiricists have claimed not merely that *concepts* of objects can be so analysed, but also that *objects* are nothing but collections of actual or possible basic sense-experiences. (J. S. Mill defined *matter* as *a permanent possibility of sensation*.)

Usually, if a philosopher says 'empiricism', he means empiricism of this 'British empiricists' type (which is not restricted to subjects of Her Majesty).[3] The empiricism represented by Locke, Berkeley, and Hume is contrasted with the **rationalism** represented by Descartes, Spinoza, and Leibniz. See section 7.13.

D.   Humean

Adjective derived from the name of David Hume. Sometimes misprinted or misread as 'human' with interestingly disastrous results. For brief accounts of Hume's philosophy, see MacNabb, 1975; Copleston, 1959, Chs XIV–XVIII; Ryle, 1971(a), pp. 158–166. Hume has been described as 'the modern paragon of a man-centred naturalism' (Flew, 1971, p. 182) and as 'a mere – brilliant – sophist' (Anscombe, 1981, p. 28) with 'logically sluttish ways' (Geach, 1969, p. 76). See sections 9.4A (**fact and value**) and 5.13 (**deductivism**).

E.   Logical Positivism

Logical Positivism (or **Logical Empiricism**) is a philosophical movement begun by Moritz Schlick and a group of philosophers known as *the Vienna Circle* (*Wienerkreis*) in the early 1920s. The central tenet of Logical Positivism was the **Verification** (or **Verifiability**) **Principle**. See section 5.4A. Although Logical Positivism failed on the crucial matter of verification, many Logical Positivists (e.g., Carnap, Ayer, Schlick, Neurath) have made contributions to philosophy which are of great and lasting value. Occasionally, people (for the most part non-philosophers) use the term 'Logical Positivism' to include **Linguistic Philosophy**, but that is to confuse two very different things. See Ayer, 1959; Ferré, 1987; Heath, 1975; Ashby, 1964.

F.   Linguistic philosophy

It is often convenient to group philosophers into 'schools' or 'isms', but such groupings can conceal at least as much as they reveal. Certainly, the people grouped under the label 'linguistic philosophers' (or 'linguistic analysts', or 'ordinary language philosophers') are a heterogeneous collection. And the boundaries of the 'school' are very uncertain: some who regard themselves as opponents of linguistic philosophy are regarded by other opponents as practitioners. For what it is worth, we can say that those usually called 'linguistic philosophers' share these characteristics:

(i) They are influenced by the later writings of Ludwig Wittgenstein (1889–1951) and/or by J. L. Austin (1911–1960). See G. J. Warnock, 1989.
(ii) They believe that at least some philosophical problems are at least partly problems about language.
(iii) They believe that the careful study of what people say when they are *not* philosophizing or theorizing can be at least one important aspect of dealing with philosophical or theoretical problems.

It will be clear from these three points that one can be more or less of a linguistic philosopher, that philosophy can be linguistic to a greater or lesser degree. Linguistic philosophy has been pretty much restricted to Anglophone countries, though some notable practitioners have been of non-Anglophone origin. Wittgenstein, for instance, was a Viennese. The heyday of linguistic philosophy was the 1950s and 1960s, but it is still influential and important.

Black, 1972, pp. 203–205 is an excellent summary of what linguistic philosophy is about. Magee, 1973 (a collection of conversations with contemporary philosophers) contains some interesting discussions on linguistic philosophy (and much else besides). Cameron, 1962, Ch. VI, and Mehta, 1963, Chs I and II, are also worth reading. Chappell, 1964, and Caton, 1963, are collections of essays in linguistic analysis. See also section 5.22H (**phenomenology**).

G.   Andersonian

Of, like, or pertaining to the work of John Anderson (1893–1962), Challis Professor of Philosophy at Sydney University from 1927 to 1958. Anderson has been and still is a highly influential figure in Australian philosophy. See Passmore, 1967; J. A. B. Holland, 1973; A. J. Baker, 1979, 1986; Cumming, 1987; Anderson, 1962, 1980, 1982; Ryle, 1971(a), pp. 236–248.

H.   Austinian

An ambiguous word. It can mean either:

(1) Of, like, or pertaining to the work of the English legal positivist (see section 5.12B), John Austin (1790–1859). See Golding, 1975, Ch. II; Golding, 1966, Pt II.
(2) Of, like, or pertaining to the work of the English linguistic philosopher (see F above), John Langshaw Austin (1911–1960). See Passmore, 1968(a), pp. 450–458; G. J. Warnock, 1958, Ch. XII. J.L.A. is almost everyone's favourite example of a linguistic philosopher. Warnock, 1989, raises interesting doubts.

If someone says 'the Austinian theory of sovereignty', 'Austinian' has sense (1). If someone says 'an Austinian conceptual analysis', 'Austinian' has sense (2).

7.13   RATIONALISM; CARTESIANISM

A.   Rationalism

'Rationalism' is one of the most dauntingly ambiguous of all the 'ism' words. Descartes is called a rationalist, partly because of the way in which he thought he could prove the existence of God. Some brass-throated spruiker in the Sydney Domain calls himself a rationalist because he thinks he can prove the non-existence of God.

'Rationalism', then, has several senses. The one of most philosophical interest is expressed as follows by my colleague, Professor Doniela:

> What is the central core of philosophical rationalism? Very briefly, it consists of two claims. First, human cognitive powers are said to consist of two sources or faculties: *reason* as thinking or intuition, and the *senses* as they are involved in the perception of everyday visible, audible, touchable and so on objects. Secondly, rationalism also claims that reason as a type of cognition is far *superior* to the senses. This claim of reason's superiority has been responsible, historically, for the conflict between *rationalism* on the one hand and *empiricism* on the other. Empiricism ... rejected the rationalist claim by asserting that all knowledge comes from sense experience.
>
> (1984, p. 12)

The principal philosophical rationalists are René Descartes (1590–1650), Baruch (Benedictus) Spinoza (1632–1677), and Gottfried Leibniz (1646–1716). These philosophers (the 'Continental Rationalists') are traditionally contrasted with the 'British Empiricists', Locke, Berkeley, and Hume (see section 7.12C). Rationalists are hedgehogs (see section 7.12A(iii)). See Doniela, 1984; Flew, 1984, pp. 298–299; Copleston, 1958; Cottingham, 1984.

B.   Cartesianism

(i)   **Cartesian**
Of, like, or pertaining to René Descartes (1596–1650) and/or his work. The Latin form of his name is 'Renatus Cartesius'.

(ii)   ***Cogito ergo sum* and Cartesian doubt**
Descartes, like many others, was in search of absolutely unshakeable certainty. His method was one of *doubt*: he resolved, *for the purposes of investigation*, to treat *as if* false any proposition which could possibly be doubted. (The italicized qualifying phrases are important. The doubt

was 'hyperbolical' and 'methodological' (see section 5.17), rather than 'real'.)

He found it impossible to doubt his own existence. Doubting is a variety of thinking and the fact that he was thinking was sufficient proof that he existed. Expressed as an inference, that adds up to 'I think, therefore I am (exist)', or, in Latin, '*Cogito ergo sum*'. It is often referred to simply as 'The *Cogito*'. Cf. section 3.1 (**self-refutation**). See Sprigge, 1984, pp. 13–33; B. Williams, 1967.

(iii) Other characteristically Cartesian doctrines are his psychophysical dualism (see section 7.10C) and his doctrine that non-human animals are natural *automata* (i.e., natural machines).

7.14 EXISTENTIALISM

As Flew says (1984, p. 115), existentialism is a philosophical *trend* or *attitude* rather than a creed or system. Søren Kierkegaard (1813–1855) is regarded as its originator, but the term originated much later. The best-known later existentialists (though some of them reject the label) are Martin Heidegger (1889–1976), Karl Jaspers (1883–1969), Gabriel Marcel (1889–1973), and Jean-Paul Sartre (1905–1980).

Existentialists reject the rationalist view that reality is a system whose order and intelligibility it is the philosopher's business to grasp. Existentialists also reject empiricism, for though there is a *tendency* (not universal) amongst empiricists to see reality as a lot of little bits and pieces, they also see it as an object (or congeries of objects) for philosophic investigation. Existentialists reject this. In other words, they reject the 'observer-status' which both rationalism and empiricism accord the philosopher. They reject also the notion of experience as the passive reception of impressions which is common amongst empiricists. For the existentialist, reality is something in which the philosopher, like any other person, is *involved* as agent and patient, and pretending to have a grandstand view of reality is sheer self-deceitful folly even as a **heuristic pretence** (see section 5.18(ii)). There is, however, a strong **synthetical** (or **hedgehog**-like – see section 7.12A(iii)) tendency in existentialism, because, although the existentialists reject the notion of reality as an ordered system, most of them have a tremendous faith in the capacity of 'Philosophy' to give a comprehensive account of it. Few (if any) existentialists would dissent from Sartre's pronouncement: 'Philosophy is precisely the discipline which studies man as a whole: man-in-the-world' (Charlesworth, 1975, p. 25). That contrasts sharply with J. L. Austin's 'Neither a be-all nor an end-all be' (1979, p. 271n.).

Existentialists are a heterogeneous collection. The existentialisms of Heidegger and Sartre are atheistic, though not very similar (they disbelieve in *different* gods, so to speak). Marcel is a Catholic. Jaspers and Kierkegaard are much influenced by the Protestant tradition. Pertinacious investigators have been able to extract traces of hope from the extraordinary prose of

Heidegger. Sartre wallows luxuriously in misanthropic despair, enjoying every painful second of it. See also sections 9.6E (**self-deception**), 3.3(ii) (**absurd**).

Kaufmann, 1956, and Langiulli, 1971, are useful anthologies. Charlesworth, 1975, contains, amongst other things, interviews with various philosophers including Sartre. See also: Copleston, 1977, Chs XV–XVII; Crittenden, 1985; Macquarrie, 1973; Magee, 1973, pp. 249–267; Passmore, 1968(a), Ch. XIX; Sprigge, 1984, pp. 115–152; M. Warnock, 1967.

The English humorist, Paul Jennings, concocted an imaginary philosophy called **Resistentialism** which parodies Sartrean existentialism (and various other things). See Jennings, 1950, pp. 146–163, and 1952, pp. 148–160. Resistentialism (after a long hard day, the most delightful of philosophical 'isms') is tantalizingly summarized by Sibson, 1977.

7.15   EGO; EGOIST; EGOISM, EGOTIST, EGOTISM; EGOISM AND ALTRUISM; EGOCENTRIC; EGOCENTRIC PARTICULARS

A.   Ego

In psychology, the word 'ego' is used in various ways and is bound up with various theories. In Freudian theory, the ego is those aspects of a person's personality of which he is conscious and, according to the Freudians, is a very superficial thing. See Wollheim, 1971, Chs II, VI; A. C. MacIntyre, 1958.

Outside Freudian theory, the word is sometimes used for a person's concept of himself and sometimes for the 'dynamic unity' which the person *is*. Thus, it is a very ambiguous term and needs careful handling. See Drever, 1977, pp. 79–80, for a quick survey. For some theoretical deployments of the term, see Jouvenel, 1963, pp. 43–66; Lavelle, 1973; Natanson, 1970.

In popular talk 'ego' means something different. It comes, so we are told, in varying quantities. Some people have more of it than others and one's own stock of the substance can vary from time to time: in other words, '**self-esteem**'. See K. Hudson, 1977, pp. 69–70. See also section 1.24(iv) (**identity**).

B.   Egoism and egotism, egocentricity, narcissism; traits of character

(i)   One meaning of 'egoist' is: a person whose motives, choices, and actions tend preponderantly to favour his own interests and to disregard the interests of others except in so far as paying regard to them is a means to furthering his own interests. This particular trait of character is called 'egoism'. The contrast between it and **altruism** is discussed in C below. The egoist in this case is **the selfish person**.

(ii)   According to *SOED*, the original meaning of '*egotism*' is '*the too-frequent use of the word "I"* [Latin: "ego"]'. Thus an egotist is someone who talks and thinks too much *about* himself. Such a person may also think too highly *of* himself, and 'egotism' is also used as a synonym for '*self-conceit*'. Someone might be an egotist in either or both of these senses without being selfish and it is a mistake to use 'egotist' as a synonym for 'egoist' (even though *SOED* condones it).

(iii) If someone is said to be **egocentric**, it is not always clear precisely what is being said of him: he may be being called **an egoist** or **an egotist** or both.

Psychologists sometimes use the term 'egocentric responses' for responses in an association test which are 'clearly personal' (Drever, 1977, p. 80). Such responses need have nothing to do with either egoism or egotism. For Russell's curious phrase 'egocentric particulars', see section 8.12(iv). It is possible for some aspect of a person's character to be 'I-centred' without being either egoistic or egotistic, both of which words suggest or imply an excessive or at least especially notable concern with self.

(iv) Extremes of self-concern and self-centredness are called **narcissism** (from the name of the tiresome mythological youth who fell in love with his own reflection and pined away until he was turned into a flower: Ovid, *Metamorphoses*, Bk III, ll.339–510: Ovid, 1921, pp. 148–161). For discussions of narcissism as a character trait and as a social movement, see Lavelle, 1973; Lasch, 1980; Powell, 1976, pp. 122–124. For a classical example, see the opening paragraphs of Rousseau's *Confessions*.

C. Altruistic, egoistic

'Alter' is the Latin for 'other'; 'ego' means 'I'. When contrasted with 'altruism', 'egoism' usually refers to motivation. To be egoistic is to be concerned with one's own welfare as sole end and to be concerned with the welfare of others only as a means to one's own welfare. Altruism, according to *SOED*, is 'Regard for others, as a principle of action', but this definition is incomplete. 'Altruism' usually means *regard for the interests of others to the exclusion of one's own interests*.

Thus an action could not be both altruistic and egoistic, and it is often assumed that it *must* be one or the other. On this (quite popular) view, one must either be totally imprisoned within one's own self-contained self-interest *or* pursue the interests of others to the total neglect of one's own. But that is simply not true. As V. and R. Routley say:

The self-contained set of a person's interests is only a *subset* of her interests ....The full class of interests also includes a class of *relational* interests which are not defined or determined independently of those of others and which thus enable the individual to reach out beyond herself. An example of this relational class, which is quite natural and familiar, is 'My needs include the need that your basic needs should be satisfied.'

(1980, p. 255)

See also Midgley, 1979, Chs V, VI; Scruton, 1983, p. 14. See section 5.21(iii) (**false dichotomies**). On **interests**, see R. Williams, 1983, pp. 171–173. See also sections 4.29, 8.2.

D.   Egoisms: doctrines

(i) The 'isms' just discussed are primarily traits of characters, orientations of personality, 'motivational sets' rather than doctrines or theories (though, of course, they may give rise to or be encouraged by doctrines or theories). The word 'egoism' is used also to refer to certain doctrines or theories.

(ii) **Ethical egoism** is the view that each person ought to pursue his own interests and that that is an adequate foundation for morality. An ethical egoist need not be selfish or egoistic in any ordinary sense, because he may believe that it is in each person's interests to be just, generous, loving, etc. Such a theory runs the danger of vacuity (see section 5.6). If I judge that it is my duty to xify, then I am judging that I would be a better person if I xified than if I refrained from xifying. Thus it might seem that xifying is therefore in my interest, but the theory has become 'You ought to do what you ought to do.' True enough, but unhelpful. See Flew, 1984, p. 11; Frankena, 1973, Ch. II; Harman, 1977, Ch. XII.

(iii) **Psychological egoism** is a doctrine about motives. The psychological egoist holds that everyone always and unavoidably acts in order to advance his own interests as he sees them. For a particularly vigorous presentation of this doctrine, see Mandeville's 'An Enquiry into the Origins of Moral Virtue' (Mandeville, 1970, pp. 81–92).

Such a theory seems to be either false or **vacuous** (see section 5.6), since, in one sense of 'interest', wanting anything is sufficient to make having that thing in my interests. Thus, the theory becomes 'Everyone always and unavoidably acts with the intention of bringing about states of affairs which he wants to bring about.' That says very little and gives no information about the actual motives which move anyone to action. As ethical egoism ends up by telling us that we ought to do what we ought to do, psychological egoism ends up by telling us that everyone does what he does. Psychological egoism and ethical egoism both treat the word 'interest' as simple, but it is very complicated. See section 8.2. See also Paterson, 1964; Midgley, 1979, Ch. VI.

7.16   HEDONISM, HEDONIST

(i) If someone asks 'What is hedonism?', the first thing to say in reply is 'No one thing'. The words 'hedonism', 'hedonist', 'hedonistic' are used to say that someone or something (e.g., attitude, outlook, way of life, culture, theory) places a special and strong emphasis on pleasure or happiness. ('*Hedone*' is the Greek for 'pleasure'.)

(ii) The word 'hedonist' can mean 'pleasure-seeker' which, in turn, usually means someone in whose life the satisfaction of physical appetites plays a predominant part. Sir Epicure Mammon in Jonson's *The Alchemist* is a good caricature of the type, which can be characterized as 'the kind of person for whom *Playboy* is published'. That sort of thing is sometimes called '**vulgar hedonism**' in order to distinguish it from the theoretical hedonisms spoken of below.

(iii) **Psychological hedonism** is a doctrine about motives. The psychological hedonist holds that everyone always and unavoidably acts with the intention of seeking the maximum pleasure for himself. This doctrine is a variety of psychological **egoism** and faces the same problems (see 7.15D(iii)).

(iv) An **ethical hedonist** is someone who believes that pleasure and pleasure alone is intrinsically good, that, if anything else is valuable, it is valuable only in so far as it is a means to pleasure, and that to act rightly is to act in a way that maximizes pleasure. The ethical hedonist has little in common with the vulgar hedonist. Indeed, ethical hedonists are not uncommonly very earnest people. (See, e.g., John Stuart Mill's *Autobiography*.) The ethical hedonist has a way of adding 'or happiness' to his statements about pleasure. He stresses long-term satisfactoriness as opposed to spasmodic ecstasies, and usually takes the view that a moral agent has the duty of maximizing other people's happiness, not just his own. In other words, the ethical hedonist is usually a **utilitarian** (see section 7.17). For some general discussions of types of hedonism see Flew, 1984, p. 138; Frankena, 1973, Ch. II.

(v) Both ethical and psychological hedonists have a way of talking as if pleasure or happiness were *a consequence* of actions. This view has been heavily criticized. See Midgley, 1979, Ch. VI; Frayn, 1974, paras 141–144; Ryle, 1954, Ch. IV; Penelhum, 1956; Kenny, 1963, Ch. VI; Jean Austin, 1968; Duncker, 1941.

7.17   UTILITARIANISM

A type of ethical theory with many varieties and sub-varieties. Sometimes the word 'utilitarianism' is used as a virtual synonym of 'consequentialism' (see section 7.19(ii)) or of 'teleological ethics' (in one of its senses – see section 7.18). There is absolutely nothing to recommend that verbal habit. It is far better to confine the word 'utilitarianism' to what is sometimes called **hedonic** (or **hedonistic** or **pleasure**) **utilitarianism**. The central theses of utilitarianism are:

1. That the rightness or wrongness of actions is determined by the goodness or badness of their consequences and by nothing else.
2. That the only thing intrinsically (see section 1.19(vi)) good is pleasure (or happiness) and the only thing intrinsically evil is pain (or unhappiness).
3. That, therefore, actions are right or wrong in proportion to the pleasure or pain that they give to all those affected.

The 'classical' utilitarians are Jeremy Bentham (1748–1832), James Mill (1773–1836), and John Stuart Mill (1806–1873). Utilitarianism went into eclipse during the first half of our century, but has had renewed and vigorous life over the past thirty years or so. The leading contemporary utilitarian is the Australian philosopher, J. J. C. Smart. John Stuart Mill's long pamphlet or short book called *Utilitarianism* (1861) is generally regarded as the classic statement of utilitarian ethics in general or at least of nineteenth-century utilitarianism. But, though John Stuart Mill was a convinced utilitarian, he was also a rather troubled one, and reading his book as if it were a party manifesto can tend to distort both it and utilitarianism in general.

There are two main variants of utilitarianism: **Act** (or **Extreme**) **utilitarianism** and **Rule** (or **Restricted**) **utilitarianism**. Utilitarians of the former type take the view that there is one and only one binding rule: act so as to maximize happiness and/or minimize unhappiness. *Each* actual or projected action, therefore, must be assessed as to whether it maximizes happiness and minimizes unhappiness. Rule utilitarians take the view that what is to be assessed is *types* of acts, rather than *individual* acts. Thus, it might be the case that using torture in one particular case would result in immense benefits to millions of human beings. If that is the case, the act utilitarian is committed to approving of it, but the rule utilitarian would still disapprove, because the practice of torture, considered generally, does more harm than good.

The following objections are sometimes made to utilitarianism:

(1) The difficulty of predicting the effects of our actions and, consequently, of knowing what we ought to do.
(2) Is utilitarianism compatible with justice? Exploitation of a minority might have effects which are very beneficial for the majority.

(Rule utilitarianism is a response to those two objections.)

(3) Is utilitarianism compatible with human dignity and freedom? Aldous Huxley's *Brave New World* and Ray Bradbury's *Fahrenheit 451* show us societies in which unhappiness and conflict are minimized by protecting

people from 'dangerous' ideas, by trivializing human relationships, and by drugging them stupid.

(J. S. Mill's remarks about 'qualitative differences' in *Utilitarianism*, Ch. II, are a response to that objection, but some have maintained that, at that point, Mill ceases to be a utilitarian.)

(4) Does utilitarianism involve confused concepts of happiness and pleasure? (See section 7.16(v).)

There is a vast and growing literature on utilitarianism in general and on John Stuart Mill in particular. I list a small selection below. Some of the items are anthologies containing important essays.

On utilitarianism in general: J. J. C. Smart, 1967; J. J. C. Smart and B. Williams, 1973; Quinton, 1973(b); Frankena and Granrose, 1974, pp. 127–200, 295–366; Moore, 1903, Chs II–III, and 1912, Chs I–II; Hare, 1963, Ch. VII; Hearn, 1971.

On John Stuart Mill: Mill, 1965; McCloskey, 1971, pp. 56–95; Norman, 1983, Ch. VII; Ryan, 1974, Ch. IV; Schneewind, 1968; J. M. Smith and Sosa, 1969.

7.18 TELEOLOGY; TELEOLOGICAL ETHICS AND DEONTOLOGICAL ETHICS

A. Teleology, teleological

These words are derived from the Greek word '*telos*' (plural: '*tele*') which, depending on the context, can be translated as 'goal', 'purpose', 'function', 'end'. Thus '*telos*' is an ambiguous word (as, indeed, are some of the English words which are possible translations of it). See Beckner, 1967; Parry, 1965; Wuellner, 1956, pp. 39–41, 47; D. Emmet, 1972.

B. Teleological ethics and deontological ethics

'Teleological ethics' is also an ambiguous term.
  (i) An ethical theory which judges the rightness or wrongness of actions in terms of their results is said to be **teleological**. 'Teleological' here is synonymous with 'consequentialist' (see section 7.19(ii)). Such theories are opposed to **deontological** theories which make rightness or wrongness of actions a function of their intrinsic nature. See Olson, 1967; Horsburgh, 1956.

The distinction between teleological theories and deontological theories sounds as if it is mutually exclusive – even perhaps as if it is, within the universe of ethical theories, mutually exclusive and collectively exhaustive (see section 1.28). But things are more complicated than that. There are extreme utilitarians (see section 7.17) who believe that *any* action – regardless of its intrinsic nature – is the right thing to do if there is good reason to believe that it would produce more beneficial results than any available alternative action. This attitude, certainly, is as teleological as it is possible to be, since it implies that inflicting the most excruciating tortures on an innocent man would be the right thing to do if it produced very beneficial results for most people.

On the other hand the attitude expressed by John Henry Newman in a famous passage sounds almost fanatically deontological in its heavy stress on the intrinsic nature of actions and its insistence that there are some kinds of acts which no kind of consequences can make right or permissible:

> The Catholic Church holds it better for the sun and moon to drop from heaven, for the earth to fail, and for all the many millions on it to die of starvation in extremest agony, as far as temporal affliction goes, than that one soul, I will not say, should be lost, but should commit one single venial sin, should tell one wilful untruth, or should steal one poor farthing without excuse.

(1912, p. 222)

But Newman would also maintain that right acts are right because they contribute to a good end and wrong acts are wrong because they derogate from that good end. (Of course, he and the extreme utilitarian would specify the good end rather differently.)

The standard example of a deontological theory is the theory of Immanuel Kant (see Copleston, 1960, Ch. XIV). A deontologist is not committed to saying that consequences are never morally relevant. His contention is that they are *not always* morally decisive. The words 'deontological' and 'teleological' make a rhyming couplet. That alone is probably enough to ensure the survival of 'teleological' in this sense. But 'consequentialist' is much clearer.

(ii) The phrase 'teleological ethics' can have a quite different sense. A theory like the Thomist Natural Law theory can be styled *teleological* on the ground that it is based on the notion of 'in-built' purposes in nature which human beings are required to treat with respect. (See sections 5.12B, 7.6B. See also W. D. Hudson, 1983, pp. 333–370; Sparkes, 1973, pp. 263–269.) There is a similar (though not identical) teleologism in Socrates's thinking. See W. K. C. Guthrie, 1950(a), pp. 72–80.

C.

For **teleological explanation**, see section 5.14(iii). For **teleological argument**, see section 8.20D.

7.19   ABSOLUTELY; ABSOLUTISM

(i) In ordinary talk, 'Absolutely!' is a term of emphatic agreement:

Primus: 'The Government should crack down on tax-evaders.'
Secundus: 'Absolutely!'

Used with an adjective, the word is an intensive, a special kind of 'very', perhaps a 'very, very, very' or 'thoroughly'. This use frequently occurs in hyperbolical utterances. If a teenage schoolgirl wants to say that something is not as good as it should be, she is quite likely to say 'It's absolutely foul.' (See P. Howard, 1978, pp. 25–27.)

In philosophical discussion of moral issues, 'absolutely' needs to be used more carefully. To say that torture is absolutely wrong is to say that once any action **falls under the concept of** torture (see section 1.9A(ii)), you need no further information (about, e.g., the motives of the agent, the identity of the victim, or the outcome of the act) to know that it is wrong. Someone who regards torture as *absolutely wrong* is likely to regard it as *very wrong*. It is important to notice, however, that the two expressions are not identical in meaning. As Herbert McCabe says:

A man might hold that lying is absolutely wrong while at the same time regarding it as often a rather trivial offence. All that 'absolutely' says is that whatever makes it wrong is independent of circumstances.
(1979, p. 8)

To say that an action is *absolutely wrong* in this sense is not the same as saying that it has no good aspects. It is to say that any good aspects it has are not sufficient to make it right or permissible.

(ii) An absolutist in ethics is simply someone who believes that there are types of action which it can never be right to do. He is not to be confused with an absolutist in politics, i.e., a supporter of government not limited by institutional checks and balances (see Scruton, 1983, pp. 1–2). Indeed, an absolutist in ethics might well be looked upon by the supporters of such forms of government as a dangerously disloyal person.

Ethical relativism is the denial of **ethical absolutism**; i.e., a relativist is one who denies that there are any ethical standards which hold regardless of circumstances. Perhaps the most influential form of relativism is **consequentialism**: the view that the basis for morally judging an action is not its intrinsic nature but its actual or likely or intended consequences. See Kenny and Hare, 1974; McCabe, 1979, Ch. I; Ladd, 1973; Lukes, 1977, Ch. VIII. See also section 7.18B (**deontological and teleological ethics**).

Popularly, however (and popularly amongst philosophers), the term 'ethical relativism' tends to call to mind ethical theories which see moral criteria as being relative to *specific cultures* (or *specific historical periods*), a view which has also been called 'moral isolationism'. See Bambrough, 1979; Flew, 1984, p. 303; Flew, 1971, Ch. III; Ladd, 1973; Midgley, 1981, pp. 69–75.

(iii) Ethical relativism has nothing whatsoever to do with Einstein's theory of relativity and to think that the latter requires us to adopt the former is to allow one's thinking to be dominated by a mere pun. For a very brief account of Einstein's theory, see Flew, 1984, pp. 303–304. J. J. C. Smart, 1964, pp. 1–23, is an introductory discussion of a range of related issues.

(iv) For a related, but different sense of 'absolutely', see section 10.7.

7.20   EMOTIVISM

Emotivism (or *the emotive theory of value*) is the view that value predicates (e.g., 'good', 'right', 'beautiful') and value-judgments have no descriptive meaning and are merely manifestations of emotion. Ayer originally (1936, Ch. VI) presented emotivism as a corollary of the Verifiability Principle (see section 5.4). He later maintained that it could survive independently of verificationism (1946, pp. 20–22; 1954, pp. 231–249). C. L. Stevenson, 1944, presents an emotivism which is independent of verificationism. Sellars and Hospers, 1952, Pt V, is a selection of important articles for and against emotivism. See also M. Warnock, 1960, Ch. IV; G. J. Warnock, 1967(a), Ch. III; Urmson, 1968; Harman, 1977, Pt II. Emotivism is a **non-cognitivist** theory of value. See section 8.14A(ii).

7.21   BRANCHES OF PHILOSOPHY; OLOGIES

A.   Branches of philosophy

Philosophy is the study of intellectual foundations. 'And hence,' some might say, 'foredoomed to messiness.' One way of classifying philosophical endeavours is the following:

1. Ontology (see section 7.23).
2. Epistemology (see section 7.24).
3. Value theory, which includes **ethics** or **moral philosophy, aesthetics** (philosophy of art, the beautiful, etc. – see Osborne, 1972, pp. 1–24), **social and political philosophy**.

4. Theory of rationality, which includes **logic** (see section 6.26), **decision theory**[4] (Are there general rules of rational choice? etc.), **philosophy of language** (What is meaning? What are the relations between language and non-linguistic reality? etc. – see sections 1.1–1.29).

Although these different endeavours are *distinguishable* from one another, they are not sharply *separable*. Attempts to solve problems in one have a way of creating problems in at least one of the others.

B. Ologies

The suffix 'ology' is derived from '*logos*', a Greek word of extraordinary versatility (see Pépin, 1987). In the names of sciences and branches of philosophy, it can be interpreted as 'discourse [see section 1.1] about ...'. Thus epistemology is discourse about *episteme* (knowledge) [and kindred matters]; biology, discourse about [certain aspects of] *bios* (life), etc.

7.22 METAPHYSICS; META

A. Metaphysics

The word '**metaphysics**' has a strange history. Literally, it means simply 'after physics'. Most of the surviving works of Aristotle (384–332 BC) are lecture notes which were arranged for publication after his death. Some fell neatly into conventional classifications (ethics, politics, physics, etc.). One batch of lectures, however, dealt with far more general questions. The arrangers put them into the collection after the lectures on physics and called them 'The ones after the *Physics*', '*Metaphysica*'.

Such a title would then have given no clue as to the content of the lectures. They dealt, on the whole, with the notion of *existence*: what does it mean to say that various kinds of thing exist? The title 'metaphysics' stuck to these and similar investigations. It would be reasonably accurate to say that:

Metaphysics is that branch of philosophy concerned with the most fundamental questions: existence, essence, space and time, the nature of universals, cause and effect, etc.

Because it deals with *first principles*, metaphysics is sometimes called **first philosophy**. From time to time, philosophers have raised the very metaphysical question of whether such an enterprise has any hope of saying anything significant at all, and, in some circles, 'metaphysical' has become a term of very severe reproach. See sections 7.12E, 5.4A (**Logical Positivism, Verifiability Principle**). **Ontology** and **epistemology** (sections 7.23, 7.24) are branches of metaphysics. See Strawson, 1975; Walsh, 1968; K. Campbell, 1976; I. Ramsey, 1961.

Metaphysics is not the study of astrology, the I Ching, and vampires.

B.   Meta, metalanguage, meta-ethics, meta-theory, metapolitics

'Meta' is the Greek for 'after', but, probably because of its association with **metaphysics**, it has acquired other senses as a prefix for technical terms in English (and several other languages).

(i) A **metalanguage** is a language used in discourse about language or about *a* language. ('*A* language' here refers less to (e.g.) English, French, Urdu, etc., than to the languages of (e.g.) moral judgment, literary criticism, political persuasion, scientific investigation, etc.)

(ii) **Meta-ethics**

The word 'ethics' is somewhat ambiguous (see *SOED* and section 9.3A), but one of its meanings is *the philosophical study of moral conduct and moral reasoning*. It deals with questions about goodness and badness, rightness and wrongness (etc.) of actions.

Meta-ethics is the philosophical study of the language used in making moral judgments. See Frankena, 1973, Ch. VI; Vesey, 1974(a), Ch. IV; M. Warnock, 1960, Chs V, VI; Wallace and Walker, 1970. Some have held that meta-ethics is itself morally neutral, i.e., it presupposes or implies no moral judgments. Others have wondered whether things are quite so simple.

A look at the words 'metalanguage' and 'meta-ethics' suggests that the modern meaning of 'meta' is 'about'. That is not its *only* meaning.

(iii) **Metatheory**

If B is a more-or-less systematic body of belief or of belief-and-practice and F is the collection of assumptions on which B rests, then F is the metatheory of B. A related, but different, sense of 'metatheory' would make it mean *the activity* of identifying and critically evaluating the collection of assumptions on which B rests.

(iv) **Metapolitics** can be either the views about the nature of man and the universe (sections 1.25, 1.10C, 5.9) assumed by a theory of politics; OR those non-political branches of philosophical activity relevant to the philosophical investigation of politics. On some days of the month, the term 'metapolitics' includes *all* branches of philosophy.

In 'metatheory' and 'metapolitics', 'meta' seems to mean *that which is fundamental with respect to . . .*

7.23   ONTOLOGY

(i) Ontology is an important part of **metaphysics** (see section 7.22A). In fact, when philosophy courses have titles like 'Metaphysics and Epistemology', the word 'metaphysics' is being used as a virtual synonym for 'ontology'. (For **epistemology**, see section 7.24.)

The word 'ontology' is derived from the Greek word for 'exist', 'is', etc. Ontology is concerned with questions about *existence* and *being*:

What kinds of thing can be said to exist? What does it mean to say that something exists? Are there different senses of the verb 'to exist', different types of existence?

(ii) To worry about the **ontological status** of something is not to worry about *whether* it exists but about *what it would mean to say that it exists or that it does not exist.* If I wonder whether there is a monster in Loch Ness, I am not wondering about the ontological status of the Loch Ness monster. But if I wonder whether greenness, the number five, the pen with which I am writing, electrons, and the average plumber all exist in the same sort of way, then I am wondering about the ontological status of these things. (The ontological status of the Loch Ness monster is presumably the same as that of any other aquatic creature: that is why people try to test the hypothesis that the monster exists in ways in which they would test similar hypotheses about other aquatic creatures.)

(iii) If a theory implies that Xs and Ys exist, that implication is the **ontological commitment** of that theory. The precise ontological commitment of a theory is not always immediately clear. As Keith Campbell remarks: 'A theory of planetary orbits pretty certainly involves a commitment to the reality of planets, but its commitment to orbits is perhaps not so unconditional. And what must the world contain in order to validate the random walk theory of stock market prices?' (1976, p. 174).

One can also raise the question of the ontological commitment of common *ways of talk*: does talk about *the average plumber* commit the talker to the existence of the average plumber? If I say 'Australia is a parliamentary democracy', am I committed to the existence of something, Australia, distinct from individual Australians? See Lacey, 1976, pp. 128–130; K. Campbell, 1976, Ch. XII.

(iv) '**Ontic**' is sometimes used as a synonym for 'ontological' (e.g., in the phrase 'ontic commitment'). Less frequently, '**ontics**' is used as a synonym for 'ontology'.

(v) **Ontological argument**: see section 8.20A.

7.24 EPISTEMOLOGY

(i) The branch of philosophy concerned with questions about knowledge, belief, opinion, certainty, doubt, etc. **Epistemology** is sometimes called **theory of knowledge** but **theory of cognition** would be better (see section 8.14A). 'Epistemic' and 'epistemological' are virtually synonymous.

(ii) A **blik** (see section 5.10), a *Weltanschauung* (see section 5.9), or a **paradigm** (in one sense of that word: see section 5.11) is called an **epistemological framework** not primarily because of its *content*, but because of its *function*; i.e., because it is in terms of such a framework that its holder understands what happens, explains and interprets, makes knowledge-claims, etc. An **epistemological framework** (see section 5.11) is not a merely epistemological theory in the sense of (i) above. Rather, it is a metaphysics, perhaps primarily an ontology (see sections 7.22–7.23), though often one of an unreflective kind. The phrase 'epistemological framework', itself quite legitimate, has sometimes led sociologists and philosophers of sociological bent to say 'epistemology' when they should be saying 'ontology', 'metaphysics', or 'philosophy of science'. It is an unfortunate habit.

7.25   COSMOLOGY; COSMOGONY

For 'cosmos', see section 1.10D.

A.   Cosmology

There are two different (but sometimes overlapping) intellectual enterprises which go by this name:

  (i) One is the critical examination of 'the most universal conceptions [by] which we seek to understand the nature of the individual objects which make up the experienced physical world' (A. E. Taylor, 1961(a), p. 43). These notions include *time* and *space, causality, existence, thinghood,* etc. In other words, cosmology in this sense of the word is **ontology** (see section 7.23) and **philosophy of science**. (The word 'cosmology' is rarely used in this sense now. Taylor's book was first published in 1902.) See Weiss, 1955.

 (ii) The other cosmology is a scientific, rather than philosophic, enterprise, though it raises philosophical problems. It is a joint effort of astronomers and theoretical physicists and the aim is to give 'an account of the large-scale properties of the astronomical or physical universe [see section 1.10C, D] as a whole' (Munitz, 1967, p. 238).

B.   Cosmogony

This word can be used in a wide or narrow sense.

  (i) In the wide sense, it includes *any* account of or hypothesis about the origins and/or nature of the universe: scientific, religious, folkloric, poetic, fictional.

 (ii) In the narrower (and much more frequent) sense, it *ex*cludes scientific theories and hypotheses and *in*cludes non-scientific and pre-scientific accounts of the origin and/or nature of the universe (e.g., *Genesis*, the theories of such pre-Socratics as Anaximander, and traditional origin stories of the kind collected by anthropologists). Not all cosmogonies are intended as literal explanations. See Cornford, 1967, pp. 81–116; Cornford, 1957; W. K. C. Guthrie, 1950(b), Ch. V; Middleton, 1967; Diamond, [1964?]; Long, 1987.

8   Arguing and investigating again

8.1   CRITICAL; OBJECTIVE

A.

'He was **critical** about it' often means 'He took an unfavourable view of it', but there is another sense of 'critical': 'Involving or exercising careful judgement or observation' (*SOED*). Philosophy MUST be a critical activity in this sense. In other words, the **primary** task of someone doing philosophy is to be an *investigator* rather than an *advocate*. An advocate's task is to present as many arguments and as much evidence as he can to support his own side and to discredit the case of the other side. An investigator may be committed to one side or other of a dispute and he may be concerned to defend that side. BUT he will be especially concerned to clarify the concepts involved in the dispute, to state all the relevant options as clearly, as accurately, and as strongly as he can. He will also be especially concerned to search for weaknesses, obscurities, and paradoxes **in the views which he himself favours** as well as in those which he is inclined to reject.

Does this mean that people doing philosophy have to be **objective**? Probably, but 'objective' is a very slippery word. See B below. See also sections 7.3A (**sceptics** and **scepticism**), 8.4C (**forensic**), and 8.3 (**bias**). Those who exhort the public about 'parenting' use the word 'criticize' as a synonym for the mere monosyllables 'nag' and 'blame'. They should not.

B.   Objective, subjective

These are really dreadful words and anyone tempted to use them should stop and ask himself what he really means and whether he means anything at all.

There are circumstances in which the words are quite unproblematical. Take a simple perceptual situation: Tom sees an apple on the table. A subject (in the sense related to 'subjective') is one who thinks, feels, perceives, desires, is conscious, so here, **the subject** is Tom and **the object** is the-apple-on-the-table. The situation has **subjective factors**: those contributed to it by Tom

212

(the state of his eyesight, his background knowledge of apples, etc.). The situation has **objective factors**: those contributed to it by the object, the-apple-on-the-table.

Notice that there is no reason for saying that the subjective factors are *bad* and the objective factors are *good*. But the words are often used that way. The reason is, I think, that not all subjective factors are relevant to the situation or problem being considered and, if irrelevant considerations influence someone's judgment, that judgment is likely to be defective. If, for example, the grade I give to a student's essay is influenced by the fact that I have a headache, then my judgment has been influenced by irrelevant subjective factors. That is a bad thing, but it is bad *not because the factors are subjective but because they are irrelevant*.

We are told: 'Be objective!' What does this mean? If it means anything worth being, it means 'Try to understand things as they are, not simply as you would like them to be.' But some seem to think that you cannot be objective about anything concerning which you have any beliefs or attitudes. That makes 'Be objective' mean 'Be ignorant and apathetic.' I doubt very much whether that is a sound 'method of directing one's reason and of seeking truth' (to borrow a phrase from Descartes). Because of the sheer nonsense which often goes with the word 'objective', it is better not to use it as a term of commendation. '**Critical**' is a far more useful and far less confusing word (see A above), and so are 'fair-minded' and 'honest'.

(To confuse things still further, the word 'objective' seems to have done a complete about-turn in meaning some time in the eighteenth century. As Rose says: 'Descartes uses "x is objective" to mean the same as "x is a mode of consciousness", i.e., x depends on the subject, a conscious mind, for its existence. This is what many modern philosophers after Kant seem to mean by "subjective".' (Rose, 1978, p. 2).)

See R. Williams, 1983, pp. 308–312; Devitt, 1984, p. 13; Popper, 1976, Chs XIX, XXXI, XXXII, XXXIV; Rose, 1978; Deutscher, 1983, Chs I–III, VI; Polanyi, 1973, Ch. I. See also sections 8.2 (**interest**, etc.) and 8.3 (**bias**).

8.2   INTEREST, INTERESTED, DISINTERESTED, UNINTERESTED

'Interest' is a curious word. The *OED*'s entry on it is well worth reading. It is a direct borrowing from Latin, in which it means something like: 'It makes a difference', 'It is of importance'. Obviously, a great variety of things can make a difference or be of importance and they can do so in a variety of ways. This indeterminacy is reflected in a phrase like 'Tom's interests'. On the one hand, **Tom's interests** are his health, wealth, comfort, etc. – that is to say, his wellbeing. On the other hand, **Tom's interests** are the things Tom likes doing and/or likes finding out about; e.g. reading detective stories, collecting butterflies, doing symbolic logic (and, perhaps, doing some things which are *not* good for his wellbeing).

In careful English, this duality of meaning is reflected in a distinction between 'disinterested' and 'uninterested'. If someone is **dis**interested, he has no ulterior motive, no axe to grind, he is not out for his own advantage, he is unbiased. 'Disinterested' is a near-synonym of 'impartial'. If someone is **un**interested in something, he does not care greatly about it. It does not attract his attention, it may bore him, etc. A judge trying a case ought to be **dis**interested. On the other hand, he must not be **un**interested in it: he should be following it very closely and paying close attention to it. Someone engaged in the **dis**interested search for truth may be engaged in something which is of quite absorbing and passionate concern to him. He is disinterested because he is prepared to follow the argument where it leads and to consider all relevant factors, however awkward some of them may be for him.

The distinction is a very useful one, but it is frequently overlooked and, very often, someone who claims to be 'disinterested' is merely trying to say that he doesn't care. As Gowers says, 'A valuable differentiation is thus in need of rescue, if it is not too late' (Fowler, 1968, p. 134). See sections 8.1B (**objective/subjective**); 8.3 (**bias**); 7.15 (**egoism**, etc.).

8.3   BIAS

Doctor Samuel Johnson, in his young days, 'reported' parliamentary debates for *The Gentleman's Magazine*. Later in his life, he said that, when he wrote the reports, 'he always took care to put Sir Robert Walpole in the wrong, and to say everything he could against the electorate of Hanover' (June 1784: Boswell, 1980, p. 1308).

Sir Winston Churchill, as Leader of the Opposition, asked his party's Research Department to provide statistics on infant mortality for use in a debate on the National Health Service. He was given detailed figures of which he made very little use. Later, he said to the research officer who compiled them: 'I gather, young man, that you want to be a Member of Parliament. The first lesson you must learn is that, when I call for statistics about the rate of infant mortality, what I want is proof that fewer babies died when I was Prime Minister than when anyone else was Prime Minister. That is a political statistic' (Fairlie, 1968, pp. 203–204).

A person can report the speeches of his political enemies accurately, even though he knows that that will make life easier for them and harder for him. It is possible to investigate statistics with the intention of discovering truth and to accept results which are unwelcome. That being so, it is possible to resist one's biases and to make unbiased judgments – often extremely hard, but not impossible. There is a popular argument that goes something like this:

No one can approach anything without preconceptions.
Anyone who approaches something with preconceptions is biased.

∴   Everyone is biased.

∴   It is unreasonable to complain about any instance of bias and futile
to try to be unbiased.

The argument is weak. It uses the word 'biased' in two senses (see section
4.24 (**figura dictionis**)). In one sense, **bias** is simply an inclination this way or
that, and having a preconception is, in *that* sense, to be biased. But there is
another sense of '**bias**' according to which **being biased** implies that one's
judgment is distorted, that one cannot see straight or talk straight. Of course,
anyone who claims that there is absolutely no chance of his judgment being
distorted is a vainglorious ass, but that does not imply that all judgments are
always distorted. The thesis that all judgments are biased in the second sense
is a great comfort to unscrupulous political enthusiasts and other crooks. See
Andreski, 1974; Montefiore, 1975. See also sections 8.2 (**interest**, etc.), 8.1B
(**objective/subjective**).

8.4   RHETORIC; ERISTIC; FORENSIC

A.   Rhetoric, rhetorical, rhetorically

(i) One meaning of the word 'rhetoric' is *the art of public speaking* and
also (by extension) *the art of writing*: i.e., the art of 'getting one's
message across'. Such an art can be abused for the sake of deceiving
people ('Making the worse case seem the better one', as the Athenians
grumbled) or for the sake of making mere empty self-indulgent noise
sound like profound and interesting truth. So it is not surprising that
the words 'rhetoric', 'rhetorical', and 'rhetorically' often have a pejorative ring to them. But there is no reason why that should always be
so. The fact that an art can be abused does not imply that it has no
legitimate use. See Dixon, 1971; I. A. Richards, 1965. See also sections
7.3E (**Sophists**), 4.19 (**persuasion**). For **rhetorical question**, see section
1.2B(ii).

(ii) To say that something someone has said or written is a **rhetorical
flourish** is to say that it adds nothing significant to his argument or
claim, that it is purely decorative, etc. Logicians sometimes use the
phrase in an attempt to discredit whatever they cannot express in their
notation. (See also section 5.19A on **Procrustes**.)

B.   Eristic

There are two characteristic aims of argument: (1) to establish a conclusion
as worth believing or a prescription as worth following; and (2) to persuade

the audience. Sometimes, however, an argument may establish without persuading or persuade without establishing.

The persuasive aspect of arguing is sometimes called **eristic** and is contrasted with the establishing aspect which is *sometimes* called **dialectic** (but 'dialectic' is an appallingly ambiguous word – see Flew, 1984, pp. 94, 111; R. Williams, 1983, pp. 106–108). 'Eristic' can be either a noun or an adjective. 'Dialectic' is a noun. Its adjectival form is 'dialectical'.

There is nothing intrinsically wrong with trying to persuade one's audience or in succeeding in doing so. But, since it is possible to persuade without really establishing, the phrase 'merely eristic' is derogatory. One may speak of *the merely eristic success* of someone's argument and be impugning only his logic or the truth of his premises, but 'eristic' is frequently a term of moral condemnation as well, implying a disregard for truth, an intention to *win*, regardless of truth.

From the point of view of a merely eristic arguer, bamboozling the opposition and confusing the audience are acceptable tactics (provided it is he or someone he agrees with who does it). Confidence tricksters have a similar attitude, which is hardly surprising, since the merely eristic arguer, like the confidence man, is a swindler. A *philosopher* who behaves that way is guilty of (in Bertrand Russell's words) 'treachery to truth and the worst of philosophic sins' (Russell, 1961, p. 156). Cf. section 7.3E (**sophistry**).

C.   Forensic

   (i) Legal argument usually takes place in a very stylized situation. There are two opposing sides, each represented by a barrister. The judge is there to see fair play between the two sides and either to decide the issue himself or to sum up the arguments of both sides for the benefit of the jury which will make the decision.

   In such a situation, a barrister's duty is to present his client's case as strongly as he can without being deceitful. It is no part of his duty to draw attention to the weak aspects of his client's case, nor need he dwell on the strengths of his opponent's case. The opponent can be relied on to do both these things. It is hoped that out of this clash between two skilled advocates, truth and justice will emerge (*the adversary system*).

   A barrister is an advocate, rather than an investigator. His arguments are shaped and controlled by the practical requirement of securing a decision which favours his client. This style of arguing is suited to the law-courts, and, for that reason, is called **forensic**. If used in other settings, it may be out of place. In philosophy, it certainly is out of place. See section 8.1 (**critical**).

   (ii) The basic meaning of 'forensic' is *pertaining to courts of law, or resembling legal proceedings*. A forensic laboratory is a laboratory for the examination of objects likely to be used as exhibits in legal proceedings.

It differs from (e.g.) other departments of police headquarters, *not* by being forensic, but by being a laboratory. Newspapers frequently tell us of scientists giving 'forensic evidence'. All witnesses in a court case give forensic evidence. The scientist called as an expert witness gives *scientific* evidence. See section 8.5A (**legalistic**).

8.5   LEGALISTIC; PEDANTRY; SCIOLISM

A.

'Forensic' should be distinguished from '**legalistic**'. 'Forensic' draws its meaning from the argumentative cleverness, quickness, tenacity, and single-mindedness of the good courtroom advocate. 'Legalistic', on the other hand, draws its meaning from another aspect of legal practice: a concern for the making of distinctions, for precision, for following procedures regarded as established and correct.

'Legalistic' is almost always derogatory; e.g., it suggests an *undue* concern for distinctions, precision, etc. But in many individual cases, there can be reasonable disagreement over whether such a concern has reached undue proportions. 'Legalistic' can be just a lazy person's self-defensive sneer.

B.

The word '**pedant**' originally meant 'school teacher' or 'tutor' and was evaluatively neutral. Partly because teachers of all kinds can overdo things, partly because teachers of all kinds irritate those who prefer ignorance, the word acquired a pejorative ring. In twentieth-century English, the word imputes such faults as *excessive* concern with correctness and accuracy, an *undue and unnecessary* concern with detail, with adherence to rules, or with precision.

The emphasized words are important. What is excessive, undue, unnecessary will depend on circumstances. What would be undue and unnecessary precision in a recipe for salad-dressing would be no less than absolutely necessary in directions for manufacturing a pharmaceutical or an explosive. Further, it is possible to disagree over whether something is excessive, undue, or unnecessary. Just as one person may be excessively (and obsessively) precise, another may be excessively slapdash, and bolster his slapdashness by throwing the word 'pedant' at anyone who objects. 'A pedant,' Bertrand Russell once said mischievously, 'is a person who prefers his statements to be true.' (See sections 8.10B (**contestable**); 2.7 (**vague**); 2.2 (**semantic**).)

A neutral term for someone who puts a high value on precision is 'precisian' (with an 'a'). It too had a pejorative ring in religious controversy of the sixteenth and seventeenth centuries, but that is far enough away to be untroublesome. ('Purist' will not do. It is almost as pejorative as 'pedant', a 'missile word' as Fowler says (1968, p. 442).)

Pedantry, it is worth adding, is less likely to be the fruit of scholarship than of **sciolism** (see section C below). As Aristotle says, 'It is the mark of an educated mind never to expect more precision in the treatment of any subject than the nature of that subject admits' – or, one might add, the circumstances require (*Nicomachean Ethics*, Bk I, Ch. III. See Aristotle, 1976, pp. 64–65).

C.

'Sciolism' is an uncommon word for a too-common thing. A sciolist is 'a superficial pretender to knowledge; a conceited smatterer' (*SOED*). The uninformed misuse of computer terminology is a good (or bad) contemporary example of sciolism. Contributions to discussion become 'inputs'. It is far too unscientific to speak of *comments*: he who wants to enjoy his own sincere admiration must say 'feedback'. (Both of these uses are thoroughly inept. See Chandor *et al.*, 1977, pp. 173, 211–217; Handel, 1971, pp. 140–141, 194.) See also section 5.28 (**parameter**), and Fowler, 1968, pp. 460–461 on *popularized technicalities*; Horner and Horner, 1980, pp. 66–67, 159–160. Pronunciation: SYoLIZm.

8.6   POLEMIC, POLEMICS, POLEMICAL; IRENIC

One can say something controversial or set off a controversy without any intention of doing so, but a person who speaks **polemically** is one who quite intentionally speaks controversially. The word suggests (without implying – see section 4.4) a certain pugnacity and aggressiveness. A **polemic** is a polemical speech, article, etc. 'Polemics' is the abstract noun. 'Polemical' contrasts with **irenic** (or **'eirenic'**). To speak irenically is to speak with peaceful intentions, especially to speak with the *deliberate* intention of *establishing* peace. (According to oral tradition, 'Where an Oxford philosopher says "Quite. But at the same time . . .", a Sydney philosopher shouts "Bullshit!" ')

8.7   ACADEMY, ACADEMIC

(i) **'Academia'** was the name of a garden near Athens where Plato (see section 7.4) set up his school. Thus the names of various institutions ranging from senior learned bodies like the British Academy to cramming 'colleges' and driving schools are a (sort of) homage to Plato (see Flacelière, 1970).

(ii) The Academy outlived Plato by many centuries. From the fourth century BC onward, the philosophy taught at the Academy had a somewhat **sceptical** (see section 7.3A) flavour. Seventeenth and eighteenth-century writers sometimes use the word 'academic' to mean **sceptical**. Thus, when David Hume (1711–1776) says:

The wise lend *a very academic faith* to every report that favours the
passion of the reporter ...

(My emphasis)[1]

he means that the wise will not be inclined to believe it at all. But that
use of 'academic' is obsolete.

(iii) 'Academic' sometimes means *pertaining to universities*. **Academic
government** is the government of universities. An **academic** is a teacher
and/or researcher in a university or comparable institution. **Academic
freedom** is the freedom of academics to do their job (i.e., to teach,
research, and criticize). **Academic autonomy** is the right of universities
to control their own affairs and to make their own policy (and the dodo
is a bird that once lived in Mauritius). Occasionally, the noun 'academic'
is used in a wider sense and with a pejorative tone to mean someone
who is more educated than the speaker and therefore inferior to him.

(iv) **'The question is an academic one'** means that the question is not of
practical importance, that the only reason for asking it is *a desire to
know*.

(v) **'A MERELY academic question'** usually carries the belief that only
mugs are interested in knowledge when there isn't a quid in it. (See also
section 5.5E on the theoretical/practical distinction.)

8.8 PROOF; DEDUCTIVE AND NON-DEDUCTIVE PROOF; DIRECT AND INDIRECT PROOF

A. Proof

'Tom alleged that Harry doped the horse.' (A)
'Tom argued that Harry doped the horse.' (B)
'Tom proved that Harry doped the horse.' (C)
'Tom convinced (persuaded) me that Harry doped the horse.' (D)

(C) implies both (B) and (A), but, unlike (B) or (A), commits its assertor to
the propositions (i) that Harry *did* dope the horse and (ii) that Tom's argument
provided sufficient grounds for believing that Harry doped the horse and for
excluding any reasonable possibility that he did not dope the horse. 'Proof'
and 'prove' (unless qualified by scare-quotes – see section 1.6B(ii) – or by such
phrases as 'to his own satisfaction') are **achievement-words** (see section 8.13).

'Convince' and 'persuade' are also achievement-words, but are used to
report a different kind of achievement. Someone might be persuaded (convinced) by a bad argument, but a bad argument can prove nothing (not even
if its conclusion happens to be true). If the assertor of (D) adds 'but I now
know that Harry did not dope the horse', he has said something internally
consistent. If, however, he added the same clause to (C), his assertion would
be self-contradictory.

Further, *a proof can fail to persuade*. Add to (C) the clause 'but no one accepted the conclusion' and the assertion is still internally consistent. In such a case, Tom proved that Harry doped the horse, but failed to prove it *to* his audience. 'To prove to' ascribes a double achievement: (i) providing sufficient reason for accepting a proposition as true and for excluding alternatives inconsistent with it, AND (ii) winning the agreement of the audience. Thus understood, the expression 'prove to' involves no confusion of proof with persuasion and does not deserve Flew's condemnation as 'wretched' and 'deplorable' (Flew, 1971, pp. 21–23; 1975, pp. 57–58). See Shaw, 1981, Chs II, XVIII. See also sections 8.11 (**refute, confute**), 8.12 (**demonstrate**), 8.9A (**onus of proof**).

B.   Deductive proof and non-deductive proof

(i) When a logician says 'proof', he usually means **deductive** proof. Normally, a deductive proof that p is true amounts to this:

    (1) A valid argument (see section 4.9) with p as its conclusion;
    (2) Its premises are true;
    (3) Its premises are known to be true.

(ii) 'Proof' is sometimes used for non-deductive (see section 5.13) and therefore non-valid (see sections 4.9(iii), 4.19B) arguments which provide overwhelming grounds for accepting their conclusions. It might be advisable, in philosophical contexts, to avoid this use of 'proof' and use some near-but-not-entire synonym such as 'establishment'.

C.   Direct proof and indirect proof

(i) In B(i) I sketch the normal type of deductive proof. Such a proof is a **direct proof. Indirect proof** is a more complicated kind of deductive proof.

(ii) **Characteristics of an indirect proof**

    (1) You want to prove that p.
    (2) Assume (see section 5.5C) for the sake of argument that -p.
    (3) Find something following from -p which is obviously false and is agreed to be false.
    (4) It follows that -p must be false, because it leads validly to a false conclusion (*modus tollens* – see section 6.16).
    (5) Therefore p is true. *Quod erat demonstrandum* (see section 4.7(j)).

(iii) ***Reductio ad absurdum*** (reduction to absurdity) is one kind of indirect proof. In *reductio*, the conclusion is proved by showing that its negation is *self-contradictory*. The phrase *reductio ad absurdum* is, however, frequently used as a synonym of 'indirect proof'. This is a regrettable but deeply entrenched habit.

Indeed, '*reductio ad absurdum*' is used even more loosely. In an indirect proof, we prove p by proving that the only alternative to p is false. Demolition is simultaneously construction. But, frequently, when philosophers talk about *reductio* arguments, they are talking about arguments in which they take an opponent's thesis and show (or try to show) that it implies a falsehood and is therefore false itself. But that is not to give an indirect proof unless there is only one alternative to the opponent's thesis. It is to give a *modus tollens* (see section 6.16). It is demolition, but it is not simultaneously construction.

So I suggest that we reserve the title 'indirect proof' for arguments that have the characteristics listed under C(ii) and call the others **quasi-reductiones**. (The plural of '*reductio*' is '*reductiones*'.)

There is a world of difference between *quasi-reductio* and *straw man* (see section 4.26), but, in the heat of controversy, the two are often

D.

Refutation by logical analogy is a variety of *quasi-reductio*. 'If *that's* a good argument, so is *this*, but this is obviously *not* a good argument.' See section 6.23C.

E. Countering quasi-reductio

(i) Arguing that one is not committed to that to which the opponent says one is committed.

(ii) Admitting that one *is* committed to that to which the opponent says one is committed, but arguing that it is not false or absurd.

Cf. section 9.5D (**wedge argument**).

F.

A proposition can be reduced to absurdity only if it is absurd. Before the *reductio*, the absurdity may not have been evident, but it must have been *there*. Sometimes, the phrase is used differently. 'Primus has reduced X to absurdity' is used to mean that, though there is *nothing* intrinsically wrong or absurd with X (a value, a principle, a policy) Primus has so misinterpreted or exaggerated it as to make it wrong or absurd. Talking this way is **sciolistic** (see section 8.5C).

8.9   ONUS; PRO AND CON; *SIC ET NON; DISTINGUO*

A.   Onus; onus of proof

The literal meaning of the Latin word 'onus' is 'burden', but, when the word is used in English, the 'burden' is always metaphorical – a burden of responsibility. If the onus is on you to xify, then it is your responsibility to xify.

Often, 'onus' is short for *'onus probandi'* or 'onus of proof'. In almost all criminal trials under British (including Australian) systems of law, the *onus probandi* is on the prosecution, not on the defence. In other words, it is the job of the prosecutor to prove that the defendant is guilty: it is not the job of the defendant to prove that he is innocent. (See Mozley and Whiteley, 1977, pp. 47–48.)

If Mr X asserts that there are fairies at the bottom of his garden and Mr Y denies it, the *onus probandi* is on Mr X. Cf. sections 5.15 (**Ockham's Razor**), 9.12B (*prima facie* **case**). The fur can really fly when one of the issues in dispute is on whom the *onus probandi* rests. In legal matters, that is all taken care of. Outside the courts, things are not always so simple.

B.

Arguments **pro and con** something are *arguments for* it and *arguments against* it. 'Pro' is Latin for 'for'; 'con' is short for *'contra'*, 'against'. Attitudes pro and con are attitudes favourable and unfavourable. To have a pro-attitude towards X is to be favourably disposed towards X; to have a con-attitude towards X is to regard X unfavourably. See D. E. Cooper, 1973, pp. 54ff.

C.

'Sic et non' (literally 'yes and no' or 'so and not so') is similar to '**pro and con**'. It is the title of a theological work written or compiled by Abelard (1079–1142). Abelard's aim was to promote discussion by putting side by side apparently authoritative but apparently inconsistent statements on important theological topics. See Knowles, 1962, Ch. X. For another use of *'sic'*, see section 1.6D(v).

D.

Literally translated, the Latin word *'distinguo'* means 'I distinguish'. In the Middle Ages, philosophers engaged in 'disputations' – highly formalized philosophical debates. (See Hamblin, 1970, pp. 125–134.) When a participant wanted to say something like: 'There are two possible interpretations of what you say,' he would say: 'Distinguo' and then go on and make his distinction.

Hence a **distinguo** is a distinction – especially a *subtle* distinction.

8.10 ARGUABLE, DEBATABLE; CONTESTABLE

A.

'**Arguable**' and '**debatable**' need to be distinguished. If someone says 'It is arguable that p', his audience is to draw the conclusion that, though he is not prepared to commit himself to *asserting* p, he believes that a strong case can be made *in favour of* p. Cf. section 9.12B (**prima facie case**) and section 4.18B (**strong argument**).

If someone says 'p is debatable', or 'It is debatable *whether* p' (N.B. 'whether'), his audience is entitled to draw the conclusion that, though he is not prepared to commit himself to *denying* p, he believes that a strong case can be made *against* p.

If he merely means that p is controversial, he should say 'p is controversial'.

B. Contestable

In a broad sense, anything liable to be called in question or to become a matter of controversy is contestable. Thus, if the Treasurer says that the rate of inflation will be halved in the next twelve months, that is contestable.

The word is more especially used for expressions which are not themselves propositions but whose use presupposes propositions or theories or moral or quasi-moral claims which are disputable or controversial. 'Reform' and 'progress' are good examples and the language of race and community relations is full of such expressions; e.g., the noun 'native' may 'really mean' (in a *desk dictionary* fashion) someone born in a particular territory, but, in talk about colonies, it is deeply embedded in the colonialist outlook and is often (quite reasonably) regarded as offensive. See Inglis, 1975.

Adherents of belief-system A and adherents of belief-system B both use term *t*. They differ to some extent, however, over the application of that term. They agree on applying it to some things, but there are others to which adherents of A would apply the term and from which adherents of B would withhold it and *vice versa*. There are things which one group regards as pre-eminent examples of a t-thing, but the other regards as inferior examples. The dispute is not merely verbal (see section 2.11): they are not using the word in different senses. While it makes sense to talk of *the A concept of a t-thing* and the *B concept of a t-thing*, these concepts have enough in common to allow us to talk of *the concept of a t-thing* which is contestable between the groups. A concept of this kind *approximates to* what W. B. Gallie calls *an essentially contested concept*. Gallie gives as examples the concepts of *work of art, democracy,* and *Christian doctrine* (Gallie, 1964, Ch. VIII; see also Gray, 1977; Swanton, 1985). See also section 10.7 (**relevant**).

8.11   REFUTE, REFUTATION; REFUTABLE; REBUT; CONFUTE

A.   Refute, refutation

(i) When G. E. Moore called one of his essays 'The Refutation of Idealism' (Moore, 1922, pp. 1–30), he did so because he believed he had *proved* that a certain type of philosophical theory is *false*. Moore did NOT merely intend to indicate that he had *asserted* that that type of theory is false. 'Refutation' is an **achievement-word** (see section 8.13). 'Refute' is to 'deny' as 'demonstrate' or 'prove' or 'establish' is to 'allege'.

'Moore refuted idealism' implies that Moore *disproved* idealism. It would not, however, be self-contradictory to say 'Moore refuted idealism, but failed to convince his audience.' In other words, 'refute' reports a **dialectical** or **logical** achievement, rather than an **eristic** or **rhetorical** achievement. See sections 8.8 (**proof**), 8.4B (**dialectical, eristic**).

(ii) Moore used the word 'refutation' as it has been used in educated English since the sixteenth century. About 1963, however, a new and strange use of 'refutation' and 'refute' began to appear in such places as newspaper correspondence columns: 'refute' and 'refutation' as fancy synonyms for 'deny' and 'denial'. 'I thoroughly refute Mr X's assertion,' writes Mr Y. 'Mr Y's refutation of my reply is false,' replies Mr X.

The use was taken up by the media-folk, the politicians, and other arbiters of linguistic elegance and it is now very common indeed. Oddly enough, some of the people who use the words in this fashion seem to believe that by saying: 'I emphatically refute Mr X's assertion,' they are doing something much more effective than they would be doing if they merely said: 'I emphatically deny Mr X's assertion.' That is verbal superstition. Few words can be so mistreated and survive usefully. The prospects for 'refute' and 'refutation' are not very cheerful. See D below (**confute, confutation**).

B.

The ordinary meaning of '**refutable**' is simply 'capable of being refuted', i.e., 'false and can be shown to be false'. In philosophical talk, however, it is sometimes used as a synonym of 'falsifiable' in its *technical* sense; i.e., '*if* false, could in principle be shown to be false'. In this sense, a *true* proposition could be refutable. See sections 5.1–5.4 (**falsifiable**).

C.

'**Rebut**' is a word with a colourful history. See *OED*. Its ordinary correct use makes it a synonym of 'refute'; i.e., Primus rebuts Secundus's allegation IFF he *shows* Secundus's allegation to be false. A **rebuttal** is a *disproof*.

An *argument-in-rebuttal*, however, is an argument *intended* to show that another argument is unsatisfactory. Perhaps because of this, 'rebut' is sometimes used as if it meant merely 'argue against' or even merely 'deny'. That is a misuse which should not be followed. For **rebutting a dilemma**, see section 6.22(e). 'Rebut' should not be confused with 'rebuff'. In modern English, it is proposals, offers, suggestions, and the like which are *rebuffed*, i.e., rejected in an abrupt, or totally unqualified, or peremptory fashion. ('Rebuff' also has an interesting history. See *OED*.)

D.

'Confute' and 'confutation' are not often met with now. Various dictionaries present them as synonyms of 'refute', 'refutation'. As 'refute' and 'refutation' are being continually misused (see A above), this might be the time to revive 'confute' and 'confutation' and leave 'refute' and 'refutation' to the pompous vandals who have mutilated them.

8.12 DEMONSTRATE, DEMONSTRATION, DEMONSTRABLE, DEMONSTRATIVE

These words are derived from a Latin word meaning *to show, point out, indicate*. The English words preserve this etymology in their various uses. The demonstrators outside the Skandjistan Embassy are *showing* what they think of the Skandjistan Government. The salesman demonstrating the washing machine *shows* what it can do. The physics demonstrator *shows* the students how to do the experiment. As technical terms also, they come 'trailing clouds of etymology' (J. L. Austin, 1979, pp. 201–203).

(i) One sense of 'show' makes it synonymous with 'prove'. To **demonstrate** a proposition is to *show conclusively* that it is true. An argument which *shows conclusively* that a proposition is true is a **demonstration**, a **demonstrative argument**. Thus, in this sense, a demonstrative argument is a *valid argument from true premises* (see sections 4.9, 4.10), an argument which is a **deductive proof** (see sections 5.13A, 8.8B) of its conclusion.

(ii) David Hume (1711–1776) uses 'demonstration' and 'demonstrative argument' to mean a valid argument from premises which are **logically necessary** truths (see section 3.5): '... there is an evident absurdity in pretending to demonstrate a matter of fact ... Nothing is demonstrable unless the contrary implies a contradiction' (Hume, 1948, p. 58: *DNR* Pt IX; see also Hume, 1975, pp. 34–35, 163–165: *ECHU*, sections 4, Pt II, and 12, Pt III). For **matter of fact** see section 3.15.

This is not a different *sense* of 'demonstration' and 'demonstrative argument' but a philosophical *doctrine* concerning what we are entitled to regard as certain. See Passmore, 1968(b), pp. 18–41, 152–159; Flew, 1961, pp. 53–92, 116–117; Anscombe, 1962, pp. 189–190. Cf. section 5.13A (**deductivism**).

(iii) We can, however, draw a distinction between 'demonstr*ably* true' and 'demonstrat*ively* true'. A proposition is demonstr*ably* true IFF it can be *deductively proved* (section 8.8B) and a demonstr*ably* false proposition is one whose negation can be *deductively proved*.

But a demonstrat*ively* true proposition is a logically necessary proposition, a proposition whose negation is self-contradictory. A demonstrat*ively* false proposition is a self-contradictory proposition. A demonstr*ably* true factual proposition requires premisses if its truth is to be shown. A demonstratively true proposition (if fully understood) shows *itself* to be true. Cf. section 3.10 (**self-evidence**).

(iv) 'Demonstrative' as discussed in (i)–(iii) is an *adjective*. A quite different sense makes it a *noun*. This sense derives from the talk of grammarians, in which a demonstrative is an adjective, pronoun, or adverb whose function is to **point out** or **indicate** the particular thing referred to. 'That' and 'those', 'this' and 'these' are the traditional grammarian's favourite examples (see Bernard, 1975, pp. 38–39, or Humphreys, 1945, pp. 68–69). Philosophers would add 'now', 'here', and 'there' (in such utterances as 'Put it there'), and at least some uses of 'I'.

Most philosophers would prefer the wider term 'token-reflexive' ('indicator-word' and 'indexical word' are also used). Consider the sentence:

I have been living here since last February.

To understand fully what is being said here, we must know who is saying it, where he is saying it, and when he is saying it (i.e., we need to know what, amongst the virtually infinite number of possible referents, the actual referents of 'I', 'here', and 'last February' are). Russell used the expression 'egocentric particulars', which might seem (but is not intended) to suggest that the logical phenomenon he is talking about occurs only in first-person (i.e., 'I' or 'we') utterances. The etymology of 'token-reflexive' is given in section 1.8. Anyone who has ever been puzzled and irritated by a notice on a door saying:

BACK IN 45 MINUTES

has encountered token-reflexivity. See the poem in *Alice in Wonderland*, Ch. XII (Carroll, 1974, p. 116). See also Flew, 1984, p. 353; Lacey, 1976, p. 218; Quine, 1960, Ch. III, section 21, Ch. V, sections 36–39; Russell, 1940, Ch. VII, and 1948, Pt II, Ch. IV; Coval, 1966.

(v) A **demonstration** of a proposition is a deductive proof of that proposition. A **derivation** of a proposition is merely a valid argument with that proposition as its conclusion (or the activity of drawing that conclusion validly – a process-product ambiguity – cf. section 4.3(ii)).

To say that p is **derivable from** q and r is merely to say that (q & r) implies p. To say that p is **demonstrable** from q and r is to say that (q & r) implies p *and that* q and r (and therefore p) are true. Cf. section 5.13A(ii) (**deducible**).

8.13   TASK-WORDS AND ACHIEVEMENT-WORDS; ENDORSEMENT

A.   Task-words and achievement-words

(i) If you *know* that you have money in your wallet, then there *is* money in your wallet. You cannot know falsely that something is the case (though you can *believe* falsely). It is impossible to *solve* a problem unsuccessfully. If you *prove* the theorem, then the theorem is true and your proof cannot be invalid, and if you *discover* the cause of multiple sclerosis, you cannot have failed to arrive at truth.

All those propositions are true. Some have thought that, therefore, there is a special state of mind, *knowing*, which is superior to believing, and that if we attain that state of mind, then we have attained infallibility. It has also seemed to some that there must be faultproof methods of enquiry and/or argument, methods which exclude all possibility of invalidity and error. 'If you know, you can't be wrong.'

That, however, is a confusion. Knowing stands to believing, not as an absolutely reliable state of mind to a less reliable one, but rather as *hitting a target* stands to *firing at a target*. Hitting a target is firing at it successfully. Knowing that there is money in your wallet is believing 'successfully' (i.e., truly and on adequate grounds) that there is money in your wallet. Similarly *solving a problem* (or *proving a theorem* or *discovering a cause* or *curing* a disease) is performing a task successfully. It no more follows that there are infallible methods of investigation and reasoning than it follows that there are absolutely inerrant methods of hitting a target. See J. L. Austin, 1979, pp. 97–103; Geach, 1976, pp. 11–16.

(ii) Gilbert Ryle (1949, pp. 130–131, 149–153) marks this distinction by calling words which 'signify not merely that some performance has been gone through, but also that something has been brought off by the agent going through it' *words of success, achievement-words*, or *'got it'-words*. Examples are 'catch' (as in cricket), 'solve', 'find', 'cure', 'deceive', 'persuade', 'arrive'. These can be contrasted, on the one hand, with *failure-words* or *'missed it'-words* (e.g., 'drop', 'lose', 'foozle', 'miscalculate'), and, on the other hand, with *task-words* or *performance-* or *'try'-words* which imply neither success nor failure (e.g., 'argue', 'look for', 'run in a race', 'treat a patient', etc.). 'Believe' cannot comfortably be called a *task-* or *performance-word*, though *'try'-word* fits it a little better. The point is, however, that it stands to 'know' as 'argue that p' stands to 'prove that p' or 'establish that p' (where 'p' is a place-holder for any proposition).

B. Endorsement and cognitive achievement-words

An expression has an endorsing function if it implies a favourable evaluation of that to which it is being applied. Part of its function may be neutrally descriptive, but it goes beyond that to pass a favourable verdict as well. If someone calls a change *a reform*, he has endorsed it as a change for the better. To call an allegation *a revelation* is to endorse it as true. (See sections 9.2 (**value-judgment**), 9.4A (**fact and value**).)

Cognitive achievement expressions have an endorsing function. A cognitive achievement expression is an expression which, when used to make a claim about a proposition, or an object, or a piece of reasoning, implies the truth of that proposition, or the existence of that object, or the satisfactoriness of that piece of reasoning (see section 8.14A (**cognition**)). Column I below lists some cognitive achievement expressions and column II lists their neutrally descriptive counterparts.

I	II
Tom knows that Thursday is a holiday.	Tom believes that Thursday is a holiday.
Tom proved that Donald put the poison in the parsley.	Tom argued that Donald put the poison in the parsley.
Tom refuted materialism.	Tom argued against materialism.
Tom's solution to the problem is ...	Tom believes that the solution to the problem is ...
Tom felt the table.	Tom had sensations as of feeling the table.
Tom pointed out that the minutes were inaccurate.	Tom asserted (alleged, said) that the minutes were inaccurate.

8.14 COGNITION, ETC.,; KNOW

A. Cognition, affection, conation; cognitive ethical theories; cognitive science(s)

(i) An ancient, rough-and-ready, but useful classification of 'parts of the mind' or 'aspects of consciousness':

Cognition covers believing and the acquisition of beliefs, learning, knowing, reasoning.

Affection covers feeling (of all kinds, not only what is usually called 'affection'). See section 5.23 (**feeling**).

Conation (or **volition**) covers willing, striving, effort, endeavour, intending, motivation, etc.

The adjectival forms of these words are 'cognitive', 'affective' (NOT 'affectionate'), 'conative', 'volitional'.

'Cognition', though technical, is a useful word, not merely a 'learned' substitute for 'knowledge'. Epistemology (see section 7.24) is sometimes called '*theory of knowledge*', but '*theory of cognition*' would be more apt.

(ii) A **cognitive ethical theory** is one which treats moral judgments, precepts, and principles as propositions; i.e., as having truth-value. A **non-cognitive theory** treats moral judgments, etc., as *non-propositional*; e.g., as manifestations of feeling or as imperatives (see sections 5.23, 1.5). The words 'cognitivism' and 'non-cognitivism' are frequently met with in discussions of recent ethics. See G. J. Warnock, 1967(a); McGrath, 1967. See also section 7.20 (**emotivism**).

(iii) '**Cognitive science(s)**' is the name given to attempts to integrate certain methods and findings of such disciplines as philosophy, logic, decision theory, cybernetics, artificial intelligence, neurophysiology, psychology, and linguistics in order to deal with certain fundamental problems concerning mind, thinking, learning, perception, and language. The very confident proponents omit the final 's'. The more cautious insert it. See Mey, 1982; Stillings, 1987.

B.

'Know' is an important, though ambiguous word. At least three senses can be distinguished:

(i) **Acquaintance knowing**. I can know *that* there is a man called Tom Smith and know various facts *about* him, and yet not *know him*. Knowing him is, at a minimum, being able to recognize him. That is *knowing him, but not, on its own, knowing him at all well*. I begin to know him better when I have met him. Knowing him well includes knowing facts about him, but is not restricted to that.

(ii) **Knowing how** to xify is to have the skill of xifying. Someone may have a skill without being able to say much about it or about how to do it, e.g., knowing how to peel a potato or roll a cigarette. Millions of people have known how to roll a cigarette. How many of them have been able to say in detail how it is done? Probably only Dashiell Hammett (see *The Maltese Falcon*, Ch. II: 1965, p. 300).

(iii) **Knowing that** (or **propositional knowing**); e.g., 'Tom knows that Charlton is a safe Labour seat.'

The usual account of propositional knowing is as follows:

> Someone knows that p IFF
> (i)   he believes that p; and
> (ii) that belief is true; and
> (iii) he has adequate justification for that belief.

This is sometimes called 'the justified-true-belief account of knowledge'. How much justification is adequate is, of course, something about which there has been much controversy. Some have argued that this 'justified-true-belief' account is not satisfactory. See Griffiths, 1967, pp. 1–15.

For a classical account of the knowing-how/knowing-that distinction, see Ryle, 1949, Ch. II. J. L. Austin, 1979, pp. 76–116, is a painstaking and provocative investigation of knowledge-claims of various different kinds. See also D. M. Armstrong, 1973; Quine, 1987, pp. 18–21, 108–110; D. G. Brown, 1971, 1974; Brett, 1974. See section 8.13A for some remarks on the tempting but treacherous thesis, 'If I know, I can't be wrong.' See also section 7.3A (**scepticism** and **fallibilism**).

8.15   CREDENCE

A *person* gives credence to a proposition (or system of propositions such as a story) if he accepts it or thinks it has some likelihood of being true or of having some degree of verisimilitude (see section 1.3B(vi)). Events, facts, etc., do *not* give credence to a proposition, though they may give it *support*.

8.16   FOUNDATION, BASIS

A hypothesis, suspicion, allegation, or belief may be supported to some extent without being true. The detective regards Tom as a suspect because his fingerprints are found at the scene of the crime, but then other evidence turns up showing that Tom could not have been there when the crime occurred, so the detective no longer regards Tom as a suspect. His original suspicion, therefore, was false, but it was *not* **baseless** or **without foundation**. There is an unfortunate fashion for using those words as emphatic substitutes for 'false'. The fashion should not be followed because it leads people to say things that are not true and it obscures the important point that mistakes may be both honest and rational. (The detective is not even mistaken.) We need also to distinguish the ***unfounded*** from the ***ill-founded***, an ill-founded belief being one 'formed on mistaken premisses'. See *Pride and Prejudice*, Ch. LVIII. There are philosophical problems about **ultimate** foundations. See Popper, 1972(a), introduction.

8.17   CREDIBLE, INCREDIBLE, PLAUSIBLE, DESIRABLE

(i) If a proposition is credible, it is one not unworthy of belief. 'His story is credible' means not that his story is true, but that it might be true, that it would be wrong simply to dismiss his story. To say that his story is incredible is to say that it is not worthy of belief (not that *no* one would be *able* to believe it). Thus, 'incredible' (in this sense) is a word of rejection, and 'credible' is a word of provisional and qualified endorsement, falling short of agreement or belief, but not necessarily excluding them.

(ii) 'Incredible' also has some looser and hyperbolical uses. *SOED* quotes Edmund Burke (1729–1797) as saying: 'These stories do incredible harm.' Perhaps 'incredible' was a slip for 'immeasurable', but Burke rarely made mistakes of that sort. Probably what Burke meant was that the harm done was of a magnitude that one would not have believed possible without clear evidence that it had occurred.

'Incredible' in its hyperbolical use is often linked to a phrase used by people in great and unexpected fortune, good or bad: 'I just can't believe it.' Taken literally, that would mean that the speaker thinks the events did not happen, but that would be a mistaken interpretation. What he means is (i) that the event is extraordinary and unexpected, AND (ii) that it is difficult to assimilate into his existing set of beliefs and expectations, difficult to 'take on board'. He is used to living without money to spare and his big win in the lottery will mean an incalculable revision of his mental habits, or he is used to regarding Mr X as a close and trustworthy friend, so the news of his treachery is not only emotionally devastating, but also means that much of his habitual thinking has been based on a false assumption. In either case, the shape of the man's world has been changed and he must redraw most of his maps.

Such a hyperbolical use of 'incredible' is rich in meaning, so it is a pity that the habit has grown up of using the word as a mere gaudy substitute for 'surprising', 'strange', or even 'interesting'. (' "That's incredible, but it doesn't surprise me" ': *Sunday Telegraph* (Sydney), 12 March 1989, p. 3.)

(iii) 'Plausible' originally meant *worthy of applause*, but it came to mean *having the look of being true or reasonable or worthy of belief or accept-ance or approval*. That made it a term of qualified endorsement, but the endorsement has become *very* qualified indeed. Emphasis has come to be placed on *'the look of'*. 'Plausible' applied to an argument, hypoth-esis, narrative, etc. is faint praise, falling well short of committed agreement. Applied to a person, it is almost defamatory, often imputing deceitful intent or insincerity, shallowness, unreliability. Cf. **specious** (section 8.18B).

To say that something is implausible is to say that it lacks the appearance of acceptability. Again, there is a stress on appearance. 'Implausible but true' is not self-contradictory, whereas 'incredible but true' is (unless it is an elliptical version of something like 'Even though *he* would find it incredible, it is true'). See also section 5.24 (**sensible, intelligible**, etc.).

(iv) It is only in the murkier regions of Medialand that 'desirable' means *capable of being desired* or *capable of arousing desire*. In more literate English, 'desirable' means *worthy to be desired, that which is appropriately wished for*. John Stuart Mill has been accused of arguing as follows:

People desire pleasure.

Therefore, Pleasure can be desired.

Therefore, Pleasure is desirable.

But there are powerful arguments for the proposition that this interpretation is unjust. See Mill, *Utilitarianism*, Ch. IV; Schneewind, 1968, pp. 145–233.

8.18   APPARENT; SPECIOUS

A.

'**Apparent**' and '**apparently**' are awkwardly ambiguous. 'An apparent X' may mean 'a manifest X, something which is clearly and obviously an X'; it may also mean that the thing seems to be an X, but *may* not be so. *SOED* says (probably correctly) that the latter is 'the commonest sense now', but the former is not dead (and is often met with in older writers). These are words to watch carefully.

B.   Specious; specious present

(i) '**Specious**' comes from the Latin '*speciosus*'. Both words originally meant 'beautiful in appearance', but both acquired an additional and less favourable sense; 'beautiful in appearance BUT perhaps NOT (or even BUT NOT) in reality', 'skin-deep beautiful only'. 'Specious' in contemporary English always has a pejorative sense except in the technical phrase, 'specious present' (see (ii) below). The 'BUT NOT' sense is current; the 'BUT perhaps NOT' is virtually obsolete. 'Specious' is typically used to stigmatize *arguments, pieces of reasoning, excuses*, etc. A specious argument (etc.) is one which has a cogent *look* about it, but is not really cogent at all (for 'cogent', see section 4.18B).

There is, however, an unfortunate tendency to treat the phrase 'specious argument' as if it were merely an elegant version of 'bad argument'. Perhaps there is some confusion here with 'spurious'. This unfortunate tendency might well result in the devaluation of a quite useful piece of linguistic currency. Such phrases as 'a blatantly specious argument' which turn up in the editorials of some newspapers are self-contradictory and silly. See also section 8.17 (**plausible**, etc.).

(ii) How long does *the present* last? Does 'now' apply only to the split second of its utterance? Is your reading of those two questions (indeed, the beginning of this one) something not of the present but of the past?

To deal with such bothers, the notion of **the specious (i.e., seeming) present** was developed. Roughly speaking, the specious present is a short period experienced as if it were the present. That may tempt some to wonder whether all specious presents are equal in either duration-as-experienced or in actual duration. (It should not be difficult to find an example of someone using the word 'now' to refer to the whole period since the emergence of man.) Was the time spent thinking up the notion of the specious present time well spent? On these and related matters, see Lacey, 1976, pp. 203–206; Findlay, 1963(b); J. J. C. Smart, 1964.

8.19   ANALOGY AND ARGUMENT FROM ANALOGY

A.

When we talk of **analogies**, we talk of *likenesses*, or *similarities*, but the word is probably best in place when we are talking about similarities of rather special kinds: *either* resemblances cutting across what are or are alleged to be radically different kinds of things; *or* resemblances which have some important consequences for questions of what we are logically entitled to say.

Thus, while, in some of the dictionary senses of 'analogy', we could talk of an analogy between two peas in a pod or between two matches from the same box, there is probably no point in doing so, but it might be appropriate to talk of analogy when what is being compared are a human body and a motorbike. The Greek word '*analogia*' seems to have begun as a mathematicians' word meaning 'proportion' ('As A is to B, so C is to D'). To treat A as *analogous with* B is to treat A as an *analogue* of B.

B.

If I **argue from analogy**, I argue that because A and B are alike in respect of having property X and because A has the additional property Y, it is reasonable to expect that B also has property Y.

As it stands, that does not look very impressive. After all, water has some of the same properties as whisky. Does it follow that water has every one of the properties of whisky? No. But does that undermine all arguments from analogy? No. It should be noticed that, in the formal sketch of argument from analogy given above, the conclusion is not given as: 'therefore B has property Y.' The conclusion is far more guarded than that.

Even at their best, such arguments from analogy do not establish a conclusion demonstratively (see section 8.12(i)). It is always possible to assert the premisses and deny the conclusion without self-contradiction. But such an argument may give us a hypothesis worth further investigation. An argument from analogy *may* even give such strong support to a conclusion that it would be irrational to reject that conclusion unless there were additional evidence against it. In evaluating an argument from analogy, it is necessary to assess the significance of the **disanalogies** or **negative analogies** (i.e., the points of non-resemblance) between the things being compared. Do not confuse **argument from analogy** with **logical analogy** (section 6.23C). See Scriven, 1976, pp. 210–215; Shaw, 1981, Ch. IX; Copi, 1978, Ch. XI; Quine and Ullian, 1978, Ch. VII.

8.20 ARGUMENTS FOR THE EXISTENCE OF GOD

See section 5.30 for a cautionary remark about 'the' in 'the ontological argument', etc.

A.

An **ontological argument** sets out to prove *from the concept of God* that God exists, that, in other words, if someone understands the concept of God as Supreme Being or as that-than-which-nothing-greater-can-be-conceived, he is thereby committed to agree that God exists. Unlike most other kinds of argument for the existence of God, an ontological argument is an *a priori* argument: it appeals to no features of the world or of human experience, but merely to the (alleged) implications of the concept of God.

St Anselm of Canterbury (1033–1109), the first to put forward such an argument, formulated two of them. St Thomas Aquinas (1225–1274) rejected Anselm's arguments (a fact which draws attention to the elementary but important logical point that rejecting an argument is not the same as rejecting its conclusion). Other arguments of the ontological kind have been put forward by Descartes (1596–1650), Spinoza (1632–1677), and Leibniz (1646–1716). In our own time, Charles Hartshorne and Norman Malcolm have argued in the same style. Since the late eighteenth century, all writers on the ontological argument, pro and con, have had to take account of Immanuel Kant's objections.

Plantinga, 1965, and Hick and McGill, 1968, are collections of important formulations and criticisms of ontological arguments. Anselm, 1965, gives the Latin text and an English translation of Anselm's arguments and of the criticisms of his contemporary, Gaunilo. Charlesworth, 1965, and R.

Campbell, 1976, are detailed studies of those texts. Barnes, 1972, is a wide-ranging and lively discussion.

B.

The Five Ways are St Thomas Aquinas's five arguments for the existence of God, sometimes labelled:

Argument from Change
Argument from Efficient Causality
Argument from the Ground of Necessity
Argument from the Degrees of Being
Argument from Purpose

Thomas's own formulations of these (*Summa Theologiae*, Pt I, Question 2, Article 3) are very bald and terse (just three pages in the Image Books edition: Thomas Aquinas, 1969, pp. 67–70) and people reading them for the first time tend to be either greatly puzzled or greatly unimpressed. But they are not meant to be read apart from the rest of Part I of the *Summa*. For contemporary restatements and discussions of these 'Ways', see Geach, 1961, pp. 109–117; Maritain, 1955, pp. 13–57; Wicker, 1964, pp. 27–53 (much less technical than Geach and Maritain). For counter-arguments see Kenny, 1969 (very complex); Mackie, 1982 (complex); Flew, 1966, Chs III, IV (much less complex).

C.

The title '**Cosmological Argument**' is applied to two *types of* argument for the existence of God:
  (i) Arguments from changes going on in the universe (see section 1.10C) (sometimes called misleadingly *arguments from motion*).
  (ii) Arguments from the very existence of the world (sometimes called *first cause arguments* or *arguments from causality*).

D.

Teleological Argument is sometimes called: **Argument from design, Argument to design, Argument from the governance of things, Argument from order or purpose in the world**. Arguments of this type base their conclusion that God exists on premisses alleging the existence of pattern, design, and/or purpose in the universe. See McPherson, 1972; Anderson, 1962, pp. 88–100; A. E. Taylor, 1961(b), and works listed in B above and E below.

E.   Additional reading

There is no shortage of books on the question of the existence of God. A classical 'anti' work is David Hume's *Dialogues Concerning Natural Religion* which has been published in many editions. Russell, 1957, is another well-known anti-theist work and contains the script of a BBC debate between Russell and Father Copleston, SJ. See also Gaskin, 1984; Hick, 1964; Küng, 1980; Mascall, 1966; Hebblethwaite, 1988.

8.21   CREATION; CREATURE

A.

Of late, certain muscular Christians have had much to say about **creation**, considered as a series of events which allegedly occurred over a period of six days some 6,000 years ago. Not all theistic thinkers have taken that view of creation. St Thomas Aquinas, for instance, sees creation as a continuing relationship of utter dependence on God, so that the universe (see section 1.10C) would be a created thing, a creature, even if it had always existed. See Thomas Aquinas, 1951, Ch. V; 1955, pp. 74–117. See also Foster, 1935, pp. 134–141, 180–204; Gilson, 1959; Pieper, 1957(b), pp. 51–75, 94–102; Sartre, 1956(b); Sparkes, 1973; Westermann, 1974(b).

B.

By etymology **'creature'** means *a created thing*. Its contemptuous use for a fawning, slavish dependent is easily explicable in terms of the above and imputes a kind of idolatry. Its association with creepy-crawlies and with monsters of the type met with in unsophisticated science fiction imputes anomalousness and unclassifiability – only the most general word possible is available.

8.22   INFINITE, INFINITELY

(i) These words are often used as hyperbolical substitutes for 'considerable'/'considerably' and 'indefinite'/'indefinitely'. The habit is defended by Fowler (1968, p. 282). Fowler does not defend or mention the habit of using 'infinitely' as a substitute for 'very much'. I have heard people say that one kind of detergent is 'infinitely better' than some other kind. Whatever one thinks of the hyperbole defended by Fowler, this one is a dreary cheapening of a useful word.

(ii) There are important philosophical problems about **the infinite** as a mathematical and as a religious concept. Whatever is meant by 'infinitely' in mathematical and religious discourse, it is not used there as a fancy version of 'very' or even of 'considerably' or 'indefinitely'. So, unless we want to make obscurities still more obscure, we should abstain from the hyperbolical uses of 'infinite' and its cognates when talking philosophy. See Gandy, 1977; Flew, 1984, pp. 173–174.

9   Doing

9.1   AGENT; ON THE PART OF, ON BEHALF OF

A.

In contemporary English, an **agent** is usually *someone who acts on behalf of someone else*; e.g., an *estate agent*, a *private enquiry agent*, a *secret agent*. An older meaning, however, is simply *one who acts* (see *OED*). This meaning is preserved in the talk of moral philosophy and philosophical psychology. In such talk, to *consider someone as an agent* is to *consider him as someone who performs actions*. To consider someone as someone to whom things happen is to think of him as *a patient*. See Scruton, 1983, pp. 8–9; White, 1968.

B.

If Primus shoots Secundus, that is homicidal conduct **on the part of** Primus. It is NOT homicidal conduct **on behalf of** Primus, although it would be homicidal conduct on behalf of *Tertius*, if, in shooting Secundus, Primus was acting *as Tertius's agent* (in the common contemporary sense of that word – see A above). If Quartus saves Quintus's life, that is NOT acting on Quintus's behalf, but it is acting to (and for) Quintus's benefit or advantage (to Quinton's *behoof*, to use a curious archaism which I should not like to see revived – see Fowler, 1968, p. 54). See section 1.6D(ii) **(in propria persona)**.

9.2   VALUE-JUDGMENT

A value-judgment is a judgment which commits its maker to the opinion that something is good or bad, right or wrong, satisfactory or unsatisfactory. Some people talk as if making a value-judgment is something very, very bad. That is self-refuting silliness (see section 3.1). See also sections 8.13B, 3.15(iii) **(endorsing, evaluative)**.

    For the general scope of theory of value, see section 7.21A. For some theories about (primarily, *moral*) value, see sections 8.14A(ii) **(cognitivism,** non-cognitivism), 7.18B (**deontological and teleological ethics**), 7.20 (**emotiv-** ism), 7.19(ii) (**ethical relativism**), 5.25 (**intuitionism**), 7.3D (**moral scepticism**), 5.12B (**natural law theory**), 7.17 (**utilitarianism**). See also Flew, 1975, pp. 79–82.

9.3　MORAL, ETHICAL; MORES

A.

'Moral' can be contrasted either with 'immoral' or with non-moral. The second of these is the more common in philosophical talk and, in the discourse of most Anglophone philosophers, is treated as a near-synonym of 'ethical'. See *SOED* and Lacey, 1976, p. 138.

　　G. W. F. Hegel (1770–1831) distinguishes *Moralität* from *Sittlichkeit*, the former being the consciously thought-out morality of a reflective moral agent (section 9.1), the latter being the customary morality of a society or social group. The two German words are customarily translated 'morality' and 'ethics'. (See Findlay, 1962: index entries 'Ethical', 'Moral Consciousness', and 'Morality'.) The distinction can be a useful one. The translation is inept and a nuisance. See also section 7.22B(ii) (**ethics and meta-ethics**).

B.

The **mores** of a society are its generally accepted morality, the rules, values, and conventions about conduct which are generally regarded as binding in that society, even though they may often be broken (i.e., *Sittlichkeit*).

　　The word is a direct borrowing from Latin and should be pronounced as *two* syllables. It is plural. The Latin singular is '*mos*', but that is unsuitable for use in English. 'One of the *mores*' is probably the best we can do; e.g., 'The prohibition of stealing is one of the *mores* of our society.' Please do not say 'a mawray' (I have heard it said).

9.4　FACT AND VALUE; REASON AND EMOTION

A.　Fact and value; 'ought' and 'is'

　(i)　Statements of pure fact cannot *imply* (see section 4.4) a value-judgment, for the simple reason that no statement is a statement of *pure* fact if it contains any element of a value-judgment and a judgment R is implied by statements P and Q only if there is nothing in R that is not implicit in P and Q.

　　　　That is what is meant by the slogan, 'You cannot deduce an *ought* from an *is*.' (It does *not* imply that moral judgments are not influenced by matters of fact.) The classical text is in David Hume's *Treatise of*

Human Nature (THN), Book III, Pt 1, Ch. I (Hume, 1969, p. 521).

(ii) That little piece of elementary logic would not be very interesting if it were not for the conclusion which Hume and his many disciples draw from it, viz., that, in Hume's words 'Moral distinctions ... are not the offspring of reason.' That leaves morality (and other kinds of value) to be a matter merely of emotion or (for many of those who find that too much to swallow) a matter of a form of perception quite different from that which we employ in understanding ordinary matters of fact or matters such as arithmetic and logic. (Thus, there is an important respect in which even an intuitionist (see section 5.25) like Moore is a Humean, though, of coure, he is not so thoroughgoing a Humean as Ayer (see section 7.20).) See *THN*, Bk II, Pt III, Ch. III (Hume, 1969, p. 463); Bk III, Pt 1, Ch. 1 (Hume, 1969, p. 510).

(iii) This emotivist thesis does not follow directly from the logical point about 'is' and 'ought'. One could accept that judgments of value cannot be *deduced from* statements of pure fact and yet maintain that statements of pure fact might still provide *good reasons* for accepting some judgments of value. The factual statement that driving after drinking liquor increases the likelihood of accident does not *imply* the value-judgment 'It is wrong to drive after drinking liquor', but (it might be argued) the factual statement provides a good reason for accepting the value-judgment. In a similar way, 'It is raining heavily' (R) does not imply 'If you have to go outside, do so in a fashion as waterproof as possible' (W), but R provides a very good reason for doing as W directs. The reasonable person does not drive after drinking and wears a raincoat or carries an umbrella on the basis of just these facts. R gives justification to W in a way in which it would not give justification to some other practical judgments (e.g., 'If you have to go outside, wrap yourself in tissue paper and stick a gherkin in each ear'). All that is mere sanity. All that is rejected by Hume and the Humeans.

Hume has shown us that value-reasoning and practical reasoning (i.e., reasoning about what should be done) generally, do not work in the same way as reasoning from matters of fact to matters of fact. But he has not shown that there is no such thing as value-*reasoning* or practical *reasoning* at all. His claim to have found something which 'wou'd subvert all the vulgar systems of morality' can be accepted only if **deductivism** (see section 5.13 A(v)) is accepted. But, as indicated above, **deductivism** implies manifest falsehoods and so must itself be false (*modus tollens*: section 6.16).

See W. D. Hudson, 1983, Ch. VI; Magee, 1973, Ch. IX; W. D. Hudson, 1969; Hare, 1952, Pts I–II; Hare, 1963, Chs I–III; Fitzgerald, 1977; Midgley, 1979, Chs IX, XIII; Beardsmore, 1969; Pole, 1961, Chs III, IV; Lucas, 1971.

B. Reason and emotion

To say that someone is in an emotional state usually means that he is in *a particularly intense* emotional state. Often, it means rather more: that the person is in such an intense emotional state that he is unlikely to be able to take an even moderately long-term view of his needs and aspirations or to have an adequate appreciation of the relation of himself to the world of things and people.

In other words, such a person is in an emotional state which hinders or even precludes the use of reason. But none of this should be taken to imply that there are two things, Reason and Emotion, which are inherently hostile to each other, or that Reason or Rationality is something quite distinct from Emotions which are always inferior to it. As Mary Midgley says, ' "Reason" is not the name of a character in a drama. It is a name for organizing oneself' (1979, p. 258). See Midgley, 1979, Ch. XI. See also section 5.21(iii) (**false dichotomies**). For 'emotive', see section 2.4.

9.5 UNIVERSALIZABILITY; ARBITRARY; DISCRIMINATION; WEDGE ARGUMENTS

A. Universalizability

Universalizability is regarded by many philosophers as *the* or *a* criterion for identifying genuine moral judgments and as an important and indispensable rule of moral reasoning. This criterion (UC) has been formulated in many ways, but the basic notion is this:

> If you voluntarily perform some action, then you are committed to the proposition that performing that action is morally legitimate.

> It follows from this that you are committed to saying that it would be morally legitimate for anyone in the same circumstances to do the same thing.

It follows from UC that, if Mr A says that it is all right for him to xify but that xification by Mr B would be wrong, the onus is on Mr A to show good reasons for considering the cases to be different. (It also follows from UC that an agent who voluntarily performs an action which he regards as morally wrong is doing something analogous to uttering a self-contradiction. See section 9.6A (**akrasia**).) The best-known version of UC is that of Immanuel Kant (1724–1804): 'Always act so that the principle behind your action could be a good universal law for mankind.'

UC is an important criterion for distinguishing a genuine moral judgment from a piece of *selective or pseudo-moral indignation* – i.e., a mere squeal of anguish at harsh treatment of the side one favours. Flew gives the example of someone who professes disapproval of gas warfare, yet is completely silent when it is used by a side he supports (1975, p. 81). Thus UC demands the removal of arbitrary discriminations (see B and C below).

I said above that universalizability is regarded by many philosophers as *a* or *the* criterion for identifying genuine moral judgments. To take the latter view is to maintain that universalizability is a necessary-and-sufficient condition for a judgment's being a genuine moral judgment. To look on it as *a* criterion is to look on it *either* as a sufficient condition *or* as a necessary condition (see section 4.16(ii)). The view that it is a necessary condition is, I think, the most plausible option, though even that has been attacked (see, e.g., A. C. MacIntyre, 1970; Frankena, 1970).

Even if universalizability is a criterion for identifying authentically moral judgments and an important rule of moral reasoning, applying it is not always easy. Before we can apply UC to some particular action, we must have a true description of that action and that description must present all its morally relevant aspects. Only then can we state the principle behind the action and judge whether that principle would make 'a good universal law for all mankind'. In some cases, arriving at such a description might be no easy task and the question whether we have arrived at it might itself be a matter for moral controversy.

See Kant, 1948, pp. 30–32, 52–58; Norman, 1983, pp. 106–118; Acton, 1970, Ch. V; Benn and Peters, 1959, Ch. II; Mabbott, 1966, pp. 39–49; Hare, 1963, Chs II–III; Hare, 1981, Ch. VI; W. D. Hudson, 1983, pp. 179–195, 209–231.

B.

'Arbitrary' is a troublesome word on which a book or two could be written. Dictionary definitions tend to give the impression that to call something 'arbitrary' is *inevitably* to denigrate it. *The Penguin English Dictionary*'s definition is fairly typical:

> of uncontrolled power; despotic; impulsive; capricious; deciding or decided on inadequate grounds.

That suggests that if X is arbitrary, X is either bad or irrational. It suggests that an arbitrary choice is at best, a mere whim. But while 'arbitrary' does have such denigratory functions, it has other functions as well.

If you have a choice between A and B and there is nothing which renders either more choiceworthy than the other, it follows that the choice you make must be arbitrary. It does *not* follow that your choice is either bad or irrational or capricious. Neither is it true that there is no good reason for obeying a rule made as a result of arbitrary choice. Consider rules about the side of the road on which you should drive. See section 8.1B (**objective** and **subjective**). Spelling: please note that there are three 'r's in 'arbitrary'. It should be pronounced so that its last two syllables sound the same as the last two syllables of 'library'.

C. Discriminate, discrimination, discriminating, discriminatory

(i) Basically, **to discriminate** is *to differentiate, to distinguish*. To say 'That is chalk, but the other is cheese', to notice that the cover of volume VII is darker than the cover of volume I, to decide that the person getting off the bus is not, as you had at first thought, Tom, but Dick – all these are acts of discrimination. So is deciding to wear this shirt rather than that or to enrol for one subject rather than another.

(ii) But choices can be made carefully or casually, can be based on relevant knowledge and consideration or be *purely arbitrary*. So we get another sense of 'discriminate' in which to say that someone has made a **discriminating** choice is to say that his choice was based on knowledge and consideration (i.e., was *not* arbitrary). Similarly, to have a **discriminating** palate or a **discriminating** ear is not *merely* to be able to distinguish one taste or one sound from another: it is to be particularly good at making those distinctions. (Cf. 'He is a *thinking* person.' Everyone thinks, but not everyone deserves to be called a thinking person in that honorific sense. Cf. Sheed, 1953, pp. 87–89.)

(iii) Choices and differentiations can also be made unjustly and/or irrationally. Irrelevant considerations are treated as if they were relevant and, as a result, some people are given unfair advantages while others are unfairly disadvantaged. If a Highway Patrolman decides that driver A rather than driver B was to blame for the accident, he is **making a discrimination** in sense (i), which may or may not (let's hope it does) involve **discrimination** in sense (ii). But if he decides that driver A was to blame simply because driver A is a woman and driver B is a man, his decision is a **discriminatory** one in a third sense: he is awarding advantages and disadvantages on irrelevant and inadequate grounds (and *is*, therefore, being **arbitrary**). See Richmond, 1970.

So there are three senses of the word 'discriminate'. The three are related but different. It is fashionable at present to conclude that because something can be described as 'discrimination' (sense (i)), or as 'discrimination' (sense (ii)), it *must therefore* be discrimination in sense (iii). To argue this way is to treat a mere pun as an important necessary truth (see section 4.24). For some philosophical discussion of discrimination (sense (iii)), see Glazer, 1978; Kleinig, 1981; Chipman, 1980; Stone, 1979; Cohen, 1977.

D. Wedge arguments

One way of splitting blocks of stone or wood is by use of a hammer and a wedge. The thin end of the wedge is driven in first, making only a small difference to the block. A few more taps, however, drive the whole wedge in and the block is split. A wedge argument is an argument against a proposal on the ground that, though it, considered in itself, may have attractive features, adopting it would have (or would be very likely to have) consequences of a highly undesirable kind. 'Consequences', however, can be ambiguous between **logical consequences** and **causal consequences** (see section 3.17), so there are (at least) two kinds of wedge argument:

> A causal-wedge argument against a proposal alleges that the adoption of the proposal will make it more probable that more sweeping and more dangerous proposals will be adopted.

> A logical-wedge argument against a proposal alleges that the proposal *is* logically committing oneself to approving of more sweeping and more dangerous or clearly immoral proposals.

A sub-variety of causal-wedge argument alleges that performing the proposed action would or would be very likely to create a bad habit. There are certain resemblances between wedge arguments and **quasi-reductio** arguments (see section 8.8C). A logical-wedge argument is an appeal to the principle of universalizability (see A above).

A causal-wedge argument fails to prove what it sets out to prove if:

(i)   No such probability is created;

OR

(ii) The future probabilities alleged to be dangerous are not dangerous or are risks worth taking.

A logical-wedge argument fails to prove what it sets out to prove if:

(i)   The alleged implication does not hold;

OR

(ii) The proposals alleged to be dangerous or clearly immoral are not dangerous or clearly immoral.

Since there is more than one type of wedge argument, to talk of '*the* wedge argument' or '*the* principle of the wedge' is misleading. See section 5.30 (**the**). See Daly, 1962, pp. 55–58; Flew, 1969, p. 48; Cornford, 1949, Ch. VII.

9.6   AKRASIA; HYPOCRISY; SELF-RIGHTEOUSNESS; PREACHING AND PRACTISING; SELF-DECEPTION

A.

A case of **akrasia** occurs IFF

(a)   someone judges course of action X to be better than course of action Y

AND

(b) nevertheless, chooses to follow course of action Y.

A person who acts this way is called an **akratic agent**. Socrates declared that akratic action is impossible and so have many other philosophers (including a very notable contemporary, R. M. Hare). This denial of the possibility of akrasia is summed up in the slogan: 'No one willingly does wrong.' The reason for taking this line (put briefly) is that the concept of akratic action appears to involve a self-contradiction (see section 3.2):

> To judge course-of-action X to be better than course-of-action Y seems to imply preferring course-of-action X to course-of-action Y.

> To choose to follow course-of-action Y rather than course-of-action X seems to imply preferring course-of-action Y to course-of-action X.

Against this, there is the stubborn conviction of many of us that people, including ourselves, very often do act akratically. That makes akrasia a *very* philosophical problem. We seem to have reached *aporia* (see section 6.22(g)). Such problems are central to the philosophical enterprise.

Akrasia is sometimes called *weakness of the will, moral weakness, weakness*, or *incontinence*. It is less confusing to call it **akrasia**. Mortimore, 1971, is a useful collection of articles on akrasia with a helpful introduction.

B.

'Hypocrisy' is a word with a very complicated history which is dealt with in great detail by Wilckens, 1971, and more simply by F. W. Young, 1962. Three things are clear about the meaning of this word in modern English:

(1) It is a word of very strong moral condemnation.
(2) It implies that the person accused is guilty of very serious insincerity.
(3) It implies that the motives for that insincerity are particularly dis- creditable.

These are reasons for using the word very sparingly and very cautiously. Not every insincerity or inconsistency can fairly be described as **hypocrisy**. More important still, a person does not become guilty of hypocrisy merely by holding moral opinions which you do not hold.

C.   Self-righteousness

Like 'hypocrisy', this word is often misused in controversy:

Mr X expresses disapproval of something.
Mr Y does not like to hear someone disapproving of that thing.
Mr Y therefore condemns Mr X for self-righteousness.

That sort of thing is by no means uncommon. But it is not justified. If 'Mr

X is self-righteous' means no more than 'I dislike or disagree with Mr X's expression of disapproval', there is no point in the extreme indignation with which accusations of self-righteousness are made.

The self-righteous person is someone who has an unduly high estimation of his own moral rectitude and an unduly low estimation of the moral rectitude of others. Further, these two unpleasant attitudes are mutually reinforcing. Such an accusation should not be made without very good reason. Those who fling the word 'self-righteous' about as a term of abuse frequently accompany it with the accusation that their opponent is adopting a 'holier-than-thou attitude'. A suitable reply is: 'And I don't like your less-sanctimonious-than-thou attitude.'

NB. To commit yourself to disapproval of all disapprovals is to get yourself into a logically indefensible position. Cf. section 3.1 on **self-refutation**.

D. Preaching and practising

It is sometimes assumed that, if a person acts contrary to the advice which he gives to others, his advice cannot be good advice. As a general principle, this is fallacious, though there may be special cases in which the conduct of the adviser can undermine his advice. Someone might argue as follows: 'Dr Bloggs told me that I am overweight and that I need to go on a diet. But I'm not going to take any notice of him. He's even more overweight than I am. His advice on diet can't be worth anything.' The arguer makes two tacit assumptions. One is a matter of particular fact about Dr Bloggs: that his obesity is to be explained by immoderate and lax diet. That may or may not be so. If it is not, then the argument (even on the arguer's own principles) is misguided. There is, however, a basic flaw in the argument. That flaw is the arguer's other tacit assumption, a general principle about advice and advisers which can be stated like this:

> If Primus advises Secundus to xify;
> AND
> If this commits Primus to xify himself,
> AND
> If Primus does not xify,
>
> then
> Secundus has good reason to reject Primus's advice.

This does not seem to be a good argument for all cases in which an adviser fails to follow his own advice when he is committed to following it. It does not seem to be a good argument in the present case.

There *is* something logically as well as morally odd about the position of someone who gives advice which he does not follow himself, but that is no reason for saying either that the advice is bad advice or even that the adviser is insincere or deceitful. He may mean every word of it. An inconsistency between advice and practice is a fault in the adviser and need not be the slightest reason for believing that the advice is faulty.

There is a superficially similar kind of case which needs to be distinguished. Suppose that the arguer had gone instead to Dr Snooks, who, though equally corpulent, says to the arguer: 'You must reduce your weight, and the way to do it is to take one of these tablets after meals for six months. They have a pleasant taste and have no unpleasant side-effects. They are called "Snooks's Patent Potent Pills" because I invented them. Here is a box containing a full course – yours for only $100.'

The objection 'Why doesn't he follow his own advice?' has a lot more point here and is, *prima facie*, a reason for rejecting his advice. There is a very probable explanation for Dr Bloggs's failure to follow his own advice: **akrasia** or *weakness of the will* (see A above). Following a strict diet is not much fun, but there seems no such difficulty in taking Snooks's Patent Potent Pills.

The general principle of good reasoning about cases such as these is not the one assumed by Dr Bloggs's patient. Rather it is something like this:

> If Primus advises Secundus to xify,
> AND
> if Primus is thereby committed to xify,
> AND
> if Primus does not xify,
> then
> Secundus should endeavour to work out why, and then carefully consider what relevance that explanation has to the question of how he, Secundus, should act.

See also sections 3.13(iv) (**consistency**), 4.27 (**tu quoque**), 4.28 (**argumentum ad hominem**).

E. Self-deception, bad faith

Both phrases are used to translate Jean-Paul Sartre's '*mauvaise foi*', the latter being more literal, the former being more accurate. A person deceives himself when he deliberately refuses to recognize a truth which he would find uncomfortable. Like **akrasia** (see A above), this is the sort of thing which would sound logically impossible except that we know perfectly well that it happens and that we have done it ourselves.

Sartre is particularly concerned with forms of self-deception in which we seek to avoid responsibility for our actions by regarding them not as what we choose to do, but as necessities imposed on us: we try to deny that we are agents and to represent ourselves as things. Sartre's treatment of this topic is (in my opinion) a fascinating mixture of great subtlety and great perversity. I would prefer not to try to summarize it, and, since this is not an examination, I can get away with that. See Sartre, 1956(a), Pt I, Ch. II; M. Warnock, 1967, pp. 29–38; Murdoch, 1967; Hamlyn, 1971; Mounce, 1971; Szabados, 1974.

9.7   CONSCIENCE; CASUISTRY

A.

Speak of **conscience** and many people will assume that you are talking about something like Pinocchio's friend, Jiminy Cricket – a strange little creature which delivers advice and admonition to the person whose conscience it is.

Of course, such a notion is easy to ridicule, but it is not the only possible notion of conscience. It makes better sense to *begin* by thinking of Mr X's conscience as Mr X's moral values, principles, attitudes, sentiments especially as they are believed or suspected by Mr X to bear upon his own actual or possible conduct: Mr X's conscience is Mr X being concerned with the morality of his own actions. See Midgley, 1979, pp. 266–273; Donnelly and Lyons, 1973; Feinberg, 1969, pp. 11–15, 74–92; D'Arcy, 1961; C. S. Lewis, 1960, Ch. VIII.

B.

'Casuistry' originally meant *applied ethics*; the attempt to apply moral principles to particular cases, especially to new and unexpected cases, and the attempt to deal with situations in which acceptable moral principles appear to clash. (Such problem-cases are sometimes called *cases of conscience*. The Latin for 'case' is *'casus'*, hence the word 'casuist'.)

That sense of the word survives, but – partly because this sort of activity can go very badly wrong and partly because of the success of certain propagandists – 'casuistry' has also acquired a pejorative ring. As Dorothy Emmet says: 'its popular meaning is dialectical skill in finding reasons for wriggling out of principles when they are inconvenient' (1966, pp. 50–51). But that is no reason for condemning casuistry as defined in the preceding paragraph.

'Casuistry' is pronounced with the stress on the first syllable. Someone who practises casuistry (neutral sense or pejorative sense) is a **casuist**. The adjectival forms are 'casuistic' (neutral) and 'casuistical' (almost always pejorative).

9.8   DOUBLE EFFECT

The principle (or doctrine) of double effect holds that a voluntary action which has two effects, one good and one evil, is morally permissible IFF:
  (i) The voluntary action is, in itself, good;
 (ii) The good effect must follow as directly as the evil effect;
(iii) The good must be in reasonable proportion to the evil; i.e., there must be a proportionately grave reason for performing the act and allowing the evil effect;
(iv) The evil effect is not intended or desired, even though it is foreseen.

As Flew's *Dictionary* says, the principle is 'characteristic of, but not confined to, Roman Catholic moral theology' (Flew, 1984, p. 97). It is frequently met with in discussion of such moral issues as the use of analgesics which relieve the pain of the terminally ill and also shorten their lives, and destruction of hostile military targets which has as a 'side-effect' the killing of some non-combatants. The principle is highly controversial. See Steinbock, 1980; Wasserstrom, 1970, pp. 15–53; St John-Stevas, 1961, Ch. VII; G. Williams, 1958, pp. 177–187, 285–291; Daly, 1962, pp. 134–138; Uniacke, 1980; Snare, 1980; Lockwood, 1983; Anscombe, 1983.

9.9 INNOCENT, INNOCUOUS

A.

The word '**innocent**' is derived from the Latin verb '*nocere*', 'to do harm, to inflict injury, to hurt' and its basic meaning is 'not guilty of wrongdoing'. It can have a disparaging sense, i.e., when it is used to suggest that the person so characterized is too ignorant or too stupid to be held *guilty* of wrongdoing (e.g., 'a political innocent'). The use of the word which treats it as exactly equivalent to 'ignorant about sexual matters' is deplorable.

In discussions of moral issues involving the taking and preserving of human life, the term 'innocent life', or 'innocent human being' has a special sense. It does not mean *someone who is sinless* or *free from moral blame*. It usually has the sense of *someone who is not an unjust aggressor*.

B.

'**Innocuous**' is another derivative from '*nocere*'. The emphasis in 'innocent' is on *absence of guilt*. 'Innocuous' stresses *lack of harmfulness* and can be used of things which *logically* could not be guilty or innocent (trees, liquids, beetles, etc.). It can, however, be used of human beings and can serve as a replacement for 'innocent' when that word might seem to have misleading associations.

9.10 CATEGORICAL IMPERATIVE

Immanuel Kant (1725–1804) distinguished **categorical imperatives** from *hypothetical imperatives*. A hypothetical imperative prescribes a means to an end: 'If you want z, then xify.' The imperative thus derives its force from a desire for z. 'Buy the latest rock records here' has no force for (or on) me if I do not want rock records. (Notice that a hypothetical imperative need not be expressed in conditional form.) A categorical imperative, however, is one which has force on me quite independently of any desires I may have. I may ignore it or act against it, but it binds me nonetheless. Kant regarded this as the distinguishing feature of moral imperatives. Cf. **categorical proposition** (see section 4.11). See Kant, 1948, pp. 27–30, 39–54; Acton, 1970, Ch. IV; Norman, 1983, Ch. VI.

9.11   DUTY, OBLIGATION; POLITICAL OBLIGATION

A.

The laws of the land, the regulations of other groups to which I belong, and morality require certain actions of me and certain abstentions from action. I ought to keep my promises and I ought to purchase a ticket before boarding a train. I ought not spit on the footpath or make rash judgments about my neighbour.

In ordinary talk and in much moral and political philosophy, the words 'duty' and 'obligation' are used interchangeably to refer to those requirements. Some philosophers, however, have given the words special meanings. On this use, my **obligations** are *what I have undertaken* to do or to abstain from doing, and my **duties** are requirements for action or for abstention from action which apply without my having undertaken to perform them. (I have a **duty** to tell the truth, but an **obligation** to give the lectures required of me by my contract with the University of Newcastle.) See Woozley, 1971, pp. 312–315.

The distinction is a genuine one and that can be a useful way of making it, provided one announces loudly and clearly that that is how one intends to use the words 'duty' and 'obligation'. It is something worse than bad manners to pretend that these are *the* only correct meanings of the words. See Lacey, 1976, pp. 148–151; Hampshire, 1978, p. 8. For a distinction between *being obliged to xify* and *having an obligation to xify*, see Hart, 1961, Ch. V, section 2. For **prima facie duty**, see section 9.12.

B.

Broadly speaking, the problem of **political obligation** is:

Under what circumstances (if any) am I morally required to obey the laws of my country and the orders of its office-holders? Under what circumstances (if any) am I morally entitled or required to disobey those laws and orders? See also section 9.13B (**tacit consent**). See Macfarlane, 1970, Ch. III; McPherson, 1967; Chipman, Hamel-Green *et al.*, 1974.

9.12   PRIMA FACIE

A.

In moral philosophy, most talk of **prima facie rights** and **prima facie duties** is derived from the writings of Sir David Ross (e.g., Ross, 1930, pp. 17–47, 58–

64). For a good introductory treatment, see W. D. Hudson, 1983, pp. 87–99. In this context, **prima facie** does *not* merely mean 'on first appearances'.

If I say 'I promise to pay you $10.00 at 4.30 p.m. tomorrow,' I have a **prima facie** duty to pay you $10.00 at 4.30 p.m. tomorrow and you have a **prima facie** right to receive $10.00 from me at 4.30 p.m. tomorrow. That means that if the facts as stated (i.e., what was said, who said it, to whom it was said) are the only relevant facts, I actually do have this duty and you actually do have this right. But there may be other facts which alter the moral relationship between us so that I do not actually have this duty and you do not actually have this right. For instance, on my way to meet you, I see someone desperately trying to stop a grass-fire from spreading to his house. My duty to help him takes precedence over the **prima facie** right and duty spoken of above. 'Prima facie' is pronounced: 'PRYma FAYSS-e-e'.

If I have a duty/right which no circumstance could render inoperative, that duty/right is an **indefeasible** duty/right. So a **prima facie** duty or right can be called a **defeasible** duty or right. The word 'defeasible' is borrowed from English legal terminology in which it is 'used of a legal interest in property which is subject to termination or "*defeat*" in a number of different contingencies but remains intact if no such contingencies mature' (Hart, 1951, p. 148).

B.

In legal talk, **to make out a prima facie case** is to present argument and evidence which will establish a conclusion unless successfully rebutted. If a magistrate finds that there is a **prima facie** case against a defendant, he finds that the prosecution has presented argument and evidence which, unless rebutted, could be enough to lead a reasonable jury to convict the defendant. To find that there is a **prima facie** case against a defendant is to find that *he has a case to answer*. The case against him is *defeasible* (see A above), but strong.

Thus, in legal and other talk, to say that an argument establishes a **prima facie** case is to give qualified endorsement to that argument. Cf. in one sense of 'strong', **strong argument** (see section 4.19B) and **arguable** (see section 8.10). See also section 8.9A (**onus of proof**).

9.13   OVERT, COVERT; TACIT, IMPLICIT, EXPLICIT

A.   Overt, inner, covert

My **overt** behaviour is my *observable* behaviour, including my behaviour which *could* be observed *if* there were anyone about to observe it. You can see me furrow my brow, scratch my head, and look puzzled, but you cannot (or so it seems) see my puzzlement and my thinking. We make statements about other people's thoughts, feelings, and sensations, but we make those statements on the basis of statements about something that might seem quite different: other people's **overt** behaviour. This gives rise to what is called '*the problem of other minds*'. See sections 7.3C (**solipsism**), 7.11 (**behaviourism**). In philosophical talk, **overt** (or **outer**) behaviour is usually contrasted with **inner** behaviour. But sometimes 'inner' is put in scare-quotes (see section 1.6B(ii)). Magee, 1973, Ch. VI, is interesting on this.

'Covert' looks as if it should be the opposite of 'overt', but it is not, since (in its modern sense) it implies *deliberate* concealment. The pronunciation 'KOvert' has become common, though some still prefer to rhyme the first syllable with 'love'.

B.   Tacit, implicit, explicit

Our word 'tacit' comes from the Latin '*tacere*', 'to be silent'. To assume a proposition tacitly is to assume it without saying so. Bringing to light tacit assumptions is an important aspect of philosophical activity. (But merely bringing them to light is not the same as discrediting them. See section 5.5C.) If Mr X says something which makes a tacit assumption, that assumption is **implicit in** what he has said. To bring his assumption to light is **to make it explicit.**

Tacit consent plays an important (and sometimes rather dubious) role in consent theories of political obligation (i.e., theories which ground the citizen's duty to obey the government on the citizen's consent). See Macfarlane, 1970, Ch. III; Plamenatz, 1968.

'Implicit' and 'explicit', like 'explication' (see section 5.14) and 'implication' (see section 4.4) are etymologically linked to a metaphor of *being wrapped up* and *unwrapping*. Cf. section 5.14(iv) (**unpacking**). See also section 4.22 (**elliptical argument**).

It is a fairly frequent practice these days to use 'explicit' as a non-condemnatory substitute for 'obscene'. The extra syllables in 'sexually explicit' are, apparently, just too much trouble. It is to be hoped that 'explicit' does not go the way of 'promiscuous' and 'intercourse', each of which now Means (as they say) Only One Thing. Not so long ago, they were more generally useful. See *OED*.

9.14   ALIBI; EXCUSE

A.

Alibi (literally 'elsewhere') is a bit of legal Latin. When an accused person says that he could not have committed the crime because he was elsewhere at the time, his defence is called 'an alibi'. More popularly, 'an alibi' means **evidence** (see section 5.2B) showing or tending to show that an accused was elsewhere. There is no point in using the word 'alibi' as a 'learned' substitute for 'excuse'.

B. Excuse, reason, justification, extenuation

It is perhaps worth observing that sometimes excuses do excuse and that, therefore, neither 'alibi' nor 'excuse' should be regarded as a derogatory word. It is sometimes thought that **excuses** are always poor things, morally inferior to **reasons**. But that need not be so. If Primus pushes Secundus off the cliff because Secundus stands between him and a rich inheritance, he has a reason for his action, but it is not morally sufficient. If Primus pushes Secundus off the cliff because Secundus is about to shoot the innocent Tertius and there is no other way of stopping him, then he has an excuse, which is also a reason, and is morally quite sufficient. His excuse excuses because it indicates that the action was not what it might appear (a murderous assault on an innocent person) but something justified (a defence of an innocent person against murderous assault).

That excuse would be a *justification*. Not all excuses, even acceptable ones, are. Some may *extenuate* or *mitigate* the moral wrongness of the action (e.g., Tertius has been provoked to an extraordinary degree by Quartus, but he still shouldn't have done it). For a philosophical discussion of excuses, see J. L. Austin, 1979, pp. 175–204. See also Kovesi, 1967; Kolnai, 1977, pp. 211–224; Hart, 1970.

10   Relations

10.1   OPPOSITION

A.   Opposition of propositions

In the terminology of Traditional Logic (see section 6.24), two propositions are opposed IFF:

(i)   they have the same terms (see section 6.29A(ii))

AND

(ii)   they differ in quality and/or quantity (see section 6.29A(iii)–(v)).

Thus: 'Every man is mortal' and 'At least one man is mortal' are **opposed propositions**. They have the same *terms* ('man' and 'mortal'), but they differ in *quantity*. (The first is *universal*; the second is *particular*.) Similarly: 'Some people are Marxists' and 'Some people are not Marxists' are also opposed propositions. They have the same *terms*, but they differ in *quality*. (The first is *affirmative*; the second is *negative*.)

The word 'opposition' may suggest incompatibility (see section 10.2), even hostility, but as these examples indicate, two **opposed** propositions may be compatible. The sense of 'opposition' here is closely related to the original etymology: *placed facing*. The picture to have in mind is not two duellists with pistols raised but two people talking to each other on the same topic. See section 10.3 (**logical relations**). See also Luce, 1958, Ch. IV.

For **the square of opposition**, see D. Mitchell, 1964, pp. 32–33, or Luce, 1958, pp. 72–73. For a more useful **asymmetrical figure of opposition**, see Stebbing, 1950, pp. 59–60. Unless one is prepared to accept the doctrine that there are four and only four forms of proposition (see sections 5.19A(ii), 6.24(ii)), these figures are of very limited value.

B. Opposition of terms

(For **terms**, see section 6.29A(ii).)

Unfortunately, Traditional Logic has given the word 'opposition' another and quite different technical sense.

> Two *terms* 'A' and 'B' are *logical opposites* to each other within a given universe IFF every member of that universe can be described *either* as A *or* as B AND *no* member of that universe can be described as *both* A and B.

Thus, within the universe of organisms, the terms 'vertebrate' and 'non-vertebrate' are logical opposites to each other. (For **universe**, see section 1.27.) Notice that, if two terms are logically opposite to each other, they are *mutually exclusive* AND *collectively exhaustive* (see section 1.28).

Not all commonly drawn contrasts are pairs of logical opposites. *Young and old, winners and losers*: these are commonly drawn contrasts, but they are not pairs of logical opposites. In each case, the terms are mutually exclusive, but not collectively exhaustive. There are people who are middle-aged, and non-starters who neither win nor lose.

Some logicians speak of:

contradictory opposites   (terms which are mutually exclusive and collectively exhaustive)

and

contrary opposites   (terms which are mutually exclusive but not collectively exhaustive)

A different contrast is drawn between:

logical opposites   (terms which are mutually exclusive and collectively exhaustive)

and

popular opposites   (terms which are commonly contrasted, but which *may* not be logical opposites)

Students sometimes get the idea that, because *logical* opposites and *popular* opposites are contrasted, there is something *illogical* and silly about popular opposites. That is not so. There is nothing *il*logical about contrasting (e.g.) youth and age. 'Logical' here means simply that the contrast is based on a doctrine of logic. 'Popular' means simply that a contrast is *in fact* drawn by a great many speakers of the language. The only sort of 'inferiority' attaching to popular opposites is that, unlike logical opposites, there is no single basis on which the distinctions are drawn.

Pairs of logical opposites are (by definition) pairs of contradictory opposites, but pairs of popular opposites may be pairs of contradictory opposites or pairs of contrary opposites (or even something stranger such as the pair *pleasure and pain*; see Kenny, 1963, Ch. VI, especially p. 128, note 3). Popular opposites are sometimes called *Roget opposites* (after Roget's *Thesaurus*). See section 2.6A on **synonymy** and **antonymy**.

10.2   COMPATIBILITY AND INCOMPATIBILITY

The propositions p and q are **compatible** IFF the proposition (p & q) is NOT self-contradictory (i.e., is internally consistent – see section 3.2). The propositions p and q are **incompatible** IFF the proposition (p & q) IS self-contradictory. Thus, of the seven logical relations (see section 10.3), *contrariety* and *contradiction* are the two **relations of incompatibility** and each of the five others is a **relation of compatibility**.

10.3   THE SEVEN LOGICAL RELATIONS

The following questions can be asked about any pair of contingent statements p and q:

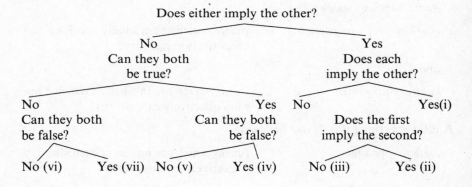

On the basis of the answers to these questions, we can say that p is in one of seven relations to q.

 (i) If p implies q and q implies p, the relation between p and q is *equivalence*; p and q are *equivalent to each other*. Equivalence is *mutual implication*.

(iii) and (ii) If p implies q, but q does not imply p, the relation of p to q is *superimplication*, and the relation of q to p is *subimplication*. (Superimplication is sometimes called *superalternation* and subimplication is sometimes called *subalternation*.)

Equivalence, superimplication, and subimplication are *implicative* relations, i.e., at least one of the statements so related implies the other.

(iv) If there are two propositions p and q, neither of which implies the other, and if p and q are compatible (see section 10.2) and if the negations of p and q are also compatible, then the relation between p and q is *indifference*; p and q are *indifferent* to each other. (For **negation** see section 6.12.)

(v) If p and q are compatible and if the negations of p and q are *in*compatible, then the relation between p and q is *subcontrariety*; p is *a subcontrary of* q and q is *a subcontrary of* p (see also section 10.5).

(vii) and (vi) If p and q are incompatible, and if their negations are compatible, then the relation between p and q is *contrariety*; p is *contrary to q* and q is *contrary to p* (see also section 10.4).

If p and q are incompatible, and if their negations are incompatible, the relation between them is *contradiction*; p is *the contradictory of* q and q *is the contradictory of* p (see also section 10.4).

Summary with examples

Conditions	*Relation*	*Example*
(i) If p is true, q must be true AND If p is false, q must be false.	**Equivalence**	Let p be: 'Today is Tuesday.' Let q be: 'Today is the day between Monday and Wednesday.'
(ii) If p is true, q must be true AND If p is false, q may be either true or false.	p is in the relation of **Superimplication** (or **Super-alter-nation**) to q.	Let p be: 'Today is Good Friday.' Let q be: 'Today is Friday.'
(iii) If p is true, q may be either true or false AND If p is false, q must be false.	p is in the relation of **Subimplication** (or **Subalterna-tion**) to q.	Let p be: 'Today is Friday.' Let q be: 'Today is Good Friday.'
(iv) If p is true, q may be either true or false AND If p is false, q may be either true or false.	**Indifference**	Let p be: 'Today is Tuesday.' Let q be: 'The passion-fruit are ready for picking.'
(v) If p is true, q may be true or false AND If p is false, q must be true.	**Subcontrariety**	Let p be: 'Today is not Tuesday.' Let q be: 'Today is not Wednesday.'
(vi) If p is true, q must be false AND If p is false, q must be true.	**Contradiction**	Let p be: 'Today is Tuesday.' Let q be: 'Today is not Tuesday.'

(vii) If p is true, q must be false AND If p is false, q may be true or false.	**Contrariety**	Let p be: 'Today is Tuesday.' Let q be: 'Today is Wednesday.'

Doing logical relations exercises is a very good way to increase your awareness of the depths, shallows, and sandbanks of language.

Hamblin, 1966, is a useful programmed text which will enable you to test your progress as you go along. For more traditional treatments, see Luce, 1958, Ch. IV, and Angell, 1964, pp. 85–103. (The 'question-tree' in this section is borrowed from Hamblin.) Lemmon, 1965, pp. 69–73 discusses logical relations with reference to the techniques of symbolic logic.

10.4   CONTRADICTION AND CONTRARIETY

(i) In ordinary talk, *to contradict someone* is to voice disagreement with something he has said. That, however, tends to obscure a distinction which needs to be noticed. Consider these two fragments of dialogue:

Fragment A
Mr X: 'Today is Wednesday.'

Mr Y: 'Today is Tuesday.'

Fragment B
Mr X: 'Today is Wednesday.'

Mr Y: 'Today is not Wednesday.'

In either case, Mr Y has told Mr X that he is wrong, so *according to ordinary talk*, Mr Y has, in either case, *contradicted* Mr X. But notice an important difference between the two cases:

In *Fragment A*, they cannot both be right, but *they can both be wrong*.

In *Fragment B*, they cannot both be right, but they can*not* both be wrong. One of them has to be right.

In the technical talk of logic, the word 'contradiction' is reserved for incompatibilities of the Fragment B type. Incompatibilities of the Fragment A type are *not* cases of contradiction, but of **contrariety**. Contradiction and contrariety are two of *the seven classical logical relations* (see section 10.3). Confusing them is a popular way of setting up a **straw man** (see section 4.26).

(ii) The **contradictory of a proposition** is the *negation of that proposition* (see section 6.12). To assert a **contrary** of p is to negate p *and do something else as well.*

(iii) All statements which are true IFF p is false and false IFF p is true are equivalent to one another; i.e., they *assert the same proposition* (see section 1.2A); hence, it is appropriate to talk of *the contradictory of p*.

But it is *not* appropriate to talk of *the contrary of p*. Let p be 'Today is Wednesday.' 'Today is Tuesday' is incompatible with p, but both might be false; hence 'Today is Tuesday' and p are contraries. 'Today is Thursday' is in precisely the same relation to p, but 'Today is Tuesday' is not equivalent to 'Today is Thursday.' Each is *a* contrary of 'Today is Wednesday.' Contrariety is **a non-transitive relation** (see section 10.6(ix)).

(iv) Avoid using sentences of the 'All Xs are not Y' type. They are ambiguous between the **contradiction** of 'All Xs are Y' (i.e., 'There are non-Y Xs') and a **contrary** of it (i.e., 'No Xs are Y' or 'There are no Y Xs'). Such idiomatic phrases as 'All is not well' and 'All that glitters is not gold' give us no problems, but 'All the members are not in favour of the proposal' fails to convey the intended information (and how would you feel if told 'All the citizens are not in favour of lynching you'?). 'All Xs are not Y' is an **ill-formed formula** (see section 6.5).

(v) Some philosophers and logicians use the phrase 'a contradiction' to mean 'a self-contradiction'. This habit is not very helpful and should not be copied. For **self-contradiction**, see section 3.2.

(vi) A **contradiction in terms** is a self-contradictory statement or description (see section 3.2). 'Round square' is a celebrated example. It is a 'description' which can describe nothing because there is a logical inconsistency between its two elements, the adjective 'round' and the noun 'square'. See also section 3.12A (**logical impossibility**).

(vii) Marxists have the habit of using the word 'contradiction' for *any* kind of contrast, opposition, conflict, or distinction. This is a very bad habit indeed as it leads to a great deal of confusion and deception. Sometimes, the deception is not intentional. On this, see Flew, 1975, pp. 18–20. (In a pamphlet published in Peking during the heyday of Maoism, a devotee tells us how the study of Mao's works enabled his comrades to Solve the Particular Contradictions of Onions: *SPD*, 1972, pp. 30–31.)

10.5 SUBCONTRARIETY

This logical relation is dealt with in section 10.3, but it deserves a section to itself as well, because it seems to be the most difficult one to grasp. It is very easy to mistake a pair of subcontraries for a pair of indifferent propositions. This comes about because of failure to grasp the logical **principle of double negation**: - - p is equivalent to p; if it is false that it is false that p, then p is true. The example of subcontrariety given in section 10.3 was:

'Today is not Tuesday.'
'Today is not Wednesday.'

Certainly if either of these is true, then the other may be true or may be false. But if one of them is false, the other *must* be true. Why? Let us assume that the first of the statements is false. We can represent that by crossing out the 'not':

'Today is ~~not~~ Tuesday.'
'Today is not Wednesday.'

If it is *false* that today is *not* Tuesday, then today is Tuesday, in which case it must be true that today is not Wednesday. Watch out for double negation. Many people get tripped up by it.

10.6 SYMMETRICAL RELATIONS, NON-SYMMETRICAL RELATIONS, ASYMMETRICAL RELATIONS, ANTI-SYMMETRICAL RELATIONS, REFLEXIVE RELATIONS, TRANSITIVE RELATIONS, NON-TRANSITIVE RELATIONS

Let R be a relation.

(i) R is **symmetrical** IFF 'X is related in R fashion to Y' implies that Y is related in R fashion to X. Of the seven logical relations (see section 10.3), **equivalence, contrariety, subcontrariety, contradiction**, and **indifference** are symmetrical. *Cousinship* is a symmetrical relation. So is *being a workmate of*. So is *being a sibling of* (but NOT *being a brother of*).

(ii) R is **non-symmetrical** IFF 'X is related in R fashion to Y' does *not* imply that Y is related in R fashion to X. **Implication** is a non-symmetrical relation, as is *being a brother of*.

(iii) R is **asymmetrical** IFF 'X is related in R fashion to Y' implies that Y is *not* related in R fashion to X. **Subimplication** and **superimplication** are asymmetrical relations, and so is *being the father of*.

(iv) R is **anti-symmetrical** IFF 'X is related in R fashion to Y and Y is related in R fashion to X' implies that X and Y are identical. Thus, *being a number not less than* is anti-symmetrical.

(v) R is **reflexive** IFF X *must* be related in R fashion to itself if X is related in R fashion to anything. Every proposition implies itself and every proposition is equivalent to itself, so **implication** and **equivalence** are reflexive relations. *Being a child of the same parents* is reflexive. (Socrates is a child of the same parents as Socrates.)

(vi) R is **irreflexive (aliorelative)** IFF nothing can be related to itself in R fashion (e.g., *being the brother of* and all the classical logical relations except equivalence).

(vii) R is **non-reflexive** IFF it is possible that something is related in R fashion to itself and possible that something is not related in R fashion to itself (e.g., *approves of*).

(viii) R is **transitive** IFF 'X is related in R fashion to Y' and 'Y is related in R fashion to Z' *together* imply that X is related in R fashion to Z. Thus, **implication** is a transitive relation.

(ix) R is **non-transitive** IFF 'X is related in R fashion to Y' and 'Y is related in R fashion to Z', taken together, do *not* imply that X is related in R fashion to Z. **Indifference** is a non-transitive relation. 'Things go better with Coke' is indifferent to 'All men are mortal.' 'All men are mortal' is indifferent to 'Things go worse with Coke.' But 'Things go better with Coke' is not indifferent to 'Things go worse with Coke'. *Being a friend of* is also non-transitive. If Tom is a friend of John, and John is a friend of Peter, it is possible that Tom is a friend of Peter, but it is also possible that Tom is not a friend of Peter.

(x) R is **intransitive** IFF 'X is related in R fashion to Y and Y is related in R fashion to Z' implies that X is *not* related in R fashion to Z; e.g., *being a parent of*.

See D. Mitchell, 1964, pp. 149–153; Flew, 1984, pp. 301–302.

10.7 RELEVANCE

Relevance is a *relation*. Nothing can be simply and absolutely above. It can only be above something else. Similarly, nothing can be simply and absolutely relevant or irrelevant. It can only be relevant or irrelevant to something else. Something can be relevant to issue A but not relevant to issue B. 'Relevant' is not a synonym of 'important', nor is 'irrelevant' a synonym of 'trivial'. Whether Bloggs has cancer and the situation in Lebanon are mutually irrelevant. Neither is a trivial matter.

If someone says 'Education must be relevant', he should always be asked 'Relevant to what?' If he replies 'Relevant to the really important issues', he should be (i) asked what he thinks these are, and (ii) reminded that there can be disagreement between reasonable people over what is 'really important'. Too often, the demand for educational 'relevance' is a demand that schools and universities should be totally devoted to the service of the demander's socio-political goals. There are also those who use 'Education must be relevant' as code for 'Do not disturb me with difficulties or unfamiliar ideas', overlooking the fact that 'Education is learning what you didn't even know you didn't know' (Boorstin, 1975, p. 51). Sometimes the demand for 'relevance' may be an expression of something more respectworthy than totalitarianism or philistine bone-laziness, but it is always an obscure demand. I for one would not think much of a form of education which encouraged people to be content with sloganistic rant. See Frankel, 1968; Cockburn and Blackburn, 1969; Boorstin, 1975; Condren, 1979. See also section 8.10B (**contestable**). For **fallacies of irrelevance**, see section 4.25. 'Irrelevant' is sometimes used as a substitute for 'ineffective'. ('Inflation was rising again and [government] controls, clearly were irrelevant' – Gwyn, 1981, p. 196.) 'Ineffective' is better.

Notes

1 SAYING THINGS

1. I am using this word in a very wide sense which includes nations or polities as well as the smaller collections of people which we normally call groups.
2. But, of course, Jefferson was thereby committing himself to more than he wanted (or, perhaps, wanted *just yet*). That's the trouble with moral principles. See sections 9.5A and 9.6A and cf. the heartfelt prayer of the not-yet-Saint Augustine: 'God, grant me chastity and continence, but not yet' (*Confessions*, Bk VIII, Ch. VII: Augustine, 1944, p. 134).

2 MEANING

1. It would be clearer to say 'declared such', but the ardent civil libertarian from whom I quote has always been stronger on moral indignation than on clarity.

3 NONSENSE, NECESSITY, AND POSSIBILITY

1. ' "X is, therefore X is possible" is a valid inference.'

4 INFERRING, IMPLYING, ARGUING, AND 'IF'

1. See *Through the Looking Glass*, Ch. VI, and Heath's note: Carroll, 1974, p. 195.
2. In this sub-section, I have borrowed some examples from Dr Paul Thom (197?, pp. 6–8).

5 INVESTIGATING

1. An American novelist called Rand, who is sometimes mistaken for a philosopher, uses the word 'objectivism' in a weird sense all her own. I mention her only to make clear that I am not talking about her 'philosophical system', on which, see Hospers, 1967 (index) and J. D. MacKenzie, 1975.
2. Reprinted as Ch. III of Maritain, 1956.
3. To posit a proposition is to assume it as a hypothesis or to treat it as a truth.
4. 'Alternation' has been used instead, would be better, but has totally failed to catch on.
5. *'Theos'* is the Greek for 'God'.

6 SYMBOLS; BASIC PROPOSITIONAL FORMS; BASIC ARGUMENTAL FORMS

1. Syllogistic reasoning involves *two* premisses and a *middle* term, and is therefore called *mediate* inference. An *immediate* inference is one involving only *one* premiss and no middle term (see section 4.3(ii)). 'Immediate' here does not mean 'quick'. See D. Mitchell, 1964, Ch. II; Luce, 1958, Ch. IV; Maritain, 1937, pp. 162–169.

7 OF ISMS, ISTS, AND OLOGIES

1. The word 'reism' has been used also for the very different philosophy that objects of belief, hope, desire, etc. (even non-existent ones) must, in *some* way, be objective (see Flew, 1984, p. 301). There is a curse on ism-words.
2. The 'taking apart'/'putting together' metaphor is at the base of the technical senses of 'analytic' and 'synthetic'. The predicate of an analytic proposition either merely 'takes apart' the subject ('A triangle is a three-sided plane figure') or extracts an element from the meaning of the subject ('A triangle is three-sided'). In a synthetic proposition, the predicate adds something not in the subject ('A triangle is the emblem of the YWCA').
3. It is also possible for a philosopher to be both British and an empiricist but not a British Empiricist in this sense (e.g. Quinton). It might be less confusing to call Locke etc. *classical empiricists*.
4. For some introductory reading on decision theory, see Audley *et al.*, 1967, or D. W. Miller and Starr, 1967. Raz. 1978, is a good collection of articles.

8 ARGUING AND INVESTIGATING AGAIN

1. *ECHU*, section X, Pt II: Hume, 1975, p. 125. See also *ibid.*, section V, Pt I, pp. 40–41; section XII, pp. 149–165.

Bibliography

ARCHR: *see* Australia – Royal Commission on Human Relationships

Ackrill, J. L. (1975) 'Aristotle', in J. O. Urmson (ed.) *The Concise Encyclopedia of Western Philosophy and Philosophers*, London: Hutchinson.

Acton, H. B. (1955) *The Illusion of the Epoch: Marxism-Leninism as a Philosophical Creed*, London: Cohen & West.

(1970) *Kant's Moral Philosophy*, London: Macmillan.

(1975) 'Materialism', in J. O. Urmson (ed.) *The Concise Encyclopedia of Western Philosophy and Philosophers*, London: Hutchinson.

Adams, E. M. (1967) 'Lewis, Clarence Irving', in *The Encyclopedia of Philosophy*, ed. Paul Edwards, New York: Macmillan & Free Press.

Aldrich, Virgil C. (1963) *Philosophy of Art*, Englewood Cliffs: Prentice-Hall.

Allers, Rudolf (1955) 'Universals', in D. D. Runes (ed.) *Dictionary of Philosophy*, Ames, Iowa: Littlefield, Adams.

Allport, Gordon W. (1958) *The Nature of Prejudice* (abridged edn), Garden City, New York: Anchor/Doubleday.

Alston, William P. (1964) *Philosophy of Language*, Englewood Cliffs: Prentice-Hall.

Anderson, John (1962) *Studies in Empirical Philosophy*, Sydney: Angus & Robertson.

(1980) *Education and Inquiry* (ed. by D. Z. Phillips), Oxford: Blackwell.

(1982) *Art and Reality: John Anderson on Literature and Aesthetics* (ed. by Janet Anderson, Graham Cullum, Kimon Lycos), Sydney: Hale & Iremonger.

Andreski, Stanislav L. (1970) 'Ideal Type', in G. D. Mitchell (ed.) *A Dictionary of Sociology*, London: Routledge & Kegan Paul.

(1974) *Social Sciences as Sorcery*, Harmondsworth: Penguin.

Angell, Richard B. (1964) *Reasoning and Logic*, New York: Appleton-Century-Crofts.

Angluin, D. J. C. (1974) 'Austin's Mistake about Real', *Philosophy* XLIX:47–62.

Anschutz, R. P. (1968) 'The Logic of J. S. Mill', *Mind* LVIII(1949):277–305; reprinted in J. B. Schneewind (ed.) *Mill: A Collection of Critical Essays*, London: Macmillan, pp. 46–83.

Anscombe, Gertrude Elizabeth Margaret (1962) 'Hume Reconsidered', *Blackfriars* XLIII:187–190.

(1981) *The Collected Papers of G. E. M. Anscombe* Vol III *Ethics, Religion and Politics*, Oxford: Blackwell.

(1983) 'Sins of Omission? The Non-Treatment of Controls in Clinical Trials', *Proceedings of the Aristotelian Society* Supplementary Vol. LVII:223–227.

Anscombe, G. E. M. and Geach, Peter T. (1961) *Three Philosophers*, Oxford: Blackwell.

Anselm, (Saint) (1965) *St Anselm's 'Proslogion' with 'A Reply on Behalf of the Fool' by Gaunilo and 'The Author's Reply to Gaunilo'* (trans. with an introduction and philosophical commentary by M. J. Charlesworth), Oxford: Clarendon Press.

Anstey, F.: *see* Guthrie, Thomas Anstey

Aquinas, (Saint) Thomas: *see* Thomas Aquinas (Saint)

Ardley, Gavin (1950) *Aquinas and Kant: The Foundations of the Modern Sciences*, London: Longmans, Green.

Aristotle (1976) *The Ethics of Aristotle: The Nicomachean Ethics* (trans. by J. A. K. Thomson; rev. with notes and appendices by Hugh Tredennick; introduction and bibliography by Jonathan Barnes), Harmondsworth: Penguin.

Armstrong, A. Hilary (1961) 'Platonism', in Ian Ramsey, (ed.) *Prospect for Metaphysics: Essays of Metaphysical Exploration*, London: Allen & Unwin, pp. 93–110.

— (1965) *An Introduction to Ancient Philosophy* (4th edn), London: Methuen.

Armstrong, David M. (1961) *Perception and the Physical World*, London: Routledge & Kegan Paul.

— (1962) *Bodily Sensations*, London: Routledge & Kegan Paul.

— (1973) *Belief, Truth and Knowledge*, Cambridge: Cambridge University Press.

— (1975) 'Towards a Theory of Properties: Work in Progress on the Problem of Universals', *Philosophy* L:145–155.

— (1978) *A Theory of Universals: Universals and Scientific Realism* (Vol. II), Cambridge: Cambridge University Press.

— (1979) 'Laws of Nature: Why They Cannot Be Mere Uniformities', *Proceedings of the Russellian Society* [Sydney University] IV:46–63.

— (1980) *'The Nature of Mind' and Other Essays*, St Lucia: University of Queensland Press.

— (1983) *What is a Law of Nature?*, Cambridge: Cambridge University Press.

Ashby, Ronald W. (1964) 'Logical Positivism', in D. J. O'Connor (ed.) *A Critical History of Western Philosophy*, Glencoe, Illinois: Free Press, pp. 492–508.

Auden, Wystan Hugh (1977) *The English Auden: Poems, Essays and Dramatic Writings 1927–1939* (ed. by Edward Mendelson), London: Faber.

Audley, R. J. *et al.* (1967) *Decision Making*, London: BBC.

Augustine, (Saint) (1944) *The Confessions of St Augustine* (trans. by F. J. Sheed), London: Sheed & Ward.

Aune, Bruce (1967) 'If', in *The Encyclopedia of Philosophy*, ed. Paul Edwards, New York: Macmillan & Free Press.

Austin, Jean (1968) 'Pleasure and Happiness', *Philosophy* XLIII:51–62. Also published as pp. 144–153 in Smith and Sosa, 1969, and as pp. 234–250 in Schneewind, 1968.

Austin, John (1954) *The Province of Jurisprudence Determined* (ed. by H.L.A. Hart), London: Weidenfeld and Nicolson.

Austin, John Langshaw (1962) *Sense and Sensibilia*, Oxford: Clarendon Press.

— (1979) *Philosophical Papers* (3rd edn), Oxford: Oxford University Press.

Australia – Royal Commission on Human Relationships (1977(a)) *Final Report* (Vol. I), Canberra: Australian Government Publishing Service.

— (1977(b)) *Final Report* (Vol. V), Canberra: Australian Government Publishing Service.

Ayer, (Sir) Alfred Jules (1936) *Language, Truth and Logic*, London: Gollancz.

— (1946) *Language, Truth and Logic* (2nd edn), London: Gollancz.

— (1954) *Philosophical Essays*, London: Macmillan.

— (1956) *The Problem of Knowledge*, Harmondsworth: Penguin.

266 *Talking Philosophy*

266 *Talking Philosophy*

(1959) (ed.) *Logical Positivism*, Glencoe, Illinois: Free Press.

(1969) *Metaphysics and Common Sense*, London: Macmillan.

(1976) *The Central Questions of Philosophy*, Harmondsworth: Penguin.

Baalman, John (1979) *Outline of Law in Australia* (4th edn by Geoffrey A. Flick), Sydney: Law Book Co.

Baker, A. James (1979) *Anderson's Social Philosophy*, Sydney: Angus & Robertson.

(1986) *Australian Realism: The Systematic Philosophy of John Anderson*, Cambridge: Cambridge University Press.

Baker, Robert (1975) ' "Pricks" and "Chicks": A Plea for "Persons" ', in R. A. Wasserstrom (ed.) *Today's Moral Problems*, New York: Macmillan, pp. 152–171.

Bambrough, Renford (1979) *Moral Scepticism and Moral Knowledge*, London: Routledge & Kegan Paul.

Barnes, Jonathan (1972) *The Ontological Argument*, London: Macmillan.

Basson, A. H. and O'Connor, D. J. (1959) *Introduction to Symbolic Logic* (3rd edn), London: University Tutorial Press.

Beardsmore, R. W. (1969) *Moral Reasoning*, London: Routledge & Kegan Paul.

Becker, Alton L.: *see* Young, Richard E., Becker, Alton L., and Pike, Kenneth L.

Beckner, Morton (1967) 'Teleology', in *The Encyclopedia of Philosophy*, ed. Paul Edwards, New York: Macmillan & Free Press.

Benn, Stanley Isaac (1976) 'Freedom, Autonomy and the Concept of a Person', *Proceedings of the Aristotelian Society* n.s. LXXVI(1975/76):109–130.

(1984) 'Abortion, Infanticide, and Respect for Persons', pp. 135–144 in J. Feinberg (ed.) *The Problem of Abortion* (2nd edn), Belmont, California: Wadsworth.

Benn, Stanley Isaac and Gaus, G. F. (eds) (1983) *Public and Private in Social Life*, London: Croom Helm.

Benn, Stanley Isaac and Peters, Richard Stanley (1959) *Social Principles and the Democratic State*, London: Allen & Unwin.

Bennett, Jonathan (1966) 'Real', *Mind* n.s. LXXV:501–515.

Benson, John (1983) 'Who is the Autonomous Man?', *Philosophy* LVIII:5–17.

Bensusan-Butt, D. M. (1978) *On Economic Man: An Essay on the Elements of Economic Theory*, Canberra: Australian National University Press.

Berlin, (Sir) Isaiah (1953) *The Hedgehog and the Fox: An Essay on Tolstoy's View of History*, New York: Simon & Schuster.

Bernard, J. R. L.-B. (1975) *A Short Guide to Traditional Grammar*, Sydney: Sydney University Press.

Bird, Graham (1962) *Kant's Theory of Knowledge: An Outline of One Central Argument in the 'Critique of Pure Reason'*, London: Routledge & Kegan Paul.

Black, Max (1949) *Language and Philosophy: Studies in Method*, Ithaca, NY: Cornell University Press.

(1950) (ed.) *Philosophical Analysis*, Ithaca, NY: Cornell University Press.

(1972) *The Labyrinth of Language*, Harmondsworth: Penguin.

(1975) *Caveats and Critiques: Philosophical Essays in Language, Logic, and Art*, Ithaca, NY: Cornell University Press.

Blackburn, Robin: *see* Cockburn, Alexander and Blackburn, Robin

Blair, Eric Arthur: *see* Orwell, George

Boehner, Philotheus (1957) Introduction: pp. ix–li in *Ockham: Philosophical Writings*, Edinburgh: Nelson.

Bok, Sissela (1980) *Lying: Moral Choice in Public and Private Life*, London: Quartet.

Boorstin, Daniel J. (1975) *Democracy and its Discontents: Reflections on Everyday America*, New York: Vantage/Random House.

Borst, C. V. (ed.) (1970) *The Mind-Brain Identity Theory: A Collection of Papers*, London: Macmillan.

Boswell, James (1980) *Life of Johnson* (ed. by R. W. Chapman; rev. by J. D. Fleeman, with a new introduction by Pat Rogers), Oxford: World's Classics/Oxford University Press.

Bourke, Vernon J. (1951) *Ethics: A Textbook in Moral Philosophy*, New York: Macmillan.

Bradbury, Ray (1957) *Fahrenheit 451*, London: Corgi/Transworld.

Brennan, Christopher John (1960) *The Verse of Christopher Brennan* (ed. by A. R. Chisholm and J. J. Quinn, with a biographical introduction by A. R. Chisholm), Sydney: Angus & Robertson.

Brett, Nathan (1974) 'Knowing How, What and That', *Canadian Journal of Philosophy* IV:293–300.

Brewer, Ebenezer Cobham (1970) *Brewer's Dictionary of Phrase and Fable* (centenary edn, rev. by I. H. Evans), London: Cassell.

Brody, Baruch A. (1967) 'Logical Terms, Glossary of', in *The Encyclopedia of Philosophy*, ed. Paul Edwards, New York: Macmillan and Free Press.

Brooker, B. (1972) 'Paranoia', in *Encyclopedia of Psychology*, ed. H. J. Eysenck and W. Arnold, London: Search Press.

Brown, D. G. (1971) 'Knowing How and Knowing That, What', in O. P. Wood and G. Pitcher (eds) *Ryle*, London: Macmillan, pp. 213–248.

—— (1974) 'Reply to Brett', *Canadian Journal of Philosophy* IV:301–303.

Buckley, Kenneth D. (1976) *All About Citizens' Rights*, West Melbourne: Nelson.

Bullock, Alan: *see The Fontana Dictionary of Modern Thought*

Burke, John: *see Osborn's Concise Law Dictionary*

Burnet, John (1964) *Greek Philosophy: Thales to Plato*, London: Macmillan.

Burnet, (Sir) Macfarlane (1978) *Endurance of Life: The Implications of Genetics for Human Life*, Melbourne: Melbourne University Press.

Burnheim, John (1978) 'Theoretical Individualism', in R. O'Donnell *et al. Paper Tigers: An Introduction to the Critique of Social Theory*, pilot edn, Sydney: Dept of General Philosophy, University of Sydney, pp. 50–70.

Burns, Arthur Lee (1977) 'Conspiracy', *Quadrant* XXII no. 6 (June):9–11.

Burnyeat, Myles: *see* Honderich, Ted and Burnyeat, Myles

Burridge, Kenelm (1979) *Someone, No One: An Essay on Individuality*, Princeton: Princeton University Press.

Butler, Joseph (1949) *'Fifteen Sermons Preached at the Rolls Chapel' and 'A Dissertation upon the Nature of Virtue'* (... with introduction, analyses and notes by ... W. R. Matthews), London: Bell.

Butterfield, John (1977) 'The Concept of a Blik', *Sophia* XVI no. 1 (April):16–22.

CODCE: see The Concise Oxford Dictionary of Current English

Cameron, J. M. (1962) *The Night Battle: Essays*, London: Burns & Oates.

Campbell, Keith (1970) *Body and Mind*, Garden City, New York: Anchor/Doubleday.

—— (1976) *Metaphysics: An Introduction*, Encino, California: Dickenson.

—— (1985) 'Self-mastery and Stoic Ethics', *Philosophy* LX:327–340.

Campbell, Richard (1976) *From Belief to Understanding: A Study of Anselm's 'Proslogion' Argument on the Existence of God*, Canberra: Faculty of Arts, ANU.

Carroll, Lewis (1974) *The Philosopher's Alice: 'Alice's Adventures in Wonderland' and 'Through the Looking-Glass'* (... with illustrations by John Tenniel; introduction and notes by Peter Heath), London: Academy Editions.

Caton, Charles E. (ed.) (1963) *Philosophy and Ordinary Language*, Urbana: University of Illinois Press.

Cavendish, A. P.: *see* Basson, A. H.

Chalmers, Alan F. (1982) *What is This Thing Called Science?: An Assessment of the Nature and Status of Science and its Methods* (2nd edn), St Lucia: University of Queensland Press.

Chandor, Anthony, *et al.* (1977) *A Dictionary of Computers* (2nd edn), Harmondsworth: Penguin.

Chapman, D. R.: *see* Uvarov, E. B. and Chapman, D. R.

Chappell, V. C. (ed.) (1964) *Ordinary Language: Essays in Philosophical Method*, Englewood Cliffs: Prentice-Hall.

Charlesworth, Maxwell John (1965) Introduction and philosophical commentary to *St Anselm's 'Proslogion' with 'A Reply on Behalf of the Fool' by Gaunilo and 'The Author's Reply to Gaunilo'*, Oxford, Clarendon Press.
  (1974) (ed.) *The Problem of Religious Language*, Englewood Cliffs: Prentice-Hall.
  (1975) *The Existentialists and Jean-Paul Sartre*, St Lucia: University of Queensland Press in association with Australian Broadcasting Commission.

Chipman, Lauchlan (1977) 'Tru-speak', *Quadrant* Vol. XXII no. 6 (June):79–80.
  (1980) 'Equality Before (and After) the Law', *Quadrant* XXIV no. 3 (March):46–51.

Chipman, Lauchlan, Hamel-Green, Michael, *et al.* (1974) *Conscience and the Law*, South Yarra: Heinemann.

Chomsky, Noam, Putnam, Hilary, and Goodman, Nelson (1971) 'Symposium on Innate Ideas', in J. R. Searle (ed.) *The Philosophy of Language*, London: Oxford University Press, pp. 121–144. Reprinted from *Boston Studies in the Philosophy of Science* III (1968):81–107.

Christenson, Reo M., *et al.* (1972) *Ideologies and Modern Politics*, London: Nelson.

Cockburn, Alexander and Blackburn, Robin (eds) (1969) *Student Power: Problems, Diagnosis, Action*, Harmondsworth: Penguin in association with *New Left Review*.

Cohen, Marshall, *et al.* (eds) (1974) *The Rights and Wrongs of Abortion: A 'Philosophy and Public Affairs' Reader*, Princeton: Princeton University Press.
  (1977) *Equality and Preferential Treatment: A 'Philosophy and Public Affairs' Reader*, Princeton: Princeton University Press.

Cohen, Morris Raphael and Nagel, Ernest (1934) *An Introduction to Logic and Scientific Method*, London: Routledge & Kegan Paul.

The Complete Cat Encyclopaedia, ed. by Grace Pond (1972) London: Heinemann.

The Concise Encyclopedia of Western Philosophy and Philosophers: *see under* Urmson, J. O.

Concise Oxford Dictionary of Current English (1976) – based on *The Oxford English Dictionary* and its Supplements (1st edn by H. W. Fowler and F. G. Fowler; 6th edn by J. B. Sykes), Oxford: Clarendon Press.

Condren, Conal (1979) *Three Aspects of Political Theory: On Confusions and Reformation of an Expression*, South Melbourne: Macmillan.

Cooper, David E. (1973) *Philosophy and the Nature of Language*, London: Longman.

Cooper, Neil (1978) 'The Law of Excluded Middle', *Mind* n.s. LXXXVII:161–180.

Copi, Irving M. (1978) *Introduction to Logic* (5th edn), New York: Macmillan.
  (1979) *Symbolic Logic* (5th edn), New York: Macmillan.

Copleston, Frederick C. (1947) *A History of Philosophy* Vol. I *Greece and Rome* (rev. edn), London: Burns, Oates & Washbourne.
  (1950) *A History of Philosophy* Vol. II *Mediaeval Philosophy: Augustine to Scotus*, London: Burns, Oates & Washbourne.
  (1955) *Aquinas*, Harmondsworth: Penguin.

(1958) *A History of Philosophy* Vol. IV *Descartes to Leibniz*, London: Burns & Oates.

(1959) *A History of Philosophy* Vol. V *Hobbes to Hume*, London: Burns, Oates & Washbourne.

(1960) *A History of Philosophy* Vol. VI *Wolff to Kant*, London: Burns & Oates.

(1972) *A History of Mediaeval Philosophy*, London: Methuen.

(1977) *A History of Philosophy* Vol. IX *Maine de Biran to Sartre*, London: Search Press.

See also Russell, Bertrand and Copleston, Frederick C.

Cornford, Francis M. (1949) *Microcosmographia Academica being a guide for the young academic politician* (4th edn), Cambridge: Bowes.

(1957) *From Religion to Philosophy: A Study in the Origins of Western Speculation*, New York: Torchbooks/Harper & Row.

(1967) *'The Unwritten Philosophy' and Other Essays*, Cambridge: Cambridge University Press.

Cornman, James (1968) 'Mental Terms, Theoretical Terms and Materialism', *Philosophy of Science* XXXV:45–63.

Cottingham, John (1984) *Rationalism*, St Albans: Paladin/Granada.

Coval, S. (1966) *Scepticism and the First Person*, London: Methuen.

Cranston, Maurice (1953) *Freedom: A New Analysis*, London: Longmans, Green.

Critchley, Julian (1986) *Westminster Blues: Minor Chords*, London: Futura.

Crittenden, Paul J. (1985) 'Sartrean Transcendence: Winning and Losing', *Australasian Journal of Philosophy* LXIII:440–450.

Crombie, I. M. (1955) 'Theology and Falsification: Arising from the *University Discussion*', in A. G. N. Flew and A. C. MacIntyre (eds) *New Essays in Philosophical Theology*, London, SCM, pp. 109–130.

(1964) *Plato: The Midwife's Apprentice*, London: Routledge & Kegan Paul.

Cross, R. C. and Woozley, A. D. (1964) *Plato's 'Republic': A Philosophical Commentary*, London: Macmillan.

Crystal, David (1980) *A First Dictionary of Linguistics and Phonetics*, Boulder, Colorado: Westview Press.

Cumming, Leila (ed.) (1987) *Andersonian Papers* Vol. XXX of *Dialectic: Journal of the Newcastle University [New South Wales] Philosophy Club*.

Daly, Cathal B. (1962) *Morals, Law and Life: An Examination of the Book: 'The Sanctity of Life and the Criminal Law'*, Dublin: Clonmore and Reynolds.

D'Arcy, Eric (1961) *Conscience and its Right to Freedom*, London: Sheed and Ward.

(1963) *Human Acts: An Essay in their Moral Evaluation*, Oxford: Clarendon Press.

Davidson, Donald and Harman, Gilbert (eds) (1975) *The Logic of Grammar*, Encino: Dickinson.

de Jouvenel, Bertrand: *see* Jouvenel, Bertrand de

de Mandeville, Bernard: *see* Mandeville, Bernard

de Mey, Marc: *see* Mey, Marc de

d'Entrèves, A. P. (1952) *Natural Law: An Introduction to Legal Philosophy* (rev. reprint), London: Hutchinson.

Descartes, René (1954) *Descartes: Philosophical Writings* (a selection trans. and ed. by Elizabeth Anscombe ... and Peter Thomas Geach ... with introduction by Alexandre Koyre), Edinburgh: Nelson.

(1986) *'A Discourse on Method', 'Meditations on the First Philosophy', 'Principles of Philosophy'* (trans. by John Veitch; new introduction by Tom Sorrell), London: Everyman/Dent.

Deutscher, Max (1983) *Subjecting and Objecting: An Essay in Objectivity*, St Lucia: University of Queensland Press.

Devambez, Pierre *et al.* (1970) *A Dictionary of Ancient Greek Civilization*, London: Methuen.

Devitt, Michael (1981) *Designation*, New York: Columbia University Press.

(1984) *Realism and Truth*, Oxford: Blackwell.

De Vries, Peter (1961) *Through the Fields of Clover*, London: Gollancz.

Diamandopoulos, P. (1967) 'Chaos and Cosmos', in *The Encyclopedia of Philosophy*, ed. Paul Edwards, New York: Macmillan & Free Press.

Diamond, Stanley (ed.) (1964?) *Primitive Views of the World*, New York: Columbia University Press.

Dixon, Peter (1971) *Rhetoric*, London: Methuen.

Dockrill, David William (1971(a)) 'The Origin and Development of Nineteenth Century English Agnosticism', *The University of Newcastle Historical Journal* I no. 4 (Feb.):1–29.

(1971(b)) 'T. H. Huxley and the Meaning of "Agnosticism"', *Theology* LXXIV:461–477.

Dodgson, Charles Lutwidge: *see* Carroll, Lewis

Doniela, William V. (1974) 'Dialectic: An Introduction', *Politics* IX:74–82.

(1984) 'Rationalism', *Dialectic* [University of Newcastle, New South Wales] XXII:12–19.

Donnellan, Keith S. (1967) 'Reasons and Causes', in *The Encyclopedia of Philosophy*, ed. Paul Edwards, New York: Macmillan & Free Press.

Donnelly, John and Lyons, Leonard (eds) (1973) *Conscience*, Staten Island: Alba House.

Downie, R. S. and Telfer, Elizabeth (1969) *Respect for Persons*, London: Allen & Unwin.

Downing, A. B. (ed.) (1969) *Euthanasia and the Right to Death: The Case for Voluntary Euthanasia*, London: Peter Owen.

Drever, James (1977) *A Dictionary of Psychology*, rev. by Harvey Wallenstein [and B. R. Singer], Harmondsworth: Penguin.

Dummett, Michael (1984) 'Frege: Sense and Reference', in T. Honderich (ed.) *Philosophy through its Past*, Harmondsworth: Penguin, pp. 433–466.

Dunbar, M. J. (1980) 'The Blunting of Occam's Razor, or To Hell with Parsimony', *Canadian Journal of Zoology* LVIII:123–128.

(1981) 'Reply to "Comment: The Blunting of Occam's Razor, or To Hell with Parsimony"', *Canadian Journal of Zoology* LIX:146.

Duncker, Karl (1941) 'On Pleasure, Emotion and Striving', *Philosophy and Phenomenological Research* I (1940/41):391–430.

Dworkin, Ronald M. (ed.) (1977) *The Philosophy of Law*, London: Oxford University Press.

Eddington, (Sir) Arthur S. (1939) *The Philosophy of Physical Science*, Cambridge: Cambridge University Press.

Edel, Abraham (1963) *Method in Ethical Theory*, London: Routledge & Kegan Paul.

Edwards, Paul (1967) 'Why', in *The Encyclopedia of Philosophy*, ed. Paul Edwards, New York: Macmillan & Free Press.

See also The Encyclopedia of Philosophy

Eliade, Mircea: *see The Encyclopedia of Religion*

Emmet, Dorothy (1962) '"That's That": or Some Uses of Tautology', *Philosophy* XXXVII:15–24.

(1966) *Rules, Roles and Relations*, London: Macmillan.

(1972) *Function, Purpose and Powers: Some Concepts in the Study of Individuals and Societies* (2nd edn), London: Macmillan.

Emmet, E. R. (1968) *Learning to Philosophize* (2nd edn), Harmondsworth: Penguin.

The Encyclopedia of Philosophy (1967) ed. Paul Edwards, New York: Macmillan & Free Press. Articles are arranged alphabetically by title.

Encyclopedia of Psychology (1972) editors H. J. Eysenck and W. Arnold, London: Search Press. Articles are arranged alphabetically by title.

The Encyclopedia of Religion (1987) Editor in Chief Mercea Eliade, New York: Macmillan.

Encyclopaedia of Religion and Ethics (1915) ed. by James Hastings with the assistance of John A. Selbie ... and Louis H. Gray ... Vol. VIII, Edinburgh: T. & T. Clark.

Entrèves, A. P. d': *see* d'Entrèves, A. P.

Evans, Illtud (ed.) (1965) *Light on the Natural Law*, London: Compass/Burns & Oates.

Ewing, A. C. (1975) 'Idealism', in J. O. Urmson (ed.) *The Concise Encyclopedia of Western Philosophy and Philosophers* (2nd edn), London: Hutchinson.

Eysenck, Hans Jürgen (1965) *Smoking, Health and Personality*, London: Four Square.

Fairlie, Henry (1968) *The Life of Politics*, London: Methuen.

Farber, Marvin (1940) 'The Function of Phenomenological Analysis', *Philosophy and Phenomenological Research* I (1940/41):431–441.

(1975) 'Phenomenology', in J. O. Urmson (ed.) *The Concise Encyclopedia of Western Philosophy and Philosophers* (2nd edn), London: Hutchinson.

Feinberg, Joel (ed.) (1969) *Moral Concepts*, London: Oxford University Press.

(1973) *The Problem of Abortion*, Belmont, California: Wadsworth.

(1984) *The Problem of Abortion* (2nd edn), Belmont, California: Wadsworth.

Ferré, Frederick (1987) 'Logical Positivism', in *The Encyclopedia of Religion*, ed. Mircea Eliade, New York: Macmillan.

Feyerabend, Paul (1978) *Against Method: Outline of an Anarchistic Theory of Knowledge*, London: Verso.

Findlay, John Niemeyer (1962) *Hegel: A Re-Examination*, New York: Collins.

(1963(a)) *Language, Mind and Value: Philosophical Essays*, London: Allen & Unwin.

(1963(b)) 'Time: A Treatment of Some Puzzles', in J. N. Findlay, *Language, Mind and Value: Philosophical Essays*, London: Allen & Unwin, pp. 39–56. Also published as pp. 37–54 in Flew, 1951 and as pp. 339–355 in J. J. C. Smart, 1964.

(1970) *Axiological Ethics*, London: Macmillan.

Finley, Moses I. (1972) *Aspects of Antiquity: Discoveries and Controversies*, Harmondsworth: Penguin in association with Chatto & Windus.

Finnis, John (1983) *Fundamentals of Ethics*, Oxford: Clarendon Press.

Fischer, Ernst: *see under* Marx, Karl

Fisher, Alec (1988) *The Logic of Real Arguments*, Cambridge: Cambridge University Press.

Fitzgerald, Ross (ed.) (1977) *Human Needs and Politics*, Rushcutters Bay: Pergamon Press.

Fitzgibbon, Constantine (1968) *The Life of Dylan Thomas*, London: Sphere Books.

Flacelière, Robert (1970) 'Academy', in P. Devambez *et al. A Dictionary of Ancient Greek Civilization*, London: Methuen.

Fletcher, Ronald (1968) *Instinct in Man in the Light of Recent Work in Comparative Psychology* (2nd edn), London: Unwin University Books.

Flew, Antony Garrard Newton (1951) (ed.) *Logic and Language* First series, Oxford: Blackwell.

(1953) (ed.) *Logic and Language* Second series, Oxford: Blackwell.

(1955(a)) 'Theology and Falsification (A)' in A. G. N. Flew and A. C. MacIntyre (eds) *New Essays in Philosophical Theology*, London: SCM, pp. 96–99. Reprinted as pp. 13–15 of B. Mitchell, 1971.

(1955(b)) 'Theology and Falsification (D)', in A. G. N. Flew and A. C. MacIntyre (eds) *New Essays in Philosophical Theology*, London: SCM, pp. 106–108. Reprinted as pp. 20–22 of B. Mitchell, 1971.

(1956) (ed.) *Essays in Conceptual Analysis*, London: Macmillan.

(1961) *Hume's Philosophy of Belief: A Study of his First 'Inquiry'*, London: Routledge & Kegan Paul.

(1964) (ed.) *Body, Mind and Death: Readings*, New York: Macmillan.

(1966) *God and Philosophy*, London: Hutchinson.

(1969) 'The Principle of Euthanasia', in A. B. Downing (ed.) *Euthanasia and the Right to Death: The Case for Voluntary Euthanasia*, London: Peter Owen, pp. 30–48.

(1971) *An Introduction to Western Philosophy: Ideas and Arguments from Plato to Sartre*, London: Thames and Hudson.

(1975) *Thinking about Thinking (Or, Do I Sincerely Want to be Right?)*, London: Fontana/Collins.

(1984) (ed.) *A Dictionary of Philosophy* (2nd edn), London: Pan in association with Macmillan.

Flew, Antony G. N. and MacIntyre, Alasdair C. (eds) (1955) *New Essays in Philosophical Theology*, London: SCM.

Fogelin, Robert J. (1978) *Understanding Argument: An Introduction to Informal Logic*, New York: Harcourt, Brace, Jovanovich.

The Fontana Dictionary of Modern Thought (1977) ed. Alan Bullock and Oliver Stallybrass, London: Fontana/Collins. Articles are arranged alphabetically by title.

Foot, Philippa (1967) (ed.) *Theories of Ethics*, London: Oxford University Press.

(1978) *'Virtues and Vices' and Other Essays in Moral Philosophy*, Oxford: Blackwell.

Foster, Michael B. (1935) *The Political Philosophies of Plato and Hegel*, Oxford: Clarendon Press.

Fowler, Henry W. (1968) *A Dictionary of Modern English Usage* (2nd edn, rev. by Sir Ernest Gowers – corrected version), Oxford: Clarendon Press.

Frankel, Charles (1968) *Education and the Barricades*, New York: Norton.

Frankena, William K. (1952) 'The Naturalistic Fallacy' in W. Sellars and J. Hospers (eds) *Readings in Ethical Theory*, New York: Appleton-Century-Crofts, pp. 103–114. Reprinted from *Mind* XLVIII (1939).

(1970) 'The Concept of Morality', in G. Wallace and A. D. M. Walker (eds) *The Definition of Morality*, London: Methuen, pp. 146–173. Reprinted from *University of Colorado Studies, Series in Philosophy* no. 3 (1967):1–22.

(1973) *Ethics* (2nd edn), Englewood Cliffs: Prentice-Hall.

Frankena, William K. and Granrose, John T. (eds) (1974) *Introductory Readings in Ethics*, Englewood Cliffs: Prentice-Hall.

Frayn, Michael (1974) *Constructions*, London: Wildwood House.

Friedrich, Gerhard (ed.) (1972) *Theological Dictionary of the New Testament*, Vol. VIII, Grand Rapids: Eerdmans.

Fuller, Lon L. (1969) *The Morality of Law* (rev. edn), New Haven: Yale University Press.

(1971) *Anatomy of the Law*, Harmondsworth: Penguin

Gale, Richard M. (1967) 'Propositions, Judgments, Sentences, and Statements', in *The Encyclopedia of Philosophy*, ed. Paul Edwards, New York: Macmillan & Free Press.

Gallie, W. B. (1964) *Philosophy and the Historical Understanding*, London: Chatto & Windus.

Gandy, Robin (1977) 'Infinite, Infinity', in *The Fontana Dictionary of Modern Thought*, ed. Alan Bullock and Oliver Stallybrass, London: Fontana/Collins.

Gaskin, J. C. A. (1984) *The Quest for Certainty: An Outline of the Philosophy of Religion*, Harmondsworth: Penguin.

Gasking, Douglas A. T. (1972) 'The Analytic-Synthetic', *Australasian Journal of Philosophy* L:107–123.

Gaunilo: *see* under Anselm (Saint)

Gaus, G. F.: *see* Benn, Stanley Isaac and Gaus, G. F.

Geach, Peter Thomas (1961) 'Aquinas', in G. E. M. Anscombe and P. T. Geach *Three Philosophers*, Oxford: Blackwell, pp. x–xvii and 65–125.

(1962) *Reference and Generality: An Examination of Some Medieval and Modern Theories*, Ithaca: Cornell University Press.

(1969) *God and the Soul*, London: Routledge & Kegan Paul.

(1971) *Mental Acts: Their Content and Their Objects* (2nd edn), London: Routledge & Kegan Paul.

(1972) *Logic Matters*, Oxford: Blackwell.

(1976) *ReasonArgument*, Oxford: Blackwell.

See also Anscombe, G. E. M. and Geach, Peter T.

Gibbs, Benjamin (1976) *Freedom and Liberation*, Falmer: Sussex University Press.

Gilby, Thomas (1975) 'Aquinas', in J. O. Urmson (ed.) *The Concise Encyclopedia of Western Philosophy and Philosophers* (2nd edn), London: Hutchinson.

Gilson, Étienne (1959) *God and Philosophy*, New Haven: Yale University Press.

Glazer, Nathan (1978)ividual Rights against Group Rights' in E. Kamenka and Alice Alice Ehr-Soon Tay (eds) *Human Rights*, London: Arnold, pp. 87–103.

Goddard, Leonard (1977) *Philosophical Problems*, Edinburgh: Scottish Academic Press.

Goddard, Leonard and Routley, Richard (1966) 'Use, Mention and Quotation', *The Australasian Journal of Philosophy* XLIV:1–49.

Golding, Martin P. (1966) (ed.) *The Nature of Law: Readings in Legal Philosophy*, New York: Random House.

(1975) *Philosophy of Law*, Englewood Cliffs: Prentice-Hall.

Goodfield, June (1977) *Playing God: Genetic Engineering and the Manipulation of Life*, London: Hutchinson.

Goodman, Nelson: *see* Chomsky, Noam, Putnam, Hilary, and Goodman, Nelson.

Gorovitz, Samuel, *et al.* (1979) *Philosophical Analysis: An Introduction to its Language and Techniques* (3rd edn), New York: Random House.

Gosling, J. C. B. (1973) *Plato*, London: Routledge & Kegan Paul.

Gowers, (Sir) Ernest: *see under* Fowler, Henry W.

Graham, Keith (1977) *J. L. Austin: A Critique of Ordinary Language Philosophy*, Hassocks: Harvester.

Granrose, John T.: *see* Frankena, William K. and Granrose, John T.

Gray, J. N. (1977) 'On the Contestability of Social and Political Concepts', *Political Theory* V:331–348.

Gregor, A. James (1965) *A Survey of Marxism: Problems in Philosophy and the Theory of History*, New York: Random House.

Grice, H. P. (1975) 'Logic and Conversation' in D. Davidson and G. Harman (eds) *The Logic of Grammer*, Encino: Dickinson, pp. 64–153. Reprinted as pp. 64–153 of Fogelin, 1978.

Grice, H. P. and Strawson, (Sir) Peter F. (1956) 'In Defense of a Dogma', *The Philosophical Review* LXV:141–158. Reprinted as pp. 111–127 in Munsat, 1971.

Griffiths, A. Phillips (ed.) (1967) *Knowledge and Belief*, London: Oxford University Press.

Guthrie, Thomas Anstey (1917) *Vice Versa or A Lesson to Fathers*, by F. Anstey [pseudonym of T.A.G.], London: Murray.

Guthrie, W. K. C. (1950(a)) *The Greek Philosophers from Thales to Aristotle*, London: Methuen.

(1950(b)) *The Greeks and their Gods*, London: Methuen.

(1969) *A History of Greek Philosophy ... Vol III The Fifth-Century Enlightenment*, Cambridge: Cambridge University Press.

(1971(a)) *Socrates*, Cambridge: Cambridge University Press. (Reprint of Guthrie, 1969, Pt II.)

(1971(b)) *The Sophists*, Cambridge: Cambridge University Press. (Reprint of Guthrie, 1969, Pt I.)

Gwyn, Richard (1981) *The Northern Magus: Pierre Trudeau and Canadians*, Toronto: Paperjacks.

Halverson, William H. (1976) *A Concise Introduction to Philosophy* (3rd edn), New York: Random House.

Hamblin, Charles Lionel (1966) *Elementary Formal Logic*, Sydney: Hicks, Smith.

(1967) 'Questions', in *The Encyclopedia of Philosophy*, ed. Paul Edwards, New York: Macmillan & Free Press.

(1970) *Fallacies*, London: Methuen.

Hamel-Green, Michael, *et al.*: *see* Chipman, Lauchlan, Hamel-Green, Michael, *et al.*

Hamlyn, D. W. (1961) *Sensation and Perception: A History of the Philosophy of Perception*, London: Routledge & Kegan Paul.

(1967) 'Empiricism', in *The Encyclopedia of Philosophy*, ed. Paul Edwards, New York: Macmillan & Free Press.

(1971) 'Self-Deception', *Proceedings of the Aristotelian Society: Supplementary Volume* XLV:45–60.

Hammett, Dashiell (1965) *The Novels of Dashiell Hammett*, New York: Knopf.

Hampshire, (Sir) Stuart (ed.) (1978) *Public and Private Morality*, Cambridge: Cambridge University Press.

Handel, S. (1971) *A Dictionary of Electronics* (3rd edn), Harmondsworth: Penguin.

Hanfling, Oswald (ed.) (1972) *Fundamental Problems in Philosophy*, Oxford: Blackwell in association with Open University Press.

Hare, Richard M. (1952) *The Language of Morals*, Oxford: Clarendon Press.

(1955) 'Theology and Falsification (B)', in A. G. N. Flew and A. C. MacIntyre (eds) *New Essays in Philosophical Theology*, London: SCM, pp. 99–103. Reprinted as pp. 15–18 of B. Mitchell, 1971.

(1963) *Freedom and Reason*, Oxford: Clarendon Press.

(1971) *Practical Inferences*, London: Macmillan.

(1981) *Moral Thinking: Its Levels, Method, and Point*, Oxford: Clarendon Press.

See also Kenny, Anthony J. P. and Hare, Richard M.

Harman, Gilbert (1977) *The Nature of Morality: An Introduction to Ethics*, New York: Oxford University Press.

See also Davidson, Donald and Harman, Gilbert

Harré, Rom (1960) *An Introduction to the Logic of the Sciences*, London: Macmillan.

(1976) (ed.) *Personality*, Oxford: Blackwell.

Hart, Herbert Lionel Adolphus (1951) 'The Ascription of Responsibility and Rights'

Rights' in A. G. N. Flew (ed.) *Logic and Language*, First series, Oxford: Blackwell, pp. 145–166.

(1958) 'Positivism and the Separation of Law and Morals', *Harvard Law Review* LXXI:593–629. Reprinted in Dworkin, 1977.

(1961) *The Concept of Law*, Oxford: Clarendon Press.

(1970) *Punishment and Responsibility: Essays in the Philosophy of Law* (corrected reprint), Oxford: Clarendon Press.

Hastings, James: *see Encyclopaedia of Religion and Ethics*

Hawkins, D. J. B. (1975) 'Neo-Thomism', in J. O. Urmson (ed.) *The Concise Encyclopedia of Western Philosophy and Philosophers* (2nd edn), London: Hutchinson.

Hearn, Thomas K. (junior) (1971) *Studies in Utilitarianism*, New York: Appleton-Century-Crofts.

Heath, Peter L. (1967) 'Nothing', in *The Encyclopedia of Philosophy*, ed. Paul Edwards, New York: Macmillan & Free Press.

(1975) 'Logical Positivism', in J. O. Urmson (ed.) *The Concise Encyclopedia of Western Philosophy and Philosophers* (2nd edn), London: Hutchinson.

See also under Carroll, Lewis

Hebblethwaite, Brian (1988) *The Ocean of Truth: A Defence of Objective Theism*, Cambridge: Cambridge University Press.

Hegel, Georg Wilhelm Friedrich (1892) *The Logic of Hegel* trans. from *The Encyclopaedia of the Philosophical Sciences* by William Wallace (2nd edn), London: Oxford University Press.

Hempel, Carl G. (1966) *Philosophy of Natural Science*, Englewood Cliffs: Prentice-Hall.

Herbst, Peter F. (1956) 'The Nature of Facts', in A. G. N. Flew (ed.) *Essays in Conceptual Analysis*, London: Macmillan, pp. 134–156.

Hesse, Mary B. (1967) 'Laws and Theories', in *The Encyclopedia of Philosophy*, ed. Paul Edwards, New York: Macmillan & Free Press.

Hick, John (ed.) (1964) *The Existence of God: Readings*, New York: Macmillan.

Hick, John and McGill, Arthur C. (eds) (1968) *The Many-Faced Argument: Recent Studies on the Ontological Argument for the Existence of God*, London: Macmillan.

Higgins, Thomas (1968) *Basic Ethics*, New York: Benziger.

Hill, Christopher (1958) *Puritanism and Revolution: Studies in Interpretation of the English Revolution of the 17th Century*, London: Secker & Warburg.

Hirst, R. J. (1967) 'Realism', in *The Encyclopedia of Philosophy*, ed. Paul Edwards, New York: Macmillan & Free Press.

(1968) (ed.) *Philosophy: An Outline for the Intending Student*, London: Routledge & Kegan Paul.

Hobbes, Thomas (1840) *The English Works of Thomas Hobbes of Malmesbury*; now first collected and edited by Sir William Molesworth, Bart. Vol. IV, London: John Bohn.

(1968) *Leviathan*, ed. with an introduction by C. B. Macpherson, Harmondsworth: Penguin.

Hodges, Wilfrid ((1977) *Logic*, Harmondsworth: Penguin.

Hofstadter, Richard (1967) *'The Paranoid Style in American Politics' and Other Essays*, New York: Vintage/Random House.

Holland, J. A. B. (1973) 'A System of Classical Atheism', *Scottish Journal of Theology* XXVI:271–294.

Holland, R. F. (1981) 'Euthyphro', *Proceedings of the Aristotelian Society* n.s. LXXXII (1981/82):1–15.

Holsinger, Kent E. (1981) 'Comment: The Blunting of Occam's Razor, or To Hell with Parsimony', *Canadian Journal of Zoology* LIX:144–146.

Honderich, Ted (ed.) (1984) *Philosophy through its Past*, Harmondsworth: Penguin.

Honderich, Ted and Burnyeat, Myles (eds) (1979) *Philosophy As It Is*, London: Allen Lane.

Hook, Sidney (1955) *Dialectical Materialism and Scientific Method*, A Special Supplement to *The Bulletin of the Committee on Science and Freedom*, Manchester: Committee on Science and Freedom.

Hooker, Clifford Allen (1984) 'Empiricism and Positivism', *Dialectic* [University of Newcastle, New South Wales] XXII:20–28.

(1987) *A Realistic Theory of Science*, Albany: State University of New York Press.

Horner, Frank and Horner, Patricia (1980) *When Words Fail: A Casebook of Language Lapses in Australia*, Melbourne: Sun Books.

Horsburgh, H. J. N. (1956) 'Purpose and Authority in Morals', *Philosophy* XXXI:309–323.

Hospers, John (1967) *An Introduction to Philosophical Analysis* (2nd edn), Englewood Cliffs: Prentice-Hall.

See also Sellars, Wilfrid and Hospers, John

Housman, Alfred Edward (1939) *The Collected Poems of A. E. Housman*, London: Cape.

Howard, Philip (1978) *Weasel Words*, London: Hamish Hamilton.

(1980) *New Words for Old*, London: Unwin Paperbacks.

Howard, Ted and Rifkin, Jeremy (1980) *Who Should Play God?: The Artificial Creation of Life and What it Means for the Future of the Human Race*, New York: Laurel/Dell.

Hudson, Kenneth (1977) *The Dictionary of Diseased English*, London: Macmillan.

Hudson, William D. (1967) *Ethical Intuitionism*, London: Macmillan.

(1969) (ed.) *The Is-Ought Question: A Collection of Papers on the Central Problem in Moral Philosophy*, London: Macmillan.

(1983) *Modern Moral Philosophy* (2nd edn), London: Macmillan.

Hughes, George E. and Londey, D. G. (1965) *The Elements of Formal Logic*, London: Methuen.

Hughes, Walter Dominic (1966(a)) 'Lying', in *New Catholic Encyclopedia*, New York: McGraw-Hill.

(1966(b)) 'Mental Reservation', in *New Catholic Encyclopedia*, New York: McGraw-Hill.

Hume, David (1948) *Dialogues concerning Natural Religion (DNR)* ed. with introduction by H. D. Aiken, New York: Hafner.

(1969) *A Treatise of Human Nature (TNN)* ed. with an introduction by Ernest C. Mossner, Harmondsworth: Penguin.

(1975) *Enquiries concerning Human Understanding and Concerning the Principles of Morals ... (ECHU)* reprinted from the posthumous edn of 1777 and ed. with introduction by L. A. Selby-Bigge ... 3rd edn with text rev. and notes by P. H. Nidditch, Oxford: Clarendon Press.

Humphreys, Gordon (1945) *Teach Yourself English Grammar*, London: English Universities Press.

Huxley, Aldous (1949) *Eyeless in Gaza: A Novel*, London: Chatto & Windus.

(1955) *Brave New World: A Novel*, Harmondsworth: Penguin.

Inglis, Kenneth S. (1975) 'Papua New Guinea: Naming a Nation', *New Guinea and Australia, The Pacific and South-East Asia* IX no. 4 (Jan.):2–20.

Innes, Michael: *see* Stewart, J. I. M.

The Interpreter's Dictionary of the Bible (1962) New York: Abingdon Press. Articles are arranged alphabetically by title.

Jackson, Frank (1977) *Perception*, Cambridge: Cambridge University Press.

(1987) *Conditionals*, Oxford: Blackwell.

Jennings, Paul (1950) *Oddly Enough*, London: Reinhardt & Evans.

(1952) *Even Oddlier*, London: Reinhardt.

Jepson, R. W. (1948) *Clear Thinking: An Elementary Course of Preparation for Citizenship* (4th edn), London: Longmans, Green.

Jouvenel, Bertrand de (1963) *The Pure Theory of Politics*, Cambridge: Cambridge University Press.

Kamenka, Eugene (ed.) (1982) *Community as a Social Ideal*, London: Arnold.

Kamenka, Eugene and Tay, Alice Erh-Soon (eds) (1978) *Human Rights*, London: Arnold.

(1979) *Justice*, London: Arnold.

Kant, Immanuel (1948) *The Moral Law: Kant's 'Groundwork of the Metaphysic of Morals'* trans. and analysed by H. J. Paton, London: Hutchinson.

Kaufmann, Walter (ed.) (1956) *Existentialism from Dostoevsky to Sartre*, Cleveland, Ohio: Meridian/World Publishing Co.

Kelley, David (1988) *The Art of Reasoning*, New York: Norton.

Kelly, Paul (1976) *The Unmaking of Gough*, Sydney: Angus & Robertson.

Kemp, J. (1970) *Ethical Naturalism: Hobbes and Hume*, London: Macmillan.

Kenny, Anthony J. P. (1963) *Action, Emotion and Will*, London: Routledge & Kegan Paul.

(1969) *The Five Ways: St Thomas Aquinas' Proofs of God's Existence*, London: Routledge & Kegan Paul.

(1980) *Aquinas*, Oxford: Oxford University Press.

Kenny, Anthony J. P. and Hare, Richard M. (1974) 'What Use is Moral Philosophy?', in G. N. A. Vesey *Philosophy in the Open*, Milton Keynes: Open University Press, pp. 45–53.

Kharin, Yu. A. (1981) *Fundamentals of Dialectics*, Moscow: Progress Publishers.

Kidd, I. G. (1975(a)) 'Cynicism', in J. O. Urmson (ed.) *The Concise Encyclopedia of Western Philosophy and Philosophers* (2nd edn), London: Hutchinson.

(1975(b)) 'Stoicism', in J. O. Urmson (ed.) *The Concise Encyclopedia of Western Philosophy and Philosophers* (2nd edn), London: Hutchinson.

(1975(c)) 'Antisthenes', in J. O. Urmson (ed.) *The Concise Encyclopedia of Western Philosophy and Philosophers* (2nd edn), London: Hutchinson.

(1975(d)) 'Diogenes', in J. O. Urmson (ed.) *The Concise Encyclopedia of Western Philosophy and Philosophers* (2nd edn), London: Hutchinson.

Kim, Jaegwon (1967) 'Explanation in Science', in *The Encyclopedia of Philosophy*, ed. Paul Edwards, New York: Macmillan & Free Press.

Kleinig, John (1981) 'Equality Before (And After) the Law: A Response to Lauchlan Chipman', *Quadrant* XXV no. 1 (March):42–44.

Klemke, E. D. (ed.) (1983) *Contemporary Analytic and Linguistic Philosophies*, Buffalo: Prometheus.

Kneale, William (1949) *Probability and Induction*, Oxford: Clarendon Press.

Kneale, William and Kneale, Martha (1962) *The Development of Logic*, Oxford: Clarendon Press.

Knopfelmacher, Frank (1968) *'Intellectuals and Politics' and Other Essays*, Melbourne: Nelson.

Knowles, David (1962) *Evolution of Medieval Thought*, London: Longmans.

Knox, Ronald Arbuthnott (1953) *Off the Record*, London: Sheed & Ward.

Koestler, Arthur (1970) *The Ghost in the Machine*, London: Pan.

Kolnai, Aurel (1977) *Ethics, Value, and Reality: Selected Papers of Aurel Kolnai*, London: University of London: The Athlone Press.

Körner, Stephan (1975) 'Kant, Immanuel', in J. O. Urmson (ed.) *The Concise Encyclopedia of Western Philosophy and Philosophers* (2nd edn), London: Hutchinson, pp. 145–152.

Kovesi, Julius (1967) *Moral Notions*, London: Routledge & Kegan Paul.

Kraushaar, Otto F. (1955) 'Kantianism', in D. D. Runes (ed.) *Dictionary of Philosophy*, Ames, Iowa: Littlefield, Adams, pp. 158–160.

Kretzmann, Norman (1967) 'Semantics, History of', in *The Encyclopedia of Philosophy*, ed. Paul Edwards, New York: Macmillan & Free Press.

Kuhn, Thomas S. (1970) *The Structure of Scientific Revolutions* (2nd edn), Chicago: International Encyclopedia of Unified Science/Chicago University Press.

Küng, Hans (1980) *Does God Exist?: An Answer for Today*, London: Fount/Collins.

Lacey, A. R. (1971) 'Our Knowledge of Socrates', in G. Vlastos (ed.) *The Philosophy of Socrates: A Collection of Critical Essays*, Garden City, New York: Anchor/Doubleday, pp. 22–49.

—— (1976) *A Dictionary of Philosophy*, London: Routledge & Kegan Paul.

Ladd, John (ed.) (1973) *Ethical Relativism*, Belmont, California: Wadsworth.

Lakatos, Imre and Musgrave, Alan (1970) *Criticism and the Growth of Knowledge: Proceedings of the International Colloquium on the Philosophy of Science, London, 1965* Vol. IV (corrected edn), Cambridge: Cambridge University Press.

Langiulli, Nino (ed.) (1971) *The Existentialist Tradition: Selected Writings*, Garden City, New York: Anchor/Doubleday.

Lasch, Christopher (1980) *The Culture of Narcissism: American Life in an Age of Declining Expectations*, London: Abacus.

Laslett, Peter, *et al.* (eds) (1972) *Philosophy, Politics and Society*, Fourth Series, Oxford: Blackwell.

Lavelle, Louis (1973) *The Dilemma of Narcissism*, London: Allen & Unwin.

Lemmon, E. J. (1965) *Beginning Logic*, London: Nelson.

Lewis, Charlton T. (1889) *A Latin Dictionary for Schools*, Oxford: Clarendon Press.

Lewis, Clive Staples (1960) *Studies in Words*, Cambridge: Cambridge University Press.

Lobkowicz, Nicholas (1973) 'Quantity and Quality', in *Marxism, Communism and Western Society: A Comparative Encyclopedia*, ed. C. D. Kernig, New York: Herder.

Lockwood, Michael (1983) 'Sins of Omission? The Non-Treatment of Controls in Clinical Trials', *Proceedings of the Aristotelian Society* Supp. Vol. LVII:207–222.

Londey, D. G.: *see* Hughes, George E. and Londey, D. G.

Long, Charles H. (1987) 'Cosmogony', in *The Encyclopedia of Religion*, ed. Mircea Eliade, New York: Macmillan.

Longman Dictionary of Psychology and Psychiatry (1984) Robert M. Goldenson, New York: Glanze/Longman.

Lucas, John Randolph (1958) 'On Not Worshipping Facts', *The Philosophical Quarterly* VIII:144–156.

—— (1971) 'Ethical Intuitionism II', *Philosophy* XLVI:1–11.

Luce, A. A. (1958) *Logic*, London: English Universities Press.

Luckmann, Thomas (ed.) (1978) *Phenomenology and Sociology: Selected Readings*, Harmondsworth: Penguin.

Lukes, Steven (1977) *Essays in Social Theory*, London: Macmillan.

Lycan, William G. and Pappas, George S. (1972) 'What is Eliminative Materialism?', *The Australasian Journal of Philosophy* L:149–159.

Lyons, Leonard: *see* Donnelly, John and Lyons, Leonard

Mabbott, J. D. (1966) *An Introduction to Ethics*, London: Hutchinson.

McCabe, Herbert (1979) *Law, Love and Language* (2nd edn), London: Sheed and Ward.

McCloskey, H. J. (1971) *John Stuart Mill: A Critical Study*, London: St Martin's Press/Macmillan.

Macfarlane, L. J. (1970) *Modern Political Theory*, London: Nelson.

McGill, Arthur C.: *see* Hick, John and McGill, Arthur C.

McGrath, Patrick (1967) *The Nature of Moral Judgement: A Study in Contemporary Moral Philosophy*, London: Sheed and Ward.

MacIntyre, Alasdair C. (1958) *The Unconscious: A Conceptual Analysis*, London: Routledge & Kegan Paul.

(1964) 'Existentialism', in D. J. O'Connor (ed.) *A Critical History of Western Philosophy*, Glencoe, Illinois: Free Press, pp. 509–529.

(1970) 'What Morality is Not', in G. Wallace and A. D. M. Walker (eds) *The Definition of Morality*, London: Methuen, pp. 26–39. Reprinted from *Philosophy* XXIV (1957):325–335.

See also Flew, Antony and MacIntyre, Alasdair C.

McIntyre, Ian, *et al.* (1975) *Words: Reflections on the Uses of Language*, London: BBC.

MacKenzie, James D. (1975) 'Randism: The Doctrine of Selfishness', *Nation Review* 21/27 March:602–603.

(1988) 'Authority', *Journal of Philosophy of Education* XXII:57–65.

See also section 1.6A(i)

MacKenzie, William J. M. (1978) *Political Identity*, Harmondsworth: Penguin.

Mackie, John L. (1974) *The Cement of the Universe: A Study of Causation*, Oxford: Clarendon Press.

(1977) *Ethics: Inventing Right and Wrong*, Harmondsworth: Penguin.

(1982) *The Miracle of Theism: Arguments for and against the Existence of God*, Oxford: Clarendon Press.

MacNabb, D. G. C. (1975) 'Hume, David', in J. O. Urmson (ed.) *The Concise Encyclopedia of Western Philosophy and Philosophers* (2nd edn), London: Hutchinson.

McPherson, Thomas (1967) *Political Obligation*, London: Routledge & Kegan Paul.

(1972) *The Argument from Design*, London: Macmillan.

Macquarrie, John (1973) *Existentialism*, Harmondsworth: Penguin.

McRobbie, Michael A.: *see* Mannison, D. S. *et al.*

Magee, Bryan (1973) *Modern British Philosophy*, St Albans: Paladin.

Malcolm, Norman (1942) 'Certainty and Empirical Statements', *Mind* n.s. LI:18–46.

Mandeville, Bernard (1970) *The Fable of the Bees* (ed. with an introduction by Phillip Harth), Harmondsworth: Penguin.

Mannison, Don S. *et al.* (eds) (1980) *Environmental Philosophy*, Canberra: Dept of Philosophy, Research School of Social Sciences, ANU.

Manser, A. R. (1967) 'Games and Family Resemblances', *Philosophy* XLII:210–225.

Maritain, Jacques (1930) *An Introduction to Philosophy*, London: Sheed & Ward.

(1937) *An Introduction to Logic*, London: Sheed & Ward.

(1954) *Man and the State*, London: Hollis & Carter.

(1955) *Approaches to God*, London: Allen & Unwin.

(1956) *The Social and Political Philosophy of Jacques Maritain: Selected Readings*, [ed.] by Joseph W. Evans and Leo R. Ward, London: Bles.

(1958) *St Thomas Aquinas*, New York: Meridian.

Marx, Karl (1963) *Selected Writings in Sociology and Social Philosophy* (ed. with an introduction by T. B. Bottomore and M. Rubel), Harmondsworth: Penguin.

(1973) *Marx in His Own Words* (Ernst Fischer in collaboration with Franz Marek; trans. by Anna Bostock), Harmondsworth: Penguin.

Marxism, Communism and Western Society: A Comparative Encyclopedia (1973) ed. C. D. Kernig, New York: Herder. Articles are arranged alphabetically by title.

Mascall, E. L. (1966) *Existence and Analogy: A Sequel to 'He Who Is'*, London: Libra/Darton, Longman & Todd.

Mehta, Ved (1963) *The Fly and the Fly-Bottle: Encounters with British Intellectuals*, London: Weidenfeld & Nicolson.

Merlan, Philip (1975) 'Neoplatonism', in J. O. Urmson (ed.) *The Concise Encyclopedia of Western Philosophy and Philosophers* (2nd edn), London: Hutchinson.

Mey, Marc de (1982) *The Cognitive Paradigm: Cognitive Science, a Newly Explored Approach to the Study of Cognition Applied in an Analysis of Science and Scientific Knowledge*, Dordrecht: Reidel.

Middleton, John (ed.) (1967) *Myth and Cosmos: Readings in Mythology and Symbolism*, Garden City, NY: Natural History Press.

Midgley, Mary (1979) *Beast and Man: The Roots of Human Nature*, Hassocks: Harvester.

(1981) *Heart and Mind: The Varieties of Moral Experience*, London: Methuen.

Mill, John Stuart (1965) *Mill's Ethical Writings* (ed. J. B. Schneewind), New York: Collier.

(1969) *Utilitarianism* (ed. J. M. Smith and E. Sosa), Belmont, California: Wadsworth.

(1971) *Autobiography* (ed. Jack Stillinger), London: Oxford University Press.

(1972) *'Utilitarianism', 'Liberty', 'Representative Government', Selections from 'Auguste Comte and Positivism'* (ed. H. B. Acton), London: Everyman/Dent.

Miller, Casey and Swift, Kate (1980) *The Handbook of Nonsexist Writing*, New York: Lippincott & Crowell.

Miller, David W. and Starr, Martin K. (1967) *The Structure of Human Decisions*, Englewood Cliffs: Prentice-Hall.

Mills, C. Wright (1963) *The Marxists*, Harmondsworth: Penguin.

Milne, Alan J. M. (1968) *Freedom and Rights: A Philosophical Synthesis*, London: Allen & Unwin.

Mitchell, Basil (1955) 'Theology and Falsification (C)', in A. G. N. Flew and A. C. MacIntyre (eds) *New Essays in Philosophical Theology*, London: SCM, pp. 103–105. Reprinted as pp. 18–20 of B. Mitchell, 1971.

(1971) (ed.) *The Philosophy of Religion*, London: Oxford University Press.

Mitchell, David (1964) *An Introduction to Logic* (2nd edn), London: Hutchinson University Library.

Mitchell, G. Duncan (ed.) (1970) *A Dictionary of Sociology*, London: Routledge & Kegan Paul. Articles are arranged alphabetically by title.

Mohanty, Subodh Kumar (1988) *The Concept of Blik: An Analytical and Applied Philosophical Exploration of the Problem of Religious Language*, Meerut: Anu Books.

Montefiore, Alan (1971) 'Final Causes', *Proceedings of the Aristotelian Society: Supplementary Volume* XLV:171–192.

(1975) (ed.) *Neutrality and Impartiality: The University and Political Commitment*, Cambridge: Cambridge University Press.

Moody, Ernest A. (1967) 'William of Ockham', in *The Encyclopedia of Philosophy*, ed. Paul Edwards, New York: Macmillan & Free Press.

Moore, George Edward (1903) *Principia Ethica*, Cambridge: Cambridge University Press.

(1912) *Ethics*, London: Oxford University Press.

(1922) *Philosophical Studies*, London: Routledge & Kegan Paul.

(1959) *Philosophical Papers*, London: Allen & Unwin.

Mortimore, G. W. (ed.) (1971) *Weakness of Will*, London: Macmillan.

Mounce, H. O. (1971) 'Self-Deception', *Proceedings of the Aristotelian Society: Supplementary Volume* XLV:61–72.

Mozley and Whiteley's Law Dictionary (1977) (9th edn by J. B. Saunders), London: Butterworths.

Munitz, Milton K. (1967) 'Cosmology', in *The Encyclopedia of Philosophy*, ed. Paul Edwards, New York: Macmillan & Free Press.

Munsat, Stanley (ed.) (1971) *The Analytic-Synthetic Distinction*, Belmont, California: Wadsworth.

Murdoch, Iris (1967) *Sartre: Romantic Rationalist*, London: Fontana/Collins.

(1968) *The Nice and the Good*, London: Chatto & Windus.

Nagel, Ernest: *see* Cohen, Morris Raphael and Nagel, Ernest

Nagel, Thomas (1971) 'The Absurd', *The Journal of Philosophy* LXVIII:716–727.

Natanson, Maurice (1970) *The Journeying Self: A Study in Philosophy and Social Role*, Reading, Massachusetts: Addison-Wesley.

Nerlich, Graham (1964) 'A Resurgence of Metaphysics', *Quadrant* VIII no. 2 (June/July):58–66.

New Catholic Encyclopedia (1966) New York: McGraw-Hill. Articles are arranged alphabetically by title.

Newman, John Henry (1912) *Apologia pro Vita Sua*, London: Everyman/Dent.

Nisbet, Robert (1982) *Prejudices: A Philosophical Dictionary*, Cambridge, Massachusetts: Harvard University Press.

Noonan, John T. (ed.) (1970) *The Morality of Abortion: Legal and Historical Perspectives*, Cambridge, Massachusetts: Harvard University Press.

Norman, Richard (1983) *The Moral Philosophers: An Introduction to Ethics*, Oxford: Clarendon Press.

Nurick, John (1989) *Wet, Dry and Privatise: a New Political Phrasebook*, Perth: Australian Institute for Public Policy.

Nuttall (1943) *The Nuttall Dictionary of English Synonyms and Antonyms: 12,000 Words Showing 100,000 Parallel Expressions with Opposite Examples* (ed. G. Elgie Christ: new edn), London: Warne.

ODEE: *see The Oxford Dictionary of English Etymology*

OED: *see The Oxford English Dictionary*

Oakeshott, Michael (1962) '*Rationalism in Politics' and Other Essays*, London: Methuen.

Ockham, William: *see* William of Ockham

O'Connor, Daniel John (1964) (ed.) *A Critical History of Western Philosophy*, Glencoe, Illinois: Free Press.

(1967) *Aquinas and Natural Law*, London: Macmillan.

See also Basson, A. H. and O'Connor, D. J.

O'Connor, Johnson (1956) *Science Vocabulary Builder*, Boston: Human Engineering Laboratory.

O'Donnell, Rod *et al.* (1978) *Paper Tigers: An Introduction to the Critique of Social Theory*, pilot edn, Sydney: Dept of General Philosophy, University of Sydney.

O'Donovan, Oliver (1984) *Begotten or Made?*, Oxford: Clarendon Press.

Ogden, Charles Kay and Richards, Ivor Armstrong (1956) *The Meaning of Meaning: A Study of the Influence of Language upon Thought and of the Science of Symbolism*, London: Routledge & Kegan Paul.

Olson, Robert G. (1967) 'Teleological Ethics', in *The Encyclopedia of Philosophy*, ed. Paul Edwards, New York: Macmillan & Free Press.

O'Neil, William M. (1969) *Fact and Theory: An Aspect of the Philosophy of Science*, Sydney: Sydney University Press.

Orwell, George (1970) *The Collected Essays, Journalism and Letters of George Orwell* Vol. IV, Harmondsworth: Penguin in association with Secker & Warburg.

Osborn's Concise Law Dictionary (1976) (6th edn by John Burke), London: Sweet & Maxwell.

Osborne, Harold (ed.) (1972) *Aesthetics*, London: Oxford University Press.

Ovid (1921) *Metamorphoses* with an English trans. by Frank Justus Miller (2nd edn) Vol. I, London: Heinemann.

The Oxford Book of Literary Anecdotes: *see* Sutherland, James

The Oxford Dictionary of English Etymology (1966) ed. C. T. Onions with the assistance of G. W. S. Friedrichsen and R. W. Burchfield, Oxford: Clarendon Press.

The Oxford English Dictionary (1933) . . . Oxford: Clarendon Press.

The Oxford English Dictionary: *Supplements* (1972–1982) ed. by R. W. Burchfield.

The Oxford English Dictionary (1989) (2nd edn), Oxford: Clarendon Press.

Parfit, Derek (1971) 'Personal Identity', *The Philosophical Review* LXXX:3–27. Reprinted as pp. 183–211 in Honderich and Burnyeat, 1979.

Parkinson, G. H. R. (ed.) (1968) *The Theory of Meaning*, London: Oxford University Press.

Parry, Adam (1965) 'A Note on the Origins of Teleology', *Journal of the History of Ideas* XXVI:259–262.

Partridge, Eric (1973) *Usage and Abusage: A Guide to Good English* (rev. edn), Harmondsworth: Penguin in association with Hamish Hamilton.

Passmore, John A. (1961) *Philosophical Reasoning*, London: Duckworth.

—— (1967) 'Anderson, John', in *The Encyclopedia of Philosophy*, ed. Paul Edwards, New York: Macmillan & Free Press.

—— (1968(a)) *A Hundred Years of Philosophy* (2nd edn), Harmondsworth: Penguin.

—— (1968(b)) *Hume's Intentions* (rev. edn), London: Duckworth.

—— (1969) *Talking Things Over* (4th edn), Melbourne: Melbourne University Press.

Paterson, R. W. K. (1964) 'Psychological Egoism', *Ratio* VI:92–103.

Paton, H. J. (1948) 'Analyses of the Argument', in *The Moral Law: Kant's 'Groundwork of the Metaphysic of Morals'*, trans. and analysed by H. J. Paton, London: Hutchinson, pp. 13–23.

Pears, David F. (1967) 'Is Existence a Predicate?', in P. F. Strawson (ed.) *Philosophical Logic*, London: Oxford University Press, pp. 97–102.

Pearson, Hesketh (1948) *The Smith of Smiths, being The Life, Wit and Humour of Sydney Smith*, Harmondsworth: Penguin in association with Hamish Hamilton.

Penelhum, Terence (1956) 'The Logic of Pleasure', *Philosophy and Phenomenological Research* XVII (1956/57):488–503.

The Penguin English Dictionary (1969) comp. by G. N. Garmonsway with Jacqueline Simpson (2nd edn), Harmondsworth: Penguin.

Pépin, Jean (1987) 'Logos', in *The Encyclopedia of Religion*, ed. Mircea Eliade, New York: Macmillan.

Perry, John (ed.) (1975) *Personal Identity*, Berkeley and Los Angeles: University of California Press.

Peters, Richard S. (1973) *Reason and Compassion*, London: Routledge & Kegan Paul.
See also Benn, Stanley Isaac and Peters, Richard Stanley

Pieper, Josef (1957(a)) *Justice*, London: Faber.
(1957(b)) *The Silence of St Thomas: Three Essays*, London: Faber.

Pike, Kenneth L.: *see* Young, Richard E., Becker, Alton L., and Pike, Kenneth L.

Pitcher, George (ed.) (1964) *Truth*, Englewood Cliffs: Prentice-Hall
(1968) *Wittgenstein: The 'Philosophical Investigations'*, London: Macmillan.
See also Wood, Oscar P. and Pitcher, George

Plamenatz, John (1968) *Consent, Freedom and Political Obligation* (2nd edn), Oxford: Oxford University Press.
(1970) *Ideology*, London: Macmillan.

Plantinga, Alvin (ed.) (1965) *The Ontological Argument from St Anselm to Contemporary Philosophers*, New York: Anchor/Doubleday.

Plato (1956) *'Protagoras' and 'Meno'* trans. by W. K. C. Guthrie, Harmondsworth: Penguin.
(1969) *The Last Days of Socrates: 'Euthyphro', 'The Apology', 'Crito', 'Phaedo'* trans. by Hugh Tredennick (rev. edn), Harmondsworth: Penguin.

Plumwood, Val: *see* Routley, Val

Polanyi, Michael (1973) *Personal Knowledge: Towards a Post-Critical Philosophy*, London: Routledge & Kegan Paul.

Pole, David (1961) *Conditions of Rational Inquiry: A Study in the Philosophy of Value*, London: University of London: Athlone Press.

Pond, Grace: *see The Complete Cat Encyclopaedia*

Pontifex, Mark and Trethowan, Illtyd (1953) *The Meaning of Existence: A Metaphysical Enquiry*, London: Longmans, Green.

Popkin, Richard H. (1967) 'Skepticism', in *The Encyclopedia of Philosophy*, ed. Paul Edwards, New York: Macmillan & Free Press.

Popper, (Sir) Karl Raimund (1959) *The Logic of Scientific Discovery*, London: Hutchinson.
(1966) *The Open Society and its Enemies* (5th edn), London: Routledge & Kegan Paul.
(1972(a)) *Conjectures and Refutations: The Growth of Scientific Knowledge* (4th edn), London: Routledge & Kegan Paul.
(1972(b)) *Objective Knowledge: An Evolutionary Approach*, Oxford: Clarendon Press.
(1976) *Unended Quest: An Intellectual Autobiography*, London: Fontana/Collins.
(1983) *A Pocket Popper* ed. David Miller, London: Fontana.

Powell, Anthony (1976) *To Keep the Ball Rolling: The Memoirs of Anthony Powell* Vol. I *Infants of the Spring*, London: Heinemann.

Prior, Arthur N. (1954) 'Entities', *The Australasian Journal of Philosophy* XXXII:159–168.
(1962) *Formal Logic* (2nd edn), Oxford: Clarendon Press.
(1967(a)) 'Existence', in *The Encyclopedia of Philosophy*, ed. Paul Edwards, New York: Macmillan & Free Press.
(1967(b)) 'Traditional Logic', in *The Encyclopedia of Philosophy*, ed. Paul Edwards, New York: Macmillan & Free Press.
(1967(c)) 'Logic, History of: Keynes', in *The Encyclopedia of Philosophy*, ed. Paul, Edwards, New York: Macmillan & Free Press.

Prior, Mary L. and Prior, Arthur N. (1955) 'Erotetic Logic', *Philosophical Review* LXIV:43–59.

Putnam, Hilary (1976) 'What is "Realism"?', *Proceedings of the Aristotelian Society* n.s. LXXVI (1975/76):177–194.

(1979) 'The "Corroboration" of Theories', in T. Honderich and M. Burnyeat (eds) *Philosophy As It Is*, London: Allen Lane, pp. 349–380.

See also Chomsky, Noam, Putnam, Hilary, and Goodman, Nelson

Quine, Willard Van Orman (1953(a)) *From a Logical Point of View: 9 Logico-Philosophical Essays*, Cambridge, Mass.: Harvard University Press.

(1953(b)) 'Two Dogmas of Empiricism', in Quine, 1953(a), pp. 20–46. Reprinted in S. Munsat (ed.) (1971) *The Analytic-Synthetic Distinction*, Belmont, California: Wadsworth.

(1960) *Word and Object*, Boston: Massachusetts Institute of Technology.

(1964) Review of P. T. Geach *Reference and Generality*, *Philosophical Review* LXXIII:100–104.

(1970) *Philosophy of Logic*, Englewood Cliffs: Prentice-Hall.

(1976) *'The Ways of Paradox' and Other Essays* (rev. and enlarged edn), Cambridge, Mass.: Harvard University Press.

(1987) *Quiddities: An Intermittently Philosophical Dictionary*, Cambridge, Mass.: The Belknap Press of Harvard University Press.

Quine, Willard Van Orman and Ullian, J. (1978) *The Web of Belief* (2nd edn), New York: Random House.

Quinton, Anthony M. (Lord Quinton) (1973(a)) *The Nature of Things*, London: Routledge & Kegan Paul.

(1973(b)) *Utilitarian Ethics*, London: Macmillan.

(1975(a)) 'Social Objects', *Proceedings of the Aristotelian Society* n.s. LXXVI (1975/76):1–27.

(1975(b)) 'Phenomenalism', in J. O. Urmson (ed.) *The Concise Encyclopedia of Western Philosophy and Philosophers* (2nd edn), London: Hutchinson.

(1975(c)) 'Nettleship', in I. McIntyre *et al. Words: Reflections on the Uses of Language*, London: BBC, pp. 107–110.

(1977(a)) 'Connotation and Denotation', in *The Fontana Dictionary of Modern Thought*, ed. A. Bullock and O. Stallybrass, London: Fontana/Collins.

(1977(b)) 'Dualism', in *The Fontana Dictionary of Modern Thought*, ed. A. Bullock and O. Stallybrass, London: Fontana/Collins.

(1977(c)) 'Idea', in *The Fontana Dictionary of Modern Thought*, ed. A. Bullock and O. Stallybrass, London: Fontana/Collins.

(1977(d)) 'Idealism', in *The Fontana Dictionary of Modern Thought*, ed. A. Bullock and O. Stallybrass, London: Fontana/Collins.

(1977(e)) 'Paradigm Case', in *The Fontana Dictionary of Modern Thought*, ed. A. Bullock and O. Stallybrass, London: Fontana/Collins.

(1977(f)) 'Platonism', in *The Fontana Dictionary of Modern Thought*, ed. A. Bullock and O. Stallybrass, London: Fontana/Collins.

(1977(g)) 'Universal', in *The Fontana Dictionary of Modern Thought*, ed. A. Bullock and O. Stallybrass, London: Fontana/Collins.

(1977(h)) 'Criterion', in *The Fontana Dictionary of Modern Thought*, ed. A. Bullock and O. Stallybrass, London: Fontana/Collins.

Rachels, James (ed.) (1979) *Moral Problems: A Collection of Critical Essays* (3rd edn), New York: Harper & Row.

Ramsey, Frank Plumpton (1931) *'The Foundations of Mathematics' and other Logical Essays*, London: Routledge & Kegan Paul.

Ramsey, Ian (ed.) (1961) *Prospect for Metaphysics: Essays of Metaphysical Exploration*, London: Allen & Unwin.

Ramsey, Paul (1978) *Ethics at the Edges of Life: Medical and Legal Intersections*: The Bampton Lectures in America, New Haven: Yale University Press.

Raz, Joseph (ed.) (1978) *Practical Reasoning*, London: Oxford University Press.

Richards, Ivor Armstrong (1965) *The Philosophy of Rhetoric*, New York: Oxford University Press.

See also Ogden, Charles Kay and Richards, Ivor Armstrong

Richards, Thomas J. (1978) *The Language of Reasoning*, Rushcutters Bay: Pergamon Press.

Richmond, A. H. (1970) 'Discrimination; Racial Discrimination', in G. D. Mitchell (ed.) *A Dictionary of Sociology*, London: Routledge & Kegan Paul.

Rifkin, Jeremy: *see* Howard, Ted and Rifkin, Jeremy

Robinson, Richard (1953) *Plato's Earlier Dialectic* (2nd edn), Oxford: Clarendon Press.

(1954) *Definition*, Oxford: Clarendon Press.

Rolbiecki, J. J. (1955) 'Perseity', in D.D. Runes (ed.) *Dictionary of Philosophy*, Ames, Iowa: Littlefield, Adams.

Rollins, C. D. (1967) 'Solipsism', in *The Encyclopedia of Philosophy*, ed. Paul Edwards, New York: Macmillan & Free Press.

Room, Adrian (1979) *Room's Dictionary of Confusibles*, London: Routledge & Kegan Paul.

Rorty, Amelie (ed.) (1976) *The Identity of Persons*, Berkeley and Los Angeles: University of California Press.

Rorty, Richard (1970) 'In Defence of Eliminative Materialism', *Review of Metaphysics* XXIV (1970/71):112–121.

Rose, Thomas (1978) 'Objectivity', *Proceedings of the Russellian Society* [Sydney University] III:1–10.

Ross, (Sir) William David (1930) *The Right and the Good*, Oxford: Clarendon Press.

Rousseau, Jean-Jacques (1953) *The Confessions . . .* trans. with an introduction by J. M. Cohen, Harmondsworth: Penguin.

Routley, Richard: *see* Goddard, Leonard and Routley, Richard; Mannison, Don S. *et al.*; Routley, Val and Routley, Richard

Routley, Val and Routley, Richard (1980) 'Social Theories, Self Management and Environmental Problems', in Don S. Mannison *et al.* (eds) *Environmental Philosophy*, Canberra: Dept of Philosophy, Research School of Social Sciences, ANU, pp. 217–332.

Runes, Dagobert D. (ed.) (1955) *Dictionary of Philosophy*, Ames, Iowa: Littlefield, Adams. Articles are arranged alphabetically by title.

Russell, Bertrand (Lord Russell) (1940) *An Inquiry into Meaning and Truth*, London: Allen & Unwin.

(1948) *Human Knowledge, its Scope and Limits*, London: Allen & Unwin.

(1957) *'Why I am not a Christian', and Other Essays on Religion and Related Subjects*, London: Allen & Unwin.

(1961) *History of Western Philosophy and its Connection with Political and Social Circumstances from the Earliest Times to the Present Day* (2nd edn), London: Allen & Unwin.

See also Whitehead, Alfred North and Russell, Bertrand

Russell, Bertrand and Copleston, Frederick C. (1957) 'The Existence of God: A Debate', in Bertrand Russell *'Why I am not a Christian', and Other Essays on Religion and Related Subjects*, London: Allen & Unwin, pp. 144–168.

Ryan, Alan (1972) ' "Normal" Science or Political Ideology?', in Peter Laslett *et al.* (eds) *Philosophy, Politics and Society*, Fourth Series, Oxford: Blackwell, pp. 86–100.
(1973) (ed.) *The Philosophy of Social Explanation*, London: Oxford University Press.
(1974) *J. S. Mill*, London: Routledge & Kegan Paul.
Ryle, Gilbert (1932) 'Systematically Misleading Expressions', in G. Ryle *Collected Papers*, Vol. II, London: Hutchinson, pp. 39–62. Also published as pp. 11–36 in Flew, 1951.
(1938) 'Categories', in G. Ryle *Collected Papers*, Vol. II, London: Hutchinson, pp. 170–184. Also published as pp. 65–81 in Flew, 1953.
(1949) *The Concept of Mind*, London: Hutchinson.
(1950) ' "If", "So", and "Because" ', in G. Ryle *Collected Papers*, Vol. II, London: Hutchinson, pp. 234–249. Reprinted from Black, 1950, pp. 302–318.
(1954) *Dilemmas: The Tarner Lectures 1953*, Cambridge: Cambridge University Press.
(1971(a)) *Collected Papers*, Vol. I *Critical Essays*, London: Hutchinson.
(1971(b)) *Collected Papers*, Vol. II, London: Hutchinson.
(1974) 'Mowgli in Babel', *Philosophy* XLIX:5–11.
(1975) 'Categories', in J. O. Urmson (ed.) *The Concise Encyclopedia of Western Philosophy and Philosophers* (2nd edn), London: Hutchinson, pp. 60–61.
SOED: see *The Shorter Oxford English Dictionary*
SPD: see *Serving the People with Dialectics*
Sainsbury, R. M. (1988) *Paradoxes*, Cambridge: Cambridge University Press.
St John-Stevas, Norman (1961) *Life, Death and the Law: A Study of the Relationship between Law and Christian Morals in the English and American Legal Systems*, London: Eyre & Spottiswoode.
Santas, Gerasimos Xenophon (1979) *Socrates: Philosophy in Plato's Early Dialogues*, London: Routledge & Kegan Paul.
Sartre, Jean-Paul (1956(a)) *Being and Nothingness: An Essay in Phenomenological Ontology*, New York: Philosophical Library.
(1956(b)) 'Existentialism is a Humanism', in W. Kaufmann (ed.) *Existentialism from Dostoevsky to Sartre*, Cleveland, Ohio: Meridian/World Publishing Co., pp. 287–311.
Schneewind, J. B. (ed.) (1968) *Mill: A Collection of Critical Essays*, London: Macmillan.
Schuhl, Pierre-Maxime (1970) 'Cynicism', in P. Devambez *et al.*, *A Dictionary of Ancient Greek Civilization*, London: Methuen.
Schulhof, J. M. (1915) 'Lying', in *Encyclopedia of Religion and Ethics*, Vol. VIII, Edinburgh, T. & T. Clark.
Scriven, Michael (1976) *Reasoning*, New York: McGraw-Hill.
Scruton, Roger (1983) *A Dictionary of Political Thought*, London: Pan in association with Macmillan.
Searle, John R. (1967) 'Proper names and descriptions', in *The Encyclopedia of Philosophy*, ed. Paul Edwards, New York: Macmillan & Free Press.
(1969) *Speech Acts: An Essay in the Philosophy of Language*, Cambridge: Cambridge University Press.
(1971) (ed.) *The Philosophy of Language*, London: Oxford University Press.
Seliger, Martin (1976) *Ideology and Politics*, London: Allen & Unwin.
Sellars, Wilfrid and Hospers, John (eds) (1952) *Readings in Ethical Theory*, New York: Appleton-Century-Crofts.

Serving the People with Dialectics: Essays on the Study of Philosophy by Workers and Peasants (1972), Peking: Foreign Languages Press.

Shaffer, Jerome A. (1968) *Philosophy of Mind*, Englewood Cliffs: Prentice-Hall.

Shapere, Dudley (1967) 'Newtonian Mechanics and Mechanical Explanation', in *The Encyclopedia of Philosophy*, ed. Paul Edwards, New York: Macmillan & Free Press.

Shaw, Patrick (1981) *Logic and its Limits*, London: Pan in association with Heinemann.

Sheed, Francis J. (1953) *Society and Sanity*, London: Sheed and Ward.

The Shorter Oxford English Dictionary on Historical Principles (1944) Prepared by William Little ... H. W. Fowler ... J. Coulson; rev. and ed. by C. T. Onions (3rd edn rev. with addenda), Oxford: Clarendon Press.

Sibson, Robin (1977) 'Resistentialism', in *The Fontana Dictionary of Modern Thought*, ed. A. Bullock and O. Stallybrass, London: Fontana/Collins.

Sinclair, William Angus (1951) *The Traditional Formal Logic: A Short Account for Students* (5th edn), London: Methuen.

Singer, Peter (1980) *Marx*, Oxford: Oxford University Press.

Sloman, Aaron (1977(a)) 'Abstract', in *The Fontana Dictionary of Modern Thought*, ed. A. Bullock and O. Stallybrass, London: Fontana/Collins.

(1977(b)) 'Explanation', in *The Fontana Dictionary of Modern Thought*, ed. A. Bullock and O. Stallybrass, London: Fontana/Collins.

Smart, John Jamieson Carswell (1956) 'The River of Time', pp. 213–227 in Flew, 1956. Reprinted from *Mind* LVIII (1949):483–494.

(1964) (ed.) *Problems of Space and Time: Readings*, New York: Macmillan.

(1967) 'Utilitarianism', in *The Encyclopedia of Philosophy*, ed. Paul Edwards, New York: Macmillan & Free Press.

Smart, John Jamieson Carswell and Williams, Bernard A. O. (1973) *Utilitarianism: For and Against*, Cambridge: Cambridge University Press.

Smart, Ninian (1969) *Philosophers and Religious Truth* (2nd edn), London: SCM.

Smith, James M. and Sosa, Ernest (eds) (1969) *Mill's 'Utilitarianism': Text and Criticism*, Belmont, California: Wadsworth.

Snare, Francis (1980) 'Comments on "The Doctrine of Double Effect" by Suzanne Uniacke', *Bulletin of the Australian Society of Legal Philosophy* no. 17 (Oct.):26–30.

Sosa, Ernest: *see* Smith, James M. and Sosa, Ernest

Spann, Richard N. (1966) 'Clichés and Other Bad Habits in Political Science', *Politics* I:3–16.

Sparkes, Alonzo William (1965) ' "Begging the Question" ', *Journal of the History of Ideas* XXVII:452–463.

(1973) 'Trust and Teleology: Locke's Politics and his Doctrine of Creation', *Canadian Journal of Philosophy* III:263–273.

(1979) 'In Defence of Bliks', *Sophia* XVIII no. 2 (July):7–9. NB: Proposition (ii) on p. 7 should read 'There are no non-religious bliks.'

Spender, Dale (1980) *Man-Made Language*, London: Routledge & Kegan Paul.

Sprigge, Timothy L. S. (1971) 'Final Causes', *Proceedings of the Aristotelian Society* Supplementary Vol. XLV:149–170.

(1984) *Theories of Existence*, Harmondsworth: Penguin.

Stallybrass, Oliver: *see The Fontana Dictionary of Modern Thought.*

Staniland, Hilary (1973) *Universals*, London: Macmillan.

Starr, Martin K.: *see* Miller, David W. and Starr, Martin K.

Stebbing, Lizzie Susan (1937) *Philosophy and the Physicists*, London: Methuen.

(1939) *Thinking to Some Purpose*, Harmondsworth: Penguin.

(1948) *Ideals and Illusions*, London: Thinker's Library/Watts.

(1950) *A Modern Introduction to Logic* (7th edn), London: Methuen.

Steinbock, Bonnie (ed.) (1980) *Killing and Letting Die*, Englewood Cliffs: Prentice-Hall.

Stevenson, Charles L. (1944) *Ethics and Language*, New Haven: Yale University Press.

Stevenson, Leslie (1983) 'Empirical Realism and Transcendental Realism', *Proceedings of the Aristotelian Society* Supplementary Vol. LVII:131–153.

Stewart, John Innes Mackintosh (1974–78) *A Staircase in Surrey* Vols I–V, London: Gollancz.

(1978) *Appleby's Other Story* [by] Michael Innes [pseudonym of J. I. M. S.], Harmondsworth: Penguin.

Stillings, Neil A. (1987) *Cognitive Science: An Introduction*, Cambridge, Mass.: M.I.T. Press.

Stone, Julius (1979) 'Justice Not Equality', in E. Kamenka and A. Ehr-Soon Tay (eds) *Justice*, London: Arnold, pp. 97–115.

Stove, David C. (1973) *Probability and Hume's Inductive Scepticism*, Oxford: Clarendon Press.

(1978) 'The Problem of Induction', *Proceedings of the Russellian Society* [Sydney University] III:11–23.

(1982) *Popper and After: Four Modern Irrationalists*, Oxford: Pergamon Press.

Strawson, (Sir) Peter F. (1952(a)) 'Ethical Intuitionism', pp. 250–259 in Sellars and Hospers, 1952. Reprinted from *Philosophy* XXIV (1949).

(1952(b)) *Introduction to Logical Theory*, London: Methuen.

(1959) *Individuals: An Essay in Descriptive Metaphysics*, London: Methuen.

(1967) (ed.) *Philosophical Logic*, London: Oxford University Press.

(1970) 'Categories', in O. P. Wood and G. Pitcher (eds) *Ryle*, London: Macmillan, pp. 181–211.

(1975) 'Metaphysics', in J. O. Urmson (ed.) *The Concise Encyclopedia of Western Philosophy and Philosophers* (2nd edn), London, Hutchinson.

See also Grice, H. P. and Strawson, (Sir) Peter F.

Sutherland, James (ed.) (1977) *The Oxford Book of Literary Anecdotes*, London: Futura.

Swanton, C. (1985) 'On the "Essential Contestedness" of Political Concepts', *Ethics* XCV:811–827.

Swift, Kate: *see* Miller, Casey and Swift, Kate

Swinburne, Richard (1970) *The Concept of Miracle*, London: Macmillan.

(1974) (ed.) *The Justification of Induction*, London: Oxford University Press.

Sylvan, Richard: *see* Routley, Richard

Szabados, Bela (1974) 'Self-deception', *Canadian Journal of Philosophy* IV (1974/75):51–68.

Tanner, Michael (1964) 'Examples in Moral Philosophy', *Proceedings of the Aristotelian Society* n.s. LXV (1964/65):61–76.

Tanner, Richard Godfrey (1982) 'The Case for Neo-Stoicism Today', *Prudentia* XIV:39–51.

Tay, Alice Erh-Soon: *see* Kamenka, Eugene and Tay, Alice Erh-Soon

Taylor, Alfred Edward (1960) *Plato: The Man and his Work*, London: Methuen.

(1961(a)) *The Elements of Metaphysics*, London: Methuen.

(1961(b)) *Does God Exist?*, London: Fontana/Collins.

Taylor, Charles (1964) *The Explanation of Behaviour*, London: Routledge & Kegan Paul.

Taylor, Daniel M. (1970) *Explanation and Meaning: An Introduction to Philosophy*, Cambridge: Cambridge University Press.

Taylor, Richard (1967) 'Causation', in *The Encyclopedia of Philosophy*, ed. Paul Edwards, New York: Macmillan & Free Press.

(1974) *Metaphysics* (2nd edn), Englewood Cliffs: Prentice-Hall.

Telfer, Elizabeth: *see* Downie, R.S. and Telfer, Elizabeth

Theological Dictionary of the New Testament: *see* Friedrich, Gerhard

Thom, Paul (197?) *Dialectic*, Canberra: Dept of Philosophy, Faculty of Arts, ANU.

Thomas Aquinas (Saint) (1951) *Philosophical Texts* sel. and trans. with notes and an introduction by Thomas Gilby, London: Oxford University Press.

(1955) *Theological Texts* sel. and trans. with notes and an introduction by Thomas Gilby, London: Oxford University Press.

(1969) *Summa Theologiae* Vol. I *The Existence of God* Part One: Questions 1–13 (general edn: Thomas Gilby), Garden City, New York: Image/Doubleday.

Thomson, James (1967) 'Is Existence a Predicate?', in (Sir) Peter F. Strawson (ed.) *Philosophical Logic*, London: Oxford University Press, pp. 103–106.

Thomson, Judith Jarvis (1974) 'A Defense of Abortion', in Marshall Cohen *et al.* (eds) *The Rights and Wrongs of Abortion: A 'Philosophy and Public Affairs' Reader*, Princeton, Princeton University Press, pp. 3–22.

Tillich, Paul (1953) *Systematic Theology* Vol. I, Digswell Place, Welwyn: Nisbet.

Trethowan, Illtyd: *see* Pontifex, Mark and Trethowan, Illtyd

Trigg, Roger (1973) *Reason and Commitment*, Cambridge: Cambridge University Press.

Ullian, J.: *see* Quine, Willard Van Orman and Ullian, J.

Unger, Peter (1976) *Ignorance: A Case for Scepticism*, Oxford: Clarendon Press.

Uniacke, Suzanne (1980) 'The Doctrine of Double Effect', *Bulletin of the Australian Society of Legal Philosophy* no. 16 (June):2–37.

Urmson, J. O. (1956) *Philosophical Analysis: Its Development Between the Two World Wars*, Oxford: Clarendon Press.

(1968) *The Emotive Theory of Ethics*, London: Hutchinson.

(1975(a)) (ed.) *The Concise Encyclopedia of Western Philosophy and Philosophers* (2nd edn), London: Hutchinson. Articles are arranged alphabetically by title.

(1975(b)) 'Logical Positivism', in J. O. Urmson (ed.) *The Concise Encyclopedia of Western Philosophy and Philosophers* (2nd edn), London: Hutchinson.

Uvarov, E. B. and Chapman, D. R. (1971) *The Penguin Dictionary of Science* (rev. for the 3rd and 4th edns by Alan Isaacs), Harmondsworth: Penguin.

Vallins, G. H. (1951) *Good English*, London: Pan.

Vesey, Godfrey N. A. (1964) (ed.) *Body and Mind: Readings in Philosophy*, London: Allen & Unwin.

(1971) *Perception*, London: Macmillan.

(1974(a)) *Philosophy in the Open*, Milton Keynes: Open University Press.

(1974(b)) *Personal Identity*, London: Macmillan.

Vlastos, Gregory (1971) (ed.) *The Philosophy of Socrates: A Collection of Critical Essays*, Garden City, New York: Anchor/Doubleday.

(1975) *Plato's Universe*, Seattle: University of Washington Press.

Vries, Peter de: *see* De Vries, Peter

Walker, A. D. M.: *see* Wallace, G. and Walker, A. D. M.

Walker, Ralph (1983) 'Empirical Realism and Transcendental Anti-Realism', *Proceedings of the Aristotelian Society* Supplementary Vol. LVII:155–177.

Wallace, G. and Walker, A. D. M. (eds) (1970) *The Definition of Morality*, London: Methuen.

Walsh, W. H. (1968) 'Metaphysics', in R. J. Hirst (ed.) *Philosophy: An Outline for the Intending Student*, London: Routledge & Kegan Paul, pp. 57–91.

Walters, Raymond S. (1967(a)) 'Contrary-to-Fact Conditional', in *The Encyclopedia of Philosophy*, ed. Paul Edwards, New York: Macmillan & Free Press. NB: On p. 212, column 1, para. 1, 'subjective mood' should be 'subjunctive mood'.

(1967(b)) 'Laws of Science and Lawlike Statements', in *The Encyclopedia of Philosophy*, ed. Paul Edwards, New York: Macmillan & Free Press.

Walton, Douglas N. (1987) *Informal Fallacies: Towards a Theory of Argument Criticisms*, Amsterdam: Benjamins.

Warnock, (Sir) Geoffrey J. (1958) *English Philosophy since 1900*, London: Oxford University Press.

(1967(a)) *Contemporary Moral Philosophy*, London: Macmillan.

(1967(b)) (ed.) *Philosophy of Perception*, London: Oxford University Press.

(1975) 'Ideas', in J. O. Urmson (ed.) *The Concise Encyclopedia of Western Philosophy and Philosophers* (2nd edn), London: Hutchinson.

(1989) 'J. L. Austin and Linguistic Philosophy', *Cogito* [UK] III:30–35.

Warnock, Mary (Baroness Warnock) (1960) *Ethics since 1900*, London: Oxford University Press.

(1967) *Existentialist Ethics*, London: Macmillan.

Warren, Mary Anne (1979) 'On the Moral and Legal Status of Abortion', pp. 35–51 in R. A. Wasserstrom (ed.) *Today's Moral Problems* (2nd edn), New York: Macmillan. Reprinted (with new postscript) from *The Monist* LVII (1973):43–61.

Wasserstrom, Richard A. (ed.) (1970) *War and Morality*, Belmont, California: Wadsworth.

(1975) *Today's Moral Problems*, New York: Macmillan.

(1979) *Today's Moral Problems* (2nd edn), New York: Macmillan.

Watkins, John W. N. (1973) 'Ideal Types and Historical Explanation' in A. Ryan (ed.) *The Philosophy of Social Explanation*, London: Oxford University Press, pp. 82–104.

Watson, Alan (1977) *The Nature of Law*, Edinburgh: Edinburgh University Press.

Waugh, Evelyn (1962) *The Life of Ronald Knox*, London: Fontana/Collins.

Weingartner, Rudolph H. (1967) 'Historical Explanation', in *The Encyclopedia of Philosophy*, ed. Paul Edwards, New York: Macmillan & Free Press.

Weiss, Paul (1955) 'Cosmology', in D. D. Runes (ed.) *Dictionary of Philosophy*, Ames, Iowa: Littlefield, Adams, pp. 68–69.

Werner, Richard (1979) 'Abortion: The Ontological and Moral Status of the Unborn', in R. A. Wasserstrom (ed.) *Today's Moral Problems* (2nd edn), New York: Macmillan, pp. 51–73. Reprinted from *Social Theory and Practice* III (1974):201–222.

Westermann, Claus (1974) *Creation* (trans. by John J. Scullion), London: SPCK.

White, Alan R. (1968) (ed.) *Philosophy of Action*, London: Oxford University Press.

(1971) 'Inference', *The Philosophical Quarterly* LXXXV:289–302.

Whitehead, Alfred North and Russell, Bertrand (1925–27) *Principia Mathematica* (2nd edn), Cambridge: Cambridge University Press.

Whitlam, Edward Gough (1970) 'Law Reform and Law and Order', *The Catholic Worker* [Melbourne] Sept.:4–5.

Wicker, Brian (1964) *God and Modern Philosophy: A Discussion of the Traditional Arguments for God's Existence in the Light of Modern Philosophy*, London: Darton, Longman & Todd.

Wilckens, Ulrich (1972) 'Hupokrinomai, sunupokrinomai, hupokrisis, hupokrites, anupokritos', in G. Friedrich (ed.) *Theological Dictionary of the New Testament*, Vol. VIII, Grand Rapids: Eerdmans, pp. 559–571.

William of Ockham (1957) *Ockham: Philosophical Writings*, a selection, ed. and trans. by Philotheus Boehner, Edinburgh: Nelson.

Williams, Bernard A. O. (1967) 'Descartes, René', in *The Encyclopedia of Philosophy*, ed. Paul Edwards, New York: Macmillan & Free Press.

(1973) *Problems of the Self: Philosophical Papers 1956–1972*, Cambridge: Cambridge University Press.

See also Smart, John Jamieson Carswell and Williams, Bernard A. O.

Williams, Glanville (1958) *The Sanctity of Life and the Criminal Law*, London: Faber.

Williams, Raymond (1983) *Keywords: A Vocabulary of Culture and Society* (rev. edn), London: Flamingo/Fontana.

Wilson, Bryan R. (ed.) (1970) *Rationality*, Oxford: Blackwell.

Winch, Peter (1958) *The Idea of a Social Science and its Relation to Philosophy*, London: Routledge & Kegan Paul.

Wisdom, John (1953) *Philosophy and Psycho-Analysis*, Oxford: Blackwell.

(1965) *Other Minds* (2nd edn), Oxford: Blackwell.

Wittgenstein, Ludwig (1958) *Philosophical Investigations* (trans. by G. E. M. Anscombe: 2nd edn), Oxford: Blackwell.

(1974) *Tractatus Logico-Philosophicus* (trans. by D. F. Pears and B. F. McGuinness with the introduction by Bertrand Russell), London: Routledge & Kegan Paul.

Wollheim, Richard (1971) *Freud*, London: Fontana/Collins.

Wood, Oscar P. and Pitcher, George (eds) (1970) *Ryle*, London: Macmillan.

Woozley, A. D. (1949) *Theory of Knowledge: An Introduction*, London: Hutchinson.

(1971) 'Socrates on Disobeying the Law', in G. Vlastos (ed.) *The Philosophy of Socrates: A Collection of Critical Essays*, Garden City, New York: Anchor/ Doubleday, pp. 299–318.

See also Cross, R. C. and Woozley, A. D.

Wright, Judith (1975) *Collected Poems 1942–1970*, Sydney: Angus & Robertson.

Wuellner, Bernard (1956) *Dictionary of Scholastic Philosophy*, Milwaukee: Bruce.

Young, F. W. (1962) 'Hypocrisy, Hypocrite', in *The Interpreter's Dictionary of the Bible*, New York: Abingdon Press.

Young, Richard E., Becker, Alton L., and Pike, Kenneth L. (1970) *Rhetoric: Discovery and Change*, New York: Harcourt, Brace & World.

Young, Robert A. (1979) 'What is So Wrong with Killing People?', *Philosophy* LIV:515–528.

Index